HISTORICAL DICTIONARIES
OF WAR, REVOLUTION, AND CIVIL UNREST
Edited by Jon Woronoff

1. *Afghan Wars, Revolutions, and Insurgencies*, by Ludwig W. Adamec. 1996.
2. *The United States–Mexican War*, by Edward H. Moseley and Paul C. Clark, Jr. 1997.
3. *World War I*, by Ian V. Hogg. 1998.
4. *The United States Navy*, by James M. Morris and Patricia M. Kearns. 1998.
5. *The United States Marine Corps*, by Harry A. Gailey. 1998.
6. *The Wars of the French Revolution*, by Steven T. Ross. 1998.
7. *The American Revolution*, by Terry M. Mays. 1999.
8. *The Spanish–American War*, by Brad K. Berner. 1998.
9. *The Persian Gulf War*, by Clayton R. Newell. 1998.
10. *The Holocaust*, by Jack R. Fischel. 1999.
11. *The United States Air Force and Its Antecedents*, by Michael Robert Terry. 1999.
12. *Civil Wars in Africa*, by Guy Arnold. 1999.
13. *World War II: The War Against Japan*, by Anne Sharp Wells. 1999.
14. *British and Irish Civil Wars*, by Martyn Bennett. 2000.
15. *The Cold War*, by Joseph Smith and Simon Davis. 2000.
16. *Ancient Greek Warfare*, by Iain Spence. 2002.
17. *The Vietnam War*, by Edwin E. Moïse. 2001.
18. *The Civil War*, by Terry L. Jones. 2002.
19. *The Crimean War*, by Guy Arnold. 2002.
20. *The United States Army, a Historical Dictionary*, by Clayton R. Newell. 2002.
21. *Terrorism, Second Edition*, by Sean K. Anderson and Stephen Sloan. 2002.
22. *Chinese Civil War*, by Edwin Pak-wah Leung. 2002.
23. *The Korean War: A Historical Dictionary*, by Paul M. Edwards. 2002.
24. *The "Dirty Wars,"* by David Kohut, Olga Vilella, and Beatrice Julian. 2003.
25. *The Crusades*, by Corliss K. Slack. 2003.
26. *Ancient Egyptian Warfare*, by Robert G. Morkot. 2003.

Historical Dictionary of the Crusades

Corliss K. Slack

*Historical Dictionaries of War,
Revolution, and Civil Unrest, No. 25*

The Scarecrow Press, Inc.
Lanham, Maryland, and Oxford
2003

SCARECROW PRESS, INC.

Published in the United States of America
by Scarecrow Press, Inc.
A wholly owned subsidiary of
The Rowman & Littlefield Publishing Group, Inc.
4501 Forbes Boulevard, Suite 200, Lanham, Maryland 20706
www.scarecrowpress.com

PO Box 317
Oxford
OX2 9RU, UK

Copyright © 2003 by Corliss K. Slack

The cover image, "Hierosolima," from Hartmann Schedel, *Liber cronicarum* (Nuremberg: Anton Koberger, 1493), is reproduced with permission from The Eran Laor Cartographic Collection at The Jewish National and University Library, Jerusalem. Woodcut by Michael Wolgemut is an imaginary representation of the temple "Templum Salomois" in the midst of walled-in Jerusalem.

All rights reserved. No part of this publication may be reproduced, stored in a retrieval system, or transmitted in any form or by any means, electronic, mechanical, photocopying, recording, or otherwise, without the prior permission of the publisher.

British Library Cataloguing in Publication Information Available

Library of Congress Cataloging-in-Publication Data
Slack, Corliss Konwiser, 1955–
  Historical dictionary of the crusades / Corliss K. Slack.
    p. cm. — (Historical dictionaries of war, revolution, and civil unrest ; no. 25)
  Includes bibliographical references.
  ISBN 0-8108-4855-4 (alk. paper)
  1. Crusades–Dictionaries. 2. Europe–History, Military–Dictionaries. 3. Europe–Church history–600–1500–Dictionaries. 4. Islamic Empire–History, Military–Dictionaries. I. Title. II. Series.
D155 .S53 2003
909.07–dc21   2003012225

∞™ The paper used in this publication meets the minimum requirements of American National Standard for Information Sciences—Permanence of Paper for Printed Library Materials, ANSI/NISO Z39.48-1992.
Manufactured in the United States of America.

This book is dedicated to Melvin Joseph Konwiser
(23 July 1926 – 11 June 2003)
Mitto angelum meum ante faciem tuam qui praeparabit viam tuam
Vulg. Mark 1: 2b

Contents

Editor's Foreword *Jon Woronoff*	ix
Preface	xi
Acknowledgments	xiii
Maps	xiv
Chronology	xvii
Introduction	1
THE DICTIONARY	11
Bibliography	231
About the Author	273

Editor's Foreword

When writing the foreword to a book dealing with warfare that occurred many centuries ago, one would expect to use all sorts of adjectives but hardly "timely." Yet, after extremely serious recent events, the topic of crusades is back, and this book tells us about the crusaders coming from the "West," "jihads" launched in the Middle East, clashes of nations and ideologies, kidnapping and ransom, assassination and what we presently call "ethnic cleansing." Alas, the parallels—while seemingly obvious to some—are rather poor and sometimes incongruous. But then again the understanding of the historical crusades in their heyday was not much clearer and it has taken a long time to get a better fix on them. That is one of the reasons why this book might just as well be characterized by adjectives like interesting, informative, even revealing.

This *Historical Dictionary of the Crusades* does enhance our understanding of a long period of intermittent warfare which lies far enough back that we should be able to regard it dispassionately but involves concepts and events that are hard to forget and harder to comprehend. There are concise dictionary entries on places (not only in the Middle East) and persons (kings and sultans, popes and warriors, preachers and chroniclers), the major campaigns, battles and sieges, the weapons and armor, relevant aspects of land and naval warfare, all of which provide the essential facts and figures as we know them. The often confusing succession of events is sorted out in the chronology. But most interesting is perhaps the introduction, which tries to make sense of a controversial and chaotic period, as much sense as can be made and certainly more than we have of the present situation. Those who want to know more, and there are bound to be many, should then resort to the bibliography.

This new volume in the War, Revolution, and Civil Unrest series was written by Corliss K. Slack who is professor of European history in the Department of Politics and History of Whitworth College. Her teaching covers the medieval period and the crusades, on which she wrote her first book, *Crusade Charters, 1138-1270*. She has also written papers on crusade topics for various international conferences and journals. This historical dictionary, which requires an impressive breadth of coverage and depth of knowledge, is her most ambitious project so far. Most readers will conclude that she has accomplished this task with skill and given us a book that is not only informative but will make us think.

Jon Woronoff, Series Editor

Preface

The crusades movement involved a number of medieval Western European communes and monarchies in an effort to conquer and colonize the Middle East and the Baltic region that lasted from 1096 until at least 1291. Attempts to summarize and categorize a multifaceted activity that was practiced over a two-hundred-year period are complicated by the range of participants, motives, and regional histories. This dictionary is meant as an introduction to students, providing an overview of events and examples of involvement by statesmen, ecclesiastical leaders, and ordinary people. The lengthy bibliography gives a sense of the wide impact of the crusade movement and its roots in a number of European institutions. The introduction sets the frame for further study.

Arabic place and proper names and alternate spellings are available in the second edition of the six-volume *History of the Crusades*, Kenneth Setton, general editor (Philadelphia, 1969-1989). Students will find considerable variation among reference works in the transliterations of Arabic words and names, and will find the Setton history in some cases outdated. In this volume Arabic words are given in the simplified form used in newspapers and journals in the United States, often without diacritical marks, glottal stops, long vowelings, etc. European and African place and proper names also appear, with some exceptions reflecting common use, in spellings familiar to American readers.

The words "Muslim" and "Islam" are used in some of the entries as shorthand to denote all followers of the teachings of Muhammad. Students should be aware that Islam in the 12th century was divided into numerous sects or denominations, reflecting an extremely diverse set of beliefs and practices. While in theory there was an Islamic theocracy based at Baghdad, in fact the political landscape was fragmented. "Muslim" is only as descriptive as "Christian," and equally problematic.

Some medieval Europeans referred to "Christendom" or the "Holy Roman Empire" as if there were a unified political entity which effectively ruled them. In fact the territorial boundaries of modern European nations were not yet set, and there was no effective political unity over the whole. The religious and political entity in the medieval Mediterranean region with the longest history of effective organization was the Byzantine Empire, a remnant of the Christianized Roman Empire.

With the benefit of hindsight, we can see that the energy driving the conquests of the crusades came from the emerging civilizations of Europe and Islam as they sought to establish themselves in the Mediterranean region. The boundaries of the territorial states with which we are now familiar were set in a contest for economic and military supremacy that was often expressed in religious terminology. While there are moments when spirituality is expressed by individuals on either side with either terrifying or inspiring effect, the main stuff of crusades history is military strategy and incident, trade treaties, propaganda, and maneuvering for political advantage. Students are encouraged to go directly to the English translations of crusade chronicles to enjoy for themselves the medieval view of the contest.

Acknowledgments

The author would like to thank Ken Pecka for tireless patience and many hours of creative work in producing camera-ready copy. Without Gail Fielding's help the research for this book could not have been done. Hans Bynagle offered valuable advice on copyright issues. I am grateful to Ayelet Rubin of The Jewish National and University Library for assistance at a crucial moment in the preparation for this volume. Professor John Yoder is certainly not responsible for, except in the sense of much improving, the entries having to do with Africa. I am also grateful to Whitworth College, which generously provided the time and technical support for this work, and to Stacy Warren of Eastern Washington University for her help and advice.

Many thanks to Jon Woronoff, Sally Craley, and Kim Tabor for their expertise and helpful suggestions, and to Scarecrow Press for sponsoring this project.

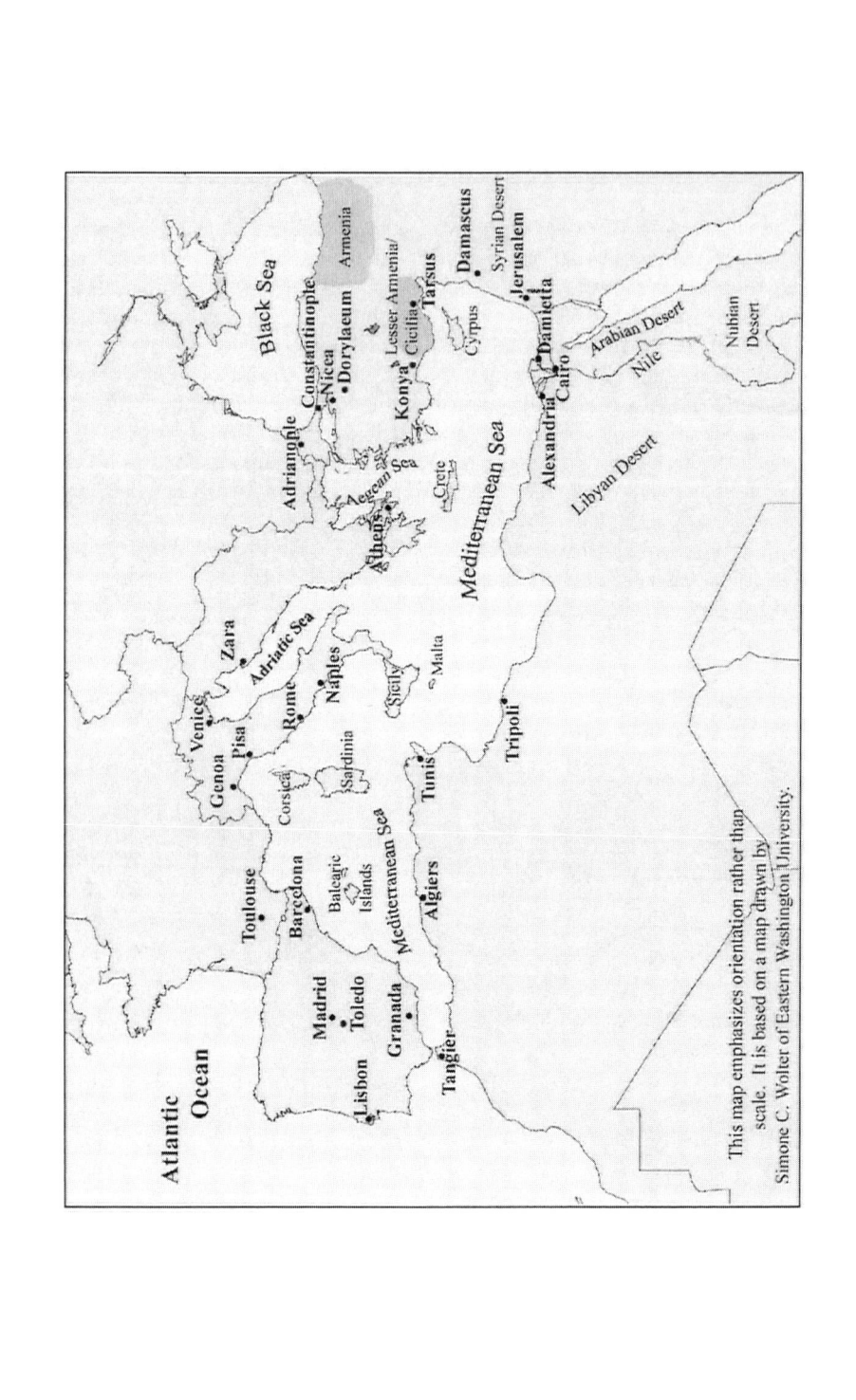

This map emphasizes orientation rather than scale. It is based on a map drawn by Simone C. Wolter of Eastern Washington University.

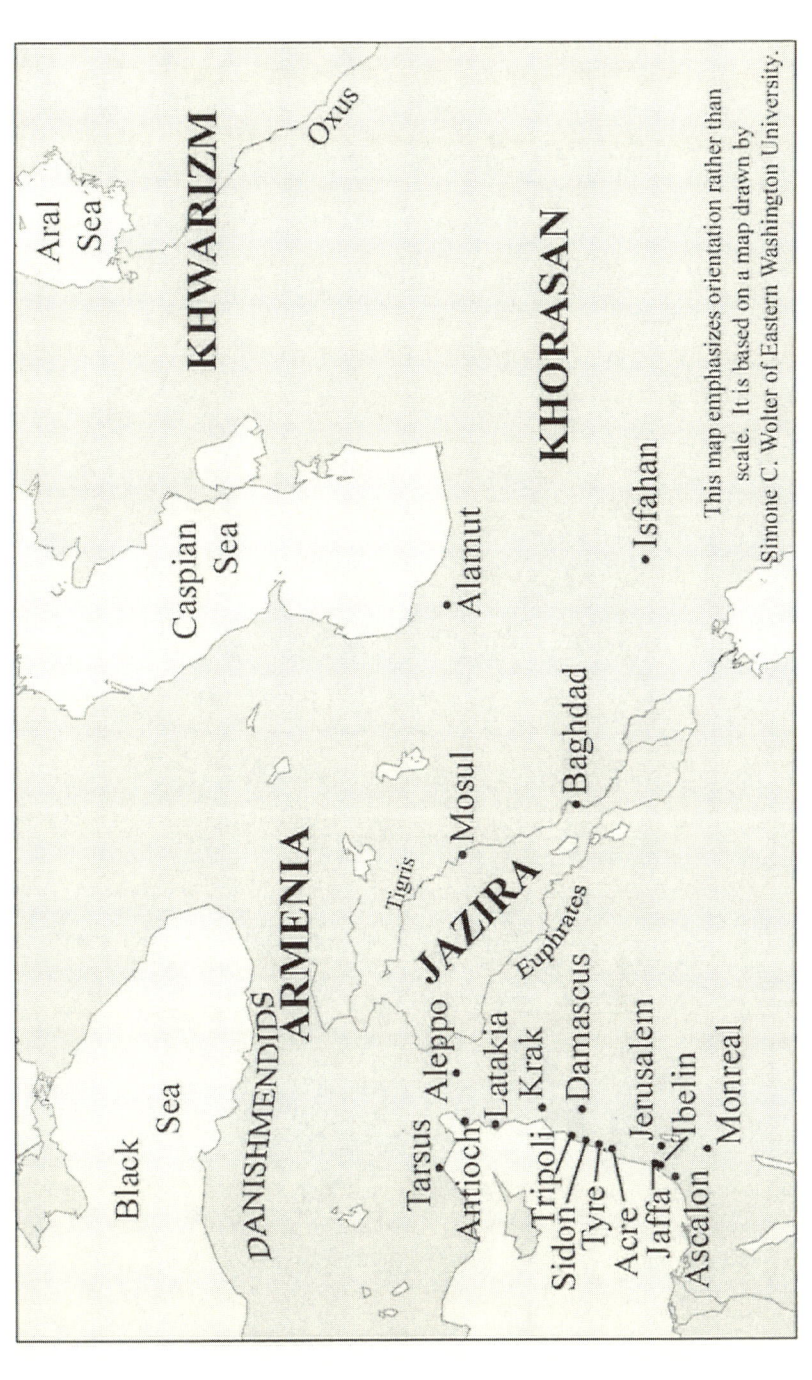

Chronology

1009 The Fatimid Caliph of Egypt destroyed Christian shrines in Jerusalem, including the church of the Holy Sepulchre.

1054 Differences in theology, language, liturgy, and organization caused a split between Rome and the other four original churches of the Christian world: Constantinople, Antioch, Jerusalem, and Alexandria. The dispute, in the first instance a disagreement between a papal legate and the Patriarch of Constantinople, was exacerbated by the events of the next two centuries, including the conquest of Constantinople by the Fourth Crusade in 1204, so that the division of the church was eventually institutionalized as the Roman Catholic vs. the Greek Orthodox denominations.

1071 The Seljuk Turks under Alp Arslan defeated the Byzantine imperial forces led by Emperor Romanus Diogenes at the battle of Manzikert, Turkey, on 26 August. Turkish conquest of much of the Byzantine eastern Mediterranean followed, including Jerusalem by 1078.

1090 Hasan al-Sabbah founded the Ismaili group known to the crusaders as the Assassins at Alamut in northern Iran.

1095 On 27 November Pope Urban II preached the First Crusade at a church council in Clermont, France, at least partially in response to a request for military assistance from the Emperor Alexius I Comnenus of Byzantium.

1096 Various crusade parties traveled towards an arranged meeting point at Constantinople, where Emperor Alexius I Comnenus expected them as mercenaries. Europeans led by Emicho of Flonheim massacred Jews in the Rhineland in May and June. A "people's crusade" led by Peter the Hermit was annihilated near Nicaea by the Turks on 21 October.

1097 The First Crusade, with assistance from the Byzantines, took Nicaea, Dorylaeum, and Tarsus during the summer. The crusade army, led by Godfrey of Bouillon started the siege of Antioch in October.

1098 Leaders of the First Crusade created lordships from conquered territory: Baldwin of Boulogne became count of Edessa in March; Bohemond of Taranto became prince of Antioch in June. Islamic power, theoretically unified, was in fact divided under regional dynasties. The Fatimids of Egypt took Jerusalem from the Seljuk Turks on 26 August.

1099 On 22 July Godfrey of Bouillon took the title of Advocate of the Holy Sepulchre after the successful First Crusade siege of Jerusalem.

1101 Seasonal expeditions from Europe continued during the years between the named crusades. In this instance crusaders from European enclaves that are now parts of Italy, France, and Germany assembled in Constantinople in April and were placed under the leadership of First Crusader Raymond of St. Gilles. They were defeated in battles with the sultan of Iconium and the Danishmends during the summer.

1109 Tripoli was taken by a crusading army on 12 July.

1119 The Muslim ruler of Mardin called for a jihad against the Christian regent of Antioch, Roger of Salerno. Roger was killed and his forces decimated at the Battle of "the Field of Blood" at Darb Sarmada west of Aleppo on 28 June.

1120 The Templars, the first military monastic order, was founded in Jerusalem by Hugh of Payns and several companions. The foundation of other military orders such as the Hospitallers, Teutonic Knights, and the Swordbrethren followed, so that in the 12th and 13th centuries crusading monks fought in Spain and the Baltic region as well as in the Holy Land.

1124 Tyre was taken by a crusading army on 7 July.

1144 Crusader Edessa was taken in December by Zengi, the Muslim governor of Mosul.

1145 Pope Eugenius III issued the bull on 1 December for what would be the Second Crusade.

1146 On 31 March St. Bernard of Clairvaux preached the crusade at Vézelay. King Louis VII of France and many of his nobles took the cross. A second Muslim attack on Edessa destroyed much of the city on 3 November.

Chronology • xix

1147 Expeditions were made by Europeans against the Slavic Wends in the Baltic area (Baltic Crusades, July-September) and Muslim cities in Iberia (Reconquista, October). The armies of King Louis VII of France and King Conrad III of Germany set off towards the Levant in the fall. Conrad's army was decimated in Asia Minor by the Turks in October. He himself was able to escape and join Louis in northern Syria.

1148 King Louis VII of France, King Conrad III of Germany, and King Baldwin III of Jerusalem unsuccessfully attacked Damascus on 24-28 July.

1149 Nur al-Din defeated the army of Antioch on 29 June. Prince Raymond of Antioch was killed in battle. Damascus accepted Nur al-Din as overlord in April of 1154.

1153 Reynald of Châtillon married Constance, regent of Antioch 1130-53, and took the title of Prince of Antioch in the spring. King Baldwin III of Jerusalem took Ascalon on 22 August.

1163 King Amalric I of Jerusalem began a series of attacks on Egypt, hoping to extend his borders and protect the Latin Kingdom. The expedition of 1163 was followed by further attacks on Egypt in 1164, 1167, 1168, and 1169.

1165 This year saw the first recorded incidence of Cathar heretics in southern France. From 1165 to 1208 the papacy attempted to deal with Catharism by ecclesiastical censure and debate. After 1208 the papacy pursued heretics by means of the Crusade, and later, the Inquisition.

1169-71 Saladin, by order of Nur al-Din, took Egypt and proclaimed the Abbasid caliphate there on 10 September 1171.

1174 Saladin took Damascus on 28 October.

1175 Saladin was invested by the caliph at Baghdad in May with Egypt and Syria.

1179 Saladin's reorganized Egyptian fleet attacked crusader seaports.

1181 Reynald of Châtillon, now lord of Kerak and the Transjordan, defied the authority of King Baldwin IV of Jerusalem by attacking a caravan to Mecca during the summer of 1181, and in 1182-83, by raiding Red Sea ports.

1182-83 Saladin's attack on Beirut failed in August 1182, but his authority was recognized by Aleppo the following June.

1186 Saladin was recognized as suzerain of Mosul on 3 March; Guy of Lusignan was crowned king in Jerusalem during the summer.

1187 Reynald of Châtillon defied King Guy by attacking a caravan from Cairo to Damascus during a truce between Saladin and the Latin Kingdom. Saladin defeated the army of the kingdom at Hattin on 4 July, and then took Jerusalem on 2 October. He held King Guy and the relic of the True Cross for ransom, and executed Reynald. Conrad of Montferrat arrived at Tyre, and successfully defended it against Saladin. Pope Gregory VIII proclaimed the Third Crusade on 29 October.

1189 Saladin had taken almost all of crusader territory. Guy of Lusignan began the siege of Acre in August with the help of a Pisan fleet as a first step in the proposed reconquest called the Third Crusade. English crusaders aided the Portuguese at Silves in September.

1190 Emperor Frederick I Barbarossa took Iconium in Turkey, defeating the Seljuk Turks. He then drowned crossing a river in Cilicia on 10 June. The Third Crusade continued, focusing on the siege of Acre. Count Henry of Champagne arrived at the siege with other European crusaders in July. Conrad of Montferrat, based at Tyre, married Isabel, claiming the throne of Jerusalem, on 24 November.

1191 King Philip II of France arrived at Acre on 20 April, joining the siege, while King Richard I of England took Cyprus from the Byzantines. Acre fell to the crusaders in July after Richard's arrival, and the king of England then defeated Saladin's army at Arsuf on 6 September.

1192 On 28 April Conrad of Monferrat was assassinated, leaving Isabel, the heir to Jerusalem, a widow. On 5 May she married Count Henry of Champagne. Guy of Lusignan bought Cyprus from the Templars, founding the Kingdom of Cyprus. King Richard I of England left Acre on 9 October, ending the Third Crusade.

1193 Saladin died on 4 March, leaving a power struggle that temporarily protected the remnants of the crusader kingdom, now based at Acre.

1197 Henry of Champagne, de facto ruler of Jerusalem, died 10 September. In October his widow married Amaury of Lusignan, king of Cyprus, thus uniting the two kingdoms. Amaury had become a vassal of the Holy Roman Empire during a crusade launched from Italy by Emperor Henry VI before the latter's death in September.

1198 Pope Innocent III proclaimed the Fourth Crusade.

1200 Saladin's brother al-Adil was proclaimed sultan of Egypt and Syria on 4 August.

1202 European crusaders joined the Venetians in October at the siege of the Christian city of Zara in order to pay for passage to the Levant. Pope Innocent III excommunicated the crusade army as a result of its attack on a Christian city.

1203 Pardoned, the crusaders proceeded to Constantinople in order to reinstate Byzantine Emperor Isaac II Angelus, who had been blinded and deposed by his brother Alexius III in 1195. Isaac's heir Alexius IV had promised aid for the Fourth Crusade in return for their assistance.

1204 Alexius V Ducas deposed Isaac II and strangled Alexius IV in February. The crusaders took and sacked Constantinople on 13 April, dividing the city with the Venetians. They then crowned Count Baldwin IX of Flanders Byzantine Emperor on 9 May. The Fourth Crusade was over, but Baldwin and other Europeans became involved in a war of conquest to take territory in order to create a new Latin Kingdom or Empire of Constantinople.

1205 Count Baldwin was captured and killed in April, leaving his brother Henry of Flanders as regent in Constantinople for the struggling Latin Empire.

1206 St. Dominic's mission to southern France resulted in his attention to the problem of heresy and the foundation of the Dominican order.

1208 Theodore I Lascaris was crowned Byzantine Emperor at Nicaea by the Greeks in opposition to the Latin occupation. Papal legate Peter of Castelnau was murdered in southern France on 14 January by Cathar heretics. Pope Innocent III launched the Albigensian Crusade in response to the murder, setting off a war that would eventually benefit the kings of France by consolidating the south under their rule.

1210 In 1205 Amaury of Cyprus and Jerusalem had died, leaving the original crusader kingdom in the hands of a regent, John of Ibelin. King Philip II of France (participant in the Third Crusade) was asked by the titular aristocracy of the Latin Kingdom of Jerusalem to nominate a warrior to rule the kingdom. He chose John of Brienne, a nobleman from Champagne. Backed financially by both the king and the pope, John arrived in Acre for his coronation on 3 October and marriage to Maria, the daughter of Isabel of Jerusalem and Conrad of Montferrat.

1212 Peasants from Germany and France participated in the ill-fated (and misnamed) Children's Crusade in which the poor attempted to recapture Jerusalem.

1213 Pope Innocent III proclaimed the Fifth Crusade.

1215 The Fourth Lateran Council laid the organizational foundation for the Fifth Crusade. The first Dominican convent was founded at Toulouse in response to the Cathar heresy.

1216 Pope Innocent III died and was replaced by Honorius III in July.

1217 The Fifth Crusade began. Crusaders from Hungary went to Acre, but were unable to recapture territory in the old Latin Kingdom.

1218 A force of Europeans arrived at Damietta, in Egypt, on 27 May intending to attack the seat of Muslim power in the Middle East as a key to the reconquest of Jerusalem. In southern France, Simon of Montfort, leader of the Albigensian Crusade forces, died at the siege of Toulouse on 25 June. Saladin's brother died 31 August, and passed the sultanate of Egypt to his son al-Kamil.

1221 The Fifth Crusaders surrendered to al-Kamil, sultan of Egypt on 30 August. Crusading after this point is even more difficult to disentangle as a separate entity from the wars of the European powers, although many of these wars were called crusades by the participants. Some key events in the history of European wars in the Levant, in Spain (the Reconquista), and in the Baltic region (the Northern or Baltic Crusades) are listed below.

1225 Holy Roman Emperor Frederick II married Isabel, daughter of John of Brienne (d.1237), and claimed the Kingdom of Jerusalem in her name. In spite of a previous agreement with John, who had expected to hold the regency of the kingdom for his daughter until his own death, Frederick immediately claimed the title and effective control of the kingdom, which was based at Acre. His delays in leaving for a promised crusade led to his excommunication by the pope from 1227-30. He finally left for what is sometimes called the Sixth Crusade in 1228, and regained Jerusalem by means of a treaty with al-Kamil, sultan of Egypt in 1229.

1229 The treaty by which Ayyubid Sultan al-Kamil gave Emperor Frederick II Jerusalem and parts of the land pilgrimage route to it has been lost, leaving us in ignorance of its details. Both rulers earned the criticism of their own followers for making the agreement. Frederick entered Jerusalem in defiance of the patriarch of the city, who had placed it under interdict to prevent Frederick's coronation as ruler of the Latin Kingdom. The Emperor's army completed their pilgrimage on March 18 by visiting the Holy Sepulchre, where Frederick crowned himself.

Frederick fought the troops of the patriarch of Jerusalem in Acre, while John of Brienne, backed by the pope, raised an army against the Emperor in Italy. Leaving a garrison to protect his interests in Acre, Frederick, pelted with garbage by the inhabitants, left for Italy on 1 May.

The Peace of Paris ended the Albigensian Crusade on 12 April.

1233 The Inquisition began operating in southern France in response to the continuing resistance of heretics, and especially the Cathars, to the authority of the pope.

1239 The crusade of Count Theobald IV of Champagne extended the treaty concluded by Emperor Frederick II during the Sixth Crusade (1240).

1240 The papacy preached a crusade against Emperor Frederick II (see above, 1229). Earl Richard of Cornwall left England for the Holy Land, where in April of 1241 he confirmed Theobald of Champagne's treaty with the sultan of Egypt and refortified Ascalon.

1244 In August Jerusalem was sacked by the Khwarizm Turks. On 17 October at the battle of La Forbie (or Harbiyya) between Egypt and a European/Syrian coalition, the army of the crusader kingdom was destroyed.

1249 Saint Louis IX, king of France, unsuccessfully attacked Egypt. He spent several years in the Levant, not sailing for home until 1254.

1258 Mongol armies sacked Baghdad in February, ending the Abbasid caliphate.

1260 Mongol armies took Aleppo and Damascus, but were prevented from entering Egypt by Mamluk sultan Baybars I.

1261 The Greeks retook the Byzantine Empire, which had been conquered by Western Europeans in 1204.

1265-71 Mamluk sultan Baybars I took Antioch and other important fortresses in the remains of the Latin Kingdom of Jerusalem, now based at Acre.

1270 Saint Louis IX, king of France, attacked Muslim North Africa at Tunisia in July. The king died on crusade on 25 August.

1291 The city of Acre fell to the Muslims on 18 May, ending the effective crusading period in the Levant.

1312 Pope Clement V abolished the order of the Templars.

Introduction

> In our time God has instituted holy wars, so that the equestrian order and the erring people, who like ancient pagans were commonly engaged in mutual slaughter, might find a new way of meriting salvation. They are no longer obliged, as used to be the case, to leave the world and to choose the monastic life and a religious rule; they can gain God's grace to no mean extent by pursuing their own profession, unconfined and in secular garb.[1]
>
> *Guibert of Nogent (d.c.1125)*

In recent years the words "**jihad**" and "holy war" have acquired a new resonance. A survey of best-sellers published in the United States after 11 September 2001 would show that there is a sudden impulse to present the history of **Islam** and its relationship or "response" to the rest of the world. The result is a number of competing views of that history. One of the commonplaces of these competing surveys is the picture of Islam as a civilization in decline, at least in comparison to the democratic states of the West. In sharp contrast, in crusades history Islam is a major power against which the emerging European polities measure their newfound strength.

Islamic response to the West doesn't begin during the crusades, but during the period of **Muslim** conquests from the mid-seventh to the 10th centuries. The world in which the crusades occurred was a place where Islam had dominated the Mediterranean for three centuries. **Baghdad** had replaced Rome as the center of a viable empire, and rivaled **Byzantium** rather than Western Europe for military and economic supremacy. The citizen of the 11th century would have seen European monarchies and communes as poor seconds to Baghdad and **Constantinople** as "world powers." The Islamic Empire's weakness in developing effective central institutions was more of a threat to its imperial status than any outside force.

The greatest of the external threats to Islam as an empire in the 10th and 11th centuries was not European conquest but the attack on its center by the **Seljuk Turks**. Internal weakness allowed regions such as **Egypt**, the **Maghrib**, and Spain to break from Baghdad's control into separate states. From the perspective of medieval Muslims, the crusades themselves were a fairly minor distraction in the more important struggle among competing Islamic powers in **Asia Minor**. The most destructive force to counter Islamic hegemony in the medieval period was not European invasion of the 11th, but the **Mongol** invasion of the 13th century.

One interpretation of the crusades is to see them as the way in which Europeans made their entrance onto the stage of world history. What may have begun as simply defense against the encroachment of Constantinople or of Islam in Italy or Spain became a movement of commercial and colonial expansion into the Mediterranean East and the Baltics. In 1096 when the crusades began Christian states were just emerging in Spain, **Sicily**, and southern Italy. The Western European states were in their infancy and the **Baltic** region was fluid and not yet Christianized. The split between the Roman and Orthodox churches that had become formalized in 1054 still looked temporary. When **Acre** fell in 1291 it was Europe that was defeated in the Middle East by a civilization that would reconstitute itself as the **Ottoman Empire**, based at Constantinople from 1453 to 1919. Hindsight sometimes erases the relative fragility of European power during the late Middle Ages.

During the 200 years of the crusades, the European monarchies consolidated their territorial and constitutional identities, claimed the Baltics, and created an ideal of Christian polity that elevated Rome in opposition to the Orthodox faith. Europe "won" in the Mediterranean, but not until the end of World War I, when it finally claimed the territory in **Levant** for which it had struggled in vain in the Middle Ages. What that victory has meant is the theme of the many current works on Islam in the world today, and there is not yet consensus on it. What can be seen now is the distance European states have come from their beginnings in the 12th century, and something of the role that the struggle with Islam played in creating them.

The medieval European crusades must be recognized as having occurred in a political and social situation strikingly dissimilar from that of the 21st century. The most salient of these differences are the role of the **papacy** in endorsing the expeditions, and the political imperatives that guided Rome's policy. The immediate goal of the **First Crusade** was the capture of the holy places in **Jerusalem** by Western European Christians. The focus of the crusade movement after the capture of Jerusalem was the existence of a tiny European kingdom in the Levant between 1099 and 1291. The implicit medieval political goal was the conquest of the Mediterranean region by Europeans who felt threatened by Muslim expansion. In the event, the crusades had as great an impact on Europe as Europeans did in Spain, Sicily, the Baltic region, and the Middle East, where the contest with Islam was played out.

The medieval papacy acquired its civil and military aspects in the third through the sixth centuries, as the Roman Empire collapsed in Western

Europe. Beginning with the reign of Emperor Diocletian (r.284-305), the Roman Mediterranean was split in two to solve problems of administration and defense. A "new Rome" was established in the East at Constantinople during the fourth century. As military needs throughout the empire increased, the Western empire was left to its own devices. From the fourth to the 10th century waves of invasions by Goths, Lombards, and Vikings threatened the survival of Western Roman political, social, and religious institutions. The bishops of Rome came to rely on their own troops or on political alliances with the invaders for protection. They were cut off from the other important churches of **Christendom** (**Alexandria**, Jerusalem, **Antioch**, and Constantinople) in doctrinal matters as well as physically and militarily. The last real attempt to reestablish the unity of the Roman Mediterranean failed when Emperor Justinian I (r.527-65) was unable to conquer the Italian peninsula from his base in Constantinople.

Rome's independence in political matters combined with its claims to religious primacy over Constantinople to sharpen the bishops' estrangement from the emperors. By 1054 Christendom as well as the Empire was split in two, and Constantinople in its turn was threatened by encroaching armies. The bishops of Rome developed their agenda in Western Europe largely independent of the church in the East. The great missionary activity of the Western European church in the centuries during and after the barbarian invasions was as much a bid for survival as it was for expansion of Rome's influence. Sacked by an Ostrogoth army in 410, Rome was trying to position itself as the ideological center of a new Christian polity by the ninth century, and by the 11th, was still struggling to create loyalty to its authority. Rome's claim to primacy and independence is expressed in the doctrine of the popes as successors to St. Peter, rather than as bishops among equals with the other founding churches of the Christian community. The crusade movement was initiated by the papacy as part of an ambitious general organizational program for Western Christendom, but grew quickly to become a popular enthusiasm beyond Rome's control.

Pope **Gregory VII** (r.1073-85) is the most famous of a circle of clerics who founded "a great international movement of reform led by the papacy from the mid-eleventh century onward."[2] The results of this movement were far-reaching in the development of Western political theory and in the history of the church. Only a small part of the pope's goals can be mentioned here. Gregory promoted the idea of "a war . . . blessed by the Church" in which **knights** could "dedicate their swords to the service of Christ and of St. Peter, and realize their Christian vocation by so doing."[3] Although the idea of the "just war" has a long history in Christian writing, this notion of a

Christian vocation for knights is more problematic and harder to trace. Bernard Lewis has recently commented that "the Crusades . . . were themselves an imitation of Muslim practice."[4] It is true that during Gregory's pontificate, well before the First Crusade in 1096, Muslims and **Christians** were at war in Spain. The theology of jihad was already well developed at this point, and is in some ways similar to Gregory's proposal. More striking is the organization of, for instance, Italian cities such as **Genoa** and **Pisa** under papal leadership in 1087 to respond to Muslim attacks on European targets.

Fear of Islam as a rival for the Mediterranean was a powerful force in European thinking from the eighth through the 17th century.[5] From the 13th century Muslim states emerged in India, Indonesia, and China as well. To the extent that Western Europeans understood its expansion, the spread of Islam in its first three centuries from Arabia through Egypt, Syria, Turkey, and Iran was impressive and frightening.

North Africa became a base of operations for control of the Iberian Peninsula by 711.[6] During the next two centuries Muslim control spread by invasion and conversion throughout southern Iberia, Sicily, and northern Africa. The idea of the jihad was developed by the 900s in the context of this Islamic expansion.[7] In the 790s the first Spanish Christian kingdoms developed in the northern portions of the peninsula. Until the 11th century there can be no comparison between the sophisticated and influential culture of Islamic Spain, or *al-Andalus*, and the emerging northern Christian kingdoms of **León-Castile** and **Aragon**. But by 1077 Alfonso VI of León was powerful enough to make a claim to the peninsula. His pretensions did not become reality until 1492, but he laid the basis for an ongoing war that came to be called the **Reconquista** by Europeans. In his search for political legitimacy, Alfonso reached an uneasy alliance with Pope Gregory VII and a closer relationship with the increasingly influential French monastic order of **Cluny**. Crusade ideology, Gregorian reform of the church, and monastic reform in imitation of Cluny all developed in the 11th century as part of a general program of renewal and reform for clergy and laity. The war with militant Islam in Iberia can be seen as one of the foundations for Pope Gregory's vision of a Christian vocation devoted to the sword.

It is not traditionally seen as the first crusade. Gregory's vision never became reality. The First Crusade was launched by Pope **Urban II** in 1095. Urban's speech is seen as groundbreaking and the crusade of 1096-99 as normative by historians seeking to understand crusading as a movement.[8]

The versions of Pope Urban's sermon that survive differ in important details, but all contain some phrases which suggest the idea of a **pilgrimage indulgence** for warfare against Muslims. Pilgrimage is a practice common to many religions and older than Christianity. The indulgence is a medieval Christian idea, as is the particular view of **martyrdom** that emerges from the crusade chronicles. Urban and his contemporaries were aware that the crusade was a new phenomenon, one that seemed best described as an armed pilgrimage. The pope himself may have been surprised by the response to his sermon. In John France's *Military History of the First Crusade*, he estimates that "an army of 50,000-60,000, plus non-combatants was set in motion in 1096. Such numbers were unknown in the west."[9] Urban's offer of forgiveness of sins in return for fighting in the army of Christ was as unprecedented as the response to it. Even the end result of the First Crusade was unexpected.

The army which gathered in 1096 did not take Jerusalem until 1099. What should have been overwhelming tactical problems, including supplies and logistical support for an army coming from such a great distance, were somehow overcome. The victorious crusaders seem themselves to have been caught off guard by their success. They celebrated their massacre of the city's inhabitants with a mass and procession, focusing on the miraculous in their explanation of their triumph: the **Holy Lance** discovered at Antioch, the posthumous appearance of the saintly **Adhémar of Le Puy** on the battlefield, their possession of the Sepulchre of Christ and the miracle of the Holy Fire that occurred there annually. Recent scholarship has emphasized their eagerness to connect their actions, and especially their massacre of the civilians in Jerusalem, both with Old Testament battles like the siege of Jericho, and with events they believed would herald the approach of the Apocalypse.[10]

This medieval characterization of military strategy in biblical terms was the moral justification for what was essentially a war of aggression. The Byzantine or East Roman Empire had made a practice of hiring mercenaries over its long and complex military history. A sizeable force of Western European mercenaries seems to have been all that Emperor Alexius I **Comnenus** (r.1081-1118) wanted when he appealed to the pope for assistance against the Seljuk Turks of western **Anatolia** in 1095. Accounts of the arrival of the various contingents of the First Crusade at Constantinople make it clear that the Emperor expected all conquered territory to be returned to him. Subsequent events make it equally clear that at least some of the leaders of the crusading army intended to hold land in the East themselves. How they expected to do so, or what they intended their relations to be with Emperor, pope, and the overwhelmingly superior number of native inhabitants remain subjects of debate. The inability of modern scholars to come to consensus on the goals of the First Crusaders is rooted in the apparent failure of

6 • Introduction

the leaders of the expedition to form any.[11] What the surviving sources offer is a heady mixture of lust for conquest, hatred of Islam, and religious enthusiasm. Pope Urban's speech initiating the movement mixes all of these elements with a desire to reunite the two halves of Christendom, and offer an alternative field of action to professional soldiers who were fighting each other at home in Europe.

The alternative field of action was effectively created. Four tiny principalities or counties at Jerusalem, Antioch, **Edessa**, and **Tripoli** were founded by the leaders of the First Crusade. Their provisioning and fortunes became the focus for crusade activity until 1291. Expeditions from Europe left for the Levant annually from 1100, and the fall of Jerusalem to **Saladin** in 1187 had an impact on the West out of all proportion to the strategic value of the crusader kingdoms. The tension between the Emperor of Constantinople, God's viceroy in the Eastern Roman Empire, and the heir to St. Peter in Rome became ever more urgent and complex, as victorious Europeans established civil and ecclesiastical jurisdiction in areas claimed by Byzantium.

Planning for the **Second Crusade** (1144-46) was more purposeful and on a greater scale than for any of the other crusades.[12] Its failure was therefore as influential a model for the movement as the success of the First Crusade had been. While future crusaders looked back to the heroes of the first expedition again and again as models, the humiliation of the great armies of France and **Flanders** at **Damascus** undermined confidence in the leadership of the papacy and the viability of the movement. One of the most influential ecclesiastics of the 12th century, **St. Bernard of Clairvaux**, had recruited the armies of the Second Crusade. Faced with their failure, he confirmed their identification with the ancient Hebrews by linking their defeat with the punishment God meted out in the Old Testament as a call to repentance. But there were some successes, notably in Iberia and in the Baltics against the pagan **Wends**, as bands of crusaders received permission to commute their pilgrimage indulgence to other fields of battle. The foundation of the **military orders**, originating in Jerusalem with the **Templars**, had fateful consequences in Eastern European and Spanish history as well as in the Levant.

The **Third Crusade** (1189-92) was also the result of impressive organization, led by the Holy Roman Emperor as well as the kings of France and England, but equally negligible in its results in the East. Participants in the **Fourth** and **Fifth Crusades** (1204, 1218) benefited from what by now was a century of experience with Islamic political realities. Strategic considerations identified **Ayyubid Egypt** as the key to the reconquest of Jerusalem, and aimed the Fourth Crusade at Byzantium itself in a struggle for its logistical support. Crucial to these efforts were the fleets of the Italian city states, Genoa, Pisa, and **Venice**, which played a significant role throughout the crusade movement in transport, supply, blockade of ports under siege, and naval battles such as the attack on Constantinople itself in 1204. The papal struggle with various European powers for control of the Italian peninsula also played an important collateral role in the fight for the Levant, beginning with the conquest of Sicily and the south by the Guiscards (*see* **Bohemond of Taranto**) as a prelude to the First Crusade, and highlighted by Emperor Frederick II's expedition (the **Sixth Crusade**) as an excommunicate in 1228.

One of the difficulties of writing a coherent narrative of the movement has been its origination in and effects on the greater landscape of European and Islamic history. Many of these causes and effects have their roots in the source of the crusade idea, the papacy itself, and its ideological centrality for the rhetoric, and to a certain extent, the reality of Western European politics and culture. The **Albigensian Crusade**, for instance, originally a response to the murder of a papal legate in the Midi in 1208, became a key event in the consolidation of French royal power and territorial integrity. The **Children's Crusade** of 1212 was essentially an exasperated response to the loss of the True **Cross** at **Hattin** in 1187 and subsequent failure of the Third Crusade to retake Jerusalem. But it is also part of a series of expeditions dominated by members of the lower classes that begin with the ill-fated People's Crusade led by **Peter the Hermit** and the massacres of **Jews** in the Rhineland initiated by **Emicho of Flonheim** in 1096.

The Northern Crusades of the **Teutonic Knights** in the Baltics fall into this category of collateral damage, as do the failed expeditions of St. **Louis, King of France**, to Egypt in 1249 (the Seventh Crusade) and Tunis in 1270. Collateral benefits might include **Sainte-Chapelle**, built to house relics from the Holy Land, and the many other churches and shrines built to imitate pilgrimage sites in the Levant. The cultural impact of the movement can be seen in a number of different areas, notably at the intersection of the arts with medieval spirituality, including pilgrim guide books, the architecture of pilgrimage churches, reliquaries and other artifacts connected with popular spirituality, and accounts of the thefts, miraculous or otherwise, of holy **relics**. The influence of the crusades on Europe for better or worse was significant, from military (*see* **Castles**; **Armor**) and medical technology borrowed from Islam to the **Inquisition**, a legal procedure developed in the course of the crusade against the **Cathars**.

The crusade movement is so intimately connected with so many aspects of European culture that histories of it do not end neatly but rather become

8 • Introduction

so diffuse as to be indistinguishable from general accounts of the late medieval era. The attempt of King Henry III of England to build his public image in imitation of and rivalry to King Louis IX of France with the relic of the **Holy Blood** crosses the boundaries between the history of the crusades and the development of the English monarchy. The establishment of chairs of Oriental Languages at European universities after 1310 is a response to problems raised by an effort that officially ended with the fall of Acre in 1291. The **Dominican** ethos of preparation for missions that was born in the early 12th century and provided so much of the energy for the medieval university owes as much to the crusades as it does to the "new" spirituality of saints **Dominic** or **Francis of Assisi**, both of whom can be found in the history of expeditions against heretics and Muslims. **Humbert of Romans**, university professor of theology in the 13th century, is known for a number of works reflecting the religious culture of his age, among them a book of model sermons to be used by crusade preachers. There is a point after which an emphasis on crusading as distinct from European politics and culture, as a phenomenon that needs a separate history, loses its meaning. Recent scholarship on crusades has emphasized that continuity with medieval culture rather than viewing the movement as an aberration.

Christopher Tyerman's recent work, *The Invention of the Crusades*, has reminded us that the definition of crusading and the interpretation of its meaning were as problematic for medieval historians as they are for us.[13] This observation brings us full circle to the raft of best-sellers on Islam being published as this dictionary is being written. Are we at war? What is the contest for, and who is the enemy? What are the possible consequences of the conflict? The circumstances are very different, but the questions are the same. Whatever view one takes of them, the crusades make up a vital piece of the puzzle presented by our own time and place.

Note: Words and terms in boldface type reference dictionary entries.

[1] Guibert of Nogent, as quoted in Alan Forey, *The Military Orders* (Toronto, 1992): 13.
[2] Brian Tierney, *Western Europe in the Middle Ages*, 6th edition (Boston, 1999): 216.
[3] H. E. J. Cowdrey, "The Genesis of the Crusades: The Springs of the Holy War," in *Popes, Monks, and Crusaders* (London, 1984): 19-20.

[4] Bernard Lewis, "The Revolt of Islam," in *The New Yorker* (19 November 2001): 60.
[5] Edward Said, *Orientalism* (New York, 1978): 59. For a discussion of responses to Said, *see* Tolan under Islam in the bibliography.
[6] Bernard F. Reilly, *The Medieval Spains* (Cambridge, 1993): 52.
[7] Abdulaziz A. Sachedina, "The Development of *Jihad* in Islamic Revelation and History," in *Cross, Crescent, and Sword*, ed. James Turner Johnson and John Kelsey (New York, 1990): 37.
[8] For several versions of Urban's sermon translated into English, see Edward Peters, *The First Crusade*, 2nd ed. (Philadelphia, 1998).
[9] John France, *Victory in the East: A Military History of the First Crusade* (Cambridge, 1994): 2.
[10] Jean Flori, *Pierre l'Ermite et la Première Croisade* (Paris, 1999). For an overview of crusade motivation in English that emphasizes the social and political rather than the religious, see Marcus Bull, "Origins," in Jonathan Riley-Smith, ed., *The Oxford Illustrated History of the Crusades* (Oxford, 1995): 13-33.
[11] Christopher Tyerman, *The Invention of the Crusades* (Toronto, 1998).
[12] Martin Hoch, "The Price of Failure: The Second Crusade as a Turning-Point in the History of the Latin East," in *The Second Crusade: Scope and Consequences*, ed. Jonathan Phillips and Martin Hoch (Manchester, United Kingdom, 2001): 193.
[13] See note 11, above.

THE DICTIONARY

-A-

ABBASID DYNASTY. (750-1258 A.D.). The Umayyad dynasty ruled Islam from **Damascus** (661-750) but was unsettled by three civil wars over the succession. The third civil war (744-50) resulted in the overthrow of the reigning caliph by the army in Syria, and then all-out war over the question of hereditary vs. elective succession. *See* **Muslim**. A Shia uprising in Khurasan (northern Iran and Afghanistan) in 747 completed the fall of the elected Umayyads. This revolt succeeded in placing a member of a collateral branch of **Muhammad**'s family on the throne. The Abbasid dynasty then had the task of resolving the essentially irresolvable succession problem. The base of their support was in Khurasan and Iraq, both of which could offer a class of bureaucrats familiar with Sassanid Persia's administrative structure. **Baghdad** was built as their capital in 762.

For the first century of its existence, the dynasty represented an Islamic dominance of the Mediterranean under local governments stretching from India to southern France, and owing at least nominal allegiance to Baghdad. Autonomous governments existed in Spain (**al-Andalus**), the **Maghrib**, Khurasan, and **Egypt**. During the 10th and 11th centuries the Islamic empire became increasingly fragmented, and the dynasty increasingly depended on slave armies recruited among the nomadic Turkic tribes. Emerging **Christian** power in Spain created the **Reconquista**, the Normans took Muslim **Sicily**, and the **Byzantine Empire** raided Syria. The **Fatimid** dynasty of Egypt intermittently controlled **Jerusalem**, and its rulers interrupted European **pilgrimage** there by destroying the Church of the **Holy Sepulchre** in 1009-10. The **Seljuk Turks**, acting as sultans in the name of the Abbasid caliphate from 1055, campaigned against the Fatimids, and the contest between the two Islamic powers helped the **First Crusaders** to take the holy city in 1099.

By the 1250s the caliphs were essentially powerless, controlling at most the city and region of Baghdad. From 1246 the **Mongols** demanded signs of submission, including troops to be sent on request. In 1258 Hulagu (d.1265) at the head of a vast army, estimated at from 70,000 to 120,000 men, besieged Baghdad. The city was taken and sacked, the inhabitants massacred first and then their caliph. Reportedly,

Qubilai Khan (r.1260-94) had given Hulagu all the land from the Oxus River to the furthest reaches of Egypt, which would have destroyed not only the Abbasids, but also the **Mamluk** Empire. The Mamluks were able to block Mongol conquest. The **Ottoman Turks** were the eventual victors in Abbasid territory starting in 1281.

The Abbasid Caliphs based in Baghdad during the crusade period were: 1094 al-Mustazhir, 1118 al-Mustarshid, 1135 al-Rashid, 1136 al-Muqtafi, 1160 al-Mustanjid, 1170 al-Mustadi, 1180 al-Nasir, 1225 al-Zahir, 1226 al-Mustansir, 1242-58 al-Mustasim.

ACRE, DESCRIPTION. A harbor town about 90 miles from **Jerusalem**, known from the Roman period as Ptolemaïs, and mentioned in the Old Testament (Judges 1:31) as a Canaanite stronghold. It became a **Muslim** city in 636. The crusaders captured it in 1104, and held it until 1291, when the city was again lost to **Islam**. After the fall of the **Latin Kingdom of Jerusalem** to **Saladin** in 1187, the Latin Kingdom was reduced to several ports and about 350 miles of the coast of Syria. Acre and other coastal cities such as **Tyre** became focal points for launching a reconquest of the Holy Land. King **Richard I** of England occupied Acre, which had surrendered to Saladin in 1187, during the **Third Crusade**. **Jacques de Vitry** was made bishop of Acre as a base for his 1217 preaching tour for the **Fifth Crusade**.

The defenses of the city were formidable. It was situated on a peninsula, so that the southern and western approaches were blocked by the sea and sea walls. There was a harbor fortification called the Tower of Flies and a stone jetty or mole to challenge naval approach. The land wall was supplemented by a deep ditch.

The Third Crusade established Acre as the center of what is sometimes called the Second Latin Kingdom of Jerusalem. It served as a new home base for those who did not return to Europe or leave for **Cyprus** after the kingdom was lost in 1187. King Richard was able to procure access to Jerusalem by truce, as was **Holy Roman Emperor** Frederick II during the **Sixth Crusade**. Both encountered some resistance by the native barons, who fought to preserve their independence from Frederick, in particular, at the same time that they tried to use the crusaders from Europe to help regain their lands. Resistance to Frederick's marshal and his fleet in 1231 created the "Commune of Acre," a sworn association or confraternity of knights and merchants dedicated to Saint Andrew. Their immediate purpose was to prevent the imperial troops from resuming control in Acre. Frederick had married the heiress to Jerusalem, and she had produced a son, Conrad, before her death in 1228.

The legitimacy of Frederick's claim did not make it easier for the barons of the kingdom to accept his direct intervention in their affairs.

ACRE, SIEGE OF 1189. In August of 1189 **Guy of Lusignan** was commanding the land forces of the **Latin Kingdom of Jerusalem** assisted by the **Pisan** navy in the siege of **Acre** that began the **Third Crusade**. Guy, desperate to regain his status since the fall of his kingdom in 1187, attempted to blockade Acre with the help of the Pisans.

He was opposed not only by the garrison, but by **Saladin**'s field army, camped close by. To protect his position, Guy had to surround it with a double line of trenches, dug while under attack from both sides. He had situated his camp so as to blockade the city but was unable to completely cut Acre off from either Saladin or other **Muslim** coastal strongholds. Guy's own people were supplied from **Tyre** and southern Italy. During the winter shipping was difficult and both sides suffered from famine.

Guy was assisted in 1190-91 by a number of European forces, including those of **Conrad of Montferrat, Frederick Barbarossa, Henry of Champagne**, and **Genoa**. Even with this help, he was unable to take the city. The balance was tipped by the arrival of the kings of France and England in 1191. Both brought additional money, men, supplies, and material for siege weapons. King **Richard**'s men were able to sink a Muslim supply ship, depriving the garrison of food and reinforcements at a crucial moment. Both kings had **siege engines** constructed and manned which, according to Muslim sources, reduced the height of the city walls with a continual barrage of rock. The European troops worked together with **pilgrims** and other noncombatants to fill in the ditches that protected the walls. One woman reportedly urged that at her imminent death her body be added to the fill she had helped to carry to the defensive ditches.

In June Richard's sappers brought down the main land tower and its adjoining wall, urged on by his offer of a cash payment for each stone removed. While the crusaders were still unable to breach the walls, they did hold off Saladin's attacks in addition to maintaining the blockade and eating away at Acre's defenses. The city surrendered on 12 July 1191, benefiting from Saladin's presence in that he protected the garrison and Muslim inhabitants from sack and massacre.

ACRE, SIEGE OF 1291. In 1288 the **Egyptian** army took the port of **Tripoli**, and preparations were made to take **Acre**. The death of the sultan caused a delay until his successor consolidated the new regime, but in 1291 the **siege** began. The **Mamluks** used **siege engines** that had been shipped to **Damascus** and from there transported to Acre. The rulers of Cairo and Damascus were at odds, which weakened the **Muslim** attack. The siege lasted 80 days.

In the mid-twelfth century, the population is estimated to have been about 30,000. In 1291, when Acre fell to Egypt, there were about 700 to 800 knights and 14,000 foot soldiers to defend the city. Some were members of military orders, some were residents of the reduced **Latin Kingdom** or of **Cyprus**, and some were **pilgrims**, carrying whatever arms they had. They represented, in other words, the total fighting force of the crusader kingdoms. The total Mamluk force at this time was somewhere between 20,000 and 40,000 trained and equipped troops.

In previous crusades, the **Christian** numbers have been put at, for instance in 1239, 4,000 knights based at Acre, and in the crusade of 1250, 2,500 knights, 5,000 bowmen, and other foot soldiers. Without help from the West, the crusader kingdom could not defend itself against Egypt or any other indigenous force. The residents, perhaps expecting defeat, had removed what might otherwise have been plundered by the victors. The remaining crusader strongholds at **Tyre**, Beirut, Athlith, Tortosa, and Jebail quickly surrendered.

ADHÉMAR OF MONTEIL, BISHOP OF LE PUY. (d.1098). Pope **Urban II** apparently consulted with a number of secular and ecclesiastical lords before and during his journey through France to the council at Clermont where he preached the **First Crusade** in 1095. The bishop of Le Puy was one of these notables. He had been raised in a noble family, and was an excellent horseman with training in arms. He had made the **pilgrimage** to **Jerusalem**, and had a name in his diocese as an energetic defender of the territorial rights and jurisdiction of the church. Adhémar came forward immediately after the pope announced the crusade to a crowd assembled to hear him in a field outside the town of Clermont. The bishop was on the spot designated leader of the expedition. This dramatic moment was presumably prearranged.

Adhémar was made papal legate and traveled with the crusade through the **siege of Antioch** in 1098. There he was one of the few who refused any credence to Peter Bartholomew's visions and the discovery of the **Holy Lance**. He was willing to use the enthusiasm of the princes and the army for the relic to encourage an oath by which they promised not to abandon the expedition at a moment when success seemed impossible. He also held the princes, as long as he led the expedition, to their oaths to Alexius **Comnenus** to return any **Byzantine** territory they conquered. Adhémar died on 1 August 1098 of typhoid at Antioch. His death signaled the end of the already tenuous cooperation with the Byzantines and an increase in the intensity of the infighting among the princes who continued on crusade, notably **Godfrey of Bouillon, Bohemond of Taranto,** and **Raymond of Saint Gilles.**

AL-ADIL. (d.1218). For the early career of al-Adil, *see* **Ayyubid.** Al-Adil held much of upper Mesopotamia from 1186-1198, and was governor of **Damascus** from 1198-1200, when he succeeded to the sultanate of **Egypt.**

In 1204 al-Adil was in Damascus when Europeans who had declined to be diverted with the **Fourth Crusade** to **Constantinople** landed in **Acre** and used it as a base for raids in the Jordan valley. The sultan assembled an army vastly superior to the crusade forces but used it to impose a generous truce on them and then retired to Cairo. In 1207 the destructive raids from crusader **Tripoli** and **Hospitaller Krac des Chevaliers** impelled him to gather the largest army since **Saladin**'s campaigns, a force of perhaps 10,000 cavalry. Sieges of Krac and Tripoli failed, and the Egyptians retreated with a truce in place.

Al-Adil's lack of interest in the Europeans could not survive the arrival of 15,000 knights at Acre in 1217 for the **Fifth Crusade.** His army was numerically inferior, and he was forced to abandon the citizens of Baysan and several inland villages to the invaders. As he rushed towards Damascus he ordered the governor to ready the city for a siege, and put out a general call to arms in the region. The Europeans surprised him by heading for his recently rebuilt fortifications at Mount Tabor, under the leadership of King **John of Brienne.** Their attack startled the garrison, but the crusaders were repelled with some difficulty and forced back to Acre to raid from that base through the winter of 1217.

In May of 1218 the crusade landed upstream of Damietta, its leaders having decided that Egypt was the key to the reconquest of the old **Latin Kingdom of Jerusalem.** Al-Adil was in Syria when the crusaders arrived, and sent the army back to assist **al-Kamil** in defending Egypt. Meanwhile he ordered the destruction of the fortifications at Mt. Tabor, in case there should be another attempt on it. He was chiefly occupied in trying to keep the sultan of Rum (an independent **Seljuk** Turkish kingdom in **Anatolia**) from taking **Aleppo**. He was forced to leave for Egypt when the crusaders captured the Chain Tower in the middle of the Nile that protected Damietta from enemy approach. He died in 1218 on his way to relieve Egypt.

ALAMUT. The headquarters of the Ismailis, or **Assassins**, as they were known to the crusaders, was located north of Tehran (Iran) at Alamut in the Elburz Mountains.

ALBERT OF AACHEN. Albert was one of the historians of the **First Crusade** and of the early years of the **Latin Kingdom** (1096-1119). Albert's chronicle makes **Godfrey of Bouillon** the central figure of the expedition. The chronicle has not been translated into English, and nothing is known of its author beyond what can be surmised from his work. Albert identifies himself as a canon at Aachen/Aix, and says that he did not go on the expedition but spoke to many who returned. The original manuscript is lost. The earliest copy dates from the first half of the 12th century. Parts of the chronicle are translated into English in collections of sources on the expedition and on crusading.

ALBERT VON BUXHÖVDEN. (d.1229). Albert or *Albrecht* was bishop of Livonia and founder of the order of the **Swordbrethren** in 1202 at Riga. Albert was unable to spread **Christianity** without the help of a crusade army. After each expedition of the Northern or **Baltic Crusades**, his diocese rejected their forced baptisms, making a permanent force of crusading knights a necessity. They were based at Riga and garrisoned fortresses as territory was conquered.

Albert was active in Livonia before 1200, when he led a crusade up the Düna River and founded the city of Riga (1201). The first bishop of Livonia was Meinhard, who died in an effort to convert the inhabitants of the area in 1196. The second bishop was Berthold, the Cisterican abbot of Lockum in Hanover, who was martyred in 1198 during a crusade backed by Bremen and Lübeck. The missions to Livonia brought German colonists as well as clerics, posing a dual threat to the interests of the indigenous people. The military order of Swordbrethren consolidated Albert's gains, making possible the establishment of the dependent bishoprics of Semgall-Kurland, Dorpat, and Oesel. Albert is credited with the conversion of his diocese by 1206.

ALBIGENSIAN CRUSADE. As early as the Third Lateran Council in 1179 the **papacy** had noted the rise of **Catharism** in southern France and offered an **indulgence** to those willing to fight heretics and bandits there. Pope **Innocent III**, from his accession in 1198, worked to end Cathar heresy in southern France through a series of papal legates who were to preach, run public debates, and in general support orthodox clergy. Among these legates was Peter of Castlenau, from the Cistercian monastery of Fontfroide who was archdeacon of the cathedral of Maguelonne (a medieval Mediterranean port).

Peter was appointed legate in 1199, and by 1206 he himself had requested permission to retire. The local clergy warned that he would be assassinated by heretics, and he was allowed six months of retreat, after which he returned to his post. 1206 was also the year St. **Dominic** arrived to preach in the Midi, as an assistant to his bishop, Diego of Osma (northern Spain). Count Raymond VI of **Toulouse** (r.1194-1222), who had been excommunicated by the legate, was suspected of engineering Peter's assassination on 14 January 1208. Innocent held Raymond responsible both for the murder and for failing to prosecute heretics in his district.

The pope offered the same indulgence for the crusade in southern France as for expeditions to the **Levant**. An army described by medieval chronicles as the largest in **Christendom** gathered in the spring of 1209 in response to his call. Raymond's negotiations with the new legate, Arnold Amalric, abbot of Cîteaux (r.1200-12), led to a temporary reconciliation, and Raymond was able to join the crusade. Arnold had been the leader of a Cistercian preaching mission to the Midi which began in 1206, and he went on to become archbishop of Narbonne (r.1212-25). The Albigensian Crusade began under his leadership as legate.

The charges to which Raymond was forced to plead guilty in order to lift the ban of excommunication are indicative of the mixture of issues behind the crusade. The charges ranged from levying unjust tolls, hiring mercenaries, and conferring public office on **Jews**, to disputes with local clergy over property rights. The response of King Philip II of France (r.1180-1223) also shows the mixture of issues. The king refused to lead the crusade, due to his own commitments, and tried to limit recruitment. When the pope appealed to Philip to enforce the decree of excommunication against his vassal, the king suggested that Raymond should be tried and convicted of heresy before his land was confiscated.

Béziers fell to the crusading army in July 1209. The pillage and slaughter of both heretics and orthodox citizens was impressive enough to cause other cities to surrender without a struggle. Carcassonne offered a resistance of only two weeks in early August. At this point a military commander was chosen from among the nobles of northern France who made up the bulk of the army: Simon, eventually earl of Leicester and baron of Montfort (r.1181-1218), whose ancestral lands lay southwest of Paris. He was already a notable crusader, having refused to follow the **Fourth Crusade** in its attack on Christian **Zara** and **Constantinople**, instead traveling to the Holy Land to fight the **Muslims**. His campaign in the winter of 1209-10 was unsuccessful. Crusaders normally agreed to serve only for a set time period, in this case 40 days, so that Simon was constantly hampered by recruitment and low numbers.

A council held at Montpellier in January and February of 1211 renewed the estrangement between Raymond of Toulouse and the papal legates. Accounts of the dispute vary. The crusade turned to the lands of Raymond and his allies. Assisted by Bishop Peter of Paris (r.1208-19) and an army from northern France, Simon laid **siege** to the stronghold of Lavaur in March 1211. Accounts of his victory in May have him burning 400 heretics, hanging over 80 knights, and throwing the countess of Lavaur into a well which was then covered with stones. The brutality may have been an attempt to encourage quick surrenders in neighboring towns and to curb the tendency of strongholds once taken from turning their allegiance back to Raymond as soon as Simon's army was out of sight.

On 12 September 1213 Simon won the battle of Muret, where King Peter II of **Aragon** (r.1196-1213), a notable crusader against Islam who had intervened on behalf of Raymond of Toulouse, was killed. By 1214 Simon was effectively in control of much of Raymond's territory. Lands won by Simon were to be distributed according to the decisions of the Fourth Lateran Council (1215), where plans were also made for the **Fifth Crusade**. After considerable debate, the bulk of the conquered territory went to Simon, in spite of the fact that Count Raymond VI of Toulouse had once again been reconciled to the church.

Over the next 10 years Raymond and his heir set about winning Toulouse back. Simon was able to keep the territory of Narbonne. His continued war against Raymond ended with Simon's death at the siege of St. Cyprien on 25 June 1218. Simon's son Amalric vainly attempted to step into his father's role. In January 1226 Louis VIII, king of France (r.1223-1226), led a new crusade to the south, essentially against the resurgent counts of Toulouse. In November the king died at Montpensier in Auvergne, leaving a 12-year-old heir.

In 1229 Pope Gregory IX was able to arrange for a settlement. Count Raymond VII (r.1222-49) was able to retain part of his ancestral lands on harsh terms. His obligations to the king of France were strengthened, his ability to pass on his inheritance was limited, and he was ordered to pay reparations which may have equaled his entire income over a four-year period. Part of the agreement required him to donate funds for what would eventually be a university at Toulouse, in order to train clergy in the south. Even more fatefully, a process for identifying and prosecuting heretics was spelled out at the council of Toulouse in November 1229. Led by Cardinal Romanus (papal legate 1225-29), the archbishops of Narbonne, Bordeaux, and Auch, and including Count Raymond, the company laid the foundation for the **Inquisition**. For more information on heresy, *see also* **Waldensians**.

ALEPPO. A city-commune in Syria, like **Damascus** held during the crusade period by a series of **Muslim** warriors, starting with Aq Sunqur, **Seljuk** Turk governor (r.c.1087-1094), Ridwan (r.1095-1113), **Zengi** (r.1128-1146) and **Nur al-Din** (r.1146-1174). Saladin, a Muslim **Kurd** who categorized himself as Nur al-Din's successor, took Aleppo in his turn as ruler of **Syria**. His successors, the **Ayyubid** (1193-1250), technically held it as his heirs.

Aleppo was heavily fortified, boasting a walled citadel raised 150 feet above the surrounding city. The citadel's entrance was protected by a moat, bridge, and gate defended by two towers. A well, arsenal, mosque, gardens, and palace were constructed to help withstand a **siege** and provide a residence suitable to the status of the city's rulers. Even Aleppo's defenses, arguably the most impressive in the **Levant**, were not proof against the **Mongols**, who were able to mine the walls of the citadel and so take the city in 1260. Neither the Mongols nor the sultans of **Egypt** were able to effectively rule the largely Sunni Muslim population of Aleppo for any length of time.

Syria was not a political unit during the crusade period. Damascus and Aleppo were effectively independent principalities, theoretically held in turn by the Ayyubid and **Mamluk** Dynasties, but at no point securely under the rule of any power. The territory of Aleppo was threatened not only by Egypt and the Mongols, but by the closer and settled principalities of crusader **Antioch**, the kingdom of Cilician **Armenia**, and the Rum Seljuks of **Anatolia**. For them, as for other Sunni rulers, the **Assassins** based at mountain strongholds in northern Syria were a continuing problem.

ALEXANDER III, POPE. (r.1159-81). Alexander's election was disputed by Victor IV (r.1159-64). Alexander was supported by the **Byzantines, Sicily,** and most of Western Europe with the exception of **Holy Roman Emperor Frederick I,** who backed Victor instead. During the dispute a crusade could not effectively be preached, which affected the ability of the **Latin Kingdom of Jerusalem** to defend crusader territory in the **Levant** against the **jihad** of **Nur al-Din.** On 16 January 1181 the pope did issue a crusade encyclical, but he died in August without having done enough to promote a crusade. The encyclical, *Cor nostrum*, puts an emphasis on leprosy as the "just judgment" of God that somewhat undermines its theme of support for **Jerusalem** and its ruler King **Baldwin IV,** "the Leper." Alexander's support for the **Baltic Crusades** enabled the conquest of territory in that region by Western Europeans. *See also* **Papacy.**

ALEXANDRIA. Alexandria was **Egypt's** most important port throughout the medieval period, and regarded as a dangerous rival by the Italian city-communes which also relied on Mediterranean trade. It had been the center of **Byzantine** government of Egypt, and was replaced for administrative purposes with Cairo by the **Fatimids.** Situated to the west of the Nile River delta, it was connected to the river by a canal that necessitated constant maintenance to work properly. These and other public works projects were crucial to commercial success and therefore a major concern of Egyptian government regardless of political affiliation.

The conquest of Egypt was a major objective of the **Latin Kingdom of Jerusalem** under **Amalric I** (r.1163-74), whose plans for an attack on Alexandria 28 July-2 August 1174 relied on the combination of an internal Shia **Muslim** revolt, European land forces, and **Sicilian** naval support. Amalric died before the plan could come to fruition, and **Saladin's** Kurdish and Turkish troops established effective military control in time to subdue the revolt, leaving the Sicilian **naval** forces to make the effort in vain. They arrived at the city with more than 150 galleys, 36 horse transports, and six ships carrying materials for **siege** warfare, including rock to use for missiles. The Normans were able to land and take down part of the city walls before withdrawing in haste at the approach of Saladin's army.

ALFONSO ENRÍQUES, KING OF PORTUGAL. (d.1185). Alfonso was the son of Henry of Burgundy, and the nephew of Duke Odo I. The latter was on crusade in the **Levant** in 1101. One of Alfonso's daughters married Count Philip of **Flanders**; an illegitimate son served briefly as Grand Master of the **Hospitallers**.

Alfonso, who described himself as a brother of the **Templar order**, ruled Portugal from 1128. He won a major battle against the **Muslims** in Iberia in 1139 and took the title of king. Supported by the Templars in his early career, he agreed to hold his kingdom under the direct protection of the **papacy** in 1143. The Cistercian order, which specialized in establishing monasteries in frontier or wastelands, began its expansion in Portugal during his reign. He asked for **Bernard of Clairvaux**'s help in raising an army as part of the **Second Crusade**, which resulted in the conquest of Lisbon in 1147.

ALMOHAD. The Spanish name of the **Muwahhid** dynasty, which originated in northern Africa. *See also* **Reconquista**.

ALMORAVID. The Spanish name of the **Murabit** dynasty, which originated in northern Africa. *See also* **Reconquista**.

ALP ARSLAN. (1029-72). The **Seljuk** Turk Empire was based at Isafahan in Iran by 1043. Alp Arslan assumed control after his uncle, Toghril-Beg, died without heirs in 1063. Moving away from the pattern of raids for plunder, he created a centralized monarchy, and solidified the goals of his father and uncle to replace the **Baghdad** caliphs as the supreme power in the **Islamic** world. In 1064 he invaded **Armenia**, and in 1068 Georgia. He defeated the **Byzantines** at Manzikert in 1071, but was assassinated in 1072. During his rule he created a protectorate over **Aleppo**. His successors were his son Malik-Shah and then **Kilij Arslan**. Malik-Shah divided his realm with his brother, and they established a Seljuk ruler, Artuq, in **Jerusalem**. Artuq's sons were ousted from the city by a **Fatimid** commander, Afdal, in 1098. After 1095 successors to Malik-Shah's rule were members of his dynasty, Ridwan in Aleppo and Duqaq in **Damascus**.

ALSACE. *See* **Flanders**.

AMALRIC/AMAURY I. (d.1174). King in **Jerusalem** 1163-74, Amalric was the second son of **Fulk** and Melisend, and the brother of **Baldwin III**. Under Baldwin III, Amalric held the title of Count of **Ascalon** and **Jaffa**. Amalric was an energetic monarch who opened an offensive on the **Muslims** by attacking **Egypt**. The expeditions of 1163, 1164, and

1167 were unsuccessful and expensive but they show a clear understanding of contemporary **Islamic** politics and they carried the struggle into enemy territory. Amalric died in the midst of preparations for an attack on **Alexandria** in alliance with **Sicily**. Amalric's marriage to Agnes Courtenay, by whom he had **Baldwin IV** and Sybil (d.1190), was annulled at the insistence of the patriarch of Jerusalem and the High Court of the kingdom before his coronation. The children of the first marriage were legitimized, and inherited in turn, Baldwin in his own right and Sybil with her husband **Guy of Lusignan**. Amalric married Maria Comnena, great-niece of **Byzantine Emperor** Manuel I **Comnenus** in 1167. In 1171, after several vain appeals to Western Europe, Amalric made a state visit to **Constantinople** and obtained a promise of military help by accepting officially a status previous rulers of the kingdom had strenuously resisted: vassal of the emperor. Maria's daughter Isabel (d.1205) eventually inherited the kingdom, passing it on to her second through fourth husbands in turn: **Conrad of Montferrat, Henry of Champagne**, and Amaury/Aimery of **Lusignan**. After Amalric's death, Maria married Balian of **Ibelin**.

In 1173-74 Amalric received an offer from the Syrian **Assassins** to ally against **Nur al-Din**, ruler of Syria, whose **jihad** against the Christians was part of a program of expansion that alarmed all his neighbors. The **Templar** march in Tortosa had allowed them to collect annual tribute from the Assassins. According to **William of Tyre**, the historian of the kingdom who was at court at this time, the Templars opposed the agreement reached with Amalric because it deprived them of the tribute. In retaliation, they murdered the envoy from the Assassins, making further negotiations difficult.

Amalric had sent a mission to Western Europe in 1173, possibly in the expectation of assistance from **Henry II** of England, and was planning an assault on Egypt in conjunction with the Sicilian navy for the summer of 1174. On 15 May Nur al-Din died suddenly, leaving a succession crisis. Amalric decided to use the opportunity to attempt the reconquest of Banias (Banyas) in June. He contracted dysentery and died on 11 July at the age of 38.

ANATOLIA. The western peninsula of Asia that forms modern Turkey is situated between the Black and Mediterranean Seas. In crusader history this area, also called Asia Minor, or Romania, was contested by the **Byzantine Empire, Armenia**, and the **Seljuk Turks**. A Seljuk state called Rum existed in western Anatolia between 1077 and 1308, based first at the city of **Nicaea**. The **First Crusaders** took Nicaea in 1097, and continued to put pressure on Anatolia. Seljuk armies defending Anatolia contributed to the failure of the **Second Crusade**, winning a battle against the combined armies of Germany (the **Holy Roman Empire**) and France. In 1176 they were also able to defeat the Byzantine army under Emperor Manuel **Comnenus**. In the second half of the 13th century, Seljuk Anatolia gradually became dominated by the **Mongols**, so that by 1308 it effectively ceased to exist as a separate entity. It eventually became part of the **Ottoman Empire**. *See also* **Iconium**.

AL-ANDALUS. Muslim Spain. Muslim conquest of Spain occurred during the first wave of Arabic invasions, by 711. In 756 a descendent of the ousted Umayyad dynasty of **Damascus** took all of Muslim Spain and established a capital at Córdoba. Under Abd al-Rahman III (r.912-61) al-Andalus reached its greatest extent and wealth, putting annual pressure on its **Christian** frontiers. Internal weakness caused rival claimants to the Spanish caliphate (founded in 929) to appeal for help to Muslim northern Africa. Córdoba was sacked by **Berbers** in 1013, opening a period of internal rivalry that left al-Andalus unable to resist Christian incursions. *Andalusia* means a region of southwestern Spain bordering the Atlantic and the Mediterranean. *See also* **Reconquista**.

ANTIOCH, DESCRIPTION. (Turkey). One of the great cities of the ancient world, Antioch ranked third among the most important and populous urban centers of the Roman Empire. According to tradition, it was the first Christian bishopric, founded by St. Peter and presided over by him (33-40 A.D.) before he went to Rome. As one of the five chief cities of **Christendom**, in the fourth through the sixth centuries it held ecclesiastical jurisdiction over 11 metropolitan provinces and 127 episcopal dioceses. It was invaded by Persia in 538 and conquered by **Islam** in 638.

Antioch changed hands again before it was captured by the **First Crusaders** in 1098. It was claimed by the Byzantines but had fallen to the Muslims at **Aleppo** in 1085. According to **William of Tyre** it had two miles of walls defended by 400 towers. Two hills stood within the walls, with the citadel on one, rising 1,000 feet over the town. The city, now called Antakya is about 12 miles from the sea.

Until 1268 the city was the base for one of four principalities or counties into which the crusader-conquered territory was divided (**Jerusalem**, Antioch, **Edessa**, **Tripoli**). **Saladin** inflicted considerable damage on but was not able to take Antioch and the Christian north, including **Cilicia**, Tripoli, Tortosa, and major fortresses such as **Krac des Chevaliers**. These places were confirmed as remaining in crusader hands by the truce arranged at the close of the **Third Crusade** in 1192. In 1268, however, Antioch was taken by the **Mamluks**.

ANTIOCH, PATRIARCHATE. In 1098 when the **First Crusade** reached Antioch, the **Greek** Orthodox patriarch (senior ecclesiastical authority) of the city was John IV, who had been appointed in 1091. In response to the mixed force of **Byzantines** and Europeans besieging him, the Turkish governor desecrated the cathedral of St. Peter and suspended John in an iron cage from the city walls. In 1100 **Bohemond of Taranto** fought his former allies, the Byzantines, for control of the conquered city. John retired to a monastery. He was replaced by a **Latin** cleric.

Below this highest level of the ecclesiastical hierarchy, Greek Orthodox priests and monks were allowed to retain their positions, subject to the Latin patriarchs. The crusader patriarch of Antioch had three secular lords within his jurisdiction: the prince of Antioch, and the counts of **Edessa** and **Tripoli**. When Bernard of Valence was elected in 1100, his see took precedence over all the other sees in **Christendom** except for the pope and the patriarchs of **Constantinople** and **Alexandria**. His duties included secular ones such as riding with the armies of the principality on campaign, and the defense of the city when its regent and army were massacred by the Turks in 1119. Bernard died in 1135.

In 1100, the crusaders established the five dioceses of the patriarchate: Albara, Edessa, Tarsus, Mamistra, and Artah. By 1110 the see of Albara had been transferred to Apamea, and Tripoli had been conquered and added to the list of bishoprics. In the following two decades sees were also established at Marash, Jabala, Tortosa, and Gibelet. By 1135 there were 14 sees. The crusaders were trying to reestablish the sixth century boundaries of the Byzantine patriarchate. **Muslim** reconquest soon turned the tide, most notably in 1144 at Edessa, and the patriarchate at Antioch began to shrink. By the following year only six bishoprics were still in European hands.

Aimery of Limoges, patriarch from 1140, acted as regent for the principality during the minority of Bohemond III. In 1154 the patriarch fell out with the new husband and consort of the prince's mother Constance. **Reynald of Châtillon** demanded financial support from Aimery for his military expenses, and the patriarch refused. In the heat of the quarrel, the prince had Aimery beaten, stripped, smeared with honey, and exposed to the summer sun and to insects on the citadel of the city.

Reynald was made to repent by a delegation of bishops, but Aimery retired to the protection of the king at **Jerusalem**. Reynald attacked Byzantine **Cyprus** in 1156. He was punished by Emperor Manuel **Comnenus**, who led an army to the principality in 1159. Aimery returned during this dispute. Reynald was captured by **Nur al-Din** in 1161 and imprisoned at **Aleppo**.

The young Bohemond III was crowned but was taken captive by Nur al-Din in 1164. Aimery took over the government of the principality. Emperor Manuel agreed to help Bohemond pay his ransom if a Greek Orthodox patriarch was restored to Antioch. Bohemond returned to his principality in 1165 with Athanasius III, and Aimery was expelled from the cathedral. In 1170 an earthquake damaged the cathedral and killed Athanasius, after which Aimery returned.

He was again forced into exile in 1181 when he excommunicated Bohemond for repudiating his first wife in order to marry again. Again, notables from Jerusalem convened a conference to resolve the issues. Aimery was still in office when **Saladin** conquered the Latin Kingdom and took part of the principality of Antioch. The patriarch appealed to King **Henry II of England**, but only a small portion of his diocese was returned to him as a result of the **Third Crusade**. He was buried in his cathedral in 1193.

Patriarchs and the dates during which they held office include: Ralph of Domfront (1135-40); Aimery of Limoges (d.1193); Ralph II (r.1193-96); and Peter of Angoulême, who was first bishop of Tripoli, became patriarch in 1196 and was deposed in the winter of 1205-06. He was imprisoned and died in 1208. He was replaced by Peter, bishop of Ivrea 1209-17. *See below*, **Antioch, principality**. After this crisis two very able men tried to remedy the problems in the patriarchate: Ranier, vice-chancellor to Pope Honorius III (1219-25); Albert of Rizzato, bishop-elect of Brixen (1227-45). The last Latin patriarch before the fall of **Acre** in 1291 was Opizo dei Fieschi (1247-92).

ANTIOCH, PRINCIPALITY. The events of the **First Crusade** created an independent principality at **Antioch**, openly hostile to the **Byzantine** emperor because of his competing claim to it, and with an uncertain relationship to **Jerusalem** because of the indecision over its status. Before the death of **Godfrey of Bouillon** in 1100, many crusaders still imagined a victory that would deliver **Muslim** Palestine to the rule of the **papacy** and other previously Byzantine territory to its emperor. The crusade leaders took an oath to Alexius I **Comnenus** upon their arrival in **Constantinople** to return his land and to hold any fiefs they might carve out for themselves as his vassals. The implication was that Orthodox clergy would remain in control of churches within his empire. The establishments of Latin bishoprics at Albara and **Ramla-Lydda** after the **siege of Antioch** are important points in the shift of thinking to the creation of regional European lordships with **Latin** rite churches instead.

Christian princes of Antioch and their reigning dates include: **Bohemond I**, 1099-1111; Bohemond II, 1126-30; Raymond of Poitiers, 1136-49; Bohemond III, 1163-1201; Bohemond IV, 1201-16, 1219-33; Raymond Roupen, 1216-19; Bohemond V, 1233-52; Bohemond VI, 1252-68; Bohemond VII, 1275-87; Princess Lucia, 1287-89. Regents and their terms of office include: **Tancred**, 1101-03, 1104-12; Roger of Salerno, 1112-19 (*see* **Mosul**); Constance, 1149-53, 1160-63; **Reynald of Châtillon**, 1153-60 (from Setton, vol. 2, p. 817, *see* Crusades in the bibliography).

The relationship between the princes and patriarchs of Antioch was embittered by their relative wealth. The patriarch's resources were greater, which led to an open breach between Reynald of Châtillon and the church, and a civil war between the secular and ecclesiastical powers in 1180-81. Antioch was under constant pressure from neighboring Muslim powers and from Christian **Cilicia**, and was also expected to field troops at the request of the kings of Jerusalem. In the first years of the 12th century, Antioch could field 700 knights. As the century progressed and the principality lost territory, that number decreased.

In 1193 Bohemond III was taken captive by the king of Cilicia, Leo II. The quarrel between the two Christian rulers was soon resolved, but the citizens of Antioch had meanwhile formed a commune under the leadership of the patriarch of the city (*see* **Antioch, patriarchate**). The commune survived the original dispute, and came to claim jurisdiction over clergy in levying taxes and judging civil and criminal offenses. The majority of the citizens were **Greek** Orthodox rather than Roman Catholics, and in 1205-06 attempted to install an Orthodox patriarch. Their prince, Bohemond IV, who had seized power in 1201 during a succession crisis with the help of the commune, sided with them. The Latin patriarch was imprisoned in the citadel and died in 1208. This presented a knotty problem for Pope **Innocent III** to resolve, and he placed the arbitration in the hands of St. Albert, **patriarch of Jerusalem**. In 1209 Albert installed Peter, a monk from the Cistercian house of La Ferté who was serving as bishop of Ivrea (Italy). The succession and the resources of the principality were constantly challenged in the 13th century by Cilicia and other neighboring powers. Sultan **Baybars I** of **Egypt** took the city in 1268.

ANTIOCH, SIEGE. The siege of Antioch (21 October 1097-28 June 1098) makes up an important component of chronicle accounts of the **First Crusade**. Some of the events that immediately followed it set the context for decisions made at the **siege** of **Jerusalem** and for the early political arrangements after its conquest.

The crusade army had been weakened and impoverished by the siege of **Nicaea** (1097), and was unable to effectively blockade Antioch until April. Starvation set in, especially among the foot soldiers, who reportedly resorted to cannibalism. The walls at Antioch enclosed more than three-and-a-half square miles, with gardens, wells, and cisterns to supply the inhabitants. These defenses were augmented by 400 towers and a citadel that rose 1,000 feet above the surrounding countryside. There were six major gates for the attackers to cover, and the Orontes River blocked access to the northern walls. Two of the gates could be approached only by bridges over the river. The large Turkish garrison had been augmented with troops sent from **Muslim** rulers in northern Syria. These defenses, remodeled by **Byzantine** Emperor Justinian I (r.527-65), had been vulnerable only to treachery, which was the key to crusader victory there as well.

The European blockade was slowly extended from the original encampments to a tighter control over the city by means of constructed counter-forts. Supplies became a problem over the winter due to the repeated sorties of the Turkish garrison's cavalry, raids on foraging parties from nearby Muslim strongholds, and attacks by three relieving armies. Numbers of those who deserted the army or died of want are unknown, but there was considerable attrition, and a crisis in the loss of horses. An earthquake on 30 December prompted a three-day ritual penance, led by the papal legate and putative commander of the army **Adhémar of Le Puy**. Morale improved in February of 1098 when a Muslim relief force was defeated and plunder was taken.

In May **Bohemond of Taranto** was able to open negotiations with a captain of the garrison to betray the city. On 2 June a party of crusaders deserted under **Stephen of Blois**, unsettled by the approach of **Kerbogha**, ruler of **Mosul**, with a large army. By sunrise of the following day Bohemond and a party of knights were able to take a section of the wall with scaling ladders and open the Gate of St. George to the crusade army. During the day on 3 June the army looted the city and slaughtered the garrison. Unfortunately the siege had emptied the city of food and extensive fortifications had to be manned against Kerbogha's troops. The crusaders were in their turn besieged inside Antioch.

Kerbogha arrived on 5 June, invested the city by the seventh, and defeated a sortie on the 10th. A Byzantine relief force turned back on hearing reports from Stephen of Blois and other deserters. During this crisis a peasant from southern France claimed to have had a vision that would deliver an important **relic** to the crusaders, the lance which had been used to pierce Christ's side at the crucifixion. Somewhat shaken by their knowledge of the presence of the same relic in the Chapel of the Virgin at Pharos in **Constantinople**, the leadership split over the legitimacy of the divine encouragement. The army embraced the story after a Provencal priest backed it with accounts of his own vision, and a meteor was seen falling into the Turkish camp (14 June). A piece of iron was duly discovered the next day in the cathedral of St. Peter with the help of the original peasant, supposedly guided by St. Andrew the Apostle.

Morale was high on 28 June when Bohemond staged the pitched field battle against Kerbogha. **Raymond of Aguilers**, whose chronicle of the First Crusade covers the history of Antioch to 1128, carried the **Holy Lance** into battle. The crusaders were able to defeat Kerbogha and slaughter many of his retreating troops. Bohemond took control of the government of the city in spite of the original commitment, made during his stay in Constantinople, to deliver it to the Byzantines. The decision to rest at Antioch until 1 November put the Europeans in danger from an epidemic, possibly of typhoid, which further depleted their ranks over the summer. Adhémar of Le Puy died on 1 August.

In October **Raymond of Saint Gilles** took the nearby town of Albara and set up the first Latin bishopric in the east in its mosque. He and Bohemond were rivals for control of Antioch, and beyond that, for leadership of the crusade. When the army left to complete their **pilgrimage** vow in November, a tentative agreement had been reached whereby Bohemond kept control of three-quarters of the city, and Raymond kept the remaining portion for himself. Both were to complete the crusade before any further arrangements could be made.

This agreement fell apart after the successful siege of Marrat-an-Noman (28 November-12 December) 40 miles southeast of Antioch. Adhémar's death had left the position of leader vacant, and the princes could not agree on a successor. **Godfrey of Bouillon**, **Robert of Normandy**, Robert of **Flanders**, and Bohemond's nephew **Tancred** all resisted Raymond's attempt to buy their support in January. The army split when Raymond set out for **Jerusalem** on 13 January 1099. Tancred and Robert of Normandy followed him, while the rest lingered as Bohemond established himself as sole ruler of Antioch.

In February Raymond took Tortosa and Maraclea and besieged Arqua, 15 miles from **Tripoli**. His victories brought the rest of the crusade to the siege except for Bohemond. Their quarrels over the leadership continued until April, when a message arrived promising a Byzantine relief force to take them the rest of the way to Jerusalem at the end of June. The **Fatimids** of **Egypt** offered an alliance against Byzantium for the second time, and were again rebuffed.

Raymond refused to give up the siege of Arqua until 13 May. The army's support for him had been shaken by the events of April 8. One of Raymond's most outspoken supporters was the peasant who had found the Holy Lance, Peter Bartholomew. His continued visions of St. Andrew backed the count of St. Gilles's desire to complete the siege. Peter insisted on proving his veracity in a trial by fire on Good Friday. He died of the injuries he sustained in this public display, and Raymond's prestige, based in some sense on possession of the Lance, suffered when its authenticity was discredited by Peter's failure.

The army left Tripoli, provisioned by its relieved garrison, on 14 May. With the exception of a brief sortie from **Sidon** the coastal cities ignored the European plunder of their suburbs in the hope that the crusade would pass quickly from their territory. Above **Jaffa** the army turned inland and arrived at **Ramla** on 3 June. This had been the administrative center of Muslim Palestine, but it was abandoned by its citizens. A Norman priest was made bishop and administrator of Ramla-Lydda. On 6 June Tancred and **Baldwin of Le Bourg** took **Bethlehem** while the main army moved on to Jerusalem.

AL-AQSA MOSQUE. *See* **Temple**.

ARAB. Saracen, Turk, Moor, **Muslim**. These are terms which may be used specifically, for instance Arab to denote an Arabian or Muslim to denote a follower of **Islam**. However in the European crusade chronicles they may also be used indiscriminately to refer to an enemy, regardless of ethnic, religious, or political allegiance. "Saracen" is more likely to be found in European accounts of the Holy Land, while "Moor" is seen more frequently in reference to the Iberian peninsula. For similar generic terms to refer to multiethnic groups, *see* **Greek**, **Frank**, and **Latin**. The word Muslim reflects a complex reality, in the sense that Islam was not in the 12th century, any more than it is now, monolithic as either a religion or a political construct.

ARAGON. Spain. Originally a province of the medieval **Christian** kingdom of **Navarre**, Aragon is a valley at the base of the western Pyrenees, which emerged as a separate principality under Ramiro I (r.1035-63). Jaca was its principal town, situated at a mountain pass that made it the main route from Western Europe to the **pilgrimage** church of **Santiago de Compostela.**

Count Sancho Ramírez I (r.1063-94), in his efforts to expand his territories at the expense of the neighboring **Muslims**, made a pilgrimage to Rome in 1068 and arranged to hold his fief from the pope. He hoped that this connection would enable him to call on military help from beyond Iberia. In 1073 Pope **Gregory VII** (*see* the introduction) unsuccessfully attempted to call in such assistance from southern France.

Pedro I, king of Aragon (r.1094-1104) renewed the allegiance to the **papacy** in 1096 in return for help from southern France in taking Muslim Huesca. Alfonso I (r.1104-34) continued to expand Aragon in the direction of the county of **Barcelona**, enabling the eventual union of the two Christian principalities. His marriage with Queen Urraca (d. 1126) of **León-Castile** produced war between them (1111-17) and competing claims to control of the Iberian Peninsula. In spite of this setback, in 1118-19 Alfonso defeated Muslim armies to take Córdoba and Tudela. Pope Gelasius II's grant of a crusade **indulgence** brought help from southern France, including veterans of the **First Crusade.** By 1120 the leadership of the **Murabit** in Spain was in its turn fractured, and Alfonso, with European assistance, won a major battle at Cutanda. He created the **military order** of **Monreal** in 1124 to help patrol the southern boundaries of his territory. In 1125-26 he accumulated a major force for a season of raids into Muslim territory from Valencia to Granada. The purpose seems to have been intimidation rather than conquest.

The forward momentum of Aragon came to a temporary halt with Alfonso's death in 1134. He had no heirs, and divided his territory in 1131 among the canons of the **Holy Sepulchre**, and the new military orders of the **Hospitallers** and **Templars.** The eventual settlement bought out the claims of the three orders by ceding them property, and created the combined principality of Aragon/Barcelona. After 1134, the dynasty of the latter controlled the fortunes of both, along with territory in the Balearics, Valencia, **Sicily**, and southern Italy. *See also* **Reconquista.**

ARMENIA. Ancient Armenia was thought to extend from the Caucasus to the Taurus Mountains, from the Caspian to the Black Sea, and to have included both the Garden of Eden and Mount Ararat, where Noah's Ark was supposed to have rested after the biblical flood. The Roman province of Armenia was probably only a small part of **Asia Minor**, south of the Black and Caspian Seas. In essence, the Romans held the Euphrates as the border of their empire, beyond which was the frontier province of Armenia.

The country produced its own line of kings, was converted to **Christianity** in 303, and developed a liturgy in the national language. Armenia, like the **Copts**, **Jacobites**, and **Nestorians**, broke with the Melkites, or Greek Orthodox, at the Council of Chalcedon in 451. The Persian Sassanid Empire, with which the **Byzantines** had split Armenia in 387, fell in 642 to **Islam**. The caliph at **Baghdad** appointed governors for Armenia, which was otherwise left semiautonomous. The Byzantine Empire continued to claim this region after **Seljuk** conquest (from 1020), and into the **Mongol** era (from 1240). What the crusaders called "Armenia" is not well-defined because of these competing territorial claims, and is now split between the former Soviet republic of Armenia, Turkey, and Iran. *See also* **Cilicia, Edessa**.

ARMOR. During the Middle Ages **knights** were responsible to provide their own equipment, which meant that there was considerable variation, especially as plunder after a battle was an important source of **weaponry**. European knights wore felt, padded, or leather coats, sometimes with leggings or cap, to take the weight of metal armor. A hauberk or coat of chain links (*mail*: the links could be single or double and were expensive to forge) was basic equipment, along with a metal, cloth, or wooden shield, and some form of helmet. Shoulder, knee, and foot guards of metal could also be worn, with a surcoat over the hauberk, and gauntlets to protect the wrists and hands. A steel cap might be supplemented with a mail covering of various lengths, and possibly with a helmet as well. The pot helmet, with a visor to protect the mouth and marked to distinguish the wearer, was used from the end of the 12th century. *See also* **Heraldry**.

ARSENAL. By the 13th century **Venice**'s fleet was a state-directed institution. The city was a center for shipbuilding long before 1104, when the government built the Arsenal, a walled enclosure for the manufacture of ships and arms. Its size was doubled between 1303 and 1325.

Next door was a government-owned rope factory, and the area around them both was densely populated by private shipyards. Eventually shipowners would be forbidden by law to sell useful ships to foreigners. Venice's goals were commercial expansion at the expense of neighboring rivals, and specifically trade agreements that would open new markets. *See also* **Naval Warfare.**

ASCALON. This port city controlled by the **Fatimids** of **Egypt** acted as a check on the main European **pilgrim** road from **Jaffa** to **Jerusalem.** Its capture preoccupied the crusaders until 1153, when King **Baldwin III** of Jerusalem was able to take it. Baldwin used **castles** built by his father, King **Fulk** (Blanche Garde, **Ibelin,** and Beth Gibelin) as bases from which to attack the city, adding Gaza in 1149 to complete a ring of fortresses around it.

Upon capturing the city, the crusaders reconsecrated the largest mosque as the cathedral of St. Paul. Ascalon was technically subject to the crusader bishopric of **Bethlehem** in the ecclesiastical organization of the **Latin Kingdom of Jerusalem.** Along with other port cities, Ascalon changed hands several times after 1187, but was definitively returned to Egyptian control under **Baybars I** in 1270.

ASIA MINOR. This phrase refers to the western peninsula of Asia, lying between the Black Sea and the Mediterranean, which is now Turkey. *Anatolia* means "the country east of the Aegean Sea" or western Asia Minor. These terms are used to designate these areas before 20th century national boundaries were set, when there were still several contenders, such as the **Armenians, Byzantines,** and the **Seljuk Turks,** for land in this region. *See also* **Kilij Arslan**; **Danishmends**; **Anatolia**; **Iconium.**

ASSASSINS, ISMAILI ORIGINS. The word "Assassins" is derived from the Arabic word for hashish. Medieval authors told stories of this sect's daring political assassinations, their use of disguise, and their willingness to die for their leader. The name "Assassin" was given by Sunni and European opponents to the Nizarite Ismailis, who represent a division among the Shia **Muslims.** For the Ismailis, the legitimate line of succession belonged to the **Fatimid** dynasty in **Egypt** (and eventually to their own imam or religious leader in northeastern Persia) rather than to the **Abbasid** caliphs at **Baghdad.**

The origins of the Fatimid dynasty go back to 902 in northern Africa, from which they conquered Egypt with the help of **Berber** tribes in 969. Al-Aziz conquered **Damascus** during his reign (975-96), and his successor al-Hakim (r.996-1021) took **Aleppo**. In 1021 a succession crisis precipitated another split, between the Ismailis and the Druze. In 1060 Baghdad itself was briefly under Fatimid rule, but by 1070 the **Seljuk Turks** had conquered Iraq, Aleppo, and by 1075, much of **Asia Minor**. The Seljuks thus became rivals with Egypt for the Middle East.

A new succession crisis in Egypt in 1094 produced another division between the Ismailis and the Nizari, the followers of Nizar, who was passed over for the throne of Egypt. The leader of this group was Hasan al-Sabbah (d. 1124), who in 1090 established himself in the Elburz (Alborz) Mountains north of Tehran near the Caspian Sea at a fortress called Alamut. From this and other strongholds in Iran the movement spread to Syria.

Ismailism was both a religious and a political movement. Its difference from Sunni can be summed up as a divergent view of the way to interpret the Quran. For the Sunni the consensus of the group, expressed by scholars, is definitive. For the Ismailis, there is a universal order, expressed by God through a series of interpreters, from Adam through Jesus to **Muhammad**, who expressed the final revelation. The messages of these men might seem contradictory, and some passages from the Quran might seem archaic or lacking in consistency. These seeming contradictions or irrelevancies can be shown to be both consistent and meaningful only by a true teacher, of the line begun by Muhammad and continued through Ali and Nizar. The true succession is therefore the key to true interpretation, the rope that extends salvation to the human intellect from the divine.

Some Ismailis believed in the transmigration of souls. Those who refused true interpretation degenerated, returning as animals, while those who understood the universal order increased their status in the next life. Ismailis saw their activities as missionary work, when necessary backed by military action.

ASSASSINS, SYRIA. In the early 1100s, under the protection of Sunni **Seljuk** rulers, the Ismailis were able to establish a house in **Aleppo** for a preaching mission.

From this date, they were also suspected of carrying out political assassinations in Syria and **Egypt**. There is support for this supposition from the sources beginning in 1106, when the Ismailis based in Aleppo attempted to take a fortress in the upper Orontes valley. They were defeated by the combined local forces of the family of an Egyptian governor and **Tancred**, prince of **Antioch**. The Ismailis were exiled from Aleppo in 1124, and sought a foothold in southern Syria.

In 1125 Ismaili warriors helped the Sunni Turkish ruler of **Damascus** hold off the forces of the **Christian** crusader kingdom, hoping to earn his protection or at least tolerance for their existence in southern Syria. Their political loyalties were always suspect however, and in 1129 the residents of Damascus slaughtered possibly as many as 6,000 Ismailis. The response of the survivors was to develop a string of **castles** in inaccessible mountainous areas between **Tripoli** and Aleppo, situated in such a way as to bring them into conflict with both the European crusaders and the Sunni Turkish rulers of Aleppo. The notable **Hospitaller** fortress of **Krac des Chevaliers** was 25 miles south of Misyaf, the most important Naziri stronghold. The **Templars** were also neighbors in their march at Tortosa.

The leaders of the Naziri Ismailis in southern Syria, whose string of fortresses and villages are called the Emirate of Misyaf, were sent out from **Alamut**, and information about them is minimal. Sarim al-Din, also known as Abu Muhammad, may have been the first ruler of the Syrian community, followed by Rashid al-Din Sinan, known to the crusaders as the Old Man of the Mountain. Sinan followed the orders of the Imam in Alamut, Hassan II, to announce that believers were released from **Islamic law**. Syrians obedient to Sinan destroyed mosques and publicly displayed their freedom from fasting and from taboos on pork and wine.

Rashid al-Din Sinan is thought to have been born c.1135 in Basra, educated in Iran (Persia), and sent from Alamut in 1162-63 to take leadership of the Syrian community. His cult, developed in the 14th century, combined with the secrecy of the community in the 12th century make it difficult to disentangle fact from pious fiction. Sinan is said to have trained his warriors in collecting information, which necessitated fluency in several languages, and to have set up a system of communications between the Ismaili fortresses, based on pigeons and coded messages. Normally, their missions were aimed at important Muslim rulers, but the Assassins were supposed to have murdered the Christian count of Tripoli in 1151.

Sinan is also reported to have reached a truce with **Amalric I**, king of **Jerusalem**, in c.1173, a truce almost immediately broken by the Templars. During the winter of 1174-75, the ruler of Aleppo, besieged by **Saladin**, asked Sinan for help. The response was the attempted assassination of Saladin that winter and again in May 1176. Both attempts failed. Saladin made a raid into Ismaili territory and briefly attempted a siege of Misyaf in July. A temporary truce seems to have followed these hostilities. Ismaili sources allege that members of the community fought in alliance with Saladin at **Hattin** in 1187, and that European prisoners taken during that battle were held in Ismaili fortresses.

There are too many acts attributed to the Naziri to list them all here. The one that caused the greatest stir among the crusaders was the murder of **Conrad of Montferrat** in 1192, after which, his successor, **Henry of Champagne**, is supposed to have visited Sinan, who died in 1193. Stories circulated that the Assassins had been sent by Philip Augustus of France against King **Richard I** of England in 1195, and that they had murdered Raymond of Antioch in 1213 and Duke Ludwig of Bavaria in 1231. They were said to have received a handsome sum of money from **Holy Roman Emperor** Frederick II in preparation for the **Sixth Crusade** in 1226-27.

In Alamut, the most important of the successors to Hasan al-Sabbah (r.1090-1124) was Jalal al-Din Hasan III (r.1210-21), who attempted to gain toleration for the Ismailis from the caliphs of Baghdad. In order to do this, he laid emphasis on the necessity of obeying religious law and observing ritual behavior. "Externals" such as law and ritual were certainly important to the Ismailis, but not as crucial as the allegorical or spiritual meaning of the Quran. These overtures were accepted by Caliph al-Nasir (r.1180-1225), for whom unity in Islam was essential in the face of the threat offered by Jingiz [Genghis] Khan (1162-1226).

Alamut's approach to the caliph earned the southern Syrian Ismaili community a breathing space with the **Ayyubid** dynasty. When Raymond, heir to Antioch, was murdered in 1212, his father, Bohemond IV (r.1187-1223) laid siege to one of their fortresses in 1214-15. Aleppo sent a relief force to aid the Ismailis. In 1250 the Assassins sent an embassy to King **Louis IX** of France during his stay in **Acre**, requesting to be released from an expectation, which may have gone back to 1150, that they would pay annual tribute to the Hospitallers and Templars. Louis sent emissaries to both the Assassins and the **Mongols** during his stay at Acre, apparently with the intention of gathering information on their beliefs and possibly forming an alliance. Neither of these efforts bore fruit.

By 1250 the Mongols had taken northern Iran, becoming a threat to Baghdad and Alamut, both of which fell to them in the next decade. The Ismailis of Syria first submitted to Mongol control, but after **Mamluk** Sultan **Baybars** of Egypt defeated the Mongols in 1260, the Assassins offered him their loyalty. In 1261 he gave their territory to his own governor at Hama. In 1262-63 they sent another emissary to the sultan, and were courteously received, but Baybars was clearly more concerned to consolidate his own power in Syria than to indulge the Assassins. In about 1266 Baybars, now focused on driving the Europeans out of his domain, put a stop to the tribute payments the Ismailis had been making to the **military orders**, but ordered that they should be paid to himself instead. From 1271 any resistance to his orders led to military reprisals. All of the Ismaili castles in Syria surrendered to him in 1273.

Legend has it that after this point the Ismailis worked for Baybars as spies and assassins. They were supposed to have attempted the murder of King **Edward I** of England in 1272 when he visited Acre. They continued to exist, without much of a political impact, under the Mamluk and **Ottoman Empires**.

Early in the history of the Ismailis, another line of leaders or imams had been established in India. In 1842 Hasan Ali Shah, a contender for legitimacy as an Ismaili leader, left Iran and settled in India. He and his successors are known as Agha Khan. Agha Khan III (1885-1957) and his descendants were accepted as leaders by many Ismailis after 1885.

AYYUBID DYNASTY. (1171-1250). The dynasty was created by **Saladin** as he consolidated **Nur al-Din**'s holdings in **Syria** and **Egypt** and destroyed the **Latin Kingdom of Jerusalem**. As Saladin conquered territory, he placed it under the control of various family members, in a confederation of states nominally loyal in the first place to the Turkish ruler of **Aleppo**, Nur al-Din (r.1146-74), and after his death to the **Abbasid** dynasty in **Baghdad**. After Saladin's death, his family continued to hold Syria, Egypt, and parts of Mesopotamia, but to a large extent left the remaining crusader states based at **Acre** to their own devices. It was up to the **Mamluks**, their successors, to drive the last of the Europeans off the mainland to the island kingdom of **Cyprus** by 1291.

Saladin's rule offers a contrast to the North African **Fatimid** dynasty, which he replaced, on several levels. He himself was a **Kurd**, expanding the hold of the **Seljuk Turks** over Syria and Egypt. The Turks had entered Islam first as mercenaries, and then as conquerors of parts of Abbasid territory. Under Nur al-Din and Saladin, the veneer of loyalty to the Abbasids was scrupulously maintained in Syria and Egypt. The Shia Fatimids had been both political and religious rivals to Sunni Baghdad. Saladin created a Sunni Muslim government in Cairo that became a center of learning and culture in the Islamic world.

European crusades launched against Egypt were a focus of attention in 1218 (the **Fifth Crusade**), in 1228 (the **Sixth Crusade**), and in 1249 (under **Louis IX**, king of France 1226-70). The Ayyubid dynasty fell to the Mamluks in 1249-50, who revived the **jihad** against the Europeans while fighting off **Mongol** incursions.

The most notable of the Ayyubid rulers for the crusaders were **al-Adil**, Saladin's brother (d.1218), who ruled Egypt when the Fifth Crusade arrived there; **al-Kamil**, al-Adil's son (d.1238), who actually fought the Fifth Crusade and made a treaty with the **Holy Roman Emperor** Frederick II in 1229 to end the Sixth Crusade; and al-Salih (d.1249), sultan of Egypt during an important battle with crusading forces in 1244 at Harbiyya, near **Ascalon**.

The Ayyubid period is notable for the increasing militarization of Egypt, and its link with Syria as a base for military operations. Foreigners were used in freeborn as well as *mamluk*, or military slave, regiments, either as individuals or as tribal units. The state functioned as a loose confederation of principalities under various branches of the dynasty. The principalities themselves did not have stable political boundaries. They were conglomerations of lands collected by princely houses, and traded for family advantage without any regard for ethnic identities or even geography, beyond the immediate goal of commercial or diplomatic gain. Only the sultanate of Egypt and the lordship of the largest cities of Syria kept a territorial identity or centralized financial administrations, as they were passed about among various princes. Histories of the Ayyubid reign therefore focus on Egypt, **Damascus**, and **Aleppo**, with lesser cities playing a lesser role. The military resources available during Saladin's reign have been estimated at 16,000 cavalry for the whole area under his control, with an additional force of 1,000 from his personal estates. He essentially destroyed the Fatimid army as part of his bid for power in 1169, and installed instead the force of Turks and **Kurds** who had backed him. The Syrian military establishment was of recent date (12th century, *see* **Seljuk Turks**), and consisted of the same mixed **Turcoman** and Kurdish warriors who had put Saladin in power. Without a centralized treasury or administration for his entire empire, he was unable to create a larger military force or impose obedience to his decrees. His rule rested on his personal influence and his generosity in awarding conquered territory to his adherents. Technically, he had usurped power from the **Zengid** rulers of Syria for whom he had taken Egypt. The legitimacy of his rule was therefore a serious question in both Egypt and Syria. The Ayyubid inherited his problems along with his possessions.

The Ayyubid, like the Zengids of Syria before them, looked to the caliph of **Baghdad** for formal confirmation of their status as rulers. The embassy they sent in 1193 presented the caliph with Saladin's arms as a reminder of his own claim to political power as the leader of the jihad against Shia Fatimid Egypt and the **Christian** crusader kingdoms. Ayyubid commitment to jihad was tested when the truce made by Saladin and King **Richard I** of England expired in 1195. Holy Roman Emperor Henry VI (r.1190-97) sent a force to Acre in 1197 led by Duke Henry of Brabant (r.1190-1235). Saladin's brother al-Adil held much of upper Mesopotamia from 1186 to 1198, and was governor of Damascus from 1198 to 1200, when he succeeded to the sultanate of Egypt. He tried to engage the German force near Tiberias, but when they avoided the engagement, he instead took and razed **Jaffa**. He was also able to raze **Sidon**, but the crusaders took Beirut before he could follow the destruction of its walls with the razing of its citadel.

The crusaders had met their objective, which was to control the coast between Acre and the county of **Tripoli**. They moved on to the fortress of Toron in November of 1197, their first attempt to take some of the inland territory that they had lost to Saladin. Al-Adil was unable to oust them, and appealed to Egypt. The sultan's troops did not arrive until February 1198. By then the crusade army had received the news that Henry VI had died in **Sicily**. They retreated in haste to **Tyre**, chased by the two Muslim armies, and the crusaders left for home. The **Lusignan** king of **Cyprus** and **Jerusalem** was left to negotiate a truce with al-Adil.

In 1200, due to a reshuffle in the Ayyubid world, al-Adil was sultan of Egypt. The skirmish of 1197 paled in comparison to the problem of the Fifth Crusade which he faced in Egypt as sultan (r.1200-18). The Europeans were never his choice for the focus of his activities. The maintenance of his regime in Egypt and Syria and expansion into Mesopotamia and **Armenia** were his policies. The chief impact of the Fifth Crusade for al-Adil, and the Sixth Crusade for al-Kamil after him, was as a distraction from these more important goals.

The failure of the dynasty to realize these goals is apparent in al-Kamil's appointment of two heirs, one for Egypt, and one for an area called the Jazira, which was at various points in medieval times an independent principality, made up of parts of modern-day Syria and Iraq. This division shows the prevalence of the pattern of consolidating the Egyptian hold on southern Syria through the governorship of Damascus and using it as a springboard from which to move north to Aleppo and then to the region of the Tigris and Euphrates Rivers. The succession to al-Kamil also presented the problems common to the Ayyubid: the jockeying for position among the various members of the family, stationed throughout the empire, complicated by the actual election procedure, which was a negotiation among the most powerful generals to either confirm or overturn al-Kamil's own choice for his successor.

The next member of Saladin's dynasty to play a major role in the crusades was al-Kamil's son al-Salih Ayyub, ruler of Damascus (1238-39), and sultan of Egypt (1240-49). His rule of both areas was hotly contested, so much so that in 1239 the crusade army of Count **Theobald IV of Champagne** (1201-53) became a factor in the dispute among the Ayyubid. The count was offered Jerusalem and a corridor of land to the coastal cities in exchange for an alliance, first with al-Salih's rival for Damascus, and then with al-Salih, who made a counteroffer just as he took office as sultan in Egypt. Theobald made his peace with the sultan in 1240 and left for home.

A new army arrived in 1241 with Earl **Richard of Cornwall**. He confirmed the treaty with Egypt in April, leaving the titular barons of Jerusalem, based at Acre, to hold the promised territory in the face of a hostile Damascus. Just at this crisis in the struggle between Damascus and Egypt both were diverted by attacks on northern Syria by Turks from the region of the Oxus River near the Aral Sea called Khorezm or Khwarizm. Their cavalry of 12,000 easily outmatched the Aleppan forces of 1,500, and Damascus was raising forces against Richard of Cornwall. The necessity for coordinated action in the north led to a truce among the Ayyubid in 1243, by which the sultan's authority was to be recognized by Damascus and Aleppo.

The peace was immediately broken and Jerusalem changed hands at least twice in the resulting struggle among the Ayyubid. To European eyes the most important factor in these events was that in July 1244 Jerusalem was looted and the Christian shrines destroyed by the Khwarizm Turks, for the moment allied with Egypt. The full force of the crusader kingdom joined in alliance with the Syrian Muslims against the sultan of Egypt at the battle of La Forbie or Harbiyya, near Ascalon on 17 October 1244. The army of the crusader kingdom was destroyed, but the sultan's real objective was the **siege** of Damascus which followed. He was joined by the Khwarizm forces and the Aleppans. He was able to reduce the city to the status of an Egyptian province. He followed this with an attack on the remains of the crusader kingdom, still clinging to the coastal cities. In the summer of 1247 he took a number of important fortresses and razed Ascalon. The crusade of King Louis IX of France was the last attempt to save the remnants of the crusader kingdom. The king's forces landed in Egypt and took Damietta in June

1249. On 22 November 1249 al-Salih died, leaving a succession crisis faced with the invasion of the French.

In order to build his strength against his family, the sultan had resorted not only to a series of alliances like the ones with the crusaders and Khwarizm, but to the construction of regiments of military slaves personally loyal to himself. It was one of these regiments, made up of Kipchak (Qipchaq) Turks, that succeeded him as the **Mamluk** dynasty.

-B-

BAGHDAD. Iraq's capital sits on the Tigris River in the center of the country. During the caliphate of al-Mansur (r.754-75) the city was built to serve as the center of the **Abbasid** dynasty's **Islamic** empire. It was conquered by the **Seljuk Turks** in 1059 under the command of Tughrul Beg (r.1040-63), but was still perceived as the nominal center of **Islam**, even when under Seljuk control. The Seljuk capital was Isfahan, and the successor to Tughrul Beg was his nephew **Alp Arslan**. Caliph al-Muqtafi (r.1136-60) was able to establish independence from the Turks for himself and his successors, but was still in alliance with them as Sunni **Muslim** rulers. The **Mongols** sacked Baghdad in 1258 and executed the last caliph. In 1261 **Baybars**, **Mamluk** sultan of **Egypt**, installed a member of the Abbasid dynasty in Cairo under his protection. Baghdad was not a capital of an independent Muslim state again until after World War I, and the imperial period passed with the Abbasids.

BAHA AL-DIN IBN SHADDAD. (1145-1234). Baha al-Din's *Life of Saladin* was written at court during the author's career there between 1188 and **Saladin**'s death in 1193. It is an important source for the **Third Crusade**, and has been translated into English.

BAIBARS. *See* **Baybars I**.

BALDRIC, ARCHBISHOP OF DOL. (France). Baldric had been abbot of Bourgueil in the early 12th century. His chronicle of the **First Crusade** relies on the anonymous **Gesta**, an eyewitness account, and includes a version of Pope **Urban II**'s speech at Clermont.

BALDWIN I (OF BOULOGNE). Baldwin was the younger brother of **Godfrey of Bouillon**. His first wife, Godechilde, daughter of the Norman Ralph of Tosny, accompanied him on the **First Crusade** and died in the Holy Land. He became count of **Edessa** (r.1098-1100), and then king in **Jerusalem** (r.1100-18), the first Western European ruler to take the title of king there.

Baldwin followed Godfrey as king so soon after the conquest of Jerusalem that much of the work of creating a territorial kingdom was still to be done. The first problem was securing ports as a key to holding and supplying the new **Latin Kingdom of Jerusalem**. Lacking a navy, he besieged but was unable to take **Acre** in 1103 (it fell in the following year) and **Sidon** in 1107-08. He developed agreements with **Genoa**, **Pisa**, and **Venice** that gave them tax-free self-regulating enclaves in cities captured with their help, along with any spoils of war they collected. He and the other veterans of the First Crusade also continued to use counter-forts to first harass and then take **Muslim** strongholds. **Raymond of Saint Gilles** was able to establish his county of **Tripoli** by building such a fortress in 1102-03 two miles from the city on Mount Pilgrim. Baldwin, with help from the Genoese, was able to work with Raymond's successors to take Tripoli in 1109. Haifa fell with Venetian help in 1100 and Beirut and Sidon in 1110. *See* **Caffaro**.

Opposition by the allied rulers of **Egypt** and **Damascus** failed in a battle at **Ramla** in 1105. Baldwin's success there was balanced by his long and initially fruitless battles on the coast and by a major defeat against the Egyptians at a battle in 1102. The coastal cities were hard-won, and the defense of the Latin Kingdom was dependent not only on the Italian communes and financial support from Europe, but also on the timely arrival of pilgrim bands such as the one in 1101. For the defeat of the forces of the kingdom under Baldwin's leadership at the battle of Lake Tiberias in 1113 *see* **Mosul**.

Moved by strategic considerations Baldwin separated from his **Armenian** queen Arda, married when he was consolidating his hold on Edessa, to replace her with Adelaide (r.1113-16). Adelaide's son by a previous marriage, Roger II of **Sicily**, seemed to offer a valuable alliance, and the lady came with a sizeable dowry. However, the new queen did not provide Baldwin with an heir, and by 1116 he feared that Roger would inherit his kingdom. In 1117 Baldwin had his marriage to Adelaide annulled but he failed to make another alliance before his death in April of 1118. The kingdom passed to his cousin **Baldwin of Le Bourg**.

Witnesses to Baldwin's acts as king include many Europeans who established lordships as a result of the **First Crusade**. These include lordships in the royal demesne of Nablus, as well as in Sidon, Caesarea, **Jaffa**, and Tripoli.

The best primary source, available in English translation, on the Latin Kingdom during its first 80 years is the chronicle of **William of Tyre**.

BALDWIN II (OF LE BOURG). King in **Jerusalem** (1118-31), Baldwin was the eldest son of Count Hugh of Rethel, cousin to both **Baldwin I** and **Godfrey of Bouillon**. His name, usually rendered as Le Bourg, refers to Bourcq, in the Ardennes region of France. The counts of Rethel held their land from the archbishop of Reims (or Rheims), as did in the first instance another crusading family, the **Coucys**.

When Baldwin I left **Edessa** to succeed Godfrey as ruler of the **Latin Kingdom of Jerusalem**, he called in his cousin to succeed him in Edessa. Upon the king's death Baldwin of Le Bourg was elected by the assembly of the lords of the Latin Kingdom to succeed him. Baldwin II was consecrated king on 14 April 1118. In May the emir of **Damascus** attacked Tiberias while the sultan of **Egypt** camped at **Ascalon**. At the same time a **Muslim** fleet landed at **Tyre**. Baldwin's forces menaced the Egyptians at Ascalon, which withdrew without a battle. His troops then raided the countryside around Damascus and **Aleppo**. The Muslim forces attacked **Antioch**. While Baldwin was en route to relieve the principality, its regent in 1119, Roger of Salerno, engaged the Aleppans at Darb Sarmada. Roger and many of his knights were slaughtered at this battle, known as the "Field of Blood."

Baldwin hurried to defenseless Antioch. The king held the region directly until the heir, Bohemond II, arrived in 1126. In 1122 Joscelin of Courtenay, who had been made lord of Edessa, was captured, leaving Baldwin as administrator of that region as well. In 1123, after five years of constant campaigning, the king himself was captured by Nur al-Daulah Belek, ruler of Aleppo in 1123-24.

Tyre was taken with the help of the **Venetians** in 1124 during a year when the kingdom was under the regency of the **Latin Patriarch of Jerusalem**, Gormond, and in the secular sphere of the constable Eustace Garnier (Grenier, *see* **Sidon**), who died in June, and after him of William of Bures, lord of Tiberias. Gormond and William negotiated the attack on Tyre with the Venetians during the winter of 1123-24. The city fell in July 1124. In August Baldwin was released from captivity.

The king immediately went to war against Aleppo, winning a field victory in June of 1125 that allowed him to pay his ransom and have his hostages released. Constant warfare allowed Baldwin II to expand the kingdom during his reign. He passed it on to **Fulk**, count of Anjou, who had married the king's eldest daughter in 1129. Fulk fought alongside

Baldwin from his arrival until the king's death in 1131, ruling newly conquered Tyre as part of his wife's dowry.

The best primary source, available in English translation, on the Latin Kingdom during its first 80 years is the chronicle of **William of Tyre**.

BALDWIN III. King in **Jerusalem** (1143-63). Baldwin's father **Fulk** died in 1143, leaving his wife Melisend as regent for their son. Melisend began to associate her son with her in royal acts in 1145 when he came of age. Baldwin contested his mother's regency in 1151. After what is normally referred to as a civil war between the two, he gained control of the kingdom in 1152. Baldwin's heir was his brother, **Amalric**.

When Fulk died, the **Latin Kingdom** had reached its greatest extent. The success of the crusaders had been built as much on the failure of the local **Islamic** powers to contest their rule as it had been on their tireless warfare. Under the rule of **Zengi**, emir of **Mosul** and then of **Aleppo**, continued European presence in the **Levant** was challenged by a formidable opponent. Zengi took **Edessa** in 1144, a disaster which prompted the **Second Crusade**. The crusade's failure made its mark on both the Latin Kingdom and European enthusiasm for future expeditions. The challenges facing Baldwin III extended well beyond those of the regency.

Much of the territory of the principality of **Antioch** was taken by Zengi's successor **Nur al-Din** in 1149, but the king was able to save the city itself and surrounding region. In 1154 Baldwin's attempts to use his alliance with **Damascus** to defend the kingdom were preempted by Nur al-Din's takeover of that emirate. Baldwin's most notable achievement was the conquest of **Ascalon** in 1153, which set the stage for his brother's several attacks on **Egypt** in the 1160s.

The best primary source, available in English translation, on the Latin Kingdom during its first 80 years is the chronicle of **William of Tyre**.

BALDWIN IV, THE LEPER. King in **Jerusalem** (1174-85). Baldwin, who was born in 1161, was the son of **Amalric I** and Agnes of Courtenay (*see* **Edessa**), whose marriage was annulled in 1163. His father's second wife was Maria **Comnena**. Maria's daughter Isabel (d.1205) had a claim on the throne after Baldwin and his sister Sybil (*see* **Guy of Lusignan**). The succession crisis arising from Baldwin's illness was a key factor in the fall of the **Latin Kingdom** to **Saladin** in 1187.

Baldwin's tutor from 1170 was **William of Tyre** (d.1185) author of the most important chronicle of the Latin Kingdom. William noticed that his charge was without feeling in and unable to use his right hand and arm. Arab doctors were called in to treat Baldwin, who was eventually diagnosed with leprosy. The boy was taught to ride and fight, using his knees to guide his mount. His diagnosis was not announced, since leprosy normally led to relative seclusion, perhaps in the **Order of St. Lazarus**, for fear of contagion.

BALDWIN IV, THE REGENCY OF MILES OF PLANCY. King **Amalric I** died suddenly in 1174. The tenants-in-chief met and decided that Baldwin should succeed him. The closest suitable male claimants were the princes of **Antioch** and **Tripoli**. Amalric's daughters Sybil and Isabel were both children. Baldwin himself was only 13. The combination of Baldwin's youth and illness, the line of succession, and the fact that the two female heirs were too closely related to the great nobles of the realm for marriages with them to be canonically legal led to an increasing rivalry for power at court. No one of the great lords wanted to see another family benefit from the succession. The resulting contest for supremacy could not be resolved in any way that was both legal and satisfactory to all parties.

The immediate crisis in the summer of 1174 was the proposed expedition to **Alexandria**, for which the **Sicilian** navy had been recruited to assist. It was too late to alert their allies of Amalric's death, and the crusader kingdom failed to muster troops to meet the Sicilian landing in **Egypt**. **Saladin** was able to block their advance as a result, and the expedition was a failure. The regency government under Miles of Plancy and Rohard of **Jaffa** was blamed for the debacle by one of the rival heirs, Raymond III of Tripoli, and a party of barons including Humphrey of Toron, Reynald of **Sidon**, Baldwin lord of **Ramla**, and his brother Balian of **Ibelin**. All of Raymond's party would have important roles to play in the fall of the kingdom in 1187. It is not known who assassinated Miles of Plancy in 1174.

BALDWIN IV, THE FIRST REGENCY OF RAYMOND OF TRIPOLI. When the High Court met on 28 October 1174 to decide on a new regency, Baldwin IV, then 13 years old, presided. Raymond of Tripoli was a dubious candidate both because of the equal claim of the princes of **Antioch** and because he had been released from captivity by **Nur al-Din** in exchange for a ransom which had not yet been paid. The

Muslim ruler of Syria was dead, but Raymond's hostages for payment were still being held by Nur al-Din's heirs. Meanwhile, **Saladin** was in **Damascus**, having marched through the **Transjordan** at the head of an Egyptian army. In spite of these disabilities, Raymond was universally admired for his intelligence and good judgment, and he was chosen by the court as regent.

One of Raymond's first acts as regent was to marry Eschiva II, heiress to the fief of Galilee. Holding the counties of **Tripoli** and Galilee made Raymond by far the most powerful of the barons, even after the regency was over. His combined knight service was 200 men, and his seat on the High Court was secured. It was Raymond who made **William** archbishop of Tyre and royal chancellor, and William's chronicle favors the regent's career. In 1175, during Raymond's regency, Baldwin IV's leprosy became common knowledge. The effects of the disease could be remarked even by casual observers. To the surprise of all, he was not isolated as a leper. Instead, his sister's marriage became an urgent matter of state, since she would be his heir.

The High Court opened negotiations with the **Montferrat** family, which offered powerful connections in Western Europe.

BALDWIN IV, THE REGENCY OF REYNALD OF CHÂTILLON.

On 15 July 1176, Baldwin came of age, ending Raymond of Tripoli's regency. The young king's first acts were to appoint his uncle Joscelin of Courtenay (*see* **Edessa**) as seneschal and to raid **Damascus** in defiance of a treaty Raymond had been trying to arrange with **Saladin**. Sybil duly married William Longsword of **Montferrat**, but during her pregnancy in the first year of the marriage, William died. The resulting uncertainty in 1177 caused Baldwin to offer the executive regency first to Count Philip of **Flanders**, and when he refused, to **Reynald of Châtillon**. Sybil's son **Baldwin V** was born during the winter of 1177-78. From this date the king began to name Sybil in public acts, signaling her impending regency for the heir.

Some scholars have argued that Baldwin's illness made him dependent on his nobles, and especially on Baldwin of **Ibelin** (c.1133-88). The young king certainly had the support of his barons in 1177, when he countered the attack of Saladin with a small force and won the battle of Mont Gisard (Tell Jazar, a hill near Ibelin). The loss of life on the **Christian** side was high, and the crusaders reported sighting St. George on the battlefield. To commemorate their victory the crusaders built a

Benedictine monastery dedicated to St. Catherine of Alexandria on the battlefield.

In 1178 Baldwin had a castle built at Jacob's Ford, Le Chastellet, on the Damascus road. The **Templars** were entrusted with its defense. In 1179 the king's forces were routed near **Sidon**. Baldwin had to be carried from the field and several important lords were captured. Saladin destroyed Le Chastellet and massacred the garrison in August of 1179. His **navy** raided **Acre** in October.

BALDWIN IV, THE REGENCY OF GUY OF LUSIGNAN.

Baldwin's sister and heir Sybil (whose first husband William of **Montferrat** had died) was married to **Guy of Lusignan** in 1180. Guy began to be associated with the king as designated heir in 1181. Raymond of **Tripoli**, the former regent of the kingdom, had entered its borders with troops in 1180, presumably to seize power. In the opinion of the native barons whose lands were at stake neither Sybil, a woman, or her brother, because of his illness, offered an effective defense for a kingdom constantly threatened by its enemies. Raymond's attempt to intervene in the succession was forestalled by the marriage of Sybil to Guy, but Raymond returned in 1182, apparently unsatisfied with Guy's performance. The High Court intervened and urged a reconciliation because the kingdom's truce with **Saladin** expired in May of 1182. The kingdom's danger was increased when the relationship between the crusader states and **Byzantium** collapsed after the 1182 coup of Andronicus **Comnenus**.

On 13 July 1182 Baldwin's forces fought a pitched battle against Saladin's much larger army at Le Forbelet in southeastern Galilee. Both sides retreated with heavy losses. Saladin moved to crusader Beirut, where his newly constituted fleet was due for an attack on the city. Baldwin went to **Tyre** to recruit ships from his ports and from his allies, the Italian city-communes, especially **Pisa**. Saladin moved his army into northern Syria, and camped outside **Mosul**, which was held by his **Zengid** rivals for power in the region. He remained there until February of 1183. During the winter of 1182-83 **Reynald of Châtillon** raided coastal areas on the Red Sea, until they were driven off by Saladin's brother **al-Adil**, who had war ships from **Alexandria** carried overland from Cairo. Those of Reynald's men who were captured by al-Adil were executed publicly as a show of Saladin's power.

The costs of defending the kingdom from Saladin during these years necessitated a special tax on property and income levied in 1183, one of the earliest examples of such a tax in **Christendom**. According to **William of Tyre**, Baldwin was blind at this point and unable to use his hands or feet. In June Saladin took **Aleppo**, which threatened the security of Antioch. Baldwin was so ill that he made Guy of Lusignan regent. Guy's failure to win a significant engagement that year with an army expanded by the tax money undermined further support for him.

Baldwin married his half-sister Isabel, who turned 12 in 1183 to Humphrey IV of Toron at Reynald of Châtillon's castle of Kerak. On 22 October Saladin besieged the wedding party at the castle, hoping to take important prisoners for ransom. The king was at **Jerusalem**, where he resumed the rule of the kingdom, dismissing Guy as regent.

BALDWIN IV, THE SECOND REGENCY OF RAYMOND OF TRIPOLI.

On 20 November 1183 the king had Sybil's son by **William of Montferrat** crowned co-king as **Baldwin V**. He discussed the possibility of having Sybil's marriage to **Guy of Lusignan** annulled. The king then went to the relief of Kerak, appointing Raymond of **Tripoli** field commander.

After their success in lifting the **siege**, the army returned to **Jerusalem**. Guy and Sybil went to **Ascalon** and refused to answer repeated summons to the court, which forestalled the attempt to annul their marriage and thus disqualify Guy from any part in a regency for Sybil's five-year-old son. Baldwin IV had himself carried to Ascalon, where he knocked on the gate and was refused admission. The king then went to **Jaffa** to begin proceedings to deprive Guy of his lordships.

In 1184 **Saladin** again besieged Kerak. Baldwin IV again had himself carried with the army, and when Saladin raised the siege the king went to **Acre**. Guy meanwhile made an unauthorized attack on **Beduins** who had been of use to the kingdom. The action showed his failure to understand the complex relationships that made the existence of the crusader territories possible. On his return to Jerusalem, the king made Raymond of Tripoli regent.

As the new year (1185) began, the king's health worsened, and he made further arrangements for the safety of his realm. Joscelin of Courtenay was appointed the guardian of Baldwin V, and the royal castles were placed under the care of the **military orders**. A crown-wearing was organized at the church of the **Holy Sepulchre**.

Baldwin IV died in 1185. He was buried in the church of the Sepulchre. The king's sister Sybil (d.1190) and half-sister, Isabel (d.1205), inherited the kingdom in turn, Sybil through her son Baldwin V, and Isabel in her own right as the last surviving member of the dynasty after 1190. Isabel was not able to hold power herself, but could pass the title on to her husbands, beginning with **Conrad of Montferrat**. The most accessible primary sources on Baldwin's reign are the chronicles of **William of Tyre** and **Ernoul**.

BALDWIN V. King in Jerusalem 1185-86. Baldwin was crowned in 1183, as heir, at the age of five, but died in 1186. He was the son of Count William of **Montferrat** and Sybil (d.1190), sister of **Baldwin IV**. When Baldwin IV died in 1185 Raymond of **Tripoli** had been appointed regent, with Joscelin of Courtenay (*see* **Edessa**) as guardian for the heir. **Guy of Lusignan** had not been successfully deprived of either his wife or his lordship, and so was a rival for the regency, if not for the throne. An embassy sent to Western Europe by Baldwin IV before his death was unsuccessful in bringing a powerful regent to stabilize the situation. When knights recruited by the embassy arrived in the **Latin Kingdom** in 1186, they were prevented from fighting by a truce between Jerusalem and **Saladin**.

Baldwin V's grandfather, William V of Montferrat, did come to reside in the Holy Land to protect the seven-year-old king's rights, and fought at **Hattin** in 1187. Baldwin died sometime during the summer of 1186, from unknown causes, and was buried in the church of the **Holy Sepulchre**.

After his death the possible heirs were Sybil (d. 1190) and Isabel (d. 1205), her half-sister. Sybil had married Guy of Lusignan in 1180. He held the title of king until his death in 1194. **Conrad of Montferrat** effectively ruled the kingdom, both because he held **Tyre** after 1187, and because of his marriage to Isabel.

BALTIC CRUSADES. The "Northern" Crusades were fought over a period of four centuries (12th-16th) in the region of the Baltic Sea essentially by Germans who wished to colonize the region from the Elbe and Saale Rivers to Lake Peipus. The **Holy Roman Empire** had no official policy that drove these crusades. They were initiatives of individual German princes and bishops against Baltic, Slavic, and Finnic tribes in this region. What makes these wars crusades is the support of the **papacy** in granting **indulgences** for service there between 1147 and 1505. However, they are in a different category from the **First Crusade**, in the sense that the aspect of **pilgrimage** to the Holy Places is missing.

From the time of the **Second Crusade** in 1147 (*see also* **Wends**) these expeditions spread German institutions through Holstein, Mecklenburg, Brandenburg, Pomerania, Silesia, Bohemia, Poland, Lithuania,

Livonia, **Estonia**, Finland, and Prussia. They led to the foundation of **military orders** such as the **Swordbrethren** and the **Teutonic Knights**, and the careers of warriors such as **Henry XII** "the Lion" (d.1195), duke of Brunswick, Saxony, and Bavaria. The bishops who brought troops to enforce **Christian** practice on the pagan Slavs include **Albert von Buxhövden**, of a noble Saxon family, who founded the diocese of Livonia.

In the same way that Christian rulers of Iberia (*see* **Reconquista**) and **Sicily** were primarily concerned with expansion, and therefore were alternatively fighting a holy war against and allied with their **Muslim** neighbors, the German princes treated pagan Slavic rulers alternately as friends and foes. In their turn, the Slavs learned to use the establishment of Christian bishoprics and monasteries as "civilizing" forces in conquest and settlement. Religious establishments collected tithes and passed some of the wealth along to their overlords in the form of hospitality and taxes. Christian settlers came voluntarily and created profitable farms from "waste" areas. Pagan pirates and slave traders were banished by the armies of the faithful.

In 1171-72 Pope **Alexander III** issued the Bull *Non parum animus noster*, which gave a crusade indulgence to those willing to fight the Finns and Estonians. Crusade expeditions were launched from Sweden in 1195 against the Estonians, to Livonia in 1198, and to Prussia in 1222 and 1223.

BARCELONA, COUNTY. A port city and the base of a small medieval **Christian** county during the **Reconquista**, Barcelona eventually became part of expanding **Aragon** (united with Catalonia in 1137). Count Raymond Berenguer I (r.1035-76) attempted to expand the trading interests of the city by building a small fleet, but was outmatched by the rise of **Genoa, Pisa**, and **Venice** in capturing Mediterranean trade. He also attempted to extend his domains into southern France.

His sons, at odds with each other and the other rulers of Iberia, had a disastrous reign from 1076 until 1097, when the survivor left for **Jerusalem**, followed by the long and successful career of Raymond Berenguer III (r.1097-1131). He allied himself with a number of neighboring counties in such a way as to expand the inheritance of his dynasty, a policy which culminated with the marriage of his daughter to Alfonso VII of **León-Castile** in 1127. His own marriage to the heiress of Provence involved him in the politics of southern France and the western Mediterranean, dominated by the counts of **Toulouse** and the city of Pisa. In 1113 Pope Paschal II authorized a crusade by the Pisans against the **Muslims** in the Mediterranean. Raymond accepted leadership of this expedition in 1114, and went on to attack and briefly hold Majorca. In 1116 Paschal proclaimed another crusade, this time to free the old Roman city of Tarragona in eastern Iberia from the Muslims.

Raymond Berenguer IV (r.1137-62) inherited his father's aspirations in Iberia, while the second son, Berenguer Raymond, inherited Provence. The succession struggle after the death of the childless Alfonso I put the count of Barcelona in control of Aragon, and the **Second Crusade** enabled him to take Muslim Tortosa and Lerida in 1148-49. His brother's death had made him regent for his nephew in Provence, and he was able to use that position to become the most powerful magnate in southern France by 1156, when he joined the king of England at the **siege** of Toulouse. These combined interests prevented any further action in the short run against **Islam** in Iberia.

BAYBARS I, MAMLUK SULTAN. (r.1260-77). In 1260 the arrival of **Mongol** ambassadors demanding the surrender of **Egypt** precipitated a crisis. Baybars's predecessor had the ambassadors murdered and gathered the forces of Egypt and Syria for a confrontation with the Mongol advance guard at Gaza. The Kipchak Syrian commander Baybars then led the attack on the Mongol army at a place near Nablus called the Spring of Goliath (Goliath's Well, Ayn Jalut). Baybars defeated the Mongols in the field, although the invaders were to return to Syria on several occasions before their final defeat there in 1303. Baybars's victory over the Mongols at Goliath's Well in 1260 stopped the latter from following the destruction of **Assassin** strongholds and the conquest of **Baghdad** and **Damascus** with the conquest of Egypt. Baybars was then able to ally himself with the Golden Horde in Russia against their rivals in Mongol Iran, so that both Mongols and refugees from their conquests entered Egypt in great numbers after 1260. Mongol refugees had an influence on Egypt's culture and administration that is still debated.

Superiority over the Mongols on the battlefield was the key to Baybars's ability to take authority in Egypt and to extend his reach into Syria, threatened by annual Mongol raids. His campaign against the remnants of the crusader kingdoms laid the foundations for their expulsion from **Acre** in 1291. Twenty-one expeditions to rout the remains of the **Latin Kingdom of Jerusalem** between 1265 and 1271 allowed Baybars to conquer crusader **Antioch**, the **Templar** fortress of Arsuf, and the **Hospitaller** fortress of **Krak des Chevaliers**, among other strategic points. Successors were able to take major holdouts such as **Tripoli**, and eventually to drive the last of the European settlers out of **Tyre**,

Sidon, and Beirut by taking **Acre** in 1291. Baybars also launched an offensive against the Assassins, who had been weakened by Mongol attacks, and was able to impose some control over them between 1265 and 1271. Baybars I used **Damascus** as a base for his military operations and died there in 1277. His son, al-Said Nasir al-Din Berke Khan, was at that point ruling Egypt. His attempts to take over upon his father's death failed, and he was forced to abdicate in 1279. The **Mamluks** returned to the practice of choosing the new sultan from among the most influential Kipchak military personnel.

BEDUIN/BEDOUIN. Pastoral nomads, usually **Arabs** who professed either **Christianity** or **Islam**, lived along the desert frontier east and south of the Crusader kingdoms. They moved across the boundaries of the kingdoms under royal protection, and were registered to make that possible. They were sometimes useful to the European or **Muslim** forces as spies or mercenaries.

BERBER. This term is used by Europeans and Arabs to refer to the indigenous inhabitants of the 2,000-mile stretch of northern Africa between the Mediterranean Sea and the Sahara Desert from **Egypt** to the Atlantic Ocean. The Berbers themselves use terms derived from their own (related) languages. Under the Romans this region was a Mediterranean province called "Africa." When Roman rule ended in the fifth century, local chiefs took control of northern Africa and benefited from trade with western Africa. By the eighth century Arab conquest had been completed, but **Islam**'s control was more effective in the cities and villages than in the countryside. The Berbers had embraced Donatism under **Christian** Rome and practiced Kharijism, often mixed with practices from local traditional religions, under their **Muslim** conquerors. They were drafted into the military in Muslim Africa and served as mercenaries in Syria and Turkey. For North African-based powers in the crusades period, *see* **Maghrib**; **Murabit**; **Muwahhid**.

BERNARD OF CLAIRVAUX, St. (1090-1153). Bernard was a Burgundian nobleman who entered the monastery of Cîteaux with 30 companions in 1113. In 1116 he became abbot of the daughter house of Clairvaux. He was a prolific writer of sermons, commentaries, and letters, and an extremely influential figure in the medieval church. Because of his reputation as a reformer, scholar, and speaker, he was chosen by

Pope **Eugenius III** (r.1145-53) to preach the **Second Crusade**. He was also instrumental in founding the Knights **Templar**, for whom he wrote a tract defining their spiritual ideal (1128). His letters are an important source for the early crusading period.

The Cistercian Order, a network of monastic houses dependent upon Cîteaux, provided many preachers and procurators of the crusade movement. There were after 1157 several houses of Cistercians in the **Latin Kingdom of Jerusalem**, including Belmont near **Tripoli**, St. John near **Jerusalem**, and a third house, Salvatio, in an unknown location. *See also* **Gervase of Prémontré**; **Robert of Arbrissel**; **Jacques de Vitry**.

BETHLEHEM. Bethlehem is a town about five miles south of **Jerusalem**, the focus of **Christian** devotion as the birthplace of Christ since at least the time of the Roman Emperor Hadrian, who desecrated the shrine there in c.132. Emperor Constantine I built a basilica there in 330. The grotto of the Nativity occupied a crypt, and nearby were the Oratory of the Manger and Altar of the Magi. **Byzantine** Emperor Justinian I built the town defenses in 531. The **First Crusaders** took it in 1099 and elevated it to a **Latin** bishopric in 1110. According to the crusade chronicles, it had been a Christian town and its chief citizens requested the help of the First Crusaders. Between 1153 and 1187 **Ascalon** was technically subject to it in the ecclesiastical hierarchy. Both cities returned to **Muslim** control in 1187, except for short periods when various areas were briefly returned to the **Latin Kingdom** as a result of treaties with Muslim powers.

Its priests (also called canons), who followed what was called the Augustinian rule for religious houses after 1112, went into exile in **Acre** until the crusader kingdom fell in 1291. Like the canons of the **Holy Sepulchre**, they sent missions to raise money and recruit men for the crusade, especially after 1187, when they were given a property in London. Over the next 200 years they built and maintained a small hospital and priory there, a focus of devotion for those who could not make the journey to the Holy Land, and a refuge for canons of their order. Beyond that house in London, by 1227 they owned 66 other churches in Western Europe. *See* **Holy Blood**.

Bishops of Bethlehem and their reigning dates include: Anschetinus (1108-25); Anselm (1129-45); Gerald (1148-53); Ralph I (1156-74); Albert (1177-81); Ralph II (1186-92).

BOHEMOND OF TARANTO, PRINCE OF ANTIOCH. (r.1098-1111). Bohemond was the son of the Norman Robert Guiscard, duke of Apulia, who invaded **Sicily** in 1071 and **Byzantine** Albania in 1081. Bohemond joined the **First Crusade** and ruled **Antioch** from its capture in 1098 until 1111. He had to defend his lordship first from the Byzantines, irritated by his failure to honor his oath to return it to them, and then from the **Armenians** and local Turkish commanders. In the summer of 1099 he attacked the Byzantine port of Latakia with the help of the **Pisan** archbishop Daimbert and his fleet. The other crusade leaders, on their return home from the **Holy Sepulchre**, successfully pressured Bohemond to lift the siege. Bohemond was captured by the **Danishmends** in 1100, so that his nephew **Tancred** assumed the regency of Antioch. Bohemond was released and resumed power in May of 1103.

After a disastrous battle against the Turkish emirs of Mardin and **Mosul** near **Edessa** in 1104, Bohemond left for Italy, appointing Tancred as regent for Antioch for the second time. He visited Pope Paschal II in 1105 to promote a crusade against the Byzantine empire. Bruno of Segni was appointed to preach as legate, and Bohemond toured Europe in 1105-06 raising troops. In 1107 he sailed from Italy to Byzantine territory in Albania with 34,000 men, and laid siege to Durazzo. He was forced to retreat and died in Apulia in 1111.

He passed the lordship on to his son, Bohemond II (r.1126-30). For further information on the lordship *see* **Antioch; Tripoli.**

BRABANT. Brabant was a principality of the Low Countries formed partially from the territories of Louvain and Brussels. Godfrey, count of Louvain, was granted the title of duke of Lower Lorraine by the **Holy Roman Emperor** in 1106. *See also* **Godfrey of Bouillon; First Crusade; Flanders.**

BYZANTINE EMPIRE. The East Roman Empire was centered at **Constantinople**, and made up originally of the Prefectures of Illyricum (the Balkan Peninsula) and the East (Thrace, the eastern Mediterranean, and **Egypt**). The original name of the capital, before it was rebuilt and renamed by Constantine I (r.306-37) was Byzantium. The term "Byzantine," meaning the East Romans based at Constantinople during the medieval period, was not coined until the seventeenth century. The strategic location of the city on the Bosporus, combined with the most impressive land walls in the Roman world, made the city unconquerable until the crusaders took it in 1204 (*see* **Fourth Crusade; Constantin-**

ople, Kingdom of). The Byzantines retook the city 1261-1453, after which **Ottoman** conquest re-created it as Istanbul, the center of an **Islamic** empire until World War I.

In 1000 the empire was far wealthier than any state in Western Europe and its culture was more influential. At its height its boundaries stretched from eastern Turkey to southern Italy and from the Crimea to Lebanon. Missionaries carried its religion and culture throughout eastern Europe and especially to Russia.

Byzantine emperors and their reigning dates during the crusade period include the **Comnenus** dynasty, as well as: Isaac II Angelus (1185-95), Alexius III Angelus (1195-1203), Isaac II and Alexius IV Angelli (1203-04), Alexius V Murzuphlus (1204), Theodore I Lascaris (1204-22), John III Ducas Vatatzes (1222-54), Theodore II Lascaris (1254-58), John IV Lascaris (1258-61), and the Palaeologus dynasty, from 1259 until 1453, interrupted by John VI Cantacuzene (1347-54).

The official language of church and state in the multilingual Byzantine Empire after the sixth century was **Greek**, which led the crusaders to refer to their Orthodox Christian allies as "the Greeks," while the crusaders from Europe were "the Latins." The original five churches sharing leadership in the early Christian world were Rome, Constantinople, **Jerusalem**, **Antioch**, and **Alexandria**. In 1054 the unity of this original organization was broken when the bishop of Rome claimed primacy over the other four. There were theological, liturgical, and organizational differences, as well as the language divergence, which made it seem reasonable to the crusaders to replace existing Greek Orthodox prelates with Europeans in territory they conquered after 1096. The decision to do so had long-term consequences not only for political relations East/West, but also for church history in the **Latin Kingdom of Jerusalem**, and more seriously, the Latin church in the crusader kingdom of **Cyprus** after the **Third Crusade**.

-C-

CAFFARO. A nobleman who sailed with a Genoese fleet to the **Levant** in 1100, Caffaro wrote a history of the **First Crusade** in addition to his history of **Genoa** from 1099-1163. Some of his estimates of numbers and other details have been challenged by historians, and in some cases appear to be unreliable. His chronicles favor his commune, and offer a valuable perspective on events in the East. They have not been translated into English, but are used by Stephen Epstein in his history of Genoa.

Caffaro records that the crusade was preached in 1097 in the church of San Siro, and that nine noblemen, whose names he lists, took the **cross**. Genoa's population has been estimated at about 10,000 at the time, making the crusade fleet of 12 galleys, each carrying a crew of 100, and a small ship which left the same year, a major venture. This fleet arrived off **Antioch** in 1098 and its leaders attached themselves to **Bohemond of Taranto**. Part of the fleet returned to Genoa in 1098 with the bones of John the Baptist, while part remained to claim their own quarter in newly conquered Antioch.

In 1099 another fleet under Guglielmo (or William, known as "Hammerhead") and Primo Embriaco arrived off **Jaffa** and took supplies and their expertise to the **siege of Jerusalem**. They were followed by a more substantial effort in August of 1100: 26 galleys and four ships, with a total crew of 3,000 men. After renewing their commune's arrangements in Antioch, they attached themselves to King **Baldwin I** of Jerusalem in the summer of 1101, and assisted him in the successful sieges of Arsuf and Caesarea. The Genoese took plunder that included a green glass bowl known to them as the Holy Basin, and returned home in October. Smaller contingents assisted at the sieges of Tortosa in 1102 and **Tripoli** over the next few years. **Acre** was taken with their help in 1104. They were rewarded by concessions in several ports by the king, and represented in these negotiations by their bishop.

Caffaro's chronicles offer information not only on the crusades, but also on the history of Genoa's commune, including its law code and the election of city consuls, the earliest form of its government.

CALIXTUS II, POPE. (r.1119-24). Guy, archbishop of Vienne, who became pope as Calixtus II, was the second son of Count William of Burgundy (d.1087). His older brother inherited the county, while the younger, Raymond, married Urraca, daughter of King Alfonso VI of **León**. Upon Raymond's death **Portugal**, part of his wife's inheritance, passed to his cousin Henry, who had married Alfonso's illegitimate daughter Teresa. *See* **Reconquista**.

Calixtus followed Popes **Urban II** and Paschal II in confirming the right of crusaders to protection of their property in Western Europe for the duration of their journey. One of Calixtus's letters, issued in 1122, was used by **canon lawyers** to construct the privileges of the crusaders.

CANON LAW. Laws established by church courts or councils. A legal status for crusaders developed in the course of the 12th and 13th centuries. **Crusade vows**, taken in the presence of a priest, created a legally binding set of obligations for the crusader, which might include limits on how long preparation could be made before departure, a specific destination to be reached on the expedition, legal protections for his family, and release from debt for a set period.

CARMELITES. The early history of the Order of Our Lady of Carmel is obscured by a lack of contemporary documents and the attempts of later medieval writers to construct the missing narrative. The order appears to have consisted in the first place of hermits following the ancient tradition of **Egyptian** monasticism by devoting themselves to prayer and contemplation without any formal rule or conventual buildings. St. Albert, **patriarch of Jerusalem** 1205-14, either wrote or approved a rule for the hermits that was based on the rule of St. Augustine, followed by the canons of the **Holy Sepulchre**. Albert's rule for the Carmelites was of a notable severity, emphasizing fasting, silence, prayer, and labor. In spite of the voluntary poverty of the order a monastery and church was built on Mount Carmel by 1263. It was burnt when the crusader kingdom fell in 1291.

As the hermits of Mount Carmel migrated to Europe in the 13th century, it became necessary to adapt their rule to the harsher climate of the west. There was also resistance after 1215 to the establishment of new orders in the west for a variety of reasons. The order expanded slowly in Western Europe in spite of these difficulties. Houses of nuns were established after 1452. The Carmelites are chiefly famous for a reform movement (the Discalced Carmelites) that arose in Spain under St. Teresa of Avila (d.1582) and St. John of the Cross (d.1591). Both wished to return to the severity of the original rule, and both wrote extensively of the practice of contemplation, based on their own experiences.

CASTLES. There were several kinds of fortifications built in the **Levant** and in Europe in the medieval era. These included simple structures (often single towers) intended for brief retreat for periods of defensive action, town walls and gates built for general security, and castles built as bases for both attack and defense over a long period. Castle construction varied with purpose: size, extent of defenses, ability to hold livestock as well as people, etc. All responded to location and purpose. Many structures were built to dominate access to roads or other key sites. Castles could be either privately owned but constructed and operated by royal license, or part of a kingdom's defenses and garrisoned by the monarch.

Crusader castles were significantly more sophisticated than **Muslim** ones because of the difference in numbers of defenders. The conquering minority depended on fortifications to dominate the vastly superior numbers of native inhabitants, and they also depended on massive financial support from Europe to build these solid masonry defenses from scratch in the Middle East. Conversely, Muslim town defenses, such as the famous walls of **Damascus**, were often far superior to those built by Europeans in the East. Like the defenses at **Aleppo**, Cairo, and **Jerusalem**, these fortification systems included citadels at the center of the city. Like rural towers, citadels were centers for supplies (often enclosing a cistern), defense (topped with battlements), and attack, as well as being highly visible symbols of the power of the warrior who controlled them. Most fortifications were built to take advantage of natural features and especially of higher ground or water as a deterrent to attackers, and of course, firm ground to support the foundation. Both Muslim and crusader forts were also used as beacons or pigeon stations to convey alarm signals.

Crusaders built more than 80 single towers in the 12th and 13th centuries to dominate lines of communication, to store supplies, and for defense. They built or fortified offshore promontories to dominate harbors, for example at **Sidon** and **Tripoli**, and extensive walls to enclose **Tyre**, completed by a chain that could prevent ships from entering or leaving the harbor. Kerak, near the Dead Sea, was built in 1142 to allow Europeans to plunder one of the routes Muslim pilgrims took to Mecca. Carole Hillenbrand, in her description of these and other fortifications, describes the 50 to 90-foot-wide gorge, 450 feet long and 60 to 130 feet high constructed by crusaders at Saone, necessitating the removal of 170,000 tons of solid rock. The gorge was only part of the defense system for this castle. **Krak des Chevaliers**, built in the 12th century, reportedly could house 6,000 people.

The most impressive Muslim castles were built by the **Assassins** in Iran and Syria in the 12th century, but their strength was in their strategic placement in mountainous areas rather than in the quality of the construction. Unlike crusader strongholds, they were built for defense and to house believers rather than as bases from which to dominate the surrounding countryside.

Castle technology adapted not only to site and purpose, but to advances in military technology. Sappers with pickaxes made corners a problem, which led to rounded walls and towers. Walls could be reinforced by using columns from previous buildings, iron bars, or iron clamps. The use of crossbows led to arrow-loops in cruciform versus strictly vertical shape. Concealed pits could be built around the castle to deter attackers from rolling **siege** towers up to the walls, but a broad ditch, in use since the Roman period, did almost as good a job at making attackers vulnerable to missile fire. The concentric castle concentrated firepower at the gate: topped by a "house," flanked by towers, and backed by three walls built so that the inner wall was in each case a bit higher than the outer. If the whole structure could be so placed that water or height prohibited an attack from any direction but the gate, the castle was very difficult to take, as the defenders could focus on the one point of advance. The moat obviously offered an obstacle, and use of the drawbridge by attackers made them subject to arrows and other missiles aimed from the towers. Normally the construction of the gate itself isolated the intruder in a small space where he could be attacked from all sides. Postern gates were often built to allow the defenders to get out in case of a siege, but they offered the attackers ingress as well, and so had to be carefully guarded.

A castle was not a static feature of the landscape. In the Latin East it was a **weapon** that had to be constantly updated, repaired, staffed, and provisioned. A water supply was critical. At Margat, the largest of the crusader castles, the **Hospitallers** were said to able to harvest 500 cartloads of crops from the surrounding land every year, and to supply the castle so that it could hold out, in terms of food and water, for five years. At Chastel Pèlerin, 4,000 men were supposed to have been fed daily during a siege in 1220.

CATHAR HERESY. The Cathars are a medieval religious sect, known from the 12th century, which was identified by the Roman Catholic church hierarchy as heretical. During the **Albigensian Crusade** (1208-29), heretics in southern France in the vicinity of the city of Albi were identified by the orthodox church as Cathars, or Dualists, in the first instance because of their resistance to established ecclesiastical authority. While theological ideas may have varied from group to group, alternative hierarchies of "good men" (and women) who lived an ascetic life were known to have existed in Languedoc, northern Italy, Catalonia, England, northern France, and the Rhineland. Dualism stresses the rejection of the material in favor of the spiritual, positing a perpetual war between the forces of Lucifer and God. Whether there was a coherent Cathar theology and effective hierarchy is still a matter of debate among scholars. Records of **Inquisition** (from 1229) proceedings emphasize a clear theology and international organization, in order to justify vigilant prosecution. The assumption was that Bogomil missionaries from Bulgaria spread something similar to the ancient doctrine of the Manicheans to Western Europe. Bosnia appears to have been the last refuge for Cathars in the 14th century as their congregations died out in France and Italy.

The significance of the heresy was a rejection of the efficacy of the sacraments and therefore of the primary function of the orthodox priesthood. Heretics were charged with a number of crimes. The most serious was their refusal to take oaths, which was viewed as a threat to social order. Those who took the rites of the Cathar church were strict ascetics (the perfecti, or "perfected"), while most of the members (the credentes, or "believers") of the sect put off their initiation (or "consolation") until they were near death.

St. **Bernard of Clairvaux** is the most famous among those who tried to combat heresy in southern France by preaching missions. He was well received at Albi in 1145, but rebuffed at a village near **Toulouse**, where a crowd of knights clashed their armor to drown out his sermon. Attempts to combat the heresy by preaching and disputation failed during the 1170s, 1180s, and 1190s, in spite of several church councils and an agreement (never activated) reached by the rulers of France and England to use force.

Pope **Innocent III** was particularly active against the Cathars, removing incompetent or suspect bishops and replacing them with people like Fulk of Marseilles, a Cistercian monk who was made bishop of Toulouse in 1206. Fulk, whose personal devotion to the ideal of apostolic poverty placed him above reproach, was in turn the patron of St. **Dominic**. Both tried to best the Cathars on their own ground, by offering a model of piety and asceticism that undercut criticism of the orthodox church. Such efforts were in vain, especially in areas where the nobility refused to prosecute heretics: Albi, Béziers, Carcassonne, Foix, and Toulouse.

Neither the crusade nor the Inquisition wiped out the Cathars, who developed a community of 400-500 believers at the mountain fortress of Montségur on the border of the county of Toulouse in 1232. It fell to orthodox besiegers in 1244, and over 200 believers were burnt. This may have been the last stand of a group of the Cathars as a civic entity, but the heresy went underground rather than disappearing altogether. The apparatus designed to combat them survived as well, especially in the missions of the **Dominican** and **Franciscan** friars.

See also **Waldensians**.

CATHERINE OF SIENA, St. (1347-80). Catherine was an Italian mystic whose letters are an important source for papal and religious history. Catherine was an advocate for the reform of the church and in particular for the removal of the **papacy** from its exile in Avignon. She was also articulate in her support for crusading. Like **Humbert of Romans**, she promoted the ideal of the movement as the reality faded, so her work represents the fully developed theology of the crusade. For other letter collections that shed light on the crusades, *see* **Gervase of Prémontré**; **Jacques de Vitry**; **Gregory VII**.

CAVALRY. The stereotypical Western European army consisted of heavily armored **knights** on powerful war **horses**, shattering their opponents with an ill-organized but overwhelming charge. The opposing stereotype was a troop of lightly armed **Muslims**, Turkish or **Mongol** archers on smaller, more nimble horses, charging straight at the enemy but then wheeling in formation at the last moment to shoot well-aimed arrows in retreat. While there is truth to both characterizations, it is also true that by the 10th century both sides had access to **armor**, infantry, **siege weapons**, pikes, lances, axes, maces, and crossbows, and could deploy all of this technology in more or less the same way.

Europeans generally left the bow to the infantry. Infantry massed together to form a shield wall or advanced armed with pikes or axes, backed by archers. Cavalry was used either to charge or to surround and harass the enemy. Both sides needed several horses to each warrior, and if heavy armor was to be used, the horses needed to be of two kinds, one for riding and the other, much heavier and slower, for the battle charge. The provision and care of horses was arguably the greatest concern for armies on both sides, and for both, horses were the first target for overwhelming the mounted enemy.

Weapons were valuable and plunder was a primary concern, as individuals were responsible to equip themselves. The mounted warrior himself was a valuable commodity, the product of a society geared to educate and support him, and he could sometimes be held at ransom more profitably than simply killed on the battlefield. Charismatic leadership was crucial to morale on both sides, and the fall of the military leader often led to the defeat of the army. Europeans and Turks were equally hesitant about risking a pitched battle; strategic engagements and cunning in general were prized by both.

Both sides used baggage trains if possible but were prepared to live off the land if necessary. Both Muslim and **Christian** armies were accompanied by noncombatants such as women and clergy. Both were skilled at siege warfare. Even more important, both were composed of troops with regional, linguistic, cultural, and sometimes religious differences. To the Middle Eastern eye, one "**Latin**" or "**Frank**" might be difficult to distinguish from any other. However, often the most important factor in any campaign was tension between factions within the army, or regional rivalries, such as the proverbial one between the French and German contingents. In the same way, an army that was simply Muslim to a crusader's eye was a coalition of groups from Syria, **Asia Minor**, **Egypt**, etc., who were as vulnerable to internal divisions as the Europeans.

Pay structures varied regionally and sometimes by commander. The early centuries of Islamic warfare were based on troops paid salaries, with income from land or revenue from tax farming playing a minimal role. In general, Europeans were in the opposite situation. By the time of the crusades, the question of pay and length of service is too complicated for both sides to be summed up here. For both sides, the variations mean that loyalties are more likely to be individual, to a leader who is directly responsible for the well-being of his troops, or regional, to a state within **Islam**, for instance, that had its own policy for payment of the army.

Hugh Kennedy, in his work on the *Early Islamic State* (2001) concluded that "one of the most obvious contrasts between the Muslim world of the early Middle Ages and contemporary **Byzantine** and Western European polities was the extent to which the Muslim world operated a monetary economy" (195). Military expenditure was the dominant expense of medieval government. Methods of payment for military service, weapons, and supplies created a structure that was a fundamental factor in medieval economies and cultures.

See also **Castles**; **Naval Warfare**.

CHARLES I OF ANJOU. (1226-85). King of Naples and **Sicily**, count of Anjou and Provence. Charles was the son of King Louis VIII of France (r.1223-26), and the brother of **Louis IX**. He married Beatrice, heiress of Raymond Berenger V, the last count of Provence, in 1246. He accompanied his brother on the crusade to **Mamluk Egypt** in 1248, and returned to Provence in 1250. He used his base in southern France to expand his territory, including Marseille in 1257 and parts of the Piedmont region in 1259. The **papacy**, immersed in a struggle for primacy with the **Holy Roman Empire**, offered Charles the kingdoms of Naples and Sicily in 1262.

With his brother's help Charles put together a land and naval force in 1264 to make good his claim to these areas. In 1265 he obtained crusade status for his invasion and set sail for his new domain. Charles was crowned in Italy and defeated the German empire's army at Benevento in February of 1266. By 1268 Charles had consolidated his hold on southern Italy and Sicily, becoming one of the most powerful rulers in Western Europe. The **Villehardouin** family, which held Achaea after the **Fourth Crusade**, accepted Charles as overlord in an attempt to protect their holdings.

To the ruler of Sicily northern Africa was a potential rival and commercial threat. Charles owed Louis military help in return for the assistance he had received in taking Sicily. Pushed by Louis to join the crusade the king vowed to undertake in 1267, Charles provided part of the motive for Louis IX's decision to carry the crusade to Tunis in 1270 rather than to a target in the **Levant**.

The **Latin Empire of Constantinople** created by the **Fourth Crusade** in 1204 had fallen to the Greeks in 1261. Charles had predatory designs on **Byzantine** territory, but had been forestalled in acting on them by the new emperor's offer to reunite the Eastern church with the papacy. Louis took the cross in 1267, with lukewarm support at best from Charles and the aristocracy of France. Crusade taxes were levied on the clergy and in some districts on the laity of France, the **Jews** were forced to ransom themselves, and the pope contributed to the costs of the projected expedition. **Genoa** was contracted for 19 and Marseille for 20 ships. No destination is named for the projected crusade in the contracts, but arrangements are made for a protracted period of campaign.

Tunisia had refused to pay Charles the same tribute the Holy Roman Emperors had received as suzerains of Sicily for trade rights in its ports and waters. It seemed an easier target than **Egypt**, and after the debacle of 1248, the French king needed a victory against **Islam**. The army and fleet assembled in Cagliari, in southern Sardinia, where many heard for the first time that they were bound for Tunis. Louis's forces landed at the fort built on the site of the ancient city of Carthage on 18 July 1270, and settled in to wait for Charles. The **Muslims** on their side waited patiently in fortified Tunis for heat, poor sanitation, and lack of supplies to do their work for them. This tactic succeeded. By 25 August the king was dead, and his army was weakened by dysentery and other illnesses brought on by their situation.

Neither Charles, who arrived soon afterwards, nor the Tunisians were eager for a pitched battle. Much to the disgust of the army, a treaty was ratified between them in November which restored the favorable trade relations between Sicily and Tunisia but did not defray the French costs of the crusade. The Prince of Wales (**Edward I** of England) arrived just as the final arrangements were being made, and unable to fight in northern Africa, set sail for the Holy Land. Philip, heir to the throne of France, had accompanied his father on the expedition. He lost both wife and newborn child on the overland journey home. He had been forced to take this longer and more difficult journey when a storm damaged most of the fleet after its return to Sicily. Crusade appeals to the French were unsuccessful after this humiliating and expensive episode.

Charles, however, remained hopeful of gaining land in the Levant. Two **Greek** claimants to the throne vied with survivors of the Latin Empire for control of Greece. The Serbs and Bulgarians were anxious to take Byzantine land with European help. By 1272 Charles had claimed the remnants of the Latin Empire of Constantinople and been crowned king of Albania. In 1277 he purchased the rights to the titular **Latin Kingdom of Jerusalem**. On paper at least he had a viable claim to land conquered by crusading Europeans in the 12th and 13th centuries. His negotiations with other potential allies were hampered by their conflicting interests.

Pope Gregory X (r.1271-76) saw Charles as an obstacle to a new crusade against the Mamluks, which would require all the resources Europe and Constantinople could offer to be successful. In 1274 Michael VIII Palaeologus, emperor at **Nicaea** 1258-61 and at Constantinople 1261-82, was able to force the union of the Roman and Orthodox churches over the bitter resistance of the Greek clergy. Charles relied on papal support and had to bide his time.

In 1281 Simon of Brie, a Frenchman with close ties to Charles's family, became pope as Martin IV (r.1281-85). The proposed union of the churches was universally unpopular, but the Greek emperor was excommunicated for failing to effect it. **Venice**, which had promoted the Fourth Crusade's conquest of Constantinople in 1204, happily joined Charles in plans for another invasion of Byzantium.

The Sicilian Vespers put an end to Charles's plans. He had taxed his Italian territories heavily to pay for his military expenses, and introduced French administrators into Sicily, making himself extremely unpopular with his subjects. The Byzantines, the German emperors Charles had defeated to take southern Italy, and the king of **Aragon**, who had a claim through marriage to Charles's throne, combined to plot against him. On 30 March 1282 a popular uprising in Sicily massacred the French garrison, and in August King Peter of Aragon arrived to claim the crown. The pope responded by excommunicating him, in theory relieving Peter of both Sicily and Aragon, and proclaimed a crusade against him.

Pope Martin offered the kingdom of Aragon to King Philip III of France (r.1270-85) for his son Charles of Valois (d.1325), and the crusade tax was collected in France to pay for the expedition. Charles of Anjou died in the beginning of 1285, on 7 January. Philip's crusade began that year, but was halted for the summer in Catalonia at the siege of Gerona. Peter's navy was superior to Philip's and forced a French retreat by inflicting serious damage on its fleet, which was supplying the **siege**, in September. In the course of withdrawing from Spain, Philip died, on 5 October. His heir, Philip IV, arranged a truce by which Charles's heirs retained southern Italy and the house of Aragon kept Sicily.

CHILDREN'S CRUSADE. (1212). The church hierarchy did not encourage this expedition, except in heightening the sense of encroaching danger by emphasizing the threat offered by **Islam**. Peasants from the **Holy Roman Empire**, the Low Countries, and France participated in the ill-fated (and misnamed) Children's Crusade in which the poor attempted to accomplish the capture of the holy places. Unable to pay for passage by either the land or sea route, most of the participants died attempting to reach the **Levant** or were captured and sold into slavery.

This was one of a series of expeditions, including the Shepherds' Crusades of 1251 and 1320, and the Popular Crusade of 1309, all of which were sparked by itinerant preachers similar to **Peter the Hermit**, who had preached the **First Crusade** and led an army of "poor knights" in 1096. Frustration with the failure of the nobility to recapture the Holy Land, combined with the desire to see **Jerusalem**, fueled these doomed expeditions. The story of the disappearance of the children of Hameln, Germany, in 1284 seems to be connected to a similar event.

CHIVALRY. (Latin: *militia*). An ideal of knighthood that shaped conduct on and off the battlefield in the Middle Ages, chivalry was a mixture of ethics derived from medieval Christianity and Western European warrior culture. The operating assumption was that violence can be an appropriate political tool when limited by ethical considerations. According to one medieval chronicler, "wrong must be done to put an end to a worse thing."

CHIVALRY • 65

The ongoing medieval discussion of the limits on and use of violence was expressed in the imaginative literature, the chronicles, and the law codes of the period, as well as in documents specifically related to the crusades, such as crusade sermons or papal letters. The authors of these documents move easily among the varying ethical codes expressed by the **Jewish** and **Christian** scriptures, Roman and **canon law**, the idea of personal honor, and the customs of various peoples. For the crusades, for instance, there is a clear invitation by the **papacy** for **knights** to internalize identification with the battle for the Holy Land by the Hebrews of the Old Testament scriptures. Secular crusade songs celebrate the duty of the knights as vassals to avenge the death of Christ as their overlord. Using a variety of such ideas as inspiration, the **First Crusaders** had no difficulty in moving from the massacre of the inhabitants of **Jerusalem** in 1099 to the liturgy of the Eucharist as a celebration of success.

A basic tension that runs through all of this literature is the relationship of "those who prayed" with "those who fought." Clerical writing of the 12th century emphasized the duty of the secular power to defend the church, lauding the superiority of the monastic life. Secular writing, by contrast, rooted the ethos of the knight in an independent relationship to the divine (using Old Testament kingship, for instance, as a model) that undercut the authority of the church. Beyond the rhetoric used by both sides, there was the simple fact that the clergy were unable to wage war or administer punishment for crime, while the laity, either through military service or the secular courts, could. Public order and defense were (and are) guaranteed by violence. In the strictest sense, to practice chivalry was to fight.

Crusade chronicles are good places to follow the ongoing medieval conversation on these issues, from **Pope Urban II**'s characterization of the knights of Europe in his sermon at Clermont, to the moment during **Louis IX**'s campaign in **Egypt** in 1250 when several knights, wounded and surrounded by enemies, take a few minutes to work through an ethical decision that threatens their honor. In fact, a close reading of crusade texts creates the impression of a conversation so involving that it interferes with the fighting: at **Antioch**, when the leaders of the First Crusade split over their responsibility to the **Byzantine Emperor**, during the **Second Crusade**, when a failure to decide who was most worthy to rule **Damascus** prevented the army from effectively attacking it, to the famous argument among the nobility of the **Latin Kingdom of Jerusalem** at **Hattin** over **Guy of Lusignan**'s fitness to command, an argument that ultimately allowed **Saladin** to take the kingdom. Geoffrey of

Villehardouin's account of the **Fourth Crusade** somewhat obsessively centers on noble behavior as opposed to its opposite, while accounts of the **Third Crusade** make Saladin more chivalrous than his Christian opponents.

CHRISTENDOM/CHRISTIAN. Like **Muslim**, these words are used in medieval and modern sources to refer collectively to a number of political and religious constructs that define themselves in terms of the New Testament. The word Christendom implies a unified culture based on a shared idealism. Even medieval Western Europe was in reality a patchwork of regional polities, beliefs, and ritual practices which the **papacy** was working to make a monolithic entity by fighting "heresy," for instance, in southern France during the **Albigensian Crusade**. The nominal alliance between **Latin** and **Greek** Christians, which looked more like rivalry in the history of missions to Eastern Europe, tipped into warfare during the **Fourth Crusade**.

In the **Levant**, Christians belonging to the **Coptic**, Maronite, **Armenian**, **Jacobite**, and Nestorian groups were regarded with suspicion by Europeans. The terms "Christian state" or "Christendom" are as problematic as "Muslim state" or **Islam**, due to sectarian, regional, ethnic, and historical divergences.

CID, EL. *See* **Reconquista**.

CILICIA. "Greater **Armenia**" refers to a region north of Lake Van, bounded by the Caucasus Mountains and the Black Sea. "Cilicia" was a Roman province bordering the Mediterranean Sea south of the Taurus Mountains in southeastern **Asia Minor**. After 1071, when the **Seljuk Turks** had completed the conquest of Greater Armenia, a region in the Taurus Mountains was settled by refugees under an Armenian dynasty as an independent principality. It eventually allied with the crusaders as a buffer between the **Byzantine** and **Islamic** rivals for their territory.

Under King Leo I (r.1129-39) Cilician Armenia conquered territory held near **Antioch** by the crusaders. Leo's Armenia received recognition from the **Holy Roman Empire**, and under his successor the kingdom was recognized by the eastern emperors as well. In 1136 the rulers of Antioch created a *march* or frontier in the Amanus Mountains to hold off Armenian expansion, and gave it to the **Templars**. The order built a series of **castles** there to strengthen their defense of the region. Prince

Thoros II (r.1145-68) was able to ally with both Byzantium and the crusader kingdoms against **Nur al-Din**.

After a coup in 1168 one of the claimants to the throne again allied with Nur al-Din and took the Templar march by 1172. Cilicia reached its peak during the reign of Leo II (r.1186-1219), when the **Latin Kingdom** was in retreat before the **Ayyubid** dynasty. In 1166 the king of Jerusalem held three castles in his own right, the rest being held by the **military orders** and great crusader lords. By contrast Leo II held 72 castles in his own right, 49 of which were major fortresses. He was able to gain recognition for his monarchy from Holy Roman Emperor Henry VI in 1198. In 1342 the **Lusignan** kings of **Cyprus** ruled Cilicia as well.

In 1375 the **Mamluks** conquered the kingdom, and the last of the Armenian dynasty died in 1393. The Armenians themselves survived under **Ottoman** rule as an ethnic and religious entity subject to taxation in exchange for toleration.

CLUNY. (Saone-et-Loire, France). Cluny was a Benedictine monastery founded by Duke William of Aquitaine in 909-10, which in its foundation charter was freed from the control of the duke's family. In 1054 the monastery obtained an exemption from oversight by any local bishop. Most religious foundations had fairly clearly defined obligations both to their secular patrons and to episcopal visitation. Over the next century more than 100 houses were founded as part of an association based on Cluny as the mother house. By the 12th century the order had 314 houses in France, the **Holy Roman Empire**, England, Scotland, and Poland. By 1614 that number had almost tripled.

The most famous abbot of Cluny was Peter the Venerable (r.1122-56); the monastery produced three popes: **Gregory VII**, **Urban II**, and Urban IV. The abbey church, built between 1089 and 1132, was the largest in Europe after St. Peter's in Rome.

Under Gregory VII a reform agenda was promoted in Spain both by papal legates who instituted the Roman liturgy at the expense of the local Mozarabic rite, and by the translation of Spanish monasteries to dependence on Cluny. Some of the earliest Cluniac houses in Iberia were Ripoll in Catalonia (1008), San Juan de la Pena in Aragon (1025), and Ona and Cardena in Castile (1032-33). Cluny continued to expand in the 12th century, under the patronage of the **papacy** and monarchs such as Alfonso VI of **León** (1030-1109), who saw the order as one of the keys to obtaining military help from France for the war against **Islam**. In 1078 Pope Gregory VII was encouraging both Alfonso and Cluny to promote the Roman rite as a way of tying Iberia to Rome, and by 1090 the process was complete. In 1088 Pope Urban II confirmed Alfonso's selection of Abbot Bernard of Sahagún as archbishop of recently conquered Toledo, naming the archbishop primate of all Spain.

Much has been written about Cluny's role in promoting the crusades. In Spain, the expansion of Cluny served the order in its desire to reform Benedictine monasticism, served the papacy's goal of uniting European dioceses in practice and obedience, and served the kings of León in legitimizing their expansion at the expense of rival **Christian** and **Muslim** princes. The crusades in this case fit into the larger goals of these different constituencies, creating a justification and strategy for the extension of jurisdiction or territory.

Pope Urban II, who had been a monk at Cluny, dedicated the main altar in the abbatial church on the preaching tour from Italy to France that led to the announcement of the **First Crusade** at Clermont in 1095. His progress was marked by a series of privileges confirmed to Cluniac houses. One of the bishops who attended him on this tour was Dalmatius, a monk from Cluny who served as bishop of **Santiago de Compostela** from 1094 to 1103. The historians of the shrine credit Cluny with promoting the **pilgrimage** to Compostela in Europe.

COMNENUS/KOMNENUS. The Comnenus dynasty ruled the **Byzantine Empire** under Isaac I (r.1057-59), Alexius I (r.1081-1118), John II (r.1118-43), Manuel I (r.1143-80), Alexius II (d.1183) under the regency of Mary of **Antioch** (r.1180-82), and Andronicus I (r.1183-85). Anna Comnena, daughter of Alexius I, wrote a chronicle which is an important source for the **First Crusade**.

Under Manuel I the empire included **Asia Minor**, **Cyprus**, Crete, the Greek islands, Greece, Thrace, and Bulgaria. Manuel rebuilt the Byzantine **navy** so that he could extend his interests in southern Italy, Syria, and **Egypt**. **Amalric I** of **Jerusalem**, hard-pressed for support against **Nur al-Din**, submitted his kingdom to the protection of Manuel in return for military assistance. Maria Comnena (d.1217), Manuel's greatniece, married Amalric I. Their daughter Isabel (d.1205) inherited the **Latin Kingdom**. Manuel also cemented ties with the princes of Antioch that had been strained since **Bohemond of Taranto** refused to acknowledge the Byzantines as his overlords in 1098. In 1161 the emperor married Mary, the sister of Bohemond III. Manuel's only daughter was married to Ranier of **Montferrat**, the first marriage of a Byzantine princess to someone not a member of a royal family.

Manuel's policy of conciliating the Western Europeans was unpopular in **Constantinople**. In 1182 Andronicus staged a coup during which

Western Europeans were massacred throughout the city, including at the hospital of St. John. Four thousand survivors were sold into slavery, and buildings which had housed the "**Latins**" were burned down. Mary of Antioch was assassinated a few months later, along with Manuel's daughter Maria and her husband Ranier. Andronicus had been governor of **Cilicia** in 1166, where he seduced the emperor's sister and was forced into exile. He had returned to Constantinople just before Manuel's death.

COMPOSTELA. *See* **Santiago de Compostela.**

CONFRATERNITIES. Very little information survives about confraternities founded to fight in the **Latin** East. They appear to have been charitable organizations which equipped foot soldiers for a season of fighting in the Holy Land, providing passage, arms, and ransom if needed. Normally such confraternities were based in Europe (the Confraternity of the Holy Spirit, for instance, founded to join the **Fifth Crusade**) but at least one, the Confraternity of St. Andrew, was founded before 1187 at **Acre**. King **Edward I** of England established the Confraternity of Saint Edward the Confessor at Acre to garrison a tower he had constructed there, and King **Louis IX** of France did the same, leaving 100 **knights**, with crossbowmen and foot soldiers behind in Acre, and promising to maintain them. Louis had trouble raising the money consistently to support this force, which accepted donations from other sources in the 1260s.

CONRAD III, KING OF GERMANY. (1093-1152). Conrad was elected **Holy Roman Emperor** and crowned at Aachen in 1138 in the presence of a papal legate. Both the **papacy** and the imperial title were contested in these years, so that Pope Innocent II was rivaled by Pope Analectus II from 1130-38. Conrad defended his throne against a number of claimants in Germany without being able to move on to the consolidation of his power as emperor by controlling Italy as well. St. **Bernard of Clairvaux**'s preaching mission for the **Second Crusade** in 1146 took place against a background of war among the German claimants. Conrad took the **cross**, had his son Henry crowned as his successor and entrusted to the guardianship of the archbishop of Mainz, and set out in the autumn of 1147. The expectation of protection for the possessions of a crusader may well have been a factor in his decision.

Conrad took a large army through Hungary to **Asia Minor**. He had been unable to enforce discipline on his soldiers as they attempted to supply themselves in **Byzantine** territory, and at **Nicaea** he was unable to force the noncombatants to separate from the army and accomplish their **pilgrimage** alone. Instead, he led an unwieldy force through the mountains in an effort to reach and attack the Turks of **Iconium**. Supplies were exhausted during the army's slow progress and a battle near Dorylaeum turned into a rout. German pilgrims and soldiers fled back to Nicaea, sustaining continuing losses from Turkish attack on the way. Those who survived the Turks fell ill due to malnourishment and fatigue. The crusaders blamed themselves for this disaster. The rivalry between the Germans and French had moved Conrad to set out to win a victory before King **Louis VII of France** and his army could arrive. Lack of discipline had created a slow-moving contingent of foraging soldiers and pilgrims.

Conrad was forced to return to **Constantinople** for the winter to recover his health, but he set out for the **Latin Kingdom of Jerusalem** in March of 1148 to gather the remnants of his army and rejoin the crusade. After the disastrous **siege** of **Damascus** in the summer of 1148 he spent another winter in the Byzantine Empire. King Louis VII of France, King Roger II of **Sicily**, and Duke Welf of Bavaria had meanwhile allied against him, so that he died in 1152 without having enforced his claim to the imperial title in Italy. He was succeeded by his nephew, Emperor **Frederick I Barbarossa**.

CONRAD, MARQUIS OF MONTFERRAT. (d.1192). Conrad was king of **Jerusalem** by virtue of his marriage in 1190 to Isabel (d.1205), daughter of **Amalric I**. In 1192, his claim was recognized by **Guy of Lusignan** and the barons of the **Latin Kingdom of Jerusalem**. Preparations for his coronation ended with his assassination in **Acre**. Isabel then married Count **Henry of Champagne**, who succeeded Conrad as king. Isabel carried the claim to the throne until her death in 1205. Isabel's daughter by Conrad, Maria, inherited the title and married **John of Brienne**.

The family of Montferrat had established a tradition of crusading before Conrad came in his turn to the **Levant**. According to David Jacoby's history of the family (listed under the Third Crusade in the bibliography), William the Elder, Conrad's father, fought in the **Second Crusade** and was captured by **Saladin** at **Hattin** in 1187. Conrad's brother William Longsword fathered the short-lived King **Baldwin V** of Jerusalem. Another brother, Ranier, had married the daughter of **Byzan-**

tine Emperor Manuel I **Comnenus** in 1180 and been assassinated in 1182. Conrad himself came to the Holy Land at the invitation of one of the Emperor Manuel's successors.

Emperor Isaac II Angelus invited Conrad to **Constantinople** in 1185, proposing a marriage with his sister Theodora. Conrad brought a contingent to the East, but in 1187 left the Byzantine Empire for Acre on a **Genoese** ship. As they approached Acre they learned that the city had been taken by Saladin, so they landed instead at **Tyre**. When they arrived, Raymond of **Tripoli**, who had twice acted as regent for the Latin Kingdom under **Baldwin IV**, was recognized as leader of the refugees who had gathered there after the fall of the kingdom at Hattin. King Guy of Lusignan had been captured by Saladin. Acting in the king's name, the members of the High Court in the city offered concessions to **Pisa** and Genoa for support in retaking the kingdom.

During the summer of 1187 Conrad presided over the defense of the city, creating a commune and operating as the foreign power of highest rank, offering hope that his connections in Europe would bring help to the **Latin** East. The support of the Genoese who had brought him from Byzantium was crucial to his success. He made one of his companions, Ansaldo Bonovicino, who had been with him in Constantinople, castellan of Tyre. In the early autumn, Saladin brought Conrad's father to the walls of Tyre, offering his release for the surrender of the city. Conrad refused.

The arrival of the **Third Crusade** was delayed by the quarrel between the kings of France and England until 1191. Emperor **Frederick Barbarossa** drowned in **Cilicia** in 1190. These delays in European response left Conrad responsible for provisioning and defending the city for five years. Poems by troubadours Peirol of Auvergne, Bertran de Born, and Hugues de Berzé celebrated the marquis as a hero and savior of the kingdom.

Guy of Lusignan, released in 1189, vainly attempted to have Tyre handed over to him. Instead, he invested Acre with the help of the Pisans, laying the foundation for the reconquest of the city on 12 July 1191. The struggle for power was exacerbated by the arrival of the king of France in April and of England in June of 1191. France and Genoa backed Conrad while **Richard I** of England and the Pisans supported Guy's claim.

War broke out between the Genoese and the Pisans over Conrad's claim in 1192, after which an agreement was made giving Guy **Cyprus** and allowing the plans to go forward for Conrad's coronation. His death at the hands of unknown assassins in Acre prevented his accession.

CONSTANTINOPLE, CITY. Situated on the Bosporus so as to command the confluence of the Aegean and Black Seas, Constantinople (now Istanbul) was the greatest city of the medieval Mediterranean, due to its control of trade in the Middle East. Customs dues from the harbor, called the Golden Horn, made the **Byzantine Emperors** rich, and the buildings and palaces of the city displayed that wealth in a way that awed contemporary travelers. From its foundation in the fourth century as the new capital of the Roman Empire until the **Fourth Crusade** in 1204 the city had never been taken by an invader. Its defenses were thought to be impregnable. The **Greeks** recaptured the city in 1261. It withstood attack until the **Ottoman Turks** took it using cannon in 1453. At that point the defenses included 13 miles of land and sea walls and 100 towers.

The church of Hagia Sophia or the Holy Wisdom was covered by the largest domed roof in the Mediterranean world, and served by a liturgy that was the most lavish in **Christendom**. The successful **siege** of the city by Western European crusaders in 1204 denuded the many churches of important **relics** and portable wealth. The establishment of a **Latin Empire or Kingdom of Constantinople**, beyond the obvious problems of occupation by a foreign power, led to enforcement of a union with the Roman church that was a continuing insult to Greek Orthodox believers. When Constantinople was recaptured by the Greeks in 1261 rituals of purification were enacted to wipe out the pollution of Latin occupation.

The contemporary explanation of how a force of perhaps 20,000 Europeans was able to take the city focused on internal weaknesses. Between 1182 and 1204 there had been five coups. Alexios V Murtzouphlos, who had held the imperial throne for 100 days, fled when the crusade forces attacked in April of 1204. He was captured by the crusaders and executed in November, to little public outcry. He had been unable to rally a defense force even while he held the city.

Greece, where the crusader states lasted until Ottoman incursion, had little loyalty to the empire. Under the rule of Byzantium it had been a backwater from which the capital drew taxes. The regional nobility were in the first instance not convinced that the crusaders would be worse overlords than the Byzantine emperors. They offered little resistance to the initial conquest. Coalitions to oust the Europeans were effective only in certain areas, in spite of the religious tensions and cultural hostilities that had existed before the conquest.

The crusaders who took Constantinople argued that the city was at least as important to the conquest of **Jerusalem** as was **Egypt**. The rhetoric of the Latin emperors continued to be of crusading, with the ultimate goal of controlling access to the **Holy Sepulchre**. This ideology was never accepted in Europe, except by the papacy, even though crusader lords from Greece did contribute to the crusades in support of the Holy Land. William II of **Villehardouin**, lord of Achaea, brought 400 knights and 28 ships to the crusade of King **Louis IX** of France in 1249. By 1267 he was unable to sustain his own lordship in the Peloponnesus, which he placed under the protection of Louis's brother, **Charles of Anjou**.

CONSTANTINOPLE, LATIN KINGDOM OR EMPIRE OF.

(1204-61). This short-lived European kingdom or "empire" was created as a result of the **Fourth Crusade**. Count Baldwin IX of **Flanders** (r.1204-05) and then his brother Henry (r.1205-1216) were the first Latin Emperors, due to the election of Baldwin by the Fourth Crusaders. The Principality of Morea, conquered as the crusaders acquired **Byzantine territory**, remained under European control until 1460.

In April of 1202 Baldwin IX left Flanders for the crusade. His wife Marie of Champagne (*see* **Henry II of Champagne**) was pregnant, and his existing heir was a two-year-old girl, Joan. He left the county in the hands of his brother Philip of Namur (d. 1212). Marie gave birth to another daughter and departed for the Holy Land, where she died before she was able to rejoin her husband. He adopted the title of emperor at his election by the victorious army in **Constantinople**, and announced his allegiance to the existing laws and institutions, with the exception, of course, of those of the **Greek** Orthodox church. It was the intention of the crusaders to restore the unity between the eastern and western halves of **Christendom** that had been lost in 1054. Their behavior was reasonably tolerant by their standards, but earned the contempt of the Greeks.

Baldwin was taken captive in 1205 and presumably died soon after. Boniface of **Montferrat** (d.1207), who had led the crusade but had not been elected as emperor, immediately founded his own domain at Thessalonika. He set about consolidating his hold on it by both warfare and politics, marrying Margaret of Hungary, the widow of Byzantine Emperor Isaac II Angelus in 1204. The crusaders had taken Thrace, Macedonia, sections of Greece, and part of **Asia Minor**. Repeated appeals by the crusaders for help from Western Europe in 1204, 1205, 1206, and 1212 met with little response. Quarrels among the crusade leaders led to internal struggles such as the campaign by which the Emperor Henry took Boniface's kingdom at Thessalonika in 1209.

After Henry's death there were also difficulties with the succession, since the claimants from the house of Flanders were reluctant to take up responsibilities in the embattled Latin Empire. Robert, one of Henry's nephews, ruled from 1221-28, at which point the throne passed to another nephew, the ten-year-old son of Peter of Courtenay (of **Namur**), who had been killed attempting to bring assistance from Flanders to Thessalonika in 1217. The regency for the young Baldwin II (r.1228-60) was offered to **John of Brienne** (d.1237), **Fifth Crusader** and titular king of **Jerusalem** 1210-25. Baldwin II made a tour of Europe trying to raise support for his empire 1236-48. Peter Lock, in his recent work on the *Franks in the Aegean*, has theorized several reasons for Baldwin's failure. First, the dynasty at Flanders did not command sufficient respect as a royal house to attract supporters. Then, even those who wished to sacrifice money and men for the crusade, such as **Richard Plantagenet, Earl of Cornwall**, did not want to spend their resources in Greece. By the mid-thirteenth century crusading had lost its initial popularity, and what popular enthusiasm remained was focused, as always, on Jerusalem. Without considerable investment from Europe, crusaders who established lordships in the Latin Empire were no more able to sustain them than the nobles of the **Latin Kingdom of Jerusalem** had been able to retain their lands. By 1261 the Latin Empire was bankrupt and unable to raise more cash in Europe.

Theodore Lascaris of Nicaea (r.1205-21) recaptured Asia Minor while Theodore Angelus **Comnenus** (d. 1254) took Thessalonika (r.1224-30). Both claimed the Byzantine throne. Michael VIII Palaeologus (d. 1282) recaptured Constantinople in 1261 with **Genoese** help. Baldwin II fled to Italy in July of 1261, and died there in 1273. The title remained a valuable commodity for at least a century and passed to the family of Valois. The last claimant died in 1382.

French lords remained at the County of Bodonitsa in central Greece, the Duchy of Athens, and the Principality of Morea (the Peloponnesus, also called the principality of Achaea), which was held by the family of **Villehardouin**. In 1265 the lord of Morea placed his domain under the lordship of **Charles I of Anjou**, king of Naples and **Sicily**. These remaining crusader lordships were conquered piecemeal by the invading **Ottoman** Turks, who controlled Greece by 1460.

COPTS. Egyptian Christians who resisted the authority of both Rome and **Constantinople** from the fifth century were called Copts. Major portions of the Bible are thought to have been translated into the Egyptian language, called Coptic, by 200 A.D. In 706 **Egypt** was conquered by **Islam** and the language of state and education became Arabic. The Coptic liturgy, which had evolved differently from either the **Greek** Orthodox or the Roman Catholic, survived.

By tradition, Egypt was converted through the efforts of St. Mark, the author of the earliest Gospel. He is the first in an unbroken line of patriarchs (bishops). He came to **Alexandria** sometime before 68 A.D., when he was martyred. Again, according to tradition, the **Venetians** stole the body of the saint for their own city in 828. From at least 190 there was a school of theology at Alexandria, which was a center of Hellenistic scholarship. Both Clement (d.215) and Origen (d.254) of Alexandria are noted theologians in the history of Christianity. Coptic missionaries followed the Nile and converted the Nubians (Sudan) and Ethiopians. Visitors to Rome in the fourth century spread the teachings of the Desert Fathers, Egyptian hermits whose ascetic lives and teachings had a major impact on Christian practice and thought, and particularly on the institution of monasticism (*see* **Carmelites**).

Before 451 **Christendom** was centered on the five major cities of its earliest success: **Jerusalem**, **Antioch**, Alexandria, Rome, and Constantinople. Councils that met from 325 attempted to impose uniformity of belief and practice on all Christians. In 451, at the Council of Chalcedon, the Copts were unable to agree to the decisions of the council of bishops, and left without signing the decrees. This marks the foundation of Coptic Christianity as a national religion.

Egypt remained a province of **Byzantium** and the Copts were therefore subject to persecution as schismatics until the Arab conquest of 640. By contrast to the Christian empire at Constantinople, **Muslim** rule offered them status as a tolerated religion. Copts were subject to periodic persecution under the Shia **Fatimid** dynasty, and to heavy taxes, periodic state-ordered restrictions, and sometimes mob violence under the **Ayyubid**. These problems were exacerbated by the crusades, which made the Copts suspect to their Muslim rulers. The European Christians were equally suspicious of anyone who did not accept the authority of Rome, so early in crusader rule Copts were forbidden to visit the Church of the **Holy Sepulchre** in Jerusalem. They were eventually given the church of the Holy **Cross** outside the walls of the city.

Saladin's victory in 1187 was something of a disaster for the Copts, beginning with the Muslim invasion of Nubia (Sudan) in 1173. Still, tolerance usually followed periods of suspicion and persecution, so the Copts fought on the Muslim side during the **Fifth Crusade** in 1218 and King **Louis IX**'s attack on Egypt in 1249. Europeans were often unable to make distinctions between the Coptic and Muslim residents of Egyptian cities, and treated both populations indiscriminately as enemies. Where settled European populations came to realize Coptic identity, they were called Nubians. *See also* **Jacobite Christians**; **Nestorians**.

COUCY. The Coucys were a crusading family, in the sense that at least one member in each generation went on an expedition. Unlike the **Lusignans** (*see* **Guy**), the **Montferrats**, the **Brienne** family (*see* **John**), or the counts of **Flanders**, the Coucys did not establish lordships in the Holy Land. They are a good example of lesser nobles who built family connections by joining royal expeditions and creating ties with **pilgrimage** churches. Thomas of Marle (d.1130) joined the **First Crusade**, and participated in massacres of the **Jews** in the Rhineland along with **Emicho of Flonheim** in 1096.

Upon his return home, Thomas, whose lordship was based on lands usurped from the archdiocese of Reims (or Rheims), so annoyed his neighbors and his bishop as to become himself the target of a crusade **indulgence** and eventually two royal expeditions. Enguerran II (r.1130-47) died on the **Second Crusade**, having accompanied King **Louis VII of France**, and was buried at the shrine church of **Nazareth**. Raoul I (r.1160-1191) died at **Ascalon** on the **Third Crusade**. Enguerran III (r.1197-1242) fought in the **Albigensian Crusade**, as well as in the famous Battle of Bouvines (1214) and an expedition led by the future King Louis VIII to England in 1216 which earned all the French participants excommunication.

CROSS. A **Christian** symbol, the cross was worn by crusaders as a sign of their vow, and eventually of their status under **canon law**. Crosses were displayed in the same way that, for instance, special clothing and symbols were worn to indicate that the bearer was under a vow of **pilgrimage**, and therefore was entitled to protection during travel. The Feast of the Exaltation of the Holy Cross (14 September), widely celebrated in the Western church, has its roots in the dedication of the church of the **Holy Sepulchre** in the fourth century. There were also Cross hymns, a liturgy of the Cross, and a feast of the Finding of the Cross (3 May) with links to **Jerusalem**, and eventually to crusading, that became popular in medieval Europe. *See also* **Crusade Vow**; and for wearing a cross as a sign of ecclesiastical censure, **Waldensians**.

The True Cross, on which Christ was believed to have been crucified, was held by the Church of the Holy Sepulchre as a frequently divided **relic**, so that stories of fragments of the wood given as gifts by the kings or patriarch are common. According to tradition, St. Helena (d.c.327), mother of the Emperor Constantine, discovered the cross, the nails and hammer used at the crucifixion, and the crown of thorns in a cave near the Holy Sepulchre. These relics were kept in a sealed chest. The crusaders had several sumptuous reliquaries made for pieces of the cross, and there was a relics keeper appointed to guard them. The church of the Holy Cross, outside the walls of Jerusalem to the west, had been built before the crusader period to memorialize the tree from which the wood of the cross had been taken. It was rebuilt in the 12th century and was served by **Copts**, Christians from **Egypt** and the Sudan (sometimes called "Nubians" by the crusaders).

According to the **Muslim** chronicler of the victory of **Saladin** at **Hattin** in 1187, the relic was a piece of wood decorated with gold and gems. Saladin was able to use it in the same way that he used high-ranking human hostages to bargain with crusade leaders. Similarly, the cross taken from the Dome of the Rock after the fall of Jerusalem was sent to the caliph in **Baghdad** as a symbol of victory, and buried under a city gate as an expression of contempt for the European invaders.

The fragment of the True Cross taken at Hattin by Saladin remained in Muslim hands after 1187, and eventually disappeared. Another portion was carried into battle by the titular patriarch of Jerusalem during the **Fifth Crusade**.

CRUSADE VOW. A crusade vow was taken before departure on an expedition, and often as a prelude to preparation for the journey. Crusading ideology developed after the **First Crusade**, so that the liturgies for these vows are not common until the early 13th century. Where they survive, they show considerable local differences rather than standardization as a ceremony or ritual. What seems to have happened during the first century of crusading, 1096-1200, is that crusaders were treated as pilgrims, and the existing rite for penitential **pilgrimage** was used. As armed pilgrims, crusaders took the **cross** as well as or instead of the traditional staff and scrip that proclaimed to all the purpose of the journey. Normally, the crusader pledged to leave by a deadline and specified the destination. He received the **cross** as a symbol of his intention, from a crusade preacher or *procurator* commissioned by the pope, or a local bishop or priest.

The earliest crusader crosses, from 1095, were pieces of cloth sewn into the clothing so as to be conspicuous. Over the course of the next two centuries, a legal status under church or **canon law** was developed which protected the crusader's property during his absence and exempted him from payment of debts until his return.

CYPRUS. When the crusaders arrived in the **Levant** Cyprus belonged to the **Byzantine Empire**. The island became a crusader kingdom, ruled by the **Lusignans** from 1192 until 1488 when the **Venetians** took it. Cyprus is the third largest island in the Mediterranean, about 50 miles south of the Turkish coast. The **Ottoman Turks** held it from 1570 until 1878.

King **Richard I** of England took the island from the Byzantines en route to the **Third Crusade**. Upon arriving in **Acre**, he sold Cyprus to the **Templars**, who vainly attempted to subdue the inhabitants with a force of 120 knights. In 1192, during the continuing succession crisis in the **Latin Kingdom of Jerusalem**, Richard negotiated its resale to **Guy of Lusignan**, who founded a crusader kingdom there. Aimery of Lusignan married the heiress to the Latin Kingdom and ruled in Cyprus from 1194-1205.

The Lusignans ruled Cyprus for 300 years, adding **Cilicia** to their domains in 1342. After 1291 their kingdom was the only remnant of the crusader conquests in the Levant. Until recently, their building projects in Cyprus were not as well-known as those in Cilicia. One of their **castles** was discovered in 2002 during excavations for a town hall in Nicosia, the capital of the island kingdom. Other Lusignan fortifications disappeared due in the first case to improvements made by the Venetians in an attempt to hold off Ottoman conquest. The **Order of St. John in Jerusalem** settled at the fortress of Kolossi in 1210 and continued to use it as the headquarters of the order until 1310, when the **Hospitallers** moved to Rhodes. Kyrenia, built to dominate the port opposite Cilicia, was expanded by the Venetians to resist artillery. The walls were at various points over 70 feet tall and 125 feet thick. Equally notable are the inland fortifications of St. Hilarion, Kantara, and Buffavento, and the cathedrals at Famagusta and Nicosia.

The dream of crusading is a constant in European history, but for Cyprus, there were serious intentions, even if never realized, to regain the Holy City as late as the mid-14th century. In 1217, for instance, the **Ibelin** brothers, who were among the tenants-in-chief of Cyprus, represented the kingdom at an assembly to plan the **Fifth Crusade**, held in Acre. Philip of Novara, a knight in the service of the Ibelins, wrote a history of Cyprus from 1218 into the 1240s (part of a compilation called the *Gestes des Chiprois*) that exalts his patrons and provides a colorful account of the kingdom at the center of the Fifth and **Sixth Crusades**.

During the crusade of King **Louis IX** of France a force of 120 knights from Cyprus joined his army in **Egypt**. Rulers of Cyprus and their ruling dates include: Guy of Lusignan (1192-94); Aimery of Lusignan (1194-1205); Hugh I (1205-18); Henry I (1218-53); Hugh II (1253-67, with regents Plaisance of Antioch, d. 1261, and Hugh of Antioch-Lusignan, who was regent until 1267 and then ruled in his own right as Hugh III until 1284); John (1284-85); Henry II (1285-1324); and Hugh IV (1324-59).

-D-

DAMASCUS. Considered to be one of the world's oldest inhabited cities, Damascus is located in southwest Syria. During the crusade period it was a semi-independent commune ruled by various commanders under nominal allegiance to **Baghdad**. The city was supported by its control over three agricultural supply centers and by its position at the junction of major trade routes to **Anatolia**, northern Syria, and India. After the initial period of **Muslim** conquest (661-750), it had been the seat of the Umayyad caliphate, which then moved to Baghdad. It was also a regional assembly point for the annual **pilgrimage** to Mecca, and heavily fortified with extensive town walls. Its citadel was notable for its position on a level with the surrounding city, for the defense system offered by its ten towers, and for its symbolic eminence as the burial place of **Saladin**. Damascus provided a crucial military base for **Egypt** in its attempt to use Syria as the key to ending the crusader kingdoms and fighting off **Mongol** attack.

Saladin took both Egypt and Syria, and established his family, the **Ayyubid**, as rulers of this region. After his death in 1193, the region again became fragmented, as the Ayyubid fought among each other for preeminence. Damascus itself was under **siege** 12 times between 1193 and 1260. A power vacuum in 1250 led **Kurdish** commanders in the city to invite the ruler of **Aleppo** to take it. An attempt by Damascus under its new prince to take Egypt failed in 1251.

Aleppo and then Damascus fell to a Mongol army in 1260. The Mongols then marched on **Mamluk** Egypt and were defeated by **Baybars I** near Tiberias. Baybars took control of Egypt (r.1260-77) and fought annual campaigns against the crusaders in Syria, using Damascus as a base of operations.

Mongol raids in Syria were a constant threat until 1303, but the sultans of Egypt continued to be its nominal rulers. Their power was never easily accepted by the local governors, and there were frequent rebellions. In 1280 the Mongols raided Aleppo essentially unopposed. In 1281 the Mongols invaded Syria with a large force, by some accounts 80,000. On 29 October a combined Egyptian and Syrian force met the Mongols at Homs. Numbers for this army are unavailable. Casualties on both sides were so heavy that even though the Mongols retreated, Egypt was unable to follow up on the victory. Further skirmishes led to the capture of Damascus by the Mongols in 1299, but they were unable to hold it for long, and suffered a major defeat in 1303 that essentially ended their attempts on Syria.

DANISHMENDS. (or Danishmendids). A Turkish dynasty based in eastern **Anatolia** was founded by Malik-Ghazi ibn-Danishmend, the emir of Sebastia (*Sivas*) from c.1097-1105. Malik-Ghazi is notable in crusades history for having captured **Bohemond of Taranto**, prince of **Antioch**, in an ambush on the road to the city of Melitene in western **Armenia** in 1100. Bohemond's captivity put his nephew **Tancred** in position as regent of Antioch. Malik-Ghazi, with the sultan of **Iconium**, defeated **Raymond of Saint Gilles** and a large army of European crusaders in 1101. They were rivals with the **Seljuk Turks** for territory in **Asia Minor** until the 1170s, when the Seljuks destroyed the Danishmend kingdom.

DOBRIN, ORDER OF. Also called the Knights of the Bishop of Prussia, or the Knights of Dobrzyn, this order was founded in Prussia by its Cistercian bishop, Christian, who began his work there in 1206. Its origins are similar to those of the **Swordbrethren**, also created by a bishop who found the going hard in Livonia. The 14 north-German **knights** who began the order's activities before 1222 were given the fort at Dobrzyn on the Vistula River as a base from which to **Christianize** the inhabitants. Like the Swordbrethren, they wore white with an emblem of the **cross** on the left shoulder, but instead of a sword their symbol was paired with a star. They were similar also in that they depended directly on their bishop, and also merged with the **Teutonic Knights** in the 1230s. *See also* **Military Orders**.

DOGE. This office derived from the seventh century, when the doge was a **Byzantine** official who ruled **Venice** as a province of the larger empire. After Byzantine rule the office was in theory elective, but in the 12th century it was routinely occupied by members of the Michiel family. After 1172 a Ducal Council was formed by the leading merchants, and it nominated men to the office. Enrico Dandalo (r.1192-1205) was the doge during the **Fourth Crusade**, the first to take a coronation oath that spelled out some of the new limits on the office.

DOME OF THE ROCK. *See* **Temple**.

DOMINIC, St. (1170-1221). Bishop Diego of Osma (Spain) and his subprior, Dominic of Guzman, were traveling in southern France in 1206 when they met with papal legates preaching against heresy there. Their suggestion to launch a preaching mission displaying asceticism and reasoned argument instead of the authority of Rome was embraced by the legates and supported by Pope **Innocent III**. Between 1206 and 1208 there was a two-year attempt by Cistercians, the legates, and the visiting Spaniards to imitate the "sending of the seventy" described in Luke 9. The Midi was divided into districts and the orthodox preachers attempted to display a piety that would undercut the **Cathar** *perfecti*'s criticism of the morals of the orthodox clergy. Conversions followed, and as early as 1206 Dominic helped to found a convent at Prouille for noble women who returned to orthodoxy.

Bishop Diego returned to **León-Castile** in 1207, while Dominic settled at Fanjeaux. In January of 1208 the papal legate, Peter of Castlenau, was murdered after excommunicating Count Raymond VI of **Toulouse**. Pope Innocent called for the **Albigensian Crusade** because he suspected Raymond of the murder and because he judged that the attack on the legate was not personal so much as it was a violent rejection of ecclesiastical authority. Count Raymond was subjected to a humiliating public display of submission to Rome's authority in order to be allowed to join the crusade: he appeared naked before the cathedral of Toulouse, took a vow of obedience, and was beaten by the papal legate as he entered the church.

Dominic continued to influence the two-pronged effort of war and missionary activity to combat heresy in the Midi. The crusaders used brutality and terror to destroy morale, but they also arranged displays of piety to convince the local inhabitants of their sincerity. The leader of the crusade army, Simon of **Montfort**, made public displays such as mass on the battlefield or a barefoot army a feature of his campaign. Burnings of 60 to over 100 professed Cathars accompanied the **sieges** of cities whose orthodox inhabitants were mutilated or massacred. Simon was reported to have close ties to Dominic, who continued his preaching mission with support from the pope. Raymond was soon again under the ban of excommunication, but the vassals who, as good Christians, ought to have abandoned their oaths to him in response to the ban instead supported him. In Raymond's contest with Fulk, bishop of Toulouse and patron of Dominic, it was the bishop who was forced into exile.

As Dominic's order expanded after it was founded in 1215, it was increasingly charged by the **papacy** both with preaching and with the identification, capture, and imprisonment of heretics. Papal bulls of 1227 show Gregory IX urging bishops to accept **Dominicans** in both roles.

DOMINICAN ORDER. This religious order was founded in 1215 by St. **Dominic** as part of a program to confound the spread of the **Cathar** heresy in southern France. Dominic favored rational dispute and reform of the orthodox clergy as a response to the anticlericalism that supported heretical belief. Emphasis on ascetic practice, improved training, and vernacular preaching characterized the early days of the expansion of the order, which grew in Languedoc from two houses of friars in 1215 to 24 in 1252. For crusade sermons and preaching, *see* **Humbert of Romans**.

-E-

EDESSA, CITY. Edessa, now called Urfa, is located in Turkey, just north of the border of Syria. It was the capital of ancient Macedonia, later becoming part of the Christian **Byzantine Empire**. It fell to the **Muslims** in 639. From the 11th century it was semi-independent, relying in emergencies for troops from Byzantium, who briefly occupied it and repaired its walls in 1032. During the next 50 years, it was increasingly threatened by the expansion of the **Seljuk Turks**, who conquered it in 1087.

The Turks placed Edessa under a **Christian** administrator, the **Armenian** Thoros (or *Toros*, d.1098). Constant attack by warring Seljuk commanders moved Thoros to invite the **First Crusader** and brother of **Godfrey of Bouillon, Baldwin of Boulogne** (d.1118), to defend Edessa. The city became the base of a crusader county (1098-1144). Edessa was one of four political entities created out of conquered territory by the crusaders, along with **Jerusalem, Antioch**, and **Tripoli**.

EDESSA, COUNTY. **Baldwin of Boulogne**, one of the leaders of the **First Crusade**, entered the city with 80 **knights** in February of 1098 and was formally accepted as the heir of Thoros, the **Armenian** administrator who had been installed by the **Seljuk Turks**. About a month after Baldwin's arrival Thoros was killed by a mob of Edessans, in circumstances that are not clear because variously reported in the sources.

The city was controlled by the Council of Twelve, a remnant of **Byzantine** rule dominated by the aristocratic families. The militia of the city was drawn from its citizens. There was considerable tension between the Council and the militia, played out in factional coups before the crusade period. The nobles were plotting against Baldwin by December. He arrested the ringleaders and confiscated their goods. In 1100, when he became ruler of the **Latin Kingdom of Jerusalem**, he made Edessa a fief of his new kingdom and installed his cousin, **Baldwin of Le Bourg** (d.1131), son of Hugh of Rethel, as count. Both Baldwins married Armenian aristocrats. Baldwin of Boulogne married an Armenian princess, Arda. Baldwin of Le Bourg married Morfia, daughter of the wealthy Gabriel of Melitene.

In 1104 both Baldwin of Le Bourg and his kinsman Joscelin of Courtenay were captured by a Turkish army at Harran. **Tancred** of **Sicily**, another First Crusader, was entrusted with Edessa, but soon had to serve as regent to his uncle in beleaguered **Antioch**. Another of King Baldwin's relatives, Richard of Salerno, stepped in as regent in Edessa (1104-08). Baldwin and Joscelin were released in 1108 and went to war with Tancred, now reluctant to give up his nominal claim to Edessa. Baldwin Le Bourg regained the city with the help of his cousin Baldwin I of Jerusalem. Richard settled in the city of Marash. Tancred returned to Antioch.

In 1110 Edessa was threatened by the forces of Mawdud of **Mosul**, who devastated the countryside and then retreated, returning to besiege the city in 1112. The attack was met with prompt action by Joscelin of Courtenay, who normally resided at the nearby fortress of Tell Bashir, ruler of a fief that stretched from the Euphrates to the boundaries of Baldwin's domain. Joscelin was in Edessa when the Turks attacked. The following year Baldwin of Le Bourg, apparently alarmed to have created so powerful a rival, expelled Joscelin from the county and he went to Jerusalem, where he was given the county of Galilee by the king.

Edessa's history continued to be turbulent. Famines in 1113 and 1114 were complicated by an earthquake in November of 1114 that collapsed 13 of the city wall's towers. In 1119 King Baldwin II of Jerusalem installed Joscelin of Courtenay as count of Edessa (r.1119-31). Joscelin was again captured by the Turks in 1122, was rescued in 1123, and died in battle in 1131. His son and namesake, Armenian on his mother's side, inherited the embattled county.

The first three kings of Jerusalem and the Courtenays were all related, so that Edessa passed from one cousin to the next until it was lost to **Zengi**, Muslim governor of Mosul, in 1144 (*see* **Second Crusade**; **Nur al-Din**). Joscelin II fought the **Muslims** for control of the city from 1131. He was blinded and held captive at **Aleppo** from 1150 until his death in 1159. His wife Beatrice was forced to sell the castles of the crusader county to Byzantine Emperor Manuel I **Comnenus** for an annual pension to support herself and her children. Her daughter Agnes married King **Amalric I of Jerusalem**, by whom she had two children, both of whom were destined to be heirs of the kingdom, **Baldwin IV** and his sister Sybil, who married **Guy of Lusignan**. Agnes's marriage was annulled by order of the High Court of the kingdom in 1163 on the grounds of consanguinity, and she married Hugh of **Ibelin**. Upon Hugh's death in c.1169 she married Reynald Grenier, lord of **Sidon**.

Edessa remained under Muslim rule under **Saladin** and the **Ayyubid** dynasty, falling to the **Mongols** in 1260 and to the **Ottoman Empire** in 1637.

Western European rulers of Edessa and their reigning dates include: **Baldwin I** (1098-1100); **Baldwin II** (1100-18); Joscelin I of Courtenay (1119-31); Joscelin II of Courtenay (1131-44, he died in 1159). Regents for parts of these reigns include: **Tancred** (1104); Richard of the Principate of Salerno (1104-08); Galeran of Le Puiset (1118-19); Geoffrey of Marash (1122-23).

EDWARD I, KING OF ENGLAND. (r.1272-1307). Edward's father Henry III took **crusade vows** which he was unable to fulfill in 1250 (*see* **Holy Blood**). As Prince of Wales, Edward sailed in 1270 to join the army of **Charles of Anjou** at Tunis, but arrived as the negotiations that ended the crusade were being concluded. With only a few hundred men, Edward sailed on to **Acre**, where he conducted raids on **Muslim** territory in 1271. The following year a truce was concluded between the **Latin Kingdom of Jerusalem**, based at Acre, and the **Mamluks** of **Egypt**. Edward arranged for a garrison to be left in the city at his expense, and sailed for home. His status as a crusader was politically useful, and he supported the idea in principle, but he invested no further resources in the crusade movement.

EGYPT. The **Fatimid** dynasty held **Jerusalem** when the **First Crusade** arrived in the **Levant** to take it, and Egypt continued to be the most effective enemy of the crusader kingdoms during the period of European occupation. The Fatimids were replaced by **Saladin**, who conquered the **Latin Kingdom** based at Jerusalem in 1187 and founded the **Ayyubid** dynasty that controlled both Egypt and Syria until 1250. The **Mamluk** dynasty then completed his work, driving the last of the European invaders off the mainland, leaving only the crusader kingdom on **Cyprus**. The island kingdom's relationship with Egypt was marked by commercial rivalry for Mediterranean trade. The **Alexandrian** Crusade of 1365 represents the culmination of resentment on both sides.

Egypt had been a province of the Roman Empire after 30 B.C. and was under **Byzantine** control when the Arabs conquered it in 639. The Egyptian Christian or **Coptic** Church had rejected the authority of **Constantinople** and Rome in 451 at the Council of Chalcedon. The Byzantines had reacted by persecuting the Copts as schismatics. Arab conquest was the more easily accepted as a result, and in any case the **Muslim** army had taken Syria as well, so help from Constantinople was ineffective. Byzantine influence and rule had been centered in the great port of Alexandria. The Arab conquerors instead built the new capital, Cairo, on the Nile. The Copts escaped Greek persecution as schismatics and instead received a limited protection and tolerance from **Islam** in exchange for high taxes. Islamic conquest stopped at the Egyptian border. An attempted invasion of Nubia (the Sudan) in 652 failed to produce anything more than a mutually beneficial trade agreement.

Between 661 and 750 the caliphate, the center of the Islamic empire, was based at **Damascus**. Beginning in the early 700s there was a shift in Egypt from Greek and Coptic to Arabic as the language of state and education. When the center of political and military gravity was moved further away to **Baghdad** under the **Abbasids**, a century of resistance to Muslim rule followed in Egypt (767-868). From the late ninth to the early 10th century the Abbasids began to rely on the **Seljuk Turks** and the Turkish slaves who were brought into the army in great numbers. These new recruits provided more or less effective government for troublesome Egypt and Syria.

A serious famine in 969 permitted Fatimid conquest. The Fatimids offered a dynastic, regional, and religious challenge from within Islam to the caliphs of Baghdad. To the Ismailis, including the Nizari or **Assassins**, they were the true successors to **Muhammad**. Their regime, based at Cairo, ushered in a period of relative peace and prosperity. They continued to push their line of conquest north into Syria, and in

1009, in the course of persecutions of Christians, had the church of the **Holy Sepulchre** destroyed. The Abbasids used the Turks and the **Kurds** against them. In 1169 the Turkish rulers of Syria conquered Egypt in the name of the caliph. Saladin (r.1171-93), a Kurdish general who led the troops of **Nur al-Din**, founded a new dynasty that controlled both areas.

Saladin's **Ayyubid** dynasty (1193-1250) developed a **cavalry** of free men who were called up for specific expeditions or could volunteer for **jihad**. Various rulers assembled their own loyal regiments of mamluks (military slaves) as well. One such group, the Kipchak (Qipchaq) Turks purchased and trained by al-Salih Ayyub (d.1249) took over after his death as the Mamluk dynasty. After 1250, under the Mamluk dynasty, mamluk and free regiments coexisted with forces of immigrants, some of whom were **Mongols**, others being **Bedouins** or **Turkmen**, who were kept out of the highest offices. Meanwhile, regular troops (possibly as many as 40,000) of free men were mustered and reviewed formally in 1264 so that their equipment could be evaluated and their training improved. In 1267 a hippodrome was constructed in Cairo for basic **weapon** training (bow, lance, mace), horsemanship, wrestling, and hunting. The dedication of the Mamluk state to warfare and jihad made them such a powerful enemy that they can be seen not only as the victors in the attempt to take the Levant by Europeans during the crusade period, but also as a deterrent to further expeditions in the 13th century.

EKKEHARD OF AURA. (d.1126). Aura is a village in Germany, 85 miles northwest of Nuremburg. Ekkehard became a monk at Corvey/ Corbie, a Benedictine monastery in the diocese of Paderborn, Westphalia. He accompanied a major crusade expedition in 1101, and was familiar with the anonymous **Gesta**, a history of the **First Crusade** by a participant. Corvey had been founded in c.820 by **Holy Roman Emperor** Louis the Pious (r.814-840), and benefited from royal patronage in its library and school. A "universal" chronicle of human history was developed there by several authors. Ekkehard reworked or recopied and added to it, producing a history of Germany from 1098 to 1125 as one portion of it. His account of the early crusade movement has been partially translated by Edward Peters in *The First Crusade*. Both Ekkehard and **Albert of Aachen** also provide information on the massacre of the **Jews** in the Rhineland by **Emicho of Flonheim** in 1096.

EMICHO OF FLONHEIM/VLANHEIM. (Also sometimes identified as Emicho of Lei[si]ningen.) The count of Flonheim, near Mainz, was notorious for his role in the attacks by a crusade army on the **Jews** of the Rhine region in 1096. Jewish and **Christian** chronicles (*see* **Albert of Aachen** and **Ekkehard of Aura**) identify Emicho only as an important local ruler, and give differing accounts of his influence on the contingents of the **First Crusade** which perpetrated the pogroms.

Groups of crusaders formed advance contingents in 1096 like the one which followed **Peter the Hermit**. Gottschalk, for instance, a priest from the Rhineland, a region surrounding the middle of the Rhine River, collected followers from eastern France, Lorraine, and southern Germany. He and another itinerant preacher, Folkmar, led their followers into Hungary, where they caused trouble in their search for provisions. The sequence of events is not clear, but violence against Jews occurred in cities of the Rhineland as these advance contingents came through, presumably with the same goal as the one which later caused them problems in Hungary: a search for money and provisions to enable the army to proceed to **Jerusalem**.

It is not clear which bands were responsible for which atrocities, but Jews who refused to be baptized were murdered at Metz in May of 1096. The same month the bishop of Speyer, faithful to canon law which protected the Jews from violence and from forced baptism, prevented a massacre by assembling them in his palace. At Worms on May 18, Jews assembled for their protection in the bishop's palace were massacred, possibly by Emicho's band of crusaders, who certainly were responsible for the similar massacre on 27 May at Mainz. Sources differ on whether he succeeded in killing another group of Jews at Cologne on 29 May. Other groups of crusaders were apparently responsible for pogroms at Neuss on 24 June, Wevelinghofen 25 June, Altenahr 26-27 June, Xanten 27 June, and Mörs 29 June-1 July.

Emicho reportedly identified himself with apocalyptic prophecies as a "last emperor" who would lead an army against the **Muslims** and lay down his crown in Jerusalem. Apocalyptic stories according to various timelines were extremely popular throughout the middle ages. In every version the punishment and/or conversion of the Jews was an element of the preparation for the Second Coming of Christ. Jean Flori's recent work on Peter the Hermit investigates the influence of apocalyptic prophecies on the members of the First Crusade armies.

Beyond the rhetoric of the crusade, there was a simple reality that made the Jews an attractive target. Emicho's followers included some of the most unsavory adventurers of the time, including William the Carpenter, viscount of Melun and Gâtinais, who had fought in the **Reconquista**, and Thomas of Marle, later lord of **Coucy**, described by

Guibert of Nogent as a brigand who tortured and robbed the poor and **pilgrims** to Jerusalem. What is clear from all the accounts of the massacres is that local authorities were either unwilling or unable to protect the Jews from crusade armies seeking plunder.

Emicho's contingent continued down the Danube River to the borders of Hungary. They were refused permission to enter the kingdom, but they attempted to cross the river at the town of Wieselburg. Most of them were killed by the Hungarians. Thomas and William escaped to Italy and joined the First Crusade contingent of Hugh of Vermandois (d.1102), brother of King Philip I of France (r.1060-1108). Thomas (d.1130) survived the **siege of Jerusalem** and returned eventually to France. His continued attacks on his family, neighbors, the king, and neighboring churches prompted a royal chronicler to label him "demonic."

Unappealing as Emicho and his band of crusaders seem, they were not alone in connecting the fight against **Islam** with punishment for the Jews. Peter the Hermit collected money from Jews along his route to support his expedition, even while restraining his army from attacking them. The army of the First Crusade set fire to the synagogue when they took Jerusalem in 1099, burning the Jews who had taken refuge there. King **Louis VII** of France released participants in the **Second Crusade** from paying the interest on debts contracted with Jewish moneylenders as a preparation for the expedition. In York, England, a mob attacked the Jews of the town before many of them joined the **Third Crusade** in 1190. King Philip II Augustus of France, who with the king of England led the **Third Crusade**, expelled the Jews from his kingdom in 1182 for moneylending and ritual murder of Christians.

ERACLES. This is the name given to one of the chronicles of the fall of the **Latin Kingdom of Jerusalem**, an Old French translation of the Latin chronicle of **William of Tyre**. It was written by an educated man, probably someone in holy orders, who visited the Latin East and wrote between 1205 and 1234. Because the translation is based on a manuscript not available now to scholars, and because there is additional material in it, it is seen as a separate source.

ERNOUL. Nothing more is known about this medieval author beyond his name. One hypothesis is that he was a squire to Balian of **Ibelin**. His account of events in the **Latin Kingdom of Jerusalem** from 1099-1228 completes that of **William of Tyre**, and offers more detail on the reign of **King Baldwin IV** (1174-85) than any other source. Ernoul seems to have been writing after the **Third Crusade**, while William apparently ceased writing by 1184. Some manuscripts offer additional information for the years 1228-32, usually attributed to Bernard the Treasurer, another author known only from his chronicle. Ernoul's chronicle favors the perspective of the Ibelins in the succession crisis of Baldwin IV's reign, blaming the fall of the kingdom on **Guy of Lusignan.**

ESTONIA. A crusade expedition was launched by Sweden in 1195 for the region of the Dvina River. It was blown off course to Estonia, where it harried the inhabitants and was bought off with tribute after three days. More effective in **Christianizing** this area were the **Swordbrethren**, a **military order** founded by Bishop **Albert** of Livonia in 1202. *See* **Baltic Crusades.**

EUGENIUS III, POPE. (r.1145-53). When Bernardo Pignateli became pope, public opinion identified St. **Bernard of Clairvaux** as the power behind the throne. The new pope, born near **Pisa**, had been a canon in the cathedral there until he met Bernard in 1130. He was then trained by the saint and served as abbot of the Cistercian monastery of Tre Fontane. St. Bernard's ideas on the duties of the pope were well developed and are laid out in an essay called "De Consideratione." He and Eugenius were the architects of the **Second Crusade**. Their preparations eclipsed those for the **First Crusade**, creating a war on three fronts: Spain, the **Baltic** region, and the **Levant**. Although the main armies of Germany and France were not successful, there were victories at Lisbon and in the Baltics. St. Bernard's response to the failure of the main armies strengthened the identification with the Hebrews of the Old Testament, idealizing the crusades as paths to repentance and reform for Western Europeans, and incidentally justifying the massacre of those who refused baptism (*see* **Wends**).

-F-

FATIMID DYNASTY. (**Egypt** and Syria, 975-1171). The Fatimids were Shia **Muslim** rivals to the **Abbasid** caliphs in **Baghdad**, based first in the central **Maghrib**, and then in Egypt. On the eve of the **First Crusade**, the war between the **Seljuk Turks** on behalf of the caliphate and the Fatimids of Egypt prevented **Islam** from defending itself against European incursion in the **Levant**. The Fatimids had destroyed the

Church of the **Holy Sepulchre** as part of the campaign of 1009-10, disrupting **Christian pilgrimage** routes and unwittingly providing a piece of the rationale for an armed European expedition to free the Holy Places. In 1097-98, as the armies of the First Crusade approached, the Fatimids were engaged in taking **Jerusalem** from the Seljuk Turks. The crusaders took the city in 1099 and then chased the Fatimid army to **Ascalon**, where the Muslim general took ship for Cairo.

Sunni sources lay the blame for the foundation of the **Latin Kingdom of Jerusalem** squarely on the Fatimids. But the willingness of the Seljuk communes in **Aleppo**, **Damascus**, and **Mosul** to go to war against each other was equally damaging. The split between the various factions in the Levant continued to be a weakness European and **Byzantine** powers could exploit until **Saladin** was able to create an effective coalition under the banner of **jihad** in the 1180s.

The Fatimids did make a number of efforts to oust the crusaders, notably in 1105, when they unsuccessfully allied with Damascus against the invaders, and at **Tripoli** in 1109, when an Egyptian fleet arrived too late to save the city. The Fatimid navy offered resistance to the extension of crusader conquests during and after the **First Crusade** but was unable in the long run to prevent the establishment of a European kingdom. The navy was organized under a commander who was an important official with an office that kept accounts of expenditure and personnel. It was expected to function at a normal strength of 75 war galleys and 10 transport ships. Problems of supply and training prevented maintenance at that level, and instead Egypt's large mercantile fleet, based at **Alexandria**, Cairo, Damietta, and Tanis, was requisitioned for some campaigns.

On paper, at least, there was a system of pay according to rank and a combat force of 5,000 men. Fatimid naval manuals and accounts of maneuvers carried out in review before the Caliph survive. The question of why they were unable to defeat the crusaders is partially answered by the organization of the crusade movement. The intermittent involvement of Byzantium, the Italian city-communes, and fleets from northern Europe meant that Egypt was fighting a number of different forces at once or in rapid succession, which quickly exhausted its resources for **naval warfare**.

Seljuk attempts to oust the Europeans during the same period were equally ineffective. The crusaders benefited from not only the inability of the various Muslim factions to work together, but also from the relative insignificance of European invasion in the context of the struggle among the various rivals within Islam for control of the Levant.

The Fatimids were northern African (**Berber**) Muslims who had invaded Egypt in 969 in an attempt to rival the Abbasid Caliphate. Like the Arabs, the Romans, and the Greeks before them, they formed a small ruling elite among the Egyptians. "Tax farms" milked the population without passing the money along to the caliph in Cairo. By the 12th century the Berber elite no longer dominated the army, as slaves of Turkish or Sudanese extraction were drafted in as cavalry and infantry, respectively. By the 1160s ethnic factions of the army fought each other or looted the countryside when their wages were overdue.

The Fatimids were overthrown by the Turkish warrior **Nur al-Din**, who conquered Syria and sent Saladin's uncle with an army to Egypt to stabilize it. Saladin, **Kurdish** hero of the **Third Crusade**, founded the **Ayyubid** dynasty in 1171.

FIFTH CRUSADE. This crusade was planned as part of a general program for the reform of the church and the world by Pope **Innocent III**, and promoted at the Fourth Lateran Council in 1215.

In 1217 the forces of King Andrew II of Hungary attacked **Muslim** strongholds on Mount Tabor. Another contingent strengthened fortifications at Caesarea. The main army arrived in **Egypt** in 1218 and laid siege to Damietta, which fell the following year. Cardinal **Pelagius**, who had been made papal legate and leader of the expedition, refused the offer of **Ayyubid** sultan **al-Kamil** to exchange Damietta for **Jerusalem**. The cardinal was opposed in his decision to attack Cairo instead by the native barons, led by the titular king of Jerusalem, **John of Brienne**. In 1221 the crusade foundered at the fortress of Mansura, and was forced to retreat at the expense of all it had gained.

See also **Gervase of Prémontré**, one of the procurators of this crusade effort, Cardinal Pelagius, who led the expedition, St. **Francis**, who visited the battlefield, and **Oliver of Paderborn**, whose chronicle is a key source for the history of the expedition.

FINLAND. *See* **Baltic Crusades.**

FIRST CRUSADE. A number of contingents from discrete regions led by local nobles advanced on **Jerusalem** starting in the year 1096, and took the city in 1099. Crusade chroniclers treat these armies as separate entities throughout the expedition, and make it clear that major decisions were made out of a process of debate as situations arose, rather than as part of a strategy, or as a result of a chain of command. This means that the military force of the only successful crusade was not, in any modern sense, an army, and not all contingents were present at each of the battles listed below.

The regional forces were led by **Peter the Hermit, Godfrey of Bouillon**, duke of Lower Lorraine, Count Robert II of **Flanders**, Duke **Robert of Normandy**, Count **Raymond of Saint-Gilles** and the Guiscards, **Bohemond** and his nephew **Tancred** (*see* **Armenia**), from southern Italy. In political terms, these forces responded to a call for military help against the **Seljuk Turks** from the **Byzantine Empire** in the 1090s. The call was published in Europe by Pope **Urban II** at the council of Clermont in 1095 (*see* the introduction). The crusade contingents won notable victories against the Turks at the Seljuk capital, **Nicaea**, and against the Turkish sultan at Dorylaeum in 1097. They moved on to the **siege of Antioch** and the conquest of **Edessa** in 1098, and the **siege of Jerusalem** in 1099. *See also* **Alp Arslan**.

The crusade established the **Latin Kingdom of Jerusalem** (1099-1187) and other crusader principalities or counties at Antioch and Edessa. The crusade leaders began the process of installing European prelates in the great shrines of **Christendom** as they were conquered from the **Muslims**. The establishment of European lordships and ecclesiastical offices was a breach of the oaths the crusade leaders made to Alexius **Comnenus**, Byzantine Emperor, when they passed through his domains to reach **Asia Minor**. The expansion of **Latin** power in the **Levant** from 1099 to 1187 continued to exacerbate tensions that already existed between East and West arising from competing commercial interests as well as doctrinal and liturgical differences.

Hostility between the Byzantines and Western Europeans would lead eventually to the conquest of **Constantinople** during the **Fourth Crusade**. The Latin states were drastically reduced by **Saladin** in 1187, and their inhabitants fled to **Acre**. They were ousted from the Levant by the **Mamluks** in 1291, and retired to the **Lusignan** kingdom on **Cyprus**.

FLANDERS, COUNTS OF. Flanders is a good example of a crusading family, as are the **Coucys, Montferrats**, and the **Lusignans**. Robert I the Frisian (r.1071-93) made the **pilgrimage** to **Jerusalem** 10 July 1086, returning before 27 April 1090. On his return trip he was received with honor by Alexius **Comnenus**, emperor of **Constantinople**, and promised to send 500 knights as mercenaries for the **Byzantine** struggle against **Islam**. His son, Robert II (r.1093-1111), acted as regent during his father's trip, and left in his turn in 1096 as one of the leaders for the

First Crusade. Robert II was married to Clementia of Burgundy, sister of Pope **Calixtus II**.

Thierry of Alsace (r.1128-68), Robert II's nephew, married Sybil, daughter of **Fulk of Anjou**, King of Jerusalem c.1134. Count Thierry took the cross with King **Louis VII** of France for the failed **Second Crusade**, missed a chance to acquire a lordship in **Damascus**, and returned home by 1150 with a relic of the "**holy blood**." His wife Sybil ended her days in the convent of the **Order of Saint Lazarus** in Jerusalem in 1165. David Nicholas, in *Medieval Flanders* (p. 71) credits Thierry with four trips to the Holy Land (1138-39, 1147-49, 1157-59, 1164-66) and his successor, Philip, with three. Before he left for the **Levant** in 1157 Thierry had Philip, then 14, installed as count, able to direct policy and to issue charters in his own name.

Philip of Alsace (r.1168-91), count of Flanders and Vermandois, Thierry's eldest son, grandson of King Fulk, made several journeys to the **Latin Kingdom of Jerusalem** (1173, 1177, 1189), dying at **Acre** on the **Third Crusade**. In 1175 he took the **cross** upon hearing of the death of King **Amalric I** of Jerusalem, and arrived in the Holy Land in 1177 during the reign of King **Baldwin IV**. The young king could not marry because it was believed that his leprosy could be communicated by physical contact. The Angevins also had a claim to the throne, so a visit to England was arranged as a prelude to Philip's pilgrimage. He visited the shrine of Thomas Becket at Canterbury in 1177 on his way to Jerusalem, and brought English crusaders and a cash gift with him to the Latin Kingdom. Because of the succession crisis, Baldwin IV offered Philip the regency of the kingdom upon his arrival.

Philip refused, and the regency was offered to **Reynald of Châtillon** instead. According to a recent study of this key period in the history of the kingdom, Philip hoped to take a leading role in the proposed conquest of **Egypt**, but only if the conquered territory were given to him. Instead, the High Court made it clear that any territory conquered would become part of the Latin Kingdom. Philip refused to act under those terms and returned home without accomplishing anything of note.

Baldwin IX (r.1194/95-1205) of Flanders and **Hainaut** married Marie, daughter of **Henry of Champagne**, titular king of Jerusalem 1192-97. Baldwin, one of the leaders of the **Fourth Crusade**, was proclaimed Emperor of Constantinople, but was captured by the Vlacho-Bulgars at Adrianople in 1205. He presumably died in captivity sometime over the next year. His brother Henry became his regent and then emperor of Constantinople (r.1205-16). Henry married Agnes of Montferrat, and when she died he married the daughter of the Bulgar king Johanitsa (d.1207).

When Henry died in 1216 his brother-in-law Peter of Courtenay traveled from Flanders with a crusade force of 160 knights and 5,500 infantry, having stopped in Rome to be crowned. He was captured and killed by the Greeks in 1217. Flanders was slow to send another heir to the empire. Robert, one of Henry's nephews, ruled from 1221-28. The **Latin Kingdom of Constantinople** lasted only until 1261.

FLANDERS, COUNTY OF. Flanders was the largest of a network of principalities formed out of Carolingian counties, each of which had courts, a tax structure, and a history of feudal defense systems such as **castles** and levies. Five major principalities existed in addition to Flanders: **Hainaut, Brabant, Namur,** Liège, and Luxembourg. Smaller principalities included at various times Limbourg, Looz, Holland, Utrecht, and Guelders. Both France and the **Holy Roman Empire** had claims as overlords over parts of Flanders, but were largely unable to enforce them during the crusades period. These principalities, often referred to as the Low Countries, took the lead in support for the **Levant**, especially during the **First** and **Second Crusades**.

FOURTH CRUSADE. This was a controversial expedition as early as 1202, when the army of French and **Venetian** crusaders turned aside from its stated goal to attack a **Christian** city on the Adriatic. Its eventual accomplishment was the sack of **Constantinople** in 1204 and the conquest of the **Byzantine Empire**. **Latin** conquest of the empire was short-lived, but the animosity engendered by the sack of the city had a permanently chilling effect on the relations between the two halves of **Christendom**.

Tensions between Byzantium and Europe were high before this crusade. In 1182 during the coup of Andronicus **Comnenus** the citizens of Constantinople massacred all the Western Europeans in the city, including the sick in the hospital of the **Order of Saint John**. Only a few escaped by sea to the crusader kingdoms to tell the story. Andronicus also arranged the murders of Mary of **Antioch**, who was regent 1180-82, Maria, the daughter of Manuel Comnenus, and her husband Ranier of **Montferrat**. The Fourth Crusade army was under the command of Ranier's brother Boniface, who became lord of Thessalonika 1204-07.

At every stage of this crusade, numbers of **pilgrims** scandalized by the diversions decided to return home or to travel on to **Jerusalem** independently, while others ran out of money during the lengthy negotiations and were left behind. One of the French leaders and chief negotiators with the Venetians, Geoffrey of **Villehardouin**, marshal of Champagne, left an account of the crusade available in an English translation. The crusade was initiated by Pope **Innocent III** in 1199, preached by Fulk of Neuilly (d.1202), attended by six abbots from the Cistercian houses of Vaux-de-Cernay, Perseigne, Loos, Cercanceaux, Locedio, and Pairis.

The crusade started in France, but its leaders moved quickly to engage Venetian transport. Their order was far larger than any previous European request to an Italian city. They expected 4,500 knights, 9,000 squires, and 20,000 foot soldiers, and promised to pay for their transport and provisions for a year, starting in 1202. The 200 ships and other supplies required would engage the energies of the whole Republic and beyond this assistance Venice promised to provide 6,000 men and 50 fully armed galleys. The crusaders were to pay 94,000 marks of silver.

The Venetians fulfilled their part of the bargain, but in 1202 only about 10,000 crusaders assembled and after they had all paid their share, the total was short by 34,000 marks. The problem had been in the original estimates. The king of France had been able to field only 650 knights and 1,300 squires during the **Third Crusade** in 1191. The agreed price would have been twice his annual income. Even with full complements from other European powers, the numbers would have been unrealistic at best.

Unable to pay cash, the crusaders were asked to pay with service as mercenaries in the Venetian quarrels with Dalmatia and Byzantium. Both were Christian powers, which led to disputes among the crusaders and with the **papacy** as the crusade went forward. **Zara**, the Dalmatian city threatening Venice's control of the Adriatic, was taken in 1202, in spite of the excommunication leveled by Pope Innocent III (r.1198-1216) on the whole army.

As the crusade wintered in Zara and negotiated with Pope Innocent, it was again deflected, this time to Constantinople, ostensibly to settle a succession dispute. Much has been written about these negotiations, but in the end the crusade took Byzantium in 1204 and established a European empire there that lasted until 1261. This victory seemed to advance the goals of the papacy, namely the hoped-for reunification of the Roman and Orthodox churches, and served immediate Venetian interests. Three days of massacre and plundering allowed the crusade army to pay off their debt to the Venetians. Constantinople was denuded of both treasure and **relics**, many of which found their way to St. Mark's. *See* **Holy Shroud**, **Naval Warfare**. Once the city was captured, plans were made to take the territory that had belonged to the Byzantines. The new **Latin Empire of Constantinople** was divided, to be shared by the leader of the crusade, the new emperor (*see* **Flanders**), the Venetians, and the French. The city itself was retaken by the **Greeks** in 1261, but the Latin states founded in central Greece lasted until the **Ottoman** invasion of the 1460s.

FRANCIS OF ASSISI, St. (d.1226). The literature on St. Francis's life and writings is vast. Francis was arguably the most important holy man of the medieval era in terms of his impact on culture and religious belief. Whereas St. **Bernard of Clairvaux** towered over contemporaries because of his writing on doctrine and spirituality (and therefore his political influence), Francis himself was more of an object of veneration because of his exemplary life. Both were involved in a reform of the church that led to the foundation and popularity of new religious orders: the Cistercian, the Premonstratensian, the Franciscan, the **Dominican**, as well as the **Templar** and other **military orders**.

Francis visited the battlefield at Damietta during the **Fifth Crusade**. He received reluctant permission from the papal legate **Pelagius**, leader of the expedition, to visit **Ayyubid** Sultan **al-Kamil** at Cairo. To the surprise and horror of the **Muslim** court, Francis was not an emissary from the army but had come to preach the gospel. The sultan refused the demand of his entourage to have Francis executed, and instead returned the holy man to the European camp unharmed, possibly under the impression that he was mentally ill.

The Franciscan Order, founded in 1209, became involved in the prosecution of heresy as **inquisitors** after Francis's death, when the order was reorganized by the **papacy** in 1254. The saint's writings do not mention the **Cathars**, but do enjoin the laity to be faithful in communion and in reverence to priests. Francis's rule for the order directs superiors to send those who are not orthodox Catholics to the proper authorities. In general, his emphasis on the beauty and value of creation and his insistence on the moral example to be given by his followers were helpful in combating dualism and anticlericalism by peaceful means. *See also* St. **Dominic**. The primary source for the story of St. Francis at Damietta is the chronicle called **Ernoul**.

FRANK. "Frank" is a term sometimes used to refer to Western Europeans. Used in Europe, for instance by Pope **Eugenius III** in the papal bull issued to promote the **Second Crusade**, it referred to the history of what is now France as an area conquered by a tribe known as the Franks after Roman occupation. Since the Franks entered Roman Gaul from beyond the Rhine, the word can also reflect German history. Used in the 12th century, it is not an accurate description of persons from either France or Germany, since both places were in fact multiethnic and multilingual. Neither was yet a sovereign territorial state in the modern sense. *See* **Arab; Greek; Latin.**

FREDERICK I BARBAROSSA. Holy Roman Emperor 1152-90. Frederick took the **cross** after the fall of the **Latin Kingdom of Jerusalem** at **Hattin** in 1187 and died in **Asia Minor** at the head of a German army that preceded the **Third Crusade** in 1190. The army disbanded after his death. Only a small number went on to join the crusade at **Acre**. The French and English forces did not reach the **Levant** until 1191.

FULCHER OF CHARTRES. Fulcher accompanied the **First Crusade** in the army of **Robert of Normandy** and served **Baldwin I**, king of **Jerusalem**, as chaplain until 1118. His chronicle was probably written between 1101 and 1128. He may have become prior of the abbey of the **Mount of Olives** before his death. The chronicle was translated into English by Frances Rita Ryan.

FULK V OF ANJOU. King of **Jerusalem** 1131-43, Fulk was the son of Fulk IV Nerra of Anjou, who had made three penitential **pilgrimages** to Jerusalem under the influence of the **Cluniac** reformers. Fulk V came to Jerusalem with a company raised by **Hugh of Payns** in 1128-29. He married Melisend (d.1161), daughter of **Baldwin II** of the **Latin Kingdom of Jerusalem**.

The kingdom passed to Melisend on Baldwin's death on 21 August 1131. First her husband and then her son contested her right to share power in the kingdom. In 1134 Melisend's cousin Hugh II of Le Puiset, angered by Fulk's exclusion of the queen from power, led a rebellion which was successfully smoothed over by the **Latin Patriarch of Jerusalem**, William of Messines. Fulk's heir was **Baldwin III**, who was 13 when his father died from a hunting accident in 1143. Melisend served as regent for her son until 1151-52, when the kingdom briefly saw civil war as the king and his mother struggled for control.

Fulk's grandson was King **Henry II** of England. The Angevin connection of the kings of Jerusalem led to repeated embassies from the **Latin Kingdom** to beg for English help during the crusade period. *See* **Guy of Lusignan**; **Montferrat**; **Flanders** for other examples of crusading families moving from **pilgrimage** to the acquisition of possessions in the Holy Land.

The best primary source, available in English translation, on the Latin Kingdom during its first 80 years is the chronicle of **William of Tyre**.

-G-

GENOA. Like **Venice**, its chief rival, Genoa was a small republic based on sea trade and plunder. Open war broke out between Genoa and Venice four times between 1253 and 1381. The rivalry was based on a desire to control the lucrative trade with the **Levant**, the **Byzantine Empire**, and the Black Sea. The roots of the rivalry went back to the early crusade period.

In 1082 Venice exchanged privileged trade status in **Constantinople** for alliance with the Byzantine Empire against the Guiscards of **Sicily**. During the **First Crusade**, in 1096-99, Genoa's assistance earned it a trade agreement with the **Latin Kingdom of Jerusalem**, finalized in 1104 in addition to the spoils of war, which included cash and two pounds of pepper each for those at the **siege** of Caesarea in 1102. During the **Fourth Crusade** Venice took three-eighths of the city of Constantinople, establishing colonies in the **Latin Empire** founded there as a result of the expedition. Genoa retaliated by supporting the deposed **Greek** emperors in 1260, and was rewarded with its own colony when Venice and the crusader kingdom were defeated. Without the support of Genoa, **Pisa**, and Venice, the crusade movement would not have been possible.

Because of their geographical position and economies based on Mediterranean trade, both Genoa and Pisa had suffered from **Muslim** attack since the 10th century. In 934-35 both cities endured raids from the **Fatimids**, based at the time in northern Africa, which involved massacres and the enslavement of women and children as well as plunder. It is possible that Genoa was a considerable settlement before this massacre, and that material remains were destroyed by it. Not much is known about the city before the 10th-century Muslim incursions.

Iberian Muslims captured Sardinia in 1015 and continued these raids. Genoa and Pisa united to take Sardinia in 1015-16 and by 1034 were carrying the fight to northern Africa. In 1087 a combined force of Genoese, Pisans, Romans, and Amalfitans, organized by Pope Victor III (1086-87) attacked the city of Mahdia (in modern Tunisia). The papal legate, Bishop Benedict of Modena, led the expedition of 300 or more ships and 30,000 men. The prize was a large indemnity in gold, trading rights in Mahdia, and the promise of an end to Muslim attacks on Italian shipping. For the Italian cities, the crusades were a natural progression from the success of this joint endeavor. For Genoa, the crusade movement was one of a number of factors which helped it to expand in the western Mediterranean in the 12th century.

Imitating its success in the crusader Levant, Genoa exchanged naval assistance against **Islam** for trading enclaves in **Barcelona** and **León-Castile**. In 1146 Genoa traded naval support and **siege engines** for commercial treaties and spoil in the projected conquest of Almeria by León and Tortosa by Barcelona. These efforts were supported by a papal **indulgence** and became part of the (short) tally of conquests in the history of the **Second Crusade**. Genoa sent more than 200 ships, materials and men to build and garrison two siege towers, and a number of armored roofs and other siege engines to Almeira in 1147. Barcelona's attack on Muslim Tortosa in 1148 was backed not only by Genoa, but also by crusaders from southern France, **Flanders**, and England, as well as members of the **Templar** order.

In 1176 when William Longsword of **Montferrat** was preparing to go to the Levant for his marriage to the heiress of the Latin Kingdom of Jerusalem, the Genoese negotiated an agreement that in return for their support, he would restore to them territories and privileges they had lost under King **Amalric I** of Jerusalem. His death from malaria put an end to those hopes, but the Genoese tried the same strategy in 1180, by backing William's brother Ranier, married to the daughter of Byzantine Emperor Manuel I **Comnenus**, in a bid for the crown of Constantinople. The support of Genoa and Pisa for the pretenders was one of the factors that led to the massacre of all the Western Europeans in the city in 1182.

In the same way, the Genoese were rewarded for their assistance at the siege of **Acre** during the **Third Crusade** by a confirmation of their trading privileges with the crusader kingdom. They supported **Conrad of Montferrat** in his struggle with **Guy of Lusignan** for control of the Latin Kingdom based at Acre. Conrad had been called to the defense of the reign of Emperor Isaac Angelus at Constantinople in 1185. Unsatisfied with the emperor's reward for his services and fearful of the unsettled atmosphere in the city after the attempted rebellion, Conrad had escaped to **Tyre** on a Genoese ship. It was the support of the Genoese that allowed him to make his bid for a kingdom in crusader territory. The fact that the Genoese switched sides at least once in the ensuing contest with Guy makes it clear that they knew how to use the politics of the crusader kingdoms to their advantage. Crusading was only one factor in the complex history of Genoese expansion.

In the early years of the 13th century the war between Genoa and Pisa prevented the former from playing any role in the **Fourth Crusade** beyond failing to honor its alliance with Byzantium for the first time since 1155. Venice outbid Genoa for Crete, captured during the crusade and sold off by Boniface of Montferrat. The rivalry with Pisa ended to Genoa's advantage at the battle of Meloria in 1284, and by that time Genoa's expansionist policy had secured it important trading posts in Byzantine and Muslim territory. In the 14th century Genoa developed a constitutional government and a permanent office of the **doge**, and continued its perennial rivalry with Venice.

See also **Caffaro**; **Naval Warfare**.

GERVASE, ABBOT GENERAL OF PRÉMONTRÉ. (r.1209-20;

bishop of Séez 1220-28). As abbot general of an order devoted to preaching, Gervase was appointed procurator (preacher with a commission to raise money and recruit men) for the **Albigensian** and **Fifth Crusades**. Papal letters promoting the crusades laid a general obligation to preach and collect funds on the hierarchy of bishops, canons, and parish priests who served the laity in the diocesan structure of the Western European church. Specific orders, such as the **Dominicans**, might receive special encouragement to join such an effort, and the **papacy** also appointed individuals, such as **Robert of Arbrissel** for the **First Crusade**, or **Jacques de Vitry** for the **Fifth**, to join the effort to promote a particular expedition. Gervase's letters offer information on the practical organization of two crusades. Two letters were analyzed by Thomas C. Van Cleve in his essay on the Fifth Crusade, published in the multivolume *History of the Crusades* edited by Kenneth Setton. For Gervase's biography, see Cheney under Crusades in the bibliography.

The Premonstratensian Order was founded in c.1120 in imitation of the spirituality of the Cistercians, with an emphasis on the reform of the diocesan churches (*see* **Bernard of Clairvaux**). In 1131 Pope Innocent II appointed Premonstratensians to preach the gospel in the **Levant** to **Muslims**. Canons of the order were established in the churches of Sts. Joseph and Habacuc near **Ramla** and St. Samuel's (on Mountjoy) near

Jerusalem. Queen Melisend gave them the church of St. John the Evangelist at Nablus, and King **Amalric** added the church of St. Longinus at Jerusalem. Like other clergy present in the kingdom in 1187, the canons moved first to **Acre** and eventually to **Cyprus**, where they settled at the monastery of Bellapaise.

GESTA FRANCORUM ET ALIORUM HIEROSOLYMYTANORUM. The *Gesta* is an anonymous chronicle of the **First Crusade**, written by a follower of **Bohemond of Taranto**. The chronicle was used by other medieval writers: **Baldric of Dol, Ekkehard of Aura, Guibert of Nogent, Tudebod,** and **Robert of Rheims**. *The Deeds of the Franks and other Pilgrims to Jerusalem* was probably written before 1103. The chronicle was edited and translated by Rosalind Hill.

GODFREY OF BOUILLON. King of Jerusalem in fact, 1099-1100, Godfrey preferred to take the title of "Defender of the **Holy Sepulchre**." He was the popularly acknowledged hero of the **First Crusade**, whose contingent left Lower Lorraine (part of the ninth-century kingdom of Lotharingia, originally extending along the North Sea between the mouths of the Rhine and the Ems Rivers) in August of 1096, following the Rhine and the Danube Rivers in turn to arrive in **Constantinople** in December. The other contingents were led by **Peter the Hermit**, Count Robert II of **Flanders**, Duke **Robert of Normandy**, Count **Raymond of Saint-Gilles**, and the Guiscards, **Bohemond** and his nephew **Tancred**, Normans from southern Italy.

Godfrey's family claimed descent from Charlemagne. Godfrey was a second son, who did not inherit his father's county of Boulogne and holdings in England, but was designated heir of Lower Lorraine by his maternal uncle. In the event of his uncle's death, **Holy Roman Emperor** Henry IV presented Godfrey with Antwerp instead, to add to his family inheritance of the county of Bouillon. He was not invested with the duchy of Lower Lorraine until 1089. For reasons that are not clear, he was forced to mortgage or sell Verdun and Bouillon to pay for the expedition to Jerusalem.

Having been elected by the other crusade leaders as *advocate* or secular protector of the greatest shrine in **Christendom**, he faced a crisis when they left for Europe or for lordships they had established in the **Levant**. By the spring of 1100 he resided in a city depopulated by the massacre of 1099 with an estimated 200 knights to defend it. His domain was limited to **Jaffa**, Lydda, **Ramla**, **Bethlehem**, and Jerusalem.

The other port cities from which help might come were in the hands of **Fatimid** commanders who could draw on naval assistance from **Egypt**. Godfrey fortified the port of Jaffa with **Pisan** assistance and negotiated truces with local **Muslim** lords.

Godfrey fell ill in June 1100, and died on 18 July. His burial set a precedent: he and his successors were buried in the chapel of Adam beneath the shrine of Calvary in the Church of the Holy Sepulchre. His successor was his brother **Baldwin I** of Boulogne.

GREEK. A term used by Europeans to denote residents of the **Byzantine Empire**. The Empire was multiethnic and multilingual, as was Europe. The official language of church and state in Byzantium after the sixth century was Greek. *See* **Arab**; **Frank**; **Latin**.

GREGORY VII, POPE. (r.1073-85). A Tuscan peasant, educated at a **Cluniac** monastery in Rome, Gregory became part of the papal curia under the reform popes. Once elected to the **papacy**, Gregory made a number of claims about the extent of papal prerogatives that are summarized in a document called the *Dictatus Papae*, contained in the papal registers for 1075. These included the claim that the pope could depose both ecclesiastical and secular rulers. Excommunication, which placed the sinner outside the community of the church, implied the invalidation of the oath of the **Christian** vassal to a ruler under the church's ban.

Gregory's claim went beyond the right to depose a ruler for sin, however. It was based instead on the ruler's fitness for office. In 1076 the **Holy Roman Emperor** deposed Gregory in the course of a quarrel between them based on this claim. Their struggle culminated in 1084 when the pope was rescued from the emperor by the Normans of southern Italy and **Sicily**. He died an exile from Rome in Norman territory.

In 1074, as he took office, Gregory had proposed an expedition to the **Holy Sepulchre** of 50,000 knights, led by himself, to rescue eastern Christians from **Seljuk Turk** incursions into **Byzantine** territory. He appealed to the western emperor who was soon to depose him to protect the Roman church in his absence. This plan was abandoned for a number of reasons, and Gregory instead gave his approval to an invasion of Byzantium by his Norman allies in 1080.

Neither the pope's view of his office nor his plan for an expedition to the east was successful during his pontificate. Gregory's idealism, however, both in his view of papal responsibility and in his suggestion for the relief of the eastern emperor, was echoed by Pope **Urban II** in his speech at the council of Clermont. Gregory's letters are an important source of information on the medieval papacy and on crusade ideology. For examples of other letter collections which shed light on the crusades, *see* **Gervase of Prémontré**; **Jacques de Vitry**; **Catherine of Siena**.

GUIBERT OF NOGENT. (c.1064-1125). Abbot of the Benedictine monastery of Nogent, in the territory dominated by the **Coucy** family, Guibert wrote two works of particular interest to crusades scholars, an autobiography, and *Dei gesta per Francos*, an account of the **First Crusade** based on the *Gesta Francorum*. The latter offers a version of **Pope Urban II**'s speech at Clermont.

GUY OF LUSIGNAN. (c.1140-1194). King of **Jerusalem** 1186-92 and of **Cyprus** 1192-94, Guy was the son of Hugh Count of La Marche in Poitou. The **Lusignans** were vassals of King **Henry II of England**, and therefore desirable connections for the **Latin Kingdom**, which suffered from a chronic lack of manpower. Guy acquired Jerusalem through his marriage to the daughter of King **Amalric I**, Sybil, in 1180.

King Amalric's marriage to Agnes of Courtenay (*see* **Edessa**) was annulled by order of the High Court as a prerequisite for his coronation. His children by that marriage were legally legitimate, but his son, the future **Baldwin IV**, was prevented by his leprosy from marrying and producing an heir. Amalric's daughter Sybil was educated at the convent of Bethany in Jerusalem where her aunt was abbess. Her first brief marriage to William of **Montferrat** produced a son, **Baldwin V**, who died at the age of eight or nine. By his second wife, Maria **Comnena**, Amalric had Isabel (d.1205), who inherited the kingdom after Sybil (d.1190).

The Lusignan brothers, Guy and Amaury, were the subject of considerable scandal in the Latin Kingdom. One explanation for Guy's presence in the Holy Land is that he had attacked the queen of England's escort and killed its leader, the earl of Salisbury, in 1168. His punishment was a **pilgrimage** to Jerusalem, where he entered the service of King Baldwin IV. Another is that Sybil's mother was so taken with Amaury that she encouraged her daughter to marry Guy. According to the chronicle of **Ernoul**, Sybil broke her engagement to Baldwin of **Ramla** in order to do so. King Baldwin's mother Agnes of Courtenay and her relations favored Guy, while his stepmother Maria Comnena and his paternal relations favored Baldwin of Ramla.

Guy took the title Count of **Ascalon** and **Jaffa** upon his marriage, and was increasingly associated with Baldwin IV and Sybil in affairs of state. He was suddenly designated regent in 1183 when Baldwin IV became too ill to rule. **Saladin** had taken Aleppo and then invaded the Latin Kingdom. Troops had been mustered to meet him at Saffuriya, a village five miles northwest of **Nazareth**, and Guy was immediately called upon to take command of them. The special tax of 1183 had been used to expand the kingdom's forces, so that an exceptionally large army of 1,300 **cavalry** and 15,000 infantry were on hand. All of the chief lords of the kingdom were present. The coastal cities were alerted and **Genoa**, **Pisa**, and **Venice** all sent troops from their quarters there. What happened is a subject of dispute among scholars. In simple terms, the two armies skirmished and then went their separate ways, with no pitched battle and no particular gains on either side. Guy could have made a name for himself on this occasion if he had possessed both the necessary skill and the support of the other leaders, many of whom had an interest in seeing him fail. The lack of incident was blamed on him.

King Baldwin IV attempted to annul the marriage between Guy and Sybil, and then to legally deprive Guy of his lordship in the kingdom. Guy and Sybil resisted these efforts, so the king had Baldwin V crowned and appointed Raymond of **Tripoli** regent. In 1185 when Baldwin IV died these arrangements came into force. The king had sent a mission to Western Europe, which made the case for a new crusade at the courts of Rome, France, and England. *See* Baldwin IV for further details on the succession crisis which began during his reign.

At the death of Baldwin V in 1186 his mother Sybil was identified by the tenants-in-chief as the legal heir. Guy had been excluded from the succession by Baldwin IV. Accounts of the details differ, but Guy was crowned with Sybil and her half-sister and rival heir Isabel agreed to the arrangement. Of the chief barons, only Raymond of Tripoli and Baldwin of **Ibelin** refused to do homage to the new king.

In March of 1187 Saladin began to muster troops against the Latin Kingdom. That winter **Reynald of Châtillon** had defied Guy's authority after attacking a caravan traveling from Cairo to Damascus through his fief of **Transjordan**. The attack broke the truce with Saladin, and Guy's demand that Reynald make restitution was refused. In April it was clear that the truce would not be renewed and the High Court of the kingdom met to make plans.

Raymond of Tripoli was pressured into making peace with Guy in the crisis. Even so, when the forces of the kingdom mustered at Saffuriya, they had only two-thirds as great a force as that of Saladin. Urged to fight by those who had been disappointed with his failure to do so in 1183, Guy lost a pitched battle with Saladin on 4 July at **Hattin** in 1187.

Guy was taken prisoner and released in 1188. He went to **Acre** to begin a two-year **siege** that laid the foundation for the **Third Crusade**. His wife Sybil through whom he had a claim to the throne died in 1190. The kingdom passed to her half-sister Isabel and **Conrad of Montferrat** by virtue of their marriage on 24 November 1190. Guy refused to yield the title until April of 1192. When Acre fell to the Third Crusade on 12 July 1191 it was Conrad who led the European forces into the city under the standards of the kings of France and England. An agreement made later in the month gave Guy the title of king for his lifetime.

The quarrel continued, Conrad refusing to serve under **Richard I** of England, and the Italian city-communes, Genoa and Pisa, coming to blows in February 1192 over their loyalties to Conrad and Guy respectively. When Conrad finally won the struggle to have his claim to the throne recognized, Guy was enabled to become king of Cyprus due to the intervention of his overlord Richard.

Guy reputedly owed his political career to his brother Amaury (or Aimery), who was taken captive in **Damascus** soon after his arrival in 1174. Amalric I ransomed him, and by c. 1179 Amaury was constable of the kingdom and had married into the **Ibelin** family. He was captured with King Guy and most of the major barons of the kingdom by Saladin at Hattin in 1187. He was released the following year, and successfully petitioned **Henry of Champagne** for the lordships of Ascalon and Jaffa. In 1194 he succeeded Guy as king of Cyprus. When Henry of Champagne died in 1197 Amaury married his widow, Isabel, and took the title of King of Jerusalem and Cyprus (1197-1205).

A treatise on the laws of the kingdom was created under Amaury's patronage (*Livre au roi*), which has been used by scholars to understand the constitutional development of the crusader kingdoms.

-H-

HAINAUT. The counts of Hainaut were powerful in the 11th and 12th centuries when both France and the **Holy Roman Empire** had claims on parts of the Low Countries but were unable to enforce them. Counts: Baldwin IV (r.1125-71) established the feudal levy, and Baldwin V (r.1171-95) could put 700 knights and thousands of foot soldiers in the field. Baldwin VI (r.1195-1205) also ruled **Flanders** as Baldwin IX, and was a leader of the **Fourth Crusade** (1202-04), in the aftermath of which he was elected Latin Emperor of **Constantinople** (r.1204-05).

His brother Henry (r.1205-16) followed him as emperor as the Europeans tried to consolidate their conquest.

HATTIN, THE BATTLE OF. This pitched field battle on 4 July 1187 between **Guy of Lusignan** at the head of the army of the **Latin Kingdom of Jerusalem** and **Saladin** leading a coalition of **Muslim** forces decided the fate of the crusader kingdom. It has been the subject of a number of analyses as a turning point in crusades history and the immediate cause of the **Third Crusade**.

According to Marshall Baldwin's account of Hattin (published in the six-volume *History of the Crusades* edited by Kenneth Setton, vol. I, p. 610), "it was a battle which perhaps need not have been fought and certainly should not have been lost." The leaders of the Latin Kingdom could have decided to delay, hoping that Saladin's fragile coalition would fall apart, or they could have chosen a defensive position that would have increased their chances of success. On 2 July the crusader army was encamped near the spring at the town of Saffuriyah, about 15 miles west of Lake Tiberias. Saladin moved his army to Tiberias, where he launched an attack on the citadel. Raymond of **Tripoli**'s wife and a small garrison of troops were there to defend the city. Raymond himself cautioned against attacking Saladin there, urging Guy to take the army to the coastal cities.

The leaders of the Latin Kingdom split over this decision, some urging Guy into battle. This latter party won, and the army approached Tiberias on 3 July. Heat and thirst led to a disastrous encampment near the hill called the Horns of Hattin. Saladin's troops surrounded the army and blocked access to water for horses and men. In the morning the two armies met on the plain south of the hill. Raymond of Tripoli, Balian of **Ibelin**, and Reginald of **Sidon** were able to escape what turned into a slaughter, especially after Saladin took advantage of the wind direction and set a grass fire.

As a result of this battle almost every crusader knight was either killed or taken captive. Saladin moved rapidly to take **Acre**, **Jaffa**, and Beirut within a few days. By September he had control of most of the kingdom and was able to take the city of **Jerusalem** with a **siege** of only two weeks. The forces of the **Third Crusade**, which arrived starting in 1189, served as a check on his advance, but the sultan's death in 1193 left the **Ayyubid** dynasty in control of Syria and **Egypt**.

After the loss of the Holy Land, Bishop Josius of Acre (r.1172-1201) sailed to Western Europe in a ship with a black sail to announce the disaster and try to raise assistance.

HELMHOLD. Saxon priest and author of the "Chronicle of the Slavs" written between 1167 and 1172, Helmhold offers one of the most important primary texts for the **Baltic Crusades**. He was a regular canon at the monastery of Faldera, afterwards known as Neumünster.

HENRY II OF CHAMPAGNE. (d.1197). De facto king of **Jerusalem** 1192-97. Henry was count of Champagne and count-palatine of Troyes 1181-87. The counts of Champagne were a crusading family, like **Flanders**. Their holdings between 1152 and 1234 included the counties of Blois, Sancerre, and Chartres, and eventually Troyes and Meaux.

Hugh, count of Troyes (r.1093-1125), gave up his lordship to join the **Templars**. Thibaut II the Great, count of Blois and Meaux (1102-52) was guardian to King **Louis VII** of France. Thibaut's son Henry (r.1152-81) accompanied Louis on the **Second Crusade** and returned to marry Louis's daughter Marie in 1164.

Henry I returned to the east in 1178-79 and was captured by the **Muslims** in **Asia Minor**, ransomed by the **Byzantine** emperor, and died in **Constantinople** in March of 1181 after his release.

Henry II married the heiress to the **Latin Kingdom**, Isabel (queen of Jerusalem 1190-1205). Isabel was the daughter of **Amalric I** and **Maria Comnena**. Her original marriage (1183-90) to Humphrey of Toron was annulled in order to recognize **Conrad of Montferrat**'s importance to the defense of what was left of the crusader kingdom after **Saladin**'s victory in 1187. Isabel was Conrad's third wife, and the marriage lasted until his death in 1192. In a similar political alliance, Isabel then married the most powerful of the Europeans who had arrived for what all hoped would be the reconquest of the Holy Land: Henry II of Champagne. Henry ruled the crusader kingdom through his marriage to Isabel from 1192 until his death in 1197.

Henry II was nephew to both **Richard I** of England and Philip Augustus of France. He arrived with the kings, and more importantly with Philip's **siege engines** at **Acre** for the **Third Crusade** in 1190. So many important feudal lords were represented at the **siege** that military leadership became a problem. The quarrels intensified when Sybil, heiress to Jerusalem and wife of King **Guy of Lusignan**, died. Guy's claim was by marriage rather than by blood, and he commanded loyalty neither among the surviving barons of the kingdom nor among the newcomers. Isabel, Sybil's younger sister, was forced by her mother and the more powerful among the native barons to annul her marriage to Humphrey of Toron and marry Conrad of Montferrat in November of 1190.

Richard I and Philip Augustus played out their hostility to each other by backing Guy and Conrad, respectively, for control of the still-to-be-reconquered Latin Kingdom, much to the detriment of the crusade. A council of the barons called by Richard on 16 April 1192 chose Conrad, and Count Henry was dispatched to inform Conrad in **Tyre** of his election. After Conrad's murder by the Assassins on 28 April, Henry of Champagne married the widow on 5 May. Richard then handed over the cities held by the **Christians**, although Guy of Lusignan was still alive and still clinging to the title of king. Henry was never crowned, and used the title only once. When Henry died in 1197, Guy's brother Amaury married Isabel and assumed the title.

Henry had accompanied Richard to **Ascalon** in January of 1192. He was rewarded by receiving the city from Richard when it fell at the end of May. Henry then followed Richard towards Jerusalem, camping about 13 miles from the city, where the king of England continued his negotiations with Saladin rather than attempt a siege he believed would not be successful. Eventually Richard retreated to Acre, and Saladin moved on to take and plunder **Jaffa** in July. Henry joined Richard in retaking the city at the end of the month. Richard's illness in Jaffa and his desire to return home prompted him to sign a three-year truce with Saladin, by which Henry would hold a narrow strip of land between the harbors of Tyre and Jaffa, with the lords of **Antioch** and **Tripoli** given an option to sign the truce as well. Ascalon would be returned to Saladin, and both **Muslims** and Christians were to be able to travel freely in all of Palestine. Only **pilgrims** from overseas bearing Richard's pass would have access to Jerusalem.

The presence of the wealthy Henry on the Third Crusade helped the European forces to take Acre, and slowed Saladin's consolidation of his victory at **Hattin**. Henry's position after Richard's departure was difficult, in spite of Saladin's death in 1193. Both the native barons and other claimants, such as the Italian communes, continued to angle for territorial rights lost in 1187. The kingdom was much reduced in size and resources, and of course surrounded by hostile forces held back only by the terms of the truce. The Lusignans were rivals not only for the Latin Kingdom, but for the newly conquered **Cyprus**, which they held. These problems came to a head in 1197, when the truce was to expire and an unruly force of crusaders led by the **Holy Roman Emperor**

Henry VI arrived. Henry of Champagne fell from a tower window on 10 September 1197, leaving his widow and the disintegrating crusader state to the Lusignans.

HENRY II, KING OF ENGLAND. (r.1154-89). In 1172 King Henry formally confessed his part in the murder of Thomas Becket, archbishop of Canterbury, and was reconciled with the church on condition that he go on crusade to the Holy Land for three years. He was unable to depart due to a succession struggle with his eldest son between 1173 and 1174. In 1173 King **Amalric I of Jerusalem** sent a mission to Western Europe to recruit for a crusade, and made plans to attack **Egypt** with the help of the **Sicilian** navy in 1174. Amalric died in the summer of the planned expedition.

Amalric's son **Baldwin IV** sent a mission to Henry in 1184-85, which left the **Latin Kingdom** during a succession crisis. **Guy of Lusignan**, one of Henry's vassals, had failed to inspire the barons of the kingdom with any great opinion of his leadership. Baldwin IV's heir was a child, the son of Guy's wife Sybil by a previous marriage to William of **Montferrat**. The envoys made such a good case for the danger posed by **Saladin** and the minority of the heir that Henry's court was reduced to tears. Henry was the grandson of King **Fulk** of Jerusalem, and was the last resort of the envoys in seeking assistance in the West. Men and money were sent, but there was no solution to the succession crisis, and no immediate help from the monarchs themselves as regents or crusaders.

Henry's second son, **Richard I** (r.1189-99), would lead the **Third Crusade**, and promote the interests of the **Lusignans**.

HENRY XII, "THE LION" OF SAXONY. Duke of Brunswick, Saxony, and Bavaria (1129-95). Henry was the son of Duke Henry of Bavaria (a descendant of Welf IV) and Gertrude of Saxony, daughter of **Holy Roman Emperor** Lothair of Supplinburg (r.1125-37). His campaign of expansion alternately pitted him against his **Christian** neighbors, including the bishops of Mecklenburg, Oldenburg, and Ratzeburg, and the pagan Slavs of the **Baltic** region.

Henry participated in the crusade of 1147 against the Slavs in the region surrounding the Baltic port of Lübeck, northeast of Hamburg. The pagan people who lived there were called **Wends**, or Abotrites (or Obotrites). Their leader was Nyklot, who, learning of the proposed crusade, took the initiative and burned Lübeck in June of 1147. There were no conclusive results of this crusade until another expedition in 1160, when the Danes harried the coast while Henry's troops moved inland, killed Nyklot, and conquered Abotrite territory. There were several rebellions in the 1160s and 1170s, after one of which the Danes received a letter of congratulation from Pope **Alexander III** for their victory against the pagans.

Henry was rewarded by Emperor **Frederick I** with Bavaria in 1156 in return for military assistance in Italy. In 1157 he campaigned against the Poles, and in 1163-64 set garrisons in Slav territory beyond the Elbe River to consolidate his conquests there. Henry divorced his first wife and then married Matilda (1156-89), daughter of Henry I of England, in 1168. He was at war with his erstwhile ally in the Slavic conquests, Valdemar I of Denmark, until 1171, after which he went on **pilgrimage** to **Jerusalem**.

In 1180 Henry was deprived of his lands due to a dispute with the emperor. He was exiled from 1181 to 1185, and again during 1189. In 1190 he was at war with the emperor, and again in 1193. He died in Brunswick on 6 August 1195. He expanded northern Germany beyond the Elbe, establishing Cistercian houses and bishoprics as civilizing agents there. His conquests benefited Denmark in the short run, because after 1180 his troubles in Germany prevented him from defending his interests in the Baltics.

HERALDRY. The herald was originally a messenger, an office with a long history in Western Europe. The word heraldry came to be used to mean "armory" or the knowledge of symbols or phrases commonly used as identification marks on coins or **armor** by members of the aristocracies of Europe. Knowledge of 12th-century "devices" or logos on armor come principally from chronicle descriptions. Coins, tomb carvings, or wax seals used to authenticate documents are also sources of information on heraldic devices. One example of such a device is the eagle used by the **Holy Roman Empire**, reportedly as far back as the ninth century. The study of coins and medals in particular is called numismatics, from the Latin word for coin. Heraldry is normally concerned with armor, badges, and banners.

Heraldic devices may have been worn on the surcoat as well as on the shield, helmet, saddle, and banner. The reason was practical: as armor developed, it became more difficult to recognize friend and foe on the battlefield. Authentication of documents made identifying seals a practical necessity for women, religious houses, city-communes, and various other institutions as well as for warriors.

Some devices, such as a **cross** or a lion, have obvious meanings, others, geometric patterns or bands of bright color, may serve to divide the shield into sections, or simply to attract attention. Other symbols or mottos were adopted for personal reasons, to commemorate achievements, for instance. Rules for heraldry were not common until the 14th century, leaving devices to individual preference. An ability to remember the devices was an advantage in battle or business. (*See* Woodcock, under Warfare in the bibliography for further information on heraldry.)

HISTORIANS. There has been no attempt to list all the histories of the crusades in this volume, or to present entries on all the medieval European (or **Muslim**) authors whose works provide information on crusading. Special effort has been made to list European historians of the **First Crusade**, for whom biographical data is scarce. These include **Albert of Aachen, Baldric of Dol, Caffaro, Ekkehard of Aura, Fulcher of Chartres, Guibert of Nogent, Raymond of Aguilers, Robert the Monk, Tudebode,** and the **Gesta. Odo of Deuil** is an important chronicler of the **Second Crusade. William of Tyre** and **Ernoul** were observers of the events leading to the **Third** through the **Fifth Crusades** from the vantage point of residents of the **Latin Kingdom of Jerusalem**. For the **Albigensian Crusade Peter of Vaux-Cernay** is noted, and for the **Fourth Crusade Robert of Clari** and Geoffrey of **Villehardouin**. For the Fifth Crusade the European source included is **Oliver of Paderborn**.

Muslim authors for whom there are entries include **Baha al-Din, Usama ibn Munqidh,** and **Imad ad-Din al-Isfahani**.

Collections of letters, sermons, and other documents are important to medieval and crusade history. Some important sources of such information include **Gregory VII, Bernard of Clairvaux, Francis of Assisi, Jacques de Vitry, Gervase of Prémontré, Humbert of Romans,** and **Catherine of Siena**.

A notable omission is the considerable troubadour literature on the crusades, but the names of several important poets are listed in the entry for **Conrad of Montferrat**.

HOLY BLOOD. In 1247 King Henry III of England (1216-72) received a **relic** of the blood of Christ as a gift from the titular patriarch of **Jerusalem**, then residing at **Acre**. The authenticity of the relic was attested by the seals of the masters of the **Templar** and **Hospitaller** Orders. The relic was stored at the church of the **Holy Sepulchre** in London, and then carried by the king himself in solemn procession from St. Paul's Cathedral to Westminster Abbey on 13 October. In the Mass that greeted the procession, a sermon was preached comparing the relic to those kept by **Louis IX**, king of France at **Sainte-Chapelle** in Paris. A **pilgrimage indulgence** of six years, 116 days was granted to anyone who made the journey to pray before the relic in the future. The historian Matthew Paris, a monk from the Benedictine abbey of St. Albans in Hertfordshire, had been called by the king to witness this event and was asked afterwards to write an account of it. (For Matthew Paris, *see* Vaughan, Richard, under Great Britain in the bibliography).

Henry did not see Sainte-Chapelle itself until 1254, when he was reportedly deeply impressed by it. One of the first acts of his personal reign was a failed expedition to regain English control of lands in western France (1230). Matthew Paris recalls a contemporary tract, attributed to Bishop Robert Grosseteste of Lincoln, which makes the argument that the Blood was a more precious relic than any of the objects (**Cross**, Crown of Thorns, **Holy Lance**) associated with the Passion of Christ. Henry was clearly interested in establishing Westminster Abbey as a rival pilgrimage site and symbol of royal power to Sainte-Chapelle. Henry continued to add to the relic collection of the abbey, giving the monks the footprint of Christ from the Ascension at the **Mount of Olives** in 1249 and during the same period a spine from the Crown of Thorns. He had received a number of such relics from the Hospitallers in 1235, including pieces of the burning bush, of the altar on which Christ had been presented in the **Temple**, of Calvary and the Sepulchre, etc.

During the years between the **Sixth Crusade** and 1244, Jerusalem had been under **Christian** control due to treaty arrangements. After 1244 Robert of Nantes, the patriarch of Jerusalem, repeatedly sent to Western Europe for help in retaking the holy places. Louis IX took the cross in 1244, followed by important nobles in France and England, including Henry's cousin and the bishop of Worcester. At the Council of Lyons in 1245 the bishops of England and Scotland promised to help finance crusades to retake Jerusalem and territories recently lost by the **Latin Empire at Constantinople**. In 1247 Emperor Baldwin II of Constantinople visited England to recruit men and collect funds. The relics were a recruitment gift, part of a several-year campaign by the Latin East to raise crusade backing.

In 1250 King Henry finally took crusade vows at Westminster Abbey, where the relic had been enshrined in a new reliquary. Richard of Croxley, abbot of Westminster, acted as crusade procurator in the 1250s (*see* **Gervase of Prémontré**). In the event, Henry became fatally involved in the affairs of **Sicily**, promising to take it from the **Holy Roman Empire** at his own expense. It was left to his heir, **Edward I**, to make an abortive crusade to Tunis in 1270 (*see* **Louis IX**). This was the last major investment in crusading made by the kings of England. *See also* **Richard Plantagenet, Earl of Cornwall**.

HOLY LANCE. This **relic** was found at the **siege of Antioch** during the **First Crusade** by a priest from southern France called Peter Bartholomew. The lance was supposed to be the weapon used to pierce Christ's side during the crucifixion (John 19:34). Tradition named the soldier who pierced Christ's side Longinus.

The crusaders' claims had to be balanced against those of a relic with an authenticated history as the lance which already existed at **Constantinople**. The leaders of the crusade had seen the **Greek** lance on their way through the **Byzantine Empire**. The Byzantine lance was held to be one of the relics discovered at **Jerusalem** (*see* **Holy Sepulchre**) by St. Helena, mother of the first **Christian** emperor, Constantine I (d.337). According to its pedigree, it had been rescued from the Persians in 614 and installed in the church of Saint Sophia. It was later moved to the imperial palace and eventually installed in the Chapel of St. Mary at Pharos.

The crusaders' relic was discredited by the death of Peter Bartholomew after he agreed to test his veracity by undergoing the ordeal of fire. **Raymond of St. Gilles** (d.1105) was the only one of the crusade leaders who continued to believe in the lance. He presented it to the Emperor Alexius I **Comnenus** (r.1081-1118) of Constantinople in 1100 on his way home from the First Crusade.

The official Byzantine explanation for the dual relics was that the piece of metal found at Antioch was one of the nails used at the crucifixion. A number of other stories circulated about the relic, especially in **Armenia**, a Christian kingdom that also claimed to possess the Holy Lance.

Saint **Louis IX**, king of France, purchased the relics of the Passion, including a Holy Lance, in 1241. This lance was kept in Paris. However a Holy Lance also remained in Constantinople and was sent by the **Ottoman** sultan to Pope Innocent VIII in 1492. Never displayed, the Roman lance was subject to an investigation by Cardinal Lambertini before he became Pope Benedict XIV (r.1740-58). He officially declared the Antioch lance a false relic when he validated the one held at Rome. The lance at Paris was destroyed during the French Revolution. *See also* **Holy Shroud**; **Holy Blood**.

HOLY ROMAN EMPIRE. In 800 A.D. Charlemagne was crowned Roman Emperor by Pope Leo III (r.795-816) in an effort to consolidate the military alliance between the **Franks** and the church. Charlemagne's empire stretched from Brittany and the Pyrenees to the Elbe River, from the "Danish March" to southern Italy. In the political rhetoric of the time, it was the successor to the Western Roman Empire. In the religious rhetoric of the time, it was **Christian** and dependent therefore on the spiritual authority of the popes in Rome. In actuality, the revival of the title of Roman Emperor in the West (*see* the introduction) was immediately a cause of considerable annoyance to the East Roman or **Byzantine** Emperor in **Constantinople**, and in the long run, a significant problem for the **papacy** as well. Charlemagne divided his empire among his heirs in such a way that the western portion became the nucleus for modern France, while the eastern part was to modern eyes an incongruous combination of principalities from the North Sea to the Mediterranean, from Saxony through the northern Italian communes. In the late 10th century, under the Ottonian dynasty it was bordered by Slavic pagans to the east and the **Muslims** of southern Italy and **Sicily** to the south, with an expanding France on its western flank.

The history of the western Empire is important to the general history of medieval Europe, and especially to the story of the **Gregorian** reform movement, but somewhat tangential to the early crusades. No European monarch joined the **First Crusade**. The **Second** and **Third** were dominated by France and England for various reasons, including the death of Emperor **Frederick I** (r.1152-90) on his way to join **Richard I** and Philip Augustus at **Acre**. Before the **Fourth Crusade**, Emperor Henry VI (r.1190-97), Frederick's son, in his turn took a crusade vow (1195). He promised more than his support for a general call and recruitment from his territory. His own contribution was to be a year's provision for 3,000 men, half knights and half squires.

In the course of negotiations for support from the Byzantines, Emperor Isaac Angelus was deposed and blinded by his brother Alexius III (r.1195-1203). In the same year, 1195, envoys from the **Lusignan** rulers of **Cyprus** arrived at Henry's court, offering to hold their new kingdom from him in return for his assistance in the east. Henry insisted that Alexius III underwrite his own costs for his proposed 3,000 men. The eastern emperor, who was far from secure on his usurped throne and apprehensive about Henry's impending arrival in the **Levant**, had to impose an unpopular "German tax" on his citizens. He was further badgered into allowing a marriage that would advantage only Henry. Irene, the daughter of the deposed Isaac, was married to Henry's brother Philip of Swabia in 1197. She was not only Isaac's heir, but also the widow of Tancred of Lecce, the ruler of Sicily Henry had ousted when he enforced his own claim to the island. In this way Henry solidified his family's claim to Sicily and opened the door for the appeal of Isaac's son to the Holy Roman Empire that started the Fourth Crusade.

Henry himself was delayed from joining his troops when they departed for the Holy Land in 1197. He stayed in Italy to put down a revolt in his new kingdom and died there in September. His army went on to **Tyre**, to attempt to regain the coastal cities and link Tyre with **Tripoli** (*see* **Ayyubid** dynasty for this crusade). Henry's death aborted the crusade, which returned to Europe in 1198.

HOLY SEPULCHRE, DESCRIPTION AND HISTORY. The Church of the Holy Sepulchre was built over what medieval people believed were the locations of the Crucifixion and Resurrection of Christ. Beneath the shrine of Calvary was the supposed tomb of Adam, where crusader kings of **Jerusalem** were buried. The original building was supposed to have been constructed by Constantine I (d. 337), under the influence of his mother, Helena, who discovered the **relic** of the True **Cross** at the site. It had a circular chapel, with an open roof over the Sepulchre, and separate enclosures for Calvary and Golgotha. This church was destroyed by **Fatimid** caliph al-Hakim bi-Amr Allah (r.996-1021) in 1009. It was rebuilt by the **Byzantines** in 1040, and in their turn the crusaders rebuilt and expanded it after 1099. Some portions remain, although the site has been considerably altered since the 12th century.

The canons of the cathedral kept the shrine of the Sepulchre as a major **pilgrimage** center. Crusaders often defined their journey by vowing to reach the Sepulchre to pray there as the end goal, and Europeans sometimes traveled there to take the religious habit as a preparation for death. After 1101 a group of at least five **Greek** Orthodox priests also served in the church, celebrating their liturgy at a large altar placed in a prominent position in the main building. They also had a chapel in the building for their relic of the Holy Cross.

The church was the center of the religious structure created by the **Latin Kingdom** of Jerusalem, with four archbishoprics (**Tyre**, Caesarea, Nazareth, Petra) and three bishoprics (**Ramla**-Lydda, **Bethlehem**, Hebron) subject to the oversight of the Patriarch of Jerusalem. The patriarch of **Antioch** had similar jurisdiction over the northern portion of the crusader kingdoms. *See* **Latin Patriarchs**.

The crusade army dispossessed the **Greek** Orthodox church in conquered territory, installing Western European clerics who had accompanied the army. The major shrines at **Mount Zion**, the **Mount of Olives**, and the *Templum Domini* (**Temple** of the Lord, housed in the Dome of the Rock), were subject to the authority of the Patriarch. The community of canons at the Sepulchre received gifts from Europeans which ranged from personal donations while on pilgrimage to grants of land and revenue in Europe. The church served as a center for coronations and other key events in the history of the Latin Kingdom, such as the vow of **Hugh of Payns**, which created the order of the **Templars**. St. Albert (d.1214), Patriarch of Jerusalem, wrote the rule for the **Carmelites**, another order founded in the Holy Land.

The most important events in the life of the church happened annually, at Palm Sunday, Easter, and the feast of the Liberation of Jerusalem. A procession of clergy and people displayed the True Cross on Palm Sunday, the miracle of the Holy Fire took place at Easter, and on 15 July another procession culminated in a service where the city walls had been breached by the **First Crusaders**. The miracle of the Holy or "New" fire, by which the lamps of the church were miraculously lit by a spark from heaven annually, was the most popular event in the pilgrimage church until it was officially discredited by Pope Gregory IX in 1238.

The church stood at the center of the Patriarch's Quarter in Jerusalem, next to the patriarch's palace, stables, and the Pool of Hezekiah (or Pool of the Patriarch, a large open reservoir). In addition to revenue from and control of the quarter, the church received property from donors in the kingdom and from pilgrims, including 21 villages nearby and a reservoir called the Mamilla Pool that fed the Patriarch's Pool through a conduit. In the city the canons held houses, mills, shops, and ovens, all of which produced revenue. There were three churches other than the Sepulchre in their quarter: St. George in the Market, St. Chariton, and St. Abraham. There was a cathedral school, where a basic education could be had, and a *scriptorium*, where manuscript copying and the art of illumination were practiced.

HOLY SEPULCHRE, INFLUENCE. The priests of the Sepulchre were a reformed community of 20 Augustinian canons who served the liturgy of the shrine. Both the shrine and the organization of the crusade **pilgrimage** site were widely imitated. The building and the iconography of its interior and exterior decoration had an impact on the lesser shrines in the kingdom, such as **Nazareth**, and on churches in Western Europe. The Augustinian rule, which emphasized communal poverty and service to the laity, was also adopted by the major shrines and bishoprics under the patriarch's control after 1112 (including **Bethlehem**, **Nazareth**, Hebron, and **Tripoli**), briefly by the **Templars**, and by the **Orders of St. Lazarus** and **St. John**. Property was given to the canons by pious donors in Western Europe, so that by the 1170s they controlled 61 churches and monasteries in Italy, France, and Spain. These houses often accepted the Augustinian rule, so that before 1187 there was an Order of the Holy Sepulchre made up of such religious institutions, which sent revenue to **Jerusalem**.

The canons in Jerusalem were forced to move to **Acre** between 1187 and 1291. When Acre fell they moved on to Perugia. Pope Urban IV (r.1261-64) was a former patriarch of Jerusalem, and assisted the order in mending its declining fortunes. Although the order was suppressed in 1489, independent houses of its canons continued to function in Europe under the direct control of the **papacy**. Members of the order in England wore a double cross in red. The equestrian Order of the Sepulchre was founded in the 1330s, but some historians accept the authenticity of documents intended to extend its roots to the time of **Godfrey of Bouillon**.

For those too poor to make the journey to the holy places, the order had in England, for instance, round churches built in imitation of the Sepulchre at Cambridge and in Newgate. Priories of the order existed as small hospitals at Warwick, Thetford, Winchester, Caldwell, Nottingham, and Stamford. Priories and churches built to commemorate the Sepulchre could be found on the continent, and many of the pilgrimage churches of Europe boasted a **relic** brought back from Jerusalem. A round church in imitation of the Sepulchre was built in the eleventh century at Neuvy-Saint-Sépulcre near Bourges on the route from Paris to **Santiago de Compostela**, for example, and given a relic of the **Holy Blood** by a participant in King **Louis IX**'s crusade of 1248.

HOLY SHROUD. The shroud is a **relic** believed to be the cloth used to wrap the body of Jesus Christ for burial. Marks on the cloth are believed to be the image of Christ and remnants of his blood. Like the True **Cross**, which was lost at the battle of **Hattin** in 1187, the Shroud was a powerful icon for Western Europeans. Legend had it that the apostles kept the shroud, and that it was placed by an empress of **Constantinople** in the church of St. Mary of the Blachernae in 436. The relic was a focus of **pilgrimage** for Europeans, and was described in **Robert of Clari**'s chronicle of the **Fourth Crusade**. The relic was traditionally thought to have been taken by the **Templars** in 1204 and transferred to France. The shroud brought to Turin, Italy, from France in 1452 is identified with this relic. It has been exhibited several times in the 20th century from the Cathedral of Saint John the Baptist in Turin.

HORSES, IMPORTANCE. The equipment and training of a mounted **knight** was so expensive as to create an aristocratic class of warriors in both **Muslim** and **Christian** societies. Both societies expected the warriors to arm and train themselves. A typical European paid more for his horses than for his other equipment: at least one battle horse and several pack animals. Members of the **military orders** normally had four horses if they were knights and one to two for sergeants.

The horse was, if anything, more important to the Muslim warrior, and especially to the Turkish **mamluk** or **Mongol** knight. The Mamluk rulers of **Egypt** regularly gave horses to their armies, and the tribes in Libya, Upper Egypt, and Syria who supplied them became wealthy enough to threaten the security of the sultans. It was a Turkish custom to eat horse flesh on state occasions. At the wedding of a member of the royal family, 50 horses might be consumed. Fermented mare's milk was a staple alcoholic drink, in one case fatal to a sultan who drank it after it had "turned." For the European or **Levantine** knight, the death or wounding of his mount in battle was often fatal to himself.

Sheep were also important to both sides, providing a staple of the army's diet. Camels were given to each mounted mamluk warrior on the Muslim side at the beginning of a major campaign, while Europeans relied on horses as pack animals. Horses were so indispensable to medieval campaigns, however, that the development of horse transport became an important component of **naval warfare**.

Stables were an important component of city life, and are described in **pilgrimage** accounts of, for instance, **Jerusalem**. The **Templars'** stables on **Temple** Mount were large enough to accommodate hundreds (the medieval sources estimate 2,000 to 10,000) of horses, camels, and asses. Other orders and institutions would have maintained their own facilities. *See also* **Cavalry**.

HORSES, TRANSPORT. There is evidence from as early as the eighth century of transporting horses by boat to military campaigns. The **Byzantines** during that period had ships that could carry 12 horses for short distances. The problems of lengthy transport for a large number of animals were obviously food, water, and the safety of the animals, but by the 12th century, judging from chronicle accounts, some of them were solved. By 960 there were horse transports with ramps allowing mounted troops to be unloaded onto beaches. In 1061 the Normans had ships that could transport as many as 21 horses for short distances. Horses continued to be shipped standing, and by the 12th century slings to keep them from lying down seem to have been used.

It is known that several of the **First Crusade** leaders shipped horses from Apulia to Durazzo (across the Adriatic Sea) but it is not known how many or what kind of ships were used. **Fulcher of Chartres** commented in 1101 that it was not possible to ship horses from Europe to **Jerusalem**. During the 12th century war galleys under oars had to put in for fresh water every few days, depending on the number of men aboard, and the addition of horses would have made that necessity even more frequent. This may be the factor that makes sense of conflicting reports of the feasibility of the sea as opposed to the land voyage.

Evidence from the 12th century indicates that at least at that point Byzantine, Western European, and **Islamic** forces were equally capable of transporting horses. Oared galleys with stern ports and ramps were necessary to land horses directly onto beaches, but these boats could carry only a small number of animals. Large transport ships under sail could carry more, but could not maneuver into position to land horses on beaches. Horses in the holds of larger ships were reserved for the second stage of an invasion, when the smaller mounted force had taken wharf facilities. When they were loaded the port was caulked behind them. There are some accounts of horses being disoriented after a long voyage below deck, and needing to be exercised before they could be used in battle. Pryor, in "Transportation of Horses," estimated that the space needed for each horse put their average length at 2.4 meters and the headroom necessary for a **knight** to mount and ride out on a gangplank at 2.25 meters. By the mid-13th century transports were built that could hold 100 horses.

HOSPITALLERS. *See* **Order of St. John.**

HUGH OF PAYNS. (d.1136). Founder (c.1120) of one of the first **military orders**, the **Templars**, he is listed as its first Master (r.1128-36). He is believed to have been related to both the counts of Champagne (*see* **Henry of Champagne**) and **Bernard of Clairvaux**. His order was dedicated to the protection of **pilgrims** traveling to **Jerusalem**. King **Baldwin II** gave the order quarters in the al-Aqsa mosque, believed by the crusaders to be the **Temple** of Solomon. The members of the order took vows, but were not ordained. They were lay members of a religious order, in which only the chaplains took vows as priests. By 1127 the order had not grown in numbers. Hugh and several companions traveled to Europe to gain papal approval at the Council of Troyes (January 1128), presided over by the legate Matthew of Albano and attended by the archbishop of Reims (or Rheims), a number of bishops, and several abbots. After this council, the order began to accumulate property in Europe due to the gifts of interested donors.

HUMBERT OF ROMANS. (d.c.1277). Crusade preacher and author of a handbook of crusade sermons, Humbert was born in the town of Romans in the diocese of Vienne, France, in about 1194. He was a student in Paris in 1215, entered the **Dominican Order** in 1224, and taught theology at Lyons 1226-63. He served as Master General of his order from 1254 until his retirement to the monastery of Valence in 1263. He wrote a number of works during his retirement, including *De paedicatione crucis contra Saracenos* after 1266, when the pope directed the order to preach the crusades. His work is important because it encapsulates fully developed crusade ideology at the end of the movement's history.

Humbert, in keeping with the ideals of his order, advocates a thorough preparation for crusade preaching, including study of the Quran and of the political map of contemporary **Islam**. Humbert's work has not been translated from the Latin. The most recent work on his life is by Brett; the evaluation of his work is by Vicaire (*see* the section on the Western European Church in the bibliography). For other examples of crusade preachers and procurators, *see* **Bernard of Clairvaux**; **Dominic**; **Robert of Arbrissel**; **Jacques de Vitry**; and **Gervase of Prémontré**. Examples of support for the crusades among contemporaries would include Sts. **Francis of Assisi** and **Catherine of Siena**.

-I-

IBELIN. This dynasty arose in the **Latin Kingdom of Jerusalem** through possession of the fortress of Ibelin in the county of **Jaffa** and then intermarriage with the lords of the great fief of **Ramla**. The lords of Ibelin played a critical role in the history of the crusader kingdoms of Jerusalem and **Cyprus**. Baldwin I (c.1133-1188), who rose to prominence under King **Baldwin IV of Jerusalem**, was captured by **Saladin** in 1179 and held for ransom in **Damascus**. When **Guy of Lusignan** was crowned king of Jerusalem in 1186 Baldwin arranged for his fief of Ramla to pass to his son Thomas, and transferred his allegiance to Bohemond of **Antioch**.

Baldwin's brother Balian was born in c.1142, reaching the age of majority before 1158. Balian married Maria **Comnena** in c.1177, and died in c.1193-94. He inherited Ramla from his nephew Thomas. His sons, John of Beirut (regent of the kingdom 1205-10) and Philip of Cyprus, were influential in the later history of the crusader kingdoms, while his daughters married the lords of Caesarea and **Sidon**. His children were related to the ruling house through their mother, who had been queen consort to **Amalric I**, and whose daughter Isabel eventually inherited the kingdom of Jerusalem. From 1177-78 his control of Maria's dower fief of Nablus made him one of the most important vassals of the crown.

Balian carried the five-year-old **Baldwin V** to his coronation in 1183. He was one of the barons who opposed **Guy of Lusignan**'s claim to the throne. He fought in the rear at **Hattin**, and so escaped capture by Saladin, instead reaching Jerusalem before the **Muslim** army in order to rescue his wife and children. The patriarch put the undefended city in his hands, and Balian was able to mount a good enough defense to encourage Saladin to offer excellent terms for the inevitable surrender of the city. Balian then joined Count Raymond of **Tripoli** for the successful defense of **Tyre**, where he supported **Conrad of Montferrat** rather than Guy of Lusignan as ruler of the surviving bits of the Latin Kingdom. He also served **Henry of Champagne** during his short reign.

Balian died in 1193, having received a fief near **Acre** in exchange for the lost lands of Ibelin and Ramla. He left four children by Maria Comnena, including two sons, John and Philip. John (d.1236) served as constable of Jerusalem and then lord of Beirut, recovered from the Muslims in 1197. He had built a substantial **castle** there by 1212 and created an essentially independent principality, granting privileges to the Italian communes in order to profit from trade. The Lusignan king of Cyprus and Jerusalem, his wife, and their only son all died in 1205. The kingdoms were separated and John of Beirut became regent for the kingdom of Jerusalem. He served for five years until the heiress to the kingdom married **John of Brienne**. By 1217 he had become one of the chief vassals of the kings of Cyprus. He and his brother Philip appear from that date on the witness lists of the Kingdom of Cyprus.

John and Philip (d.1227-28) both appear as regents for Cyprus after the death of its king in 1218. John led the resistance to direct rule over Cyprus or the Kingdom at Acre by **Holy Roman Emperor** Frederick II after the **Sixth Crusade**. The history of the Ibelins in Cyprus and Beirut was written by a **knight** in John's service, Philip of Novara, for the period from 1218 to 1242. Philip was present at John's death in 1236 after the latter had taken vows as a **Templar**, and continued to serve John's son and heir, Balian.

John's nephew, John of **Jaffa** (c.1216-66) towards the end of his life wrote a treatise on the laws of the Latin Kingdom of Jerusalem and the practices of its High Court (*Livre de Jean d'Ibelin*). He fought with King **Louis IX** of France during the crusade of 1249 in **Egypt**. The king took on the refortification of Jaffa at his own expense, and in 1253 the **papacy** took John and his family under its protection. The fortunes of the family fell with those of the crusader kingdoms, so that by the 1370s the line died out.

ICONIUM. A **Seljuk** sultanate based at Konya in Turkey, Iconium was an independent **Muslim** state and a neighbor to the crusader kingdom in the 12th century. With the **Danishmends**, the Muslims of Iconium defeated the crusade led by **Raymond of Saint Gilles** in 1101. **Kilij Arslan II** (r.1156-92) in 1157 offered an alliance against **Nur al-Din** to **Jerusalem**, **Antioch**, and **Cilicia**. Rebuffed by the crusaders, the sultan made peace with the **Byzantines** in 1162, and concentrated on taking **Anatolia** from the independent Turkish emirs who controlled territory there. In 1243 the Seljuks of Iconium were conquered by the **Mongols**.

IMAD AD-DIN AL-ISFAHANI. (1125-1201). Imad ad-Din was **Saladin**'s secretary and the author of a chronicle of his conquests that is available in a French translation (*see* the bibliography under the **Third Crusade**). He entered the sultan's service in 1174 and offers important information on the **Latin Kingdom of Jerusalem** during the years 1187 to 1193, as it was conquered and the refugees moved to **Acre** and **Cyprus**.

INDULGENCE. The theology of the forgiveness of sins and the pardon of the punishment due to sin is far beyond the scope of a dictionary entry. Speaking broadly, the teaching of the medieval church on indulgences was developing in the early crusades period, and was more clearly expressed during the pontificate of Pope **Innocent III**. What

Pope **Urban II** understood himself to be promising the **First Crusaders** and what people in the early 12th century thought he meant are possibly two different things. Both are still debated by scholars.

Forgiveness or absolution was granted only to the truly repentant through the sacrament of confession. The penance due to sin could be addressed by restitution, but the consequences of the sin could never be fully assessed. Additional penance, beyond restitution, was routinely assigned by the confessor. What Urban reportedly promised was that those who went on crusade in a spirit of true contrition would earn by the dangers and difficulties of the journey the equivalent of a full penance for their sins. Those who took **crusade vows** earned condemnation if they failed to fulfill them and many thought "remission of sin" if they honored their commitment. What this may have meant to a warrior was absolution for any sins committed before the expedition. This is why the role of the pope as key bearer, the heir of St. Peter in the office of absolution, was a crucial component of crusading. *See also* **Martyrdom**.

INNOCENT III, POPE. (r.1198-1216). Eamon Duffy, in his history of the **papacy**, has identified Lothar of Segni, elected at the age of 37 in 1198 as the representative of the office at its "pinnacle" of influence and power. Innocent presided over the planning of the **Fourth**, the **Albigensian**, and the **Fifth Crusades**. He supported the establishment of the **Dominicans** and Franciscans. The encyclical letter of 1213 that called for the Fourth Lateran Council (1215) characterized it as a venue to consider the problems of retaking the Holy Land and reforming the church.

Among the accomplishments of this council were a definition of the doctrine of Transubstantiation, reform of the monasteries and of the secular church, which was to provide preaching and catechism in the language of the laity, and new requirements for lay people to attend Communion and Confession at least once a year. Innocent's intent was a thoroughgoing initiative to take place at every level of the church hierarchy, from the establishment of orthodox teaching on the sacraments to the improvement of record keeping in church courts. The problem of the **Cathars** in southern France needed to be addressed at all of these levels: accessible orthodox preaching, an edifying example through the lives of orthodox clergy, and service to the laity in their own language.

Innocent also directed the Albigensian Crusade, offering a crusade **indulgence** to participants and funding the effort with a tax on French clergy. He called for the Fourth Crusade in 1198 and offered similar financial support for it. He offered a **pilgrimage** indulgence for further campaigns in the **Baltics**, and laid the groundwork for the Fifth Crusade.

Innocent's successors, Honorius III (r.1216-27), and Gregory IX (r.1227-41) continued his work by formally establishing the Dominicans in 1216 and canonizing **Francis of Assisi** in 1228.

INQUISITION. The offices of the **Spanish** and Roman Inquisitions were not founded until 1480 and 1542. Before the 15th century, the inquisition was not an institution but a process, used by the episcopal authority to deal with local problems, and related to the idea of auricular confession promoted by the Fourth Lateran Council (*see* **Innocent III**).

The Inquisition, like the Crusade, owed its inception to the **papacy**. The first canon of the Fourth Lateran Council (30 November 1215) laid out a number of definitions that were meant to clarify orthodox positions critiqued by **Cathar** heretics. Episcopal administration of questions about these definitions could be used to identify and punish those who refused to accede to them. Because the Cathars rejected the efficacy of the sacraments, the definitions emphasized the importance of transubstantiation, baptism, and marriage. Canon three laid out the penalties for heresy, primarily excommunication, which cut the convicted person's ties to church, family, and livelihood, as all oaths were dissolved and association with the guilty was forbidden. These canons clarified and strengthened procedures and penalties already in place.

Pope Innocent III also adapted existing procedures to identify and punish important clerics: the *accusatio*, which made the accuser subject to the penalty if the accused was not convicted, and the *infamatio*, which allowed the accused to secure acquittal if he could find witnesses who would vouch for him. Both procedures could easily be turned against the accuser by a wealthy and influential defendant. Innocent adapted these precedents by devising a process of evidentiary hearings called the *inquisitio famae*.

Pope Honorius III (r.1216-27) inherited the Cathar emergency and the **Albigensian Crusade**. Under his leadership canon three of the Fourth Lateran Council was incorporated into the law code of the **Holy Roman Empire** in 1220. The precedent for the canon and its introduction into imperial law was the Roman code of 287, which punished Manichean heretics with confiscation of goods, forced labor, and for the leaders, death (usually by burning) or the tearing out of the tongue.

This institutionalizing of **canon law** took place alongside the confirmation of local practices against heresy by papal legates. Pope Gregory IX's (r.1227-41) legate Cardinal Romanus legitimized procedures that had evolved during the crusade in southern France against the Cathars. In every parish and diocese, panels of laymen and clergy were to report regularly on suspicions of heresy. These reports were to be processed by local bishops, or papal legates when available, aided by **Franciscan** or **Dominican** friars licensed by the pope to help with this work. Under Romanus, witnesses participating in the *inquisitio famae* received anonymity, and the obligation of all to report heresy was enforced with the penalty of excommunication. Those heretics who repented only after capture faced life in prison. Those who refused to recant faced death. A local procedure developed in Rome which divided the confiscated goods of the convicted among the accusers, those who arrested the suspect, and municipal projects such as repair of town walls.

One of the "inquirers" into heresy, who was backed by the bishop of Hildesheim in a series of prosecutions licensed by the pope in 1233, commented that those who were falsely convicted of heresy and burnt were **martyrs**. By implication, this idea lifted the guilt that might be felt by those who had conducted unjust prosecutions or at least failed to protest against them.

All of these individual practices would eventually influence canon law. Constants in these early procedures were long-standing canonical conventions limiting the right to hear cases to the episcopacy and forbidding those in holy orders from participating even marginally in the actual punishment, which had to be carried out by a secular power. The basic flaws inherent in the procedure were the assumption of guilt that hampered the defense of the accused and the failure to record and register the hearings. The first notaries were used to try to remedy the latter defect in 1237. Inquisitors such as Geoffrey d'Ablis, Bernard Gui (c.1261-1331), and Jacques Fournier left records produced between 1308 and 1325 which have been widely used for the history of heresy. The most well-known is Fournier's record of the evidence gathered at the town of Montaillou in southern France, near Toulouse.

Lay enthusiasm for either the heretics or the orthodox preachers played a role in the success of either in particular districts. The murder of a Dominican inquisitor based in Milan, Peter of Verona in 1252, turned public opinion against heresy. Pope Innocent IV canonized Peter in 1253 and promoted his cult, but more importantly, he wrote a detailed list of instructions for the prosecution of heresy in May of 1252. Torture, which previously could not be used by ecclesiastical courts, was licensed in the pursuit of heretics. In 1253-54 the pope launched a series of crusades against heretics in northern Italy, and increased his reliance on Franciscans licensed as inquisitors. Italy was divided into eight districts for the prosecution of heresy, while in France from the 1240s large-scale inquiries of thousands of residents were carried out in districts where heresy was believed to be strong.

ISLAM. A term used to describe **Muslim** civilization in general, embracing a variety of political organizations, as well as belief systems based on the Quran. In reference to the medieval period, the word is used to designate all governments dominated by followers of **Muhammad**. The use of the word is similar to that of **"Christendom,"** in that it implies a coherent and effective empire where none actually existed. In that sense Islam denotes a culture or an idea rather than a political or religious unit.

Muhammad died in 632, having conquered Mecca from his base in Medina. The conquest of Arabia followed. Muslim advance caused the fall of Syria in 636, **Egypt** in 642, the Sassanid Empire of Persia (**Armenia**, Iraq, and Iran) in 650, and Khurasan (or Khorasan, eastern Iran) in 674. An attempt on **Constantinople** failed in 717. The **Mahgrib** (Mahgreb), the region of Africa north of the Sahara, stretching from Egypt to the Atlantic (parts of Libya, Tunisia, Algeria, and Morocco) was conquered, along with Spain, by 711. The central Asia (northeast of the Oxus River called Transoxiana) border was pushed to the Caucasus Mountains and the Indus River in the same century. This entire area formed "the Islamic world" tied together by the Quran, the education in Arabic that allowed full access to it and to the ruling class, and the political imperative to enshrine the precepts of Muslim belief in law.

ISLAMIC LAW. The Quran, the prophet's revelations, and the hadith, the traditions describing his life, were translated into practice in the *sharia*, or "path leading to the water (life)." This was law, systematic codes of behavior derived from God's words and the actions of **Muhammad**. Two schools of law were founded in **Baghdad** by Abu Hanifa (d.767) and Ahmad ibn Hanbal (d.855), the Hanifa, and the Hanbali. Two others developed at Medina: the Maliki from Malik bin Anas (d.795), and the Shafii, developed by one of his disciples. In the Middle Ages all four more or less recognized each other as authoritative, but each became prominent in different regions: the Hanifa in areas dominated by the **Abbasid** and **Ottoman** dynasties, the Hanbali originally in Iraq and **Syria** and eventually in Arabia, the Maliki in northern Africa, and the Shafii in **Egypt**, southeast Asia, and east Africa.

-J-

JACOBITE CHRISTIANS. Jacob Baradaeus (c.500-578) was a peripatetic saint, born near **Edessa**, who traveled throughout the **Byzantine Empire** to ordain priests and bishops for the persecuted sect of the Monophysite Christians in Syria. The word Jacobite was used for the Syrian church after a church synod in **Nicaea** in 787, to distinguish it from other forms of Monophysite belief which developed in **Jerusalem, Antioch, Alexandria,** and **Constantinople** after 451. The original disagreement was about the theological definition of the nature of Christ. Attempts to reconcile various definitions failed at the Council of Chalcedon in 451. Persecutions of the Monophysites by emperors of Byzantium resulted in regional churches grouped around the cults and ideas of holy men like Jacob. Pillar saints following the ascetic example of St. Simon Stylites (c.389-459) continued to be found in Syria through the crusade period, and are representatives of Jacobite spirituality.

Like the **Copts** and **Nestorians**, the Jacobites were outlawed as schismatics under Greek Orthodox rule. The Nestorians escaped to Persia (Iran) but the Jacobites seem to have been the majority of the inhabitants of Syria before the Arab conquest. After 658 they had the same rights as other **Christians** under **Muslim** rule, and were even allowed to do missionary work in Mesopotamia and Iran. They were less easily accepted by the Turks and Crusaders who arrived in the 11th century. European Christians were not at first able to distinguish between Muslim and Christian inhabitants of the **Levant**, and they were suspicious of even **Greek** Orthodox believers, but by the early 12th century, they seem to have been at least coexisting with the Jacobite church. Hulagu, **Mongol** conqueror of **Baghdad** and **Damascus** by 1258, also seems to have respected the church's right to exist, at least after the initial horrors of Mongol conquest. After 1295 Mongol conversion to **Islam** led to massacres of Jacobite Christians in northern Syria and Mesopotamia. Monasteries and libraries belonging to the churches were lost. The Jacobites continued to exist as a heavily taxed minority under **Ottoman** rule.

JACQUES DE VITRY. (c.1170-1240). Jacques/James was educated in Paris and ordained a priest in 1210. He served as a regular canon in the church of St. Nicholas of Oignies in the diocese of Liège in 1211-16. In 1213 he preached the **Albigensian crusade**, and in 1214 was with a party of crusaders at the siege of **Toulouse**. He then preached the **Fifth**

Crusade and was elected bishop of **Acre** (r.1216-27). He accompanied the crusade to Damietta and wrote an account of the expedition in letters to Pope Honorius III. By 1228 he had resigned his office in Acre to become auxiliary bishop of Liège. He was made cardinal-bishop of Tusculum in 1228 or 1229. His various writings (sermons, letters, narratives) are an important source of information for the early 13th century.

JAFFA. Jaffa, a commercial port mentioned in both the Old and New Testaments, was critical to supplying the **Latin Kingdom** and especially crusader **Jerusalem** after 1099. It became the base for a crusader county and was held by **Guy of Lusignan** when **Saladin** conquered the Latin Kingdom in 1187. King **Richard I of England** regained the city during the **Third Crusade**. In 1197 it was retaken by **Islam** and held until the **Fourth Crusade**, when the Europeans regained control from 1204-68. The city became part of **Mamluk Egypt** under Sultan **Baybars I** in 1268.

JAMES OF VITRY. *See* **Jacques**.

JAZIRA. The area between the Tigris and Euphrates Rivers, a region that is today part of northern Iraq, northeastern Syria, and southeastern Turkey. *See* **Aleppo**.

JERUSALEM, DESCRIPTION AND HISTORY. Jerusalem is situated about 35 miles from the Mediterranean coast in the foothills of the Judaean mountains, about 2,500 feet above sea level. The Old City, today bounded by 16th-century walls, is about the same size as the walled crusader Jerusalem of the medieval chronicles and **pilgrim** guides. The city at its greatest extent sat on two hills, **Mount Zion** and Mount Moriah (**Temple** Mount), and was served by only one water source, the Siloam Spring. In crusader times Mount Zion was outside the city walls. Jerusalem's location was not particularly suited for commerce, and population growth was possible only by expanding the water supply with reservoirs and cisterns. Both water and wood, also lacking in this location, offered supply problems for Europeans in taking and then holding the city. Food was supplied by rural villages and farmland surrounding Jerusalem.

Roman Jerusalem was conquered by Persia in 614, recaptured in 628 by **Byzantium**, and conquered by **Islam** in 638. Under **Fatimid** rule many public buildings were constructed, including the Dome of the

Rock and the al-Aqsa mosque on the Temple Mount. **Seljuk** rule from 1073-98 produced little construction, but when the Fatimids again took the city before crusader conquest in 1098-99, they strengthened the city wall. They also expelled the **Christian** population to the surrounding countryside, probably saving their lives from the crusader massacre of the city's inhabitants in July of 1099. From 1229 until 1239, and again from 1241 until 1244, European control of the city was granted by treaty with the ruling **Muslim** powers of the region, and subject to restrictions that had been negotiated in each case.

Medieval estimates on numbers are not normally accepted as reliable by scholars, and there have been a variety of estimates of the population of the city. Most sources agree that the city was depopulated after the crusader massacre, and especially when the forces of the **First Crusade** completed their pilgrimage and returned to Europe. Technically, both **Jews** and Muslims were forbidden to reside in the city during crusader rule, but some exceptions seem to have been made, possibly at the price of heavy taxation.

The building program of the Europeans during the period 1099 to 1187 is all the more impressive, given this lack of manpower. Dozens of churches, but also money exchanges, markets, hospices, housing, streets, and defense works were constructed during the crusader period, many of which survived reconstruction under Muslim rule. Medieval visitors to the city describe steep and narrow streets, in some cases covered by stone vaults with windows to let in light and air. Two-wheeled hand carts rather than larger conveyances drawn by animals had to be used to move goods to the city's several markets. By about 1150 the population of the city may have reached 30,000, including settlers from all over Europe and the **Levant**, from a multitude of Christian sects.

Under both Muslim and Christian rule, the city was divided into "quarters" to accommodate various religious groups. Under Muslim rule before 1099, there were literally four: for Muslims, Jews, **Armenians**, and Christians. When Muslims and Jews were expelled from the city by the crusaders, the divisions multiplied into districts more or less dominated by the patriarch, the **Hospitallers**, the Syrian and Armenian Christians, the German Hospital, and the **Templars**. *See* **Copts**; **Jacobites**; **Military Orders**; **Nestorians**.

From 1099 until 1187 the city was the political center of the crusader **Latin Kingdom** of Jerusalem, and the site of many of the chief pilgrimage destinations in the Holy Land. The most important of these was the Church of the **Holy Sepulchre**, built over what Christians have believed to be the sites of the crucifixion and resurrection of Christ. Medieval

European maps pictured this spot as the center of the world, and control of this preeminent shrine was the base of the authority of the **Latin patriarchs of Jerusalem**. Under the crusaders, the city had a royal palace, a mint, and a treasury. Under Muslim control, it had little political importance and did not serve as a capital, but for both, a municipal organization and services for pilgrims were well-organized and fairly sophisticated.

JERUSALEM, LATIN KINGDOM OF. *See* **Latin Kingdom of Jerusalem.**

JERUSALEM, LATIN PATRIARCHS. The patriarchs (or bishops) had seniority among the clergy of the **Latin Kingdom** and frequently acted as advisors or regents to the king. They controlled the preeminent shrine of **Christendom**, the **Holy Sepulchre**. Their role in the coronation, and relationship to the kings in terms of primacy of authority, were hotly disputed in the early days of the kingdom.

According to arrangements made with the **Byzantine** emperor as the **First Crusade** passed through **Constantinople**, any **Greek** territory recaptured from **Muslim** control was to be returned to the empire. New fiefs carved out of Muslim territory were to be held from the Byzantine emperor. By the time the army reached Jerusalem, the Byzantines had, in the crusaders' opinion, forfeited claim to it by withdrawing military support. The clergy traveling with the army elected one of their number, Arnulf from the village of Chocques in the diocese of Thérouanne, as Patriarch of Jerusalem. He had accompanied Duke **Robert of Normandy** on crusade as his chaplain. Arnulf had been appointed ancillary papal legate by Pope **Urban II** in 1096. When **Adhémar of Le Puy** died in 1198, Arnulf was the remaining legate. Upon his election, he expelled all eastern Christian clergy from the shrine of the Holy Sepulchre, and replaced them with Western Europeans.

Daimbert of **Pisa** presided over Arnulf's suspension and replaced him as patriarch. He established four **Latin** bishoprics in what had been the Greek patriarchate of **Antioch**: **Edessa**, Tarsus, Mamistra, and Artah. In 1100 the Greek patriarch of Antioch was expelled and replaced with a Western European. Gibelin of Arles and later Fulk of Tyre completed arrangements for the ecclesiastical sees of the kingdom.

Gormond of Piquigny, in conjunction with King **Baldwin II**, convened a church council at Nablus in 1120. The council was called to respond to a series of natural disasters: earthquakes, plagues of locusts, and famine. The crusaders interpreted these events in the light of similar occurrences in the Old Testament, deciding that God was angry with them. The council responded by creating a code of **canon law**, regulating morals in the kingdom.

Heraclius, the last patriarch of the kingdom before its fall in 1187, led a fund-raising and recruitment tour to Western Europe in 1184. His preaching was so effective that the court of King **Henry II of England** was reduced to tears, but aid did not arrive until the **Third Crusade**, beginning in 1189. The patriarch has taken partial blame for the succession crisis that occurred during and after the reign of King **Baldwin IV of Jerusalem**, since it was he who crowned Sibyl and **Guy of Lusignan** in 1186. He took over the defense of Jerusalem in 1187, persuading Balian of **Ibelin** to direct the defensive operations against **Saladin**, and offering himself as hostage in the eventual ransom of the poor when the sultan took the city. He joined Guy of Lusignan at the **siege of Acre** in 1189 and died there in 1190.

Latin patriarchs and their reigning dates include: Arnulf of Chocques (1099, 1112-18 [suspended 1115-16]); Daimbert, archbishop of Pisa (1099-1102); Evremar of Thérouanne (1102-08); Gibelin of Sabran, archbishop of Arles (1108-12) and papal legate; Gormond of Piquigny (1118-28); Stephen, abbot of St.-Jean-en-Vallée in Chartres (1128-30); William of Messines, prior of the Sepulchre (1130-45); Fulk, archbishop of Tyre (1145-57); Amaury of Nesles (1157-80); Heraclius (1180-91); Ralph (1191-94); Aymar the Monk, archbishop of Caesarea (1194-1202); Soffred, cardinal of Sta Prassede (1203); St. Albert Avogadro of Vercelli (1205-14); Ralph of Mérencourt (1215-24); Gerald of Lausanne, abbot of **Cluny**, bishop of Valence, patriarch (1225-39); Robert of Nantes (1240-54); James PantaLeón (1255-61, later Pope Urban IV); William of Agen (1262-70); Thomas Agni of Lentino (1272-77); Elias of Perigueux (1279-87); Nicholas of Hannapes (1288-91).

JERUSALEM, SIEGE OF. Estimates of numbers on either side at the siege of **Jerusalem** in 1099 vary. According to some accounts, there were 40,000 **Muslims** in the city, and the **First Crusade** besiegers numbered from 1,200 to 1,500 knights and 12,000 to 20,000 foot soldiers. Certainly the crusaders were outmatched and operating without a supply line in hostile territory. Steven Runciman, in his classic account of the siege, contents himself with saying that the city was adequately garrisoned and that the approaching Fatimid relief force was large. The army that arrived outside Jerusalem had left Europe in 1096 and lost a considerable number of combatants on the journey, especially at the

siege of Antioch. Bohemond of Taranto remained there to consolidate his hold on it, and **Stephen of Blois** had deserted during that siege, so attrition combined with disease and want as well as battle to weaken the crusade. On 7 June 1099 when the crusaders arrived outside the walls of Jerusalem these factors were exacerbated by the intense heat.

Jerusalem's curtain wall was protected by projecting towers, notably the Tower of David citadel on the western side. Ditches, rough terrain, and in places an outer wall added further obstacles to reaching the curtain wall. The defenders had poisoned the wells outside the city and cut nearby timber to make construction of **siege weapons** more difficult. In spite of these precautions the crusaders built towers, a battering ram, rolling and portable shields, catapults, and scaling ladders. William of Embriaco arrived from **Genoa** to assist in the building. His ships had been captured and scuttled, but he brought tools, nails, ropes, and expert carpenters to the siege (*see* **Caffaro**). A local Syrian Christian helped locate timber several miles away. Water had to be carried in from distances of up to 6 miles.

On 8 July a penitential **pilgrimage** was staged from **Mount Zion** to the **Mount of Olives**, harried by displays of derision from the Muslim garrison on the walls. The European assault beginning on 14 July focused on supporting two siege towers, commanded by **Raymond of Saint-Gilles** and **Godfrey of Bouillon**. Chronicle description puts the middle of Godfrey's tower at the height of the walls, and the top at 50 feet to cover an attempt to cross over an improvised bridge with missile fire (stones, incendiaries). On the 15th Godfrey's tower was close enough to the walls near Herod's Gate for a fierce contest with whatever either side could find to throw. **Robert of Normandy** and **Tancred**, nephew of Bohemond of Taranto, aided from below, while other contingents kept the defenders busy on the whole circuit of the defenses. Godfrey's men were successful in taking his section and bridging the walls by about 9 a.m.

Tancred's troops scaled the walls and headed for the **Temple** Mount. The gates of St. Stephen and Jehoshaphat opened to the army, which proceeded to sack the city and massacre the inhabitants with an abandon that has created a lasting memory of this siege in Muslim history. Jean Flori suggested in his history of **Peter the Hermit** that the ferocity of the crusaders can be explained by their expectation of the Apocalypse in the wake of the conquest of Jerusalem. What happened instead was that their stunning victory at the Holy City was followed by the equally impressive rout of the Egyptian relief force near **Ascalon** on 12 August. The army returned, laden with spoils, to Jerusalem on 13 August.

JERUSALEM, SYMBOLIC. Crusading is often defined as armed **pilgrimage** to Jerusalem, for medieval Europeans the symbolic center of **Christendom**, the place of Jesus Christ's death and resurrection. The city has been equally significant to **Jews** as the center of ancient Israel and location of the **Temple** of Solomon; and to **Muslims** as one of the chief holy places of **Islam**, the location of the Dome of the Rock, a shrine built to honor **Muhammad**'s Night Journey. From the vantage point of believers of all three religions it is possible to see Jerusalem as the eventual site of the Last Judgment, making apocalyptic expectations a recurring theme in political decisions.

JEWS, JUDAISM. Like the terms **Christian** and **Muslim** the word Jew is as problematic as it is descriptive. All three terms refer to major world religions which include diverse communities often at odds with each other about authority, scriptural interpretation, and the boundaries of orthodox belief. All three terms were used by medieval people to refer not only to members of a religious group, but to members of a perceived ethnic or political group as well. "Jew" is arguably the most problematic term of the three for those studying the crusade period. There were political realities behind the ideas of **Christendom** and **Islam**, but there was no territorial base for Judaism. Even in Spain and the **Levant**, where Christian and Muslim were neighbors, they could meet at a territorial boundary as crusaders or participants in **jihad** and retreat when the battle was over. By contrast, the Jews were a stable presence within both Christian and Muslim societies that at times seemed threatening.

Many Western Europeans never traveled the Mediterranean to see a Muslim state, but communities of Jews lived among them. The few places where the reader will meet Jews in this volume will be places where they were persecuted. *See* **Spanish Inquisition** for laws which isolated and stigmatized Jews; and **Emicho of Flonheim** for violence against them that was legitimized by ideas drawn from biblical texts.

In Kenneth Stow's history of the Jews as an *Alienated Minority* in medieval Europe, he emphasizes some foundational differences between Jewish and Christian society. Medieval Jews differed from Christians in that they did not develop a societal structure based on a warrior nobility and a clerical class set apart from merchants and peasants. Jews were similar to medieval Christians in that they based their personal and public ethics on the interpretation of sacred texts, some of which were shared between the two groups. In the same way that Christians tried to limit their contact with Jews by laws prohibiting intermarriage and the participation of Jews in civic life, medieval Jews tried to limit their contacts with Christians. Polemic on both sides created threatening stereotypes. Professor Stow traces the eventual expulsion of the Jews from Europe as a result of the inability of Christian secular powers to integrate them into society, rather than as a result of a war of the church on the Jews.

Only medieval Spain had a Jewish population that was over one percent of the general population. Jews lived mainly in small communities (never more than 1,500 even in urban centers) near the Mediterranean Sea. They were expelled from England in 1290, from France in 1306 and 1394, from Spain in 1492, from various German territories starting in the early 15th century, and from **Sicily** and southern Italy by 1541. By 1500 they lived mainly in central and eastern Europe.

The myth of the Jews as an organized enemy of Christian society was expressed in theological terms. It seems to have arisen from their continued presence within but critical of Christian polities. They were accused of the murder of Christ, or assigned a role in various schemes of the Apocalypse. In the same way that Christians demonized Muslims during struggles for control of Mediterranean trade or Spanish territory, Jews were isolated and accused of crimes as a prelude to expulsion and confiscation of property.

From the second century A.D. when both Jews and Christians were persecuted by the Roman state and rivals in a search for legitimacy, influential Christian writers such as Origen (c.185-250) conflated the Jewish religious observance of the Sabbath with the worship of Satan. Quaint as such an accusation may seem, it was a powerful force in the development of anti-Semitism. The accusation of the inversion of Christian worship is a reaction to Jewish difference from or opposition to Christian society. It was normally accompanied by accusations of sexual perversion, the poisoning of community wells, ritual murder, especially of children, or attacks on a Eucharistic host, which express the same opposition or threat. For a Muslim rejection of Jews as a result of their opposition within a religious polity, *see* **Murabit**; **Muwahhid**. For Jews in the context of Christian heresy, *see* **Albigensian Crusade**.

JIHAD. An **Islamic** term usually translated "holy war," meaning "struggle" for holiness on a personal as well as a societal level. The idea of jihad is central to early **Muslim** history, stemming from the military/political career of **Muhammad**. The classical theology of jihad was worked out in the ninth century, based on many injunctions from the

Quran and Hadith. The greater purpose was spiritual, the establishment of justice on earth, with conversion of the world as a secondary goal.

The obligation to join the struggle was incumbent on every believer. Even conquered nonbelievers participated in the sense that they were allowed some freedom of religion as long as they did not transgress the laws of the Muslim state, and often at the price of higher taxes than Muslim citizens. The victory of Islam over the "House of War" was inevitable, a time at which all would be invited to believe in the truth, and even those who did not would be protected under Muslim rule.

According to this classical definition, a treaty between Islam and any enemy power was not legally possible. A truce might be arranged for the cessation of warfare for a short period, not to exceed 10 years. The pious ruler was expected to make at least one expedition a year against the infidel (unbeliever). In practice, even in the medieval period, various Islamic states coexisted with foreign powers, or even allied with them. Legal theory after the 10th century kept up with practical considerations by softening the division between the House of War and the House of Islam. By the 12th century, **Saladin**'s legal advisor could allow for a treaty with the infidel in the public interest. Throughout this period, initial spiritual jihad against one's baser self was seen as essential to success in the lesser military jihad against the external enemy.

In the medieval sources, the word jihad could be used to describe war against another Islamic force, for instance to depict the wars between the Shia **Fatimid** dynasty of **Egypt** and the Sunni **Seljuk** commanders of Syria. It does not denote war against Christians necessarily. The Crusades, often characterized as a unique phenomenon in Europe, were viewed in the wider context of the ongoing history of the "House of War" by contemporary Muslim writers.

JOHN OF BRIENNE. (c.1170-1237). Brienne was a fief of Champagne (*see* **Henry of Champagne**). John's father and grandfather were crusaders, along with enough other relatives that the family of Brienne can be compared with other families such as **Coucy**, **Montferrat**, the counts of **Flanders**, etc., for whom crusading was a tradition. John was titular king of the **Latin Kingdom** of Jerusalem (r.1210-25) by virtue of his marriage to Maria, the daughter of **Conrad of Montferrat** (d.1192) and Isabel of **Jerusalem** (d.1205). Isabel was the daughter of King **Amalric I** of Jerusalem.

John's wife Maria, through whom he had a claim to the Latin Kingdom, died in 1212, leaving an infant daughter called Isabel II or

Yolanda. Through his daughter John had a continuing claim as king or at least as regent.

John led the party of native barons who wished to accept the offer of the **Ayyubid** sultan of **Egypt** to exchange Jerusalem for Damietta during the **Fifth Crusade**. His experiences in this expedition, where St. **Francis of Assisi** attempted to preach the gospel to the sultan at Cairo, apparently made a deep impression on John, who had been educated by the Cistercians of Clairvaux (*see* St. **Bernard**). John would choose to die in the habit of a Franciscan monk. He forfeited his claim to Jerusalem in 1225 when he married his daughter Isabel to **Holy Roman Emperor** Frederick II in an attempt to secure the emperor's assistance. Frederick acted immediately on Isabel's claim, leading the **Sixth Crusade** (1228-29), which briefly regained Jerusalem by treaty. Meanwhile, Isabel died in 1228, leaving her claim to Jerusalem to an infant son, Conrad.

John retreated to Italy, where he was made marshal of the papal army in Apulia. In 1229 he was offered the regency for the **Latin Empire** at **Constantinople**. The young heir, Baldwin II, of the house of **Flanders**, was to marry John's daughter Mary by his second wife Berengaria of Castile when they both came of age. John came to Constantinople in 1231, where he was crowned and the marriage was celebrated. John died there in 1237, unable to make much headway in the war to block **Greek** reconquest of the Latin Empire.

JOSAPHAT. (*Jehoshaphat* or the Kidron Valley). This was an area outside the east wall of **Jerusalem** below the **Temple** Mount. A seasonal stream, called the *Torrens Cedron*, marked the neighborhood of several **Christian** shrines. Hermit caves shared the valley with the burial ground of **knights** who fell in 1099 at the crusader conquest of the city. The valley also contained the Grotto of the Agony at Gethsemane, Job's Well, and the church of St. Savior. St. Mary of the Valley of Josaphat, a **Cluniac** Benedictine abbey, was an important **pilgrimage** shrine from 1099. The chapel was built in 1112 on the supposed site of the bodily Assumption into heaven of the Virgin Mary.

The abbey of Josaphat was able to accumulate considerable property holdings in both the Holy Land and Europe, due to gifts from pilgrims. Two knights who had traveled with **Godfrey of Bouillon** on the **First Crusade** were buried at the abbey. Queen Melisende of the **Latin Kingdom** was buried in a chapel of the church in 1161.

-K-

AL-KAMIL. (d.1238). Al-Kamil Muhammad, governor of **Egypt** (1202-18), became sultan upon the death of his father **al-Adil** in 1218. His position was contested, however, and he was forced to flee the **siege** of Damietta that was under way as the second stage of the **Fifth Crusade**. (For the opening campaign at **Acre**, *see* **Ayyubid** dynasty; **Guy of Lusignan**; **Conrad of Montferrat**.)

His flight scattered his army, and the crusaders moved into position before the city unopposed. Fortunately the relief force that had been traveling with his father from Syria arrived to assist him. The two **Muslim** armies, reassembled, were unable to dislodge the crusaders, and orders were sent to dismantle the defenses of Jerusalem, so that it could not be held by the Europeans if they managed to take it. **Saladin**'s fortifications in Jerusalem were imposing, and the citizens responded to this decision by fleeing to other strongholds in Syria in March of 1219 as the work commenced.

In November of 1219 the garrison of Damietta surrendered the city and moved to Mansura. The Syrian forces departed to defend their own territory. Each side idled until 1221, except that al-Kamil worked to create fortifications at Mansura. In August of 1221 the armies of Syria returned just in time to help al-Kamil defeat the crusader attempt to take Mansura. The Europeans had several times turned down an offer to trade Damietta for quite a bit of the old **Latin Kingdom of Jerusalem,** including **Ascalon**, **Sidon**, and Tiberias.

In October 1227 a new force of crusaders landed in Acre (*see* **Sixth Crusade**). The leader of the European forces, who had not yet arrived, was **Holy Roman Emperor** Frederick II, a canny politician who had made an informal arrangement with al-Kamil to stay out of what he hoped would become a local engagement with the ruler of **Damascus**. Relations were strained among the Ayyubid, whose goals were not tied to Jerusalem so much as they were to the integrity of Egypt-Syria and its expansion into Mesopotamia and **Armenia**. Al-Kamil was willing to offer **Christian** access to Jerusalem in exchange for pressure on Damascus to submit to Egypt's authority.

The army at Acre took **Sidon**, the walls of which al-Adil had dismantled in 1197, and started to rebuild its defenses. In August of 1128 al-Kamil arrived with the Egyptian army to meet Frederick II for their negotiations. He took Jerusalem and Hebron under his own control and settled the army at Nablus. This was as much a threat to Damascus, whose governor normally controlled these areas, as it was to the crusaders. On 7 September Frederick arrived, and he became, for the moment, the sultan's first priority. Al-Kamil used the crusade to pressure Damascus into ceding him direct control of Palestine and Transjordan. In February 1229 he signed a treaty with Frederick which outraged Europe and the **Levant**. Muslim and Christian sources do not agree on the details. Frederick was to get a secure route from Acre to Jerusalem, including many villages along the way, the city itself (although its defenses were not to be rebuilt). Muslims living in the city were to depart, but a garrison would remain there and the Muslim villages surrounding the city would be protected. The **Temple** area, the site of important **Islamic** shrines, would remain in Muslim hands, but Christians would be allowed to pray there. The treaty confirmed the crusaders' conquests at Nazareth (1204) and Sidon (1227).

The effect of these negotiations was to so undermine Ayyubid solidarity that al-Kamil took the Egyptian army to Damascus in April of 1229. By mid-June the suburbs had been burnt and the sultan's army was at the city walls. A truce was finally agreed upon that left Damascus in control of half of Palestine, including Jerusalem. Al-Kamil was then free to use Damascus as a base from which to impose obedience on Syria. Having done so, he moved on to Amida and the Tigris River area, Mesopotamian conquest being his long-term goal. In 1234 he attacked the Rum **Seljuk** Empire on the **Anatolian** plateau. In the event this campaign was a costly disaster, which led to another expedition against the victorious Seljuks the following year and the razing of **Edessa**. Once again the sultan was forced to retreat, this time because of the rumor of the approach of the **Mongols**. He was again involved in a campaign to subdue Syria when he died of dysentery in 1238.

KERBOGHA. (d.1102). Turkish ruler of the city and region of **Mosul**.

KILIJ ARSLAN. (d.1107). *See* **Iconium**.

KITBUGHA. **Mongol** commander killed at the battle of Ayn Jalut by **Baybars I**, **Mamluk** sultan of **Egypt**, in 1260.

KNIGHTS. Knights were a class of mounted warriors, normally supported by land and/or revenue granted in return for military service. Usually they were expected to equip and train themselves at their own expense. For active service there was normally an annual limit (usually 40 days) after which they might demand additional payment.

The types of arrangements made between fighting men and their overlords could vary considerably, but medieval armies were normally expected to "live off the land" while on campaign, and to take **weapons** and other valuables during or after a battle. The expectation that crusade armies would purchase supplies while crossing **Christian** territory placed an unusual financial burden on these expeditions. Violence against **Jews** in the Rhineland and Greeks in **Byzantine** territory seems to have been exacerbated by the cost of the expeditions and the difficulty of supplying the armies.

Those who farmed, labored, engaged in trade, or trained for the church were subject to different societal obligations and were, for instance, judged in a court of "burgesses" for laborers and merchants, or in an ecclesiastical court. Within the class of knights there was an additional hierarchy based on wealth: the tenants-in-chief, the barons, and the lesser knights, who in some cases were mercenaries. *See also* **Cavalry**; **Chivalry**.

KOMNENUS. *See* **Comnenus.**

KONYA. *See* **Iconium.**

KRAC DES CHEVALIERS. Krac was one of the largest and most famous of the many crusader **castles.** It was built in stages from **Muslim** fortifications after **Tancred** regent of **Antioch** captured it in 1109. It belonged to the count of **Tripoli** by 1112 and then after 1142 to the **Order of St. John in Jerusalem** (Hospitallers). The ruins stand on a spur of the Jabal an Nusayriyah Mountains in what is now southern Syria, dominating the plain between the port of Tripoli and the Orontes River.

The concentric castle was built on a spur of rock 2,100 feet above the surrounding plain that offered a sharp gradient on three sides. On the fourth side the attacker had to negotiate first a triangular outwork, then a steep ditch, an outer wall, an inner moat, and beyond the moat a talus (or sharp slope covered in rubble). Above this last barrier loomed the inner keep, set uphill again from these surrounding defenses. These defenses evolved during a number of building phases, and especially after the earthquakes of 1157, 1170, and 1202.

Estimates put the number of defenders Krac could hold at from 2,000 to 6,000 men. The castle survived **Saladin**'s month-long **siege** of it in 1188, and defenders held out through repeated Muslim attacks until 1271. In that year **Mamluk** Sultan **Baybars I** laid siege to the castle in

March, with the assistance of the **Assassins** and the emirs of Homs and Saone. The garrison was small, but held out for over a month as the attackers drove them back to the fourth and final line of defense. The Hospitallers were tricked into surrendering the castle by a forged letter from their commander at Tripoli. Their lives were spared as a result and they were allowed to escape under safe conduct.

KURDS. This is a designation for over 20,000,000 people who share a historical ethnic and cultural identity, but have never possessed a territorial state. "Kurdistan" at its greatest extent is land shared by Turkey, Syria, Iraq, Iran, and the former Soviet Union, centered on Lake Van.

Kurdistan is a crossroads between Europe and Asia. The three Kurdish kingdoms which existed in the 10th and 11th centuries in this region were destroyed by the **Seljuk Turkish** invasions of the 11th century. For the crusaders, the chief impact of the Kurds came through **Saladin** and the **Ayyubid** dynasty, which ruled **Egypt** and Syria from 1171-1250. This Kurdish dynasty was destroyed by the **Mamluks** in **Egypt** and the **Mongol** invasion in the **Levant**. In 1515 a pact between Kurdish leaders and the **Ottomans** created 17 principalities that operated autonomously in local affairs. Kurdish independence movements in 1839 and 1847 were put down by Ottoman, British, and German troops.

There are three major dialects of Kurdish, which can be written in either Roman or Arabic script. Traditional Kurdish culture is nonliterate. The chronology and mechanism of their conversion to **Islam** is unknown, but in the Middle Ages they were Sunni **Muslims**, as are the majority of them today.

-L-

LATIN. This term was sometimes used to refer to residents of Western Europe, where the official language of church and state was Latin. *See* **Arab; Frank; Greek.**

LATIN EMPIRE OR KINGDOM OF CONSTANTINOPLE. *See* **Constantinople, Latin Kingdom of.**

LATIN KINGDOM OF JERUSALEM. The crusader kingdom was based at **Jerusalem** from 1099-1187, and based at **Acre** from 1187-1291. After 1197 *see also* **Cyprus**. After 1192 the crusader territory established by a truce with **Saladin** is sometimes called the Second Kingdom or the Kingdom of Acre.

The territory the crusaders took was divided into four principalities or counties: Jerusalem, **Antioch, Edessa** (*see* **Second Crusade**), and **Tripoli**. Within the kingdom of Jerusalem there were four major fiefs: **Sidon, Jaffa-Ascalon, Transjordan,** and Galilee. There were also lordships based on fortresses, such as Kerak, and ecclesiastical domains, such as **Ramla**.

At its broadest extent, the crusader territory stretched along a narrow (from 50 to 70 miles across) strip of coast for 400 to 500 miles from the Amanus Mountains to the Sinai Desert. Its population in 1187 has been estimated at 600,000, of whom about 140,000 would have been Western Europeans. After the **Third Crusade**, the Latin Kingdom consisted of a strip of coast from **Tyre** to Jaffa until the last crusader stronghold fell to the **Muslims** in 1291. Modern estimates of the mounted military power available to the kingdom by the time it was lost in 1187 have ranged from 300 to 700 knights and 5,000 sergeants.

During the period of the first kingdom, 1099-1187, Jerusalem contained a municipal government, the institutions of a medieval kingdom, and the court of the patriarch, the highest ecclesiastical authority in crusader territory. Some participants in the **First Crusade** disputed the institution of a monarchy, arguing that the kingdom should depend on the **papacy**, with the patriarch serving as legate, in imitation of the organization of the crusade itself. The **Byzantine** emperors claimed that any territory captured by crusaders should be either returned to or held from them.

The office of king was in effect hereditary, but always subject to the approval of the tenants-in-chief, who on several occasions influenced the succession. The High Court of the kingdom served both an advisory and a judicial function. It had jurisdiction in civil and criminal cases over the aristocracy, while the lower court under the viscount dealt with commoners. The church court, headed by the patriarch, had jurisdiction over all clerics, including monks and members of **military orders**, and infractions of **canon law**. The laws of the kingdom and the taxes collected by the royal officers were kept in the church of the **Holy Sepulchre**.

The royal and city officials included the seneschal, in charge of finances, the treasury, and garrisoning fortresses, who could also convene and preside over the High Court. Next was the constable, head of the army and royal security, and the marshal, with special responsibility for the comfort of the king's household. The chamberlain and butler looked after the household's finances and wine, respectively, while the chancellor was a cleric who issued royal documents or charters.

The king of Jerusalem controlled a large area of royal demesne: about half the major fiefs in the kingdom depended directly on him. All of the crusader ports were under his control. The royal mint was a monopoly, and the king collected taxes on **Beduin** tribes, non-Christian residents, and **Muslim** trade.

The majority of the population of the crusader kingdom was Muslim or eastern rite **Christian**, and these faiths were tolerated by the Western European minority. A poll tax was charged on non-Christians. There were restrictions, variously enforced, on Muslims living in urban centers.

The kingdom's laws and customs survive only in treatises written after 1187. The *Livre au Roi* dates to the first years of the 13th century. The anonymous *Livre des Assises de la Cour des Bourgeois* dates from Acre in the mid-thirteenth century. John of **Ibelin**/Jaffa's treatise was written sometime before his death in 1266. In 1369 John's treatise was accepted as normative by the High Court of the Kingdom of Cyprus, and a commission added updated material to it. All of these treatises set out law and precedents for the Latin Kingdom, list fiefs, and establish rituals for coronations and also trial by battle, which remained the normal method of settling disputes. They are not law codes so much as advice on the rules for conducting litigation, and they say as much about the preoccupations of their 13th-century authors as they do about the realities of the 12th-century Latin Kingdom.

For kings of Jerusalem *see:* **Godfrey** (1099-1100), **Baldwin I** (1100-18), **Baldwin II** (1118-31), **Fulk** (1131-43), **Baldwin III** (1144-63) [Baldwin's mother, Melisend, acted as regent from 1143 until 1151 when her son came of age and contested her rule], **Amalric I** (1163-74), **Baldwin IV** (1174-85), **Baldwin V** (crowned 1183, died 1186), **Guy** (1186-92), **Conrad of Montferrat** (1192), **Henry II of Champagne** (1192-97), Amaury of **Lusignan** (1197-1205), **John of Brienne** (1210-25).

In 1225 John of Brienne's daughter Isabel married **Holy Roman Emperor** Frederick II. She died, leaving an infant heir to the throne of Jerusalem, Conrad, in 1228. Conrad left his claim to his son and namesake Conrad (or Conradin) in 1254. The latter died in 1268. Neither of Frederick's heirs had ever visited the **Levant**. The title reverted to the heirs of Amalric I's daughter Isabel through her marriage to Henry II of Champagne. King Hugh II of Cyprus, one of her descendants, succeeded to the title in 1258. By this time the cities of Tyre and Acre essentially operated more as independent communes than as parts of a centralized monarchy. **Charles of Anjou** tried to enforce a claim to the kingdom in 1277-85. The fall of Acre in 1291 put an end to any territorial reality that might have lent substance to the idea of the Latin Kingdom.

LEÓN-CASTILE. Alfonso VI (r.1065-1109) inherited from his father, Fernando I, a Spanish principality about the size of England, the largest of the emerging **Christian** kingdoms in Iberia. He exercised authority over **Navarre**, and collected tribute from the **Muslim** principalities of Saragossa, Toledo, and Granada.

Hoping to secure military help in the **Reconquista** from southern France, he married first Agnes, daughter of Guy, the duke of Aquitaine who had fought the Muslims in Iberia in 1064. When Agnes died in 1078 Alfonso married Constance, daughter of the duke of Burgundy. He also made a series of donations to the influential French Benedictine monastery of **Cluny**. By 1085 he had conquered Toledo, a larger city than all the towns of León-Castile combined, the conquest of which doubled his domains. He therefore became a threat both to his Muslim and Christian neighbors, and made his kingdom the target of Muslim resurgence for the next thirty years. His response to the immediate Muslim threat was to call for help to Western Europe. A major French force in fact arrived in 1087 and fought with no particular results for a year.

Alfonso attempted to secure his kingdom for his heirs by marrying his daughter to the heir of **Aragon**, and died at Toledo in 1109 in expectation of another of a long series of Muslim attacks on the city. His only son and male heir had been killed in battle with the northern African **Murabit** dynasty in 1107-08. The Murabit had taken southern Spain from Gibraltar almost to the Pyrenees. They had been called in against the Christians by the Muslim principalities, but had soon become the enemies of both and collected territory in their own right.

Between 1111 and 1117 the peninsula erupted into war among various Christian powers for Toledo: **Portugal**, León-Castile, and Aragon. Urraca, queen of León (d.1126), and her husband Alfonso of Aragon were alternately reconciled and at war, each of them claiming hegemony as "queen of all Spain" or "emperor." Portugal was in its infancy, having been created out of territory held by Alfonso VI as he made provision for Urraca's half-sister Teresa. In 1109, when her father died, Teresa had inherited an ill-defined administrative unit based at the town of Porto. Her dynasty joined the other emerging Iberian principalities in a struggle for territory and legitimacy that overshadowed the contest with **Islam**.

Alfonso VII (r.1126-57) of Castile allied himself against Portugal and Aragon by marrying the daughter of Raymond Berenguer III of **Barcelona** (r.1097-1131) in 1127. In 1135 he had himself crowned emperor, and was able to impose homage on Aragon-Barcelona and Navarre. During the **Second Crusade, Genoa** joined Alfonso VII in the siege of Almeria. Afterwards, in 1153, Alfonso continued to build a base of European support by marrying his daughter Constancia to the Second Crusade leader, King **Louis VII** of France. Louis visited **Santiago de Compostela** the following year, increasing Alfonso's prestige, if not his military reach.

In 1154-55 a papal legate visited Iberia, held a council at Valladolid, and called for the renewal of the Reconquista. Alfonso captured several strategic points that summer, but was unable to convince the other Christian powers to join him in any major engagement. As a result he made a treaty in 1156 with the local Muslim ruler of Valencia, by which ibn Mardanish became his vassal and ally. By the 1150s a newly powerful dynasty from the **Maghrib**, the **Muwahhid**, began to make conquests in Iberia. He died as their conquest of Almeria itself, hard-won during the Second Crusade, was being consolidated. Upon his death his kingdom was divided between two of his five sons: Sancho III (r.1157-58) of Castile and Fernando II (r.1157-88) of León. Sancho's sudden death at 25 left his three-year-old son, Alfonso VIII (r.1158-1214), and a dangerous regency. This instability in the most powerful of the Christian Iberian kingdoms combined with the distractions of the second power, Aragon-Barcelona, to temporarily halt the Reconquista in the mid-12th century. What continued to favor the Christian cause was less active conquest than the passive weight of immigration and settlement.

LEVANT. The Eastern Mediterranean region, also referred to by Western Europeans as *Outremer*, and including **Asia Minor**, the Middle East, and **Egypt**. See the introduction for the implications of Roman control of this region, and also the entry for the **Byzantine Empire**.

LITHUANIA. *See* **Baltic Crusades**.

LOUIS VII, KING OF FRANCE. (r.1137-80). Five successive kings of France (Louis VII in 1148–Philip III in 1270) went on crusade, but Louis VII is the only one who actually reached **Jerusalem**. His crusade was a failure, in spite of the scale of the preparations and the support of the greatest cleric of the age, St. **Bernard of Clairvaux**. *See also* **Second Crusade**.

LOUIS IX, SAINT, KING OF FRANCE. (r.1226-70).

In 1244 the last **Ayyubid** ruler of **Egypt** occupied the Holy Land and Syria, taking and sacking **Jerusalem**. At the battle of La Forbie or Harbiyya, near **Ascalon**, the remnants of the crusader kingdom allied with the ruler of **Damascus** to fight Egypt and lost. News of this disaster reached Europe, and in response, King Louis IX took the cross. This crusade, sometimes called the Seventh, was a French attempt to take Egypt's capital as the key to defeating the new military power in the region and regaining access for **pilgrims** to Jerusalem.

Louis's preparations are notable in the history of **naval warfare**, and to some extent explain the failure of this crusade. In 1246 he made arrangements with a number of individual **Genoese** contractors to lease or construct a fleet of 33 two-masted sailing ships. He also ordered from six shipbuilders 20 oared galleys to be used for landing **knights** on beaches. He made a similar order in Marseille. His nobles made their own arrangements for building and leasing further transports, and other ships were provided by the nobility of the **Levant** when they met Louis in **Cyprus** in 1248. Apparently concerned by the insufficiency of the force, Louis tried to lease or order more boats during the winter of 1248-49, creating a force of 120 large sailing ships and 80 small boats for the conquest of Egypt.

On their way to Damietta, they were hit by a storm that scattered and may have sunk some of the fleet. Small boats for landing were especially vulnerable and may have been the hardest hit. They were needed for the shallow entrance to the Nile, which was strewn with sandbanks. Both the **Fifth Crusade** and Louis's troops were forced to land on the west bank, where the river was deeper. Even there the sailing ships could not come in, but had to be anchored three leagues from shore. Many of the galleys and ship's boats could not come in any closer than the king's, and he had to disembark in water that reached his chest.

In June of 1249 Louis's army took Damietta but was forced to remain there for six months. In June the task of taking sailing ships up the narrow section of the Nile to Cairo was made impossible by the rising current of the flood season. By 20 November the flood season was ebbing but the sailing ships had to make way with variable winds and a narrow, shallow passage. The boats had to be hauled at various points to contend with these difficulties. The sources indicate that the Nile had been blocked at one point during the Fifth Crusade by sinking a half-dozen galleys in it. During both expeditions, the lack of appropriate shipping contributed to European failure.

On 22 November 1249 the last **Ayyub** sultan died as the crusader army left Damietta for Cairo. A group of relatives and advisors called in the general of the **mamluk** forces, and the main Egyptian army met the French at Mansura in late December. Part of the **Muslim** forces consisted of war galleys built for the shallow waters of the Nile. Louis's army was outnumbered and their supply line to Damietta under constant threat. In April the French king ordered a retreat, but he was captured and the army surrendered on 6 April 1250. Now Damietta was to be surrendered by the French in return for their freedom, and the king himself was to be held for ransom. During the negotiations, the mamluk general was assassinated, kicking off a struggle for power within Egypt that was not resolved until 1260/61.

Louis meanwhile was released and moved on to the coastal cities still held by the remnants of the crusader kingdoms, directing the repair of their fortifications. He had only about 1,400 knights, but these were enough to focus some attention upon him in the struggle for supremacy between Ayyubid Syria and Mamluk Egypt. Each Muslim power hoped to add the small but possibly decisive weight of the French troops to their side of the contest for power. Louis had left a number of his troops in Egypt, and needed the small leverage this situation gave him to negotiate for their release. In 1252 he accepted the Egyptian offer of the return of all prisoners and the revocation of the ransom he still owed for his own release. He formally allied with Mamluk Egypt against Ayyubid Syria. The three armies met at **Jaffa**, but the Muslims settled down for a year of negotiations. Louis used the time to refortify the city.

In 1253 the Mamluks and Ayyubid came to an agreement that did not include him. On the other hand, after a brief skirmish with his bowmen at Jaffa, the Ayyubid based at Damascus moved on for a feint at **Acre** and a more serious attack on the tiny garrison at **Sidon**. The townspeople were massacred and the Damascenes moved on. Louis finished his work at Jaffa and moved on to refortify Sidon. He did not return to France until 1254.

King Louis's interest in the Holy Land predated this crusade, as is evidenced by his construction of **Sainte-Chapelle**. He died in 1270 in the course of a failed crusade to Tunisia, once part of the **Muwahhid** empire but in the latter half of the 13th century an independent kingdom with good diplomatic and trade agreements with **Christian** Europe. Algeria and Morocco were too much at odds with each other to come to the aid of Tunis, but the Mamluks responded to the call for help, and a volunteer force was formed as well with Muslim refugees from Christian Spain. On 18 July 1270 the French fleet was allowed to land at Carthage (*see* **Maghrib**), in the expectation that they would be easier to defeat there with ground forces than resisted at less fortified places along the coast. Louis died in August, but was replaced by **Charles of Anjou** (d.1285) king of **Sicily** and Naples, and the English and Scottish troops under Prince Edward of Wales (later king of England as **Edward I**, 1272-1307).

THE LOW COUNTRIES. *See* **Flanders**.

LUSIGNAN. This family, like that of the counts of **Flanders** or the **Coucys**, made a tradition of crusading. They were from Poitou, but were vassals of the kings of England. Hugh VI came to the Holy Land in 1101 and died at **Ramla**. Hugh VII accompanied the **Second Crusade**, and Hugh VIII was captured by **Nur al-Din** in 1164 and died without being ransomed. *See* **Guy of Lusignan** for an entry on the brothers Guy and Amaury, kings of **Jerusalem** and **Cyprus**.

-M-

MAGHRIB, THE. (or *Maghreb*). The Arabic *al-Maghrib* means "the West," and is used to refer to the Mediterranean coast of northern Africa from **Egypt** to the Atlantic. The Romans had called their province of Tunisia and the city of Carthage "Africa" (to the Arabs "Ifriqiya"). The Romans lost Africa to the Vandals, but the East Romans, or **Byzantines**, reconquered it by 533, basing a fleet at Carthage. By the 690s the invading Arabs had built a fleet and destroyed Byzantine power in northern Africa and Carthage, which they replaced with the city of Tunis. **Berber** chiefs west of the new **Islamic** territory and nomads from the northern Sahara region tried in vain to oust the new conquerors.

For at least a century after Arab conquest, Islam was confined to the coastal cities taken by the conquerors, who did not push effective control into the countryside as long as the local chiefs paid tribute. Arab farming estates were staffed with Africans captured or purchased as slaves from the Maghrib and from the central and southern Sahara. Berbers were "recruited" into the army the same way. Because as soldiers they profited from Arab expansion, they converted more easily to Islam in this setting, and became an important component of the army in its invasion of the Iberian Peninsula in 711.

By the beginning of the 10th century the majority of the population of Egypt and the Maghrib had converted at least nominally to Islam. Believers had economic and cultural advantages such as lower taxes, and access to education and government. Resentment of Arab dominance led many in Africa to convert to Shia or Kharijite **Muslim** beliefs, both of which rejected the authority of **Baghdad**. The **Fatimid** dynasty was founded in the central Maghrib by believers claiming descent from **Muhammad**'s daughter Fatima. By 950 the Fatimids had conquered northern Tunisia and Algeria. Their goal was to rival the **Abbasids**, however, so in 969 they took Egypt and declared it independent of the caliphate. It is as rulers of Egypt that they had the most influence on crusade history. Their most ardent supporters in Syria were the Ismailis, or **Assassins**. Their Berber lieutenants in northern Africa succeeded them there as the Zirid dynasty.

Resistance to Arab assumption of superiority led to the rise of the Fatimids, but also to the prominence of two Berber tribes involved in the profitable Sahara trade: the Sanhaja in the west and the Tuareg in the central and southern regions. The Lamtuna branch of the Sanhaja Berbers also maintained a long-standing rivalry with the medieval African kingdom of Ghana (north of modern Ghana). A Sanhaja chief returned from his **pilgrimage** to Mecca in 1036 with a Berber scholar of the Quran, Abdalluh ibn Yasin (d.1059). Ibn Yasin's efforts to increase literacy, knowledge of the Quran, and a more dedicated practice of Islam had long-term effects on the Sanhaja, which would reverberate in the battles of the **Reconquista** in Spain.

In the short term, the scholar founded a *ribat*, or a community for religious retreat, in a fortress on the Mauritanian coast. The students who followed him there were called *al-Murabitin* (**Murabit**) or, in Spain, the *Almoravids*. During the 1040s, the Lamtuna joined the Murabit, and after 1055 began to expand their effective control into Morocco. After 1059 the stretch of territory between Ghana and the northern coast was too large for one ruler to dominate. Yusuf ibn Tashufin led the extension of Murabit power into Spain.

The Murabit were in their turn challenged by the **Muwahhids** (or *Almohads*), who succeeded in uniting the Maghrib under one Berber dynasty for the first time, from 1147 until 1269. During their reign literacy increased in Arabic through the teaching of the Quran, and northern Africa participated in the advances of Muslim civilization. After 1269 the Maghrib again fragmented into competing kingdoms, making it possible for the forces of the Reconquista to take first Ceuta in 1415, and then other northern African ports in the 15th century. *See also* **Charles of Anjou; Louis IX.**

MAMLUK. A Mamluk was a military slave, usually of Turkish origin, who was carefully trained to fill important military and political posts within **Islam.** As non-Muslims, Mamluks could not live within Islamic society except as slaves. They were trained, educated, converted, and then freed to take up political authority over other believers. Their relationship with their owner resembled that of a child to a father, even after manumission, to the extent that they could in some cases inherit goods or offices from him.

MAMLUK DYNASTY. The dynasty which ruled **Egypt** from 1250-1517 was not so much one of blood as of succession within the caste or class of Mamluks. Its principal accomplishments were keeping the **Mongols** out of Syria and Egypt and ending the last remnants of crusader power on the mainland. After 1291 only the crusader kingdom of **Cyprus** survived.

After a period of instability lasting from 1249 to about 1260, the Kipchak (Qipchaq) Turk Mamluks succeeded **Saladin**'s **Kurdish** dynasty, the **Ayyubid,** in Egypt and defended the **Levant** from the Mongols. The most powerful of the Kipchak Turkish Mamluk rulers of Egypt was **Baybars I** (r.1260-77), and the pivotal event for his rise to power was his ability to resist Mongol invasion in 1260.

In general, Mamluk troops were more heavily armed than Mongol warriors, carrying not only the bow, arrow, axe, and club, but also sword, dagger, mace, lance, shield, and sometimes body **armor.** The larger Arabian **horse** was even more expensive than the small steppe pony to provide. Mongol troops relied more on mobility, the Mamluks more on training and skill.

The Mamluk dynasty was inherently unstable, due to a failure to create a succession process other than military coup. It was also unable to command the loyalty of **Damascus** and **Aleppo** for any length of time. Mamluk rule was not popular with freeborn Egyptians. Like the **Fatimids** and Ayyubid before them, they formed a foreign elite over the indigenous population. Estimates put Mamluk numbers at 10,000, to 4,000,000 or 5,000,000 Egyptians. Sayf al-Din Qalawun al-Alfi (r.1280-90) was pelted with garbage during his first public appearance in Cairo, even after offering its residents a tax break. To add to the new ruler's

150 • MAMLUK DYNASTY

difficulties, in 1282 a mixed Egyptian and Syrian army, while technically victorious, was decimated at the Battle of Homs against the Mongols. Sultan Qalawun was thereafter hampered in any other endeavor until he had rebuilt his military forces. Qalawum, like other sultans of Egypt, supplemented regiments of free men with Mamluks purchased from the Mongol slave traders of the Crimea. Unlike the Ayyubid and Baybars I, he did not favor Kipchak slaves but bought men originating from any place between Europe and Mongolia. By the end of his reign he had succeeded in building a larger force of royal Mamluks than any other ruler of the dynasty. He was able to take **Tripoli** just before his death in 1288, and to set in motion the conquest of **Acre** by Egypt in 1291 by arranging for the **siege engines**.

After his reign the Mamluk dynasty was chiefly occupied by an internal power struggle, in which sultan after sultan took office briefly, only to be assassinated by rival claimants to the throne. The most honorable death was strangulation, in which the blood was not shed. Other methods, such as beheading, bisection lengthwise or sideways, or crucifixion, were less honorable, and much used during this period of 1293-1310. Trials, which should have been required by Muslim law, did not take place, and the oaths of loyalty administered by each sultan were disregarded. These practices reflected not only the internal weakness of the dynasty, but also its nominal connection to Islam.

Technically, each new ruler of Cairo had to be accepted by the religious leaders of Egypt and Damascus. The unpopular Mamluk rulers were eager to win over the public with displays of public piety such as the patronage of religious institutions or a **pilgrimage**. They tried to establish Egypt's reputation as the intellectual center of Islam, and themselves as the protectors of Mecca and Medina. Mamluk rulers applied to religious leaders for *fatwas*, or formal legal opinions to justify campaigns against the Mongols, the crusaders, or other Muslim powers. One of the most influential spiritual leaders of the time, Ibn Taymiyya (1263-1328), whose ideas are still important to the concept of **jihad** today, had fled from the Mongols in 1269 to take up residence in Damascus. Ibn Taymiyya was a powerful critic of the Mamluk dynasty. His arrest could lead to a riot; his approval for one of their campaigns could legitimate it as jihad.

Damascus was always a center for political opposition to the Mamluks as well, making Syria a thorn in the side of the sultans. The situation was further complicated by the Mongol presence in Iran, Iraq, and the Crimea. In the late 1290s the Mongols of Iran saw their chance in the increasingly tense relations between Egypt and Syria. Their raids into Syria, which had been a problem since the 1250s, increased. The Mamluks, on their side, frequently interfered with Mongol control of Anatolia and Iraq. In 1299 the Mamluks were in Iraq, taking Mardin. The Iranian Mongol army retaliated with a plot to assassinate the Mamluk sultan. The two armies met near Homs in December of 1299. The Mamluks were defeated and the Mongols went on to take Damascus. The conquest was difficult to consolidate, due to the hostility of the Damascenes, and after several skirmishes, the Mongols were beaten decisively in 1303 and essentially withdrew from Syria.

An earthquake in 1303 destroyed much of Cairo and led to a major building program by the dynasty to restore canals, aqueducts, mosques, and other essential public works. The bubonic plague arrived in **Alexandria** in 1347 from Central Asia. The 1340s were a particularly turbulent time for the sultans, who were assassinated and replaced with bewildering rapidity, and also a time of economic crisis for Egypt. 1347, for instance, was a famine year due to a mild flood season and therefore insufficient irrigation. The numbers for losses of human and animal lives are unknown, but estimates put it at about a third of the population of Egypt and Syria. These losses were never recouped, because the bubonic plague, which seems to have lessened in its effects by 1349, was replaced by frequent outbreaks of pneumonic plague. Robert Irwin, in his history of the dynasty, estimates that there were 55 recurrences of plague between 1347 and 1517, 20 of which were of epidemic proportions. The army, and especially the Mamluk regiments which were the guarantee of the sultans' security, was among the hardest hit.

The sultans met these challenges by continuing to insist on hegemony over Syria and by using it as a base for the conquest of ports in Asia Minor. Treaties were made with **Venice** in 1355 and 1361, in spite of papal embargoes on trade with Egypt. These activities threatened Cyprus's livelihood, and caused it to make common cause with similarly beleaguered **Armenia** against the Mamluk threat. The crusade against Alexandria in 1365 amounted to little more than a week long raid. The attackers had plundered the city and headed for home before the relief force from Cairo could arrive. Hostilities continued on both sides until the Mamluks took Armenia in 1375.

The Mamluks were succeeded by the **Ottomans** in 1517.

MARTYRDOM. In the medieval **Christian** sense this term was used with the understanding that the act was an imitation of Christ's sacrifice. Medieval authors make a clear distinction between Christian and non-Christian voluntary deaths, categorizing the latter as the crime of "self-murder." While there was a range of contemporary opinion on what constituted "true" martyrdom, some components of the act were voluntary response to God's instigation, witness to the truth of the Christian religion, and an expectation of salvation/eternal reward as the result of the self-sacrifice. In this sense it was possible to see any orthodox Christian who died on crusade as a martyr by definition, since all crusaders took vows as a condition of their departure and wore the symbol of the **cross** to indicate that their actions were a witness to their belief. *See also* **Crusade Vow.**

MILITARY ORDERS. By the 17th century, historians of military orders were stressing the antiquity of their foundations, often dating them back to the beginning of the **Christian** era. More recent scholarly histories trace them to 1120, when medieval writers hailed the foundation of the **Templars** in **Jerusalem** as the beginning of a new kind of monasticism. The new orders were a response to the crusading ideal and the military situation of the crusader kingdoms. Manpower was a perennial problem, even though many Europeans came to fight for a season in the Holy Land between the official expeditions. The orders were particularly useful in wars of invasion, as the front-runners of conquest, where the Western Europeans were vastly outnumbered: the **Reconquista**, the **Baltic Crusades**, and attempted conquest of Byzantine territory after the **Fourth Crusade**. In settled Christian lands, they tended to create instability by rivaling their rulers. *See* **Teutonic Knights.**

Many orders, such as the **Hospitallers**, started as charitable organizations which offered care for the poor and sick, or housing for **pilgrims**. Long after their transition, they were called upon to care for the wounded on the battlefield in addition to other charitable functions. They attracted gifts from Western Europe to support their work in the Holy Land. In the same way that lay people might visit a monastery or participate actively in its good works, it became possible to support the military orders with gifts of land or revenue, or to join them actively for months or years on the battlefield. As the military orders developed, they gained enough property in Western Europe so that monasteries were established there as outposts of their main activities in the **Levant**. In 1291 when the crusader kingdom fell, the headquarters of the Templars, Hospitallers, and the **Order of St. Thomas** moved to **Cyprus.**

A typical monastic house in Europe contained several types of inhabitants: ordained clerics living according to a monastic rule, monks or canons living according to the monastic rule but not ordained as priests, and lay brothers, also obeying a variation of the monastic rule. Military orders contained primarily lay brothers, with a minimum of ordained clergy. They might hire mercenaries to augment the mounted **knights** and squires, or require military service from vassals on lands belonging to the order. Traditional monasteries and military orders both often included a sister house of women who might be devoted to the charitable aims of the institution.

In the Levant, the military orders often played a key role in specific expeditions or battles, but they were also important garrisons for **castles**, and were often given these outposts as bases for defense or incursion into enemy territory. It is estimated that the **Order of St. John**, for instance, held about 56 strongholds in the crusader kingdoms during the 12th and 13th centuries. Documentation for total numbers of men in any given order is difficult to come by. One report from 1255 puts the permanent garrison of mounted knights at **Krac des Chevaliers**, a Hospitaller **castle**, at 60. Another from the 1260s puts the garrison of Safed, a Templar castle, at 50 mounted knights, 30 sergeants, 50 mercenaries, and 300 archers. Alan Forey has estimated that at their peak, the combined orders in the Holy Land could field an army of only 300 brothers, along with unknown numbers of sergeants, foot soldiers, and mercenaries (*Military Orders*, pp. 69, 79). The monastic vow of obedience combined with superior training and discipline to make the troops of the orders elite forces whose influence went beyond their numerical strength. *See also* **Dobrin, Order of; Monreal; Order of St. Lazarus; Swordbrethren.**

MILITIA OF CHRIST OF LIVONIA. *See* **Swordbrethren.**

MONGOLS. The Mongols were Eurasian steppe warriors whose society was based on tribal relationships and a nomadic, pastoral life, and whose preferred method of fighting was mounted archery. In the 12th and 13th centuries their culture was based on a mixture of Shamanism, Buddhism, and **Nestorian** Christianity. Mongol imperial idealism divided outsiders into those who gave them unconditional loyalty, and those who refused to submit to what they believed was their divine mission to rule the world.

Temüchin, known as Jingiz [Chinggis, Genghis] Khan (1162-1226/27), founded an empire in central Asia and China that by 1231 included northern Iran. By 1219 the boundaries of this advancing empire had entered the territory of the Turks of Khwarizm (Khorezm, the Khwarazm-shah), near the Aral Sea. Russia was conquered by Batu (r.1237-42), and became the province of a Mongol power called the Golden Horde, based in the region of the Crimea. A Mongol army under Hulagu (d.1265) conquered the strongholds of the Iranian Ismailis or **Assassins** in 1256, took **Baghdad**, destroying the **Abbasid** Caliphate, in 1258, and moved on to take **Aleppo** and **Damascus** in 1260. Hulagu then withdrew to Azerbaijan, near Tabriz. An army of between 10,000 and 20,000 Mongols led by Kitbugha was defeated by the army of the **Mamluk** dynasty of **Egypt** at the battle of Ayn Jalut (Goliath's Well, near Nablus) in September of 1260. Kitbugha was killed and Syria reverted to Mamluk control.

The Mongol invaders split into several groups in addition to the main force in Mongolia and China. These included Hulagu in Mongol Iran and Berke of the Golden Horde, based in South Russia (1257-61). Berke and his successor, Mongke Temur (r.1267-80) formally allied with the Mamluks of Egypt, but the distances were too great for Egypt to play a significant role in the war between Berke and Hulagu that broke out in 1262. Berke converted to **Islam** in 1260, and commercial ties between Egypt, Syria, and the Golden Horde continued to be important. Both the **Genoese** and the **Byzantines** acted as middlemen in bringing Kipchak (Qipchaq) slaves and wood to Egypt. **Baybars** is said by some commentators to have replaced Islamic law with the Mongol code for the military classes of Egypt. In 1282 Abaqa, Mongol ruler of Iran (1265-82) sent an invasion force into Syria, but it was defeated at the Battle of Homs by a Mamluk army.

Recent scholarship on the Mongol army has emphasized its size (all Mongol males were enlisted) and relative lack of training. Bows and arrows were supplemented by clubs and axes. Some, but apparently not all, of the Mongol troops had swords and helmets. The tactic of using a number of units to outflank or exhaust the enemy by charging and then wheeling away in turn, shooting arrows in retreat, wore down the Mongol **horses** as well as the enemy, making it necessary to have several mounts for each warrior, or fresh regiments to send in when horses tired. The extent to which Mongols used the **weapons**, tactics, and horses of their conquered regions is unknown, but they were certainly apt at borrowing **siege** technology, for instance, when it suited them.

MONREAL. Alfonso I of **Aragon** (r.1104-34) attempted to create a **military order** roughly based on the **Templar** example in c.1124 as an aid in the **Reconquista**. Other more successful Spanish military orders were Calatrava, founded in Castile in 1158, and Santiago, founded in León in 1170, followed by Alcántara sometime before 1176. The first military order in Portugal, called Avis, was also established in or before 1176. *See also* **Mountjoy**.

MONTFERRAT. This was a family based at a marquisate in Piedmont, with a tradition of crusading, like the **Lusignans** or the **Coucys**. They were vassals of the **Holy Roman Emperors**, and participated in the **Second Crusade**. They were also kinsmen of Emperor **Frederick Barbarossa** and of King **Louis VII** of France, and therefore offered a powerful influence in Western Europe to the kings of the beleaguered **Latin Kingdom of Jerusalem**.

Piedmont was a lordship north of **Genoa** which included the towns of Asti and Turin. The members of the house of Montferrat, like other feudal lords, collected tolls on roads and other taxes on merchants going through their domains, in this case from Genoa to continental Europe. William the Elder, whose sons were to be caught up in the fall of the Latin Kingdom, was married to Barbarossa's niece and supported the emperor's rights in northern Italy rather than those of Genoa, or the other city-communes, or the **papacy**. However, in 1150 he swore loyalty to the commune of Genoa, including a promise to provide **knight** service and counsel, and to reside in the city for part of the year. He accompanied King Louis VII of France on the Second Crusade and died in the Holy Land in c.1188 after being captured by **Saladin** at the battle of **Hattin**. The backing of the Genoese would be crucial to William's son Conrad's bid for the crown of Jerusalem.

In 1175 the leprosy of King **Baldwin IV** of **Jerusalem** became apparent, and the High Court of the Latin Kingdom opened negotiations to marry the heiress to the throne, Sybil (d.1190), to William Longsword, eldest son of William the Elder. William arrived in October of 1176 with a Genoese fleet. He was married to Sybil in November, and invested with the counties of **Jaffa** and **Ascalon**. He died in 1177 of an undiagnosed illness, leaving his wife pregnant with the future **Baldwin V**. She married **Guy of Lusignan**. King Baldwin made **Reynald of Châtillon** regent to replace William at court.

In 1180 William's younger brother Ranier married the only daughter of **Byzantine** emperor Manuel **Comnenus**. This was the first time that a Byzantine princess married someone not of royal birth. In the same year Manuel married his ten-year-old heir to the youngest daughter of King Louis VII of France. The eldest surviving brother, **Conrad of Montferrat**, would eventually marry Isabel (d. 1205), who inherited the throne of Jerusalem.

In 1182 Manuel's daughter Maria and her husband Ranier were murdered as part of the coup d'etat of Andronicus Comnenus. Conrad was assassinated in 1192 after successfully negotiating his succession to the crown of Jerusalem. William the Elder's surviving son Boniface (d.1207), succeeded to the marquisate and took the cross in 1201. After the death of Theobald of Champagne he was the acknowledged leader of the **Fourth Crusade**. He was not elected **Latin Emperor** when the crusade took Constantinople, but instead founded his own kingdom of Thessalonika in 1204, marrying the widow of the Byzantine emperor Isaac Angelus, Margaret of Hungary. Her brother was Emeric I, King of Hungary (r.1196-1204), who offered a crucial alliance for the **Latin Empire at Constantinople**.

Boniface died in battle in 1207 as the Latins were trying to consolidate their conquests in the Balkans and Greece. His daughter Agnes had just married Henry of **Flanders**, who had became Latin emperor in Constantinople (r.1205-16) when his brother Baldwin was captured (1205). His son William IV led a crusade in 1224 to relieve Thessalonika. William was delayed in starting by illness and difficulties in recruiting men and funds. He received a loan from the Holy Roman Empire in return for pledging his lands at home. His death of dysentery in 1225 ended the crusade.

MONTFORT (CASTLE OF). The **castle** of Montfort, which the **Teutonic Order** built in 1227-29 between **Acre** and **Tyre**, was also the order's administrative center.

MONTFORT (SIMON OF). Simon IV (c.1165-1218), baron of Montfort (r.1181-1218), earl of Leicester and duke of Narbonne (r.1206-18) led the **Albigensian Crusade**. His eldest son Amalric inherited the struggle and his father's claims to territory he had won in the Midi until the council of Bourges, 30 November 1225, reinforced the judgments against Count Raymond VI of Toulouse (r.1194-1222) and his heir Raymond VII (r.1222-49). As a result of a number of factors including the decision of the council, King Louis VIII of France undertook leadership of the crusade in January of 1226.

MOOR. *See* **Arab**.

MOSUL. The city of Mosul is the center of a Mesopotamian region roughly corresponding to ancient Assyria, now part of Iraq. The city, now the third largest in Iraq, is situated on the eastern bank of the Tigris River, opposite the ruins of Nineveh. During the crusade period it was ruled by a series of Turkish emirs who were nominally loyal to the **Seljuk** sultan in Iraq.

After the fall of **Tripoli** to the son of **Raymond of Saint-Gilles** in 1109 the sultan of Iraq, Muhammad, proclaimed a **jihad** against the crusaders. Commissioned by the sultan as ruler of Mosul from 1108, Sharaf-al-Din Mawdud took up this call in 1110 with an attack on crusader **Edessa**. In spite of assistance from the other European rulers at **Jerusalem** and **Antioch**, the region surrounding Edessa was devastated. Mawdud assembled a new coalition of local **Muslim** powers against Edessa in 1111 but was distracted by a contest with Ridwan, Muslim ruler of **Aleppo**. He returned in 1112, harassing the inhabitants from April through June. The poverty of the city due to these attacks weakened it fatally. It was to fall to Mosul in 1144.

Mawdud allied with the ruler of **Damascus** to face King **Baldwin I of Jerusalem** in 1113 south of Lake Tiberias. The royal army was decimated and the Muslim forces raided the kingdom without opposition through the summer.

Mawdud was murdered in October of 1113 at Damascus, possibly by the **Assassins**, although some sources blame the ruler of Damascus, Zahir al-Din Tughdakin. Damascus made a truce with the crusaders in 1114 and allied with them in 1115 against Mawdud's successor. Muslim Damascus, Aleppo, and Mardin allied with Roger of Salerno, regent of Antioch, King Baldwin, and the European lords of Tripoli and Edessa against the Seljuk ruler of Mosul. The army of Mosul staged a false retreat, withdrawing from the field only to attack Roger's domains near Antioch. Roger was able to stage an ambush in his turn at Danith between Aleppo and Apamea. The Mosul Turks were routed. Three thousand were slaughtered and prisoners were divided among the allies.

The overwhelming defeat of Mosul resulted in the dissolution of this unlikely coalition. Roger's erstwhile ally at Mardin led a holy war against him in 1119. On 28 June Roger was killed at the battle of Darb Sarmada west of Aleppo. Mosul itself recovered under the rule of **Zengi**.

MOUNTJOY (CHURCH). The church of St. Samuel, on Mountjoy near **Jerusalem**, was one of two Premonstratensian houses founded in the **Latin Kingdom** of Jerusalem after Pope Innocent II commissioned the order to preach the gospel to the **Muslims** in 1131 at the council of Reims. The other was Sts. Joseph and Habacuc near Ramla. In the confirmation of their holdings issued by the court of King **Baldwin V** in 1185 two churches are listed that had been given to them in addition: St. John the Evangelist in Nablus, given by Queen Melisend (*see* **Fulk**), and St. Longinus at Jerusalem by King **Amalric**. For the role of the order of Prémontré in the crusades *see* **Gervase**.

MOUNTJOY (ORDER OF). Count Rodrigo Alvarez of Sarria was licensed by Pope **Alexander III** in 1175 to found the **military order** of Mountjoy. He was given land for the order in **Aragon** by King Alfonso II. Beyond the assistance a military order could give to the ongoing effort of the **Reconquista**, Mountjoy concerned itself with ransoming captives. Its rule was based on that of the Cistercians (*see* **Bernard of Clairvaux**). The order eventually acquired territory in Italy and the **Levant** as well. *See also* **Monreal**.

MOUNT OF OLIVES. The Church of the Ascension and an Augustinian priory were built by the crusaders to commemorate the ascension of Christ after his resurrection. The church contained a rock with a footprint believed to be Christ's. For this **relic**, *see* **Holy Blood**.

MOUNT SION/ZION. This area was inside the city walls until the rebuilding project of the 1030s. In crusader **Jerusalem** it was reached through the Mount Zion Gate for access to the Augustinian priory and church of St. Mary. On the slope of the hill was the site where Jesus was supposed to have been imprisoned, commemorated by a church dedicated to St. Peter.

The church and abbey of St. Mary marked the supposed site of the Last Supper. This site was also connected to two other important events: Jesus' appearance to the disciples after his resurrection, and Pentecost, the descent of the Holy Spirit to the disciples. The original **Byzantine** church was destroyed by the **Fatimids** in 1009, when the church of the **Holy Sepulchre** was pulled down. Some of the stones of St. Mary's may have been used in other building projects after the earthquake in 1033. The crusaders rebuilt it by 1130, creating an enclosure bigger than any of their other shrines except for the Holy Sepulchre. It contained what the crusaders believed were the table and foot-washing basin used at the Last Supper, as well as the tombs of St. Stephen, the first martyr of the New Testament, and the Old Testament kings of Jerusalem, David and Solomon. The convent and church were torn down after 1187, leaving the chapel of the Last Supper.

MUHAMMAD. (c.570-632). The revelation given to Muhammad was the last in a long series of communications from God that included material from the Hebrew Old Testament and the Christian New Testament. The "Seal of the prophets" received these messages in Mecca starting in 610 when he was 40. Persecution prompted his removal to Medina in 622, the first year of the **Muslim** calendar. Throughout his life the Prophet recited messages as he received them from God through the angel Gabriel. The Quran, in Arabic, is the untranslatable word of God. It is not subject to textual criticism. Muhammad's actions and words, compiled by his companions as the hadith, are more comparable to the Gospels than is the Quran. There can be no successor (caliph) to Muhammad as prophet, but only as religious leader and head of state. In some medieval states, these functions were split between a caliph or a group of teachers and the sultan, rather than being combined in one person.

MURABIT. Hispanized as *Almoravid* (1056-1147). One of the Moroccan tribal confederacies, the Sanhaja **Berbers**, unified Morocco under Yusuf ibn-Tashufin (d.1106) and crossed to Andalusia in 1086, where they annihilated the army of Alfonso VI of **León-Castile**. They returned in 1090 and conquered **Muslim** Spain. To crusaders their importance is concentrated in the Iberian Peninsula, but from their perspective their base in Africa was the source of their wealth and the focus of their policies.

In the 11th century Tunisia was a relatively prosperous monarchy under the northern African Zirid dynasty, nominally loyal to the **Fatimids** of **Egypt**. Another branch of the Tunisian royal house ruled eastern Algeria, which was similarly tranquil and based on agriculture and commerce, with urban centers and schools contributing to local culture. Morocco and western Algeria were more turbulent, fragmented by rivalries among local rulers, notably the tribal confederacies of the Zanata, the Masmuda, and the Sanhaja. In c.1039, Abdalluh ibn Yasin (d.1059), who had been educated in Córdoba, was called in by one of the Sanhaja chiefs to preach a purified Muslim belief and an interpretation of **Islamic law** that was based on the writings of Malik ibn Anas (d.795).

In 1048 the ruler of Tunisia made a definitive break with Shia Egypt. The Fatimids responded by giving troublesome nomadic **Arabs** on their eastern front a reason to move on: titular claim to northern Africa. In 1052 Tunisia and Algeria were invaded by these nomads, the tribes of Banu Hilal and Banu Sulaim.

By 1056 a number of groups coalesced under the Murabit dynasty, including the Sanhaja tribes and notably the Touareg people from the western and central Sahara region, as an alternative power to these invading forces. "Murabit" is derived from an Arabic word for a fortified community of men sworn to holy war. The Touaregs are sometimes referred to in secondary sources as the "veiled" Touaregs, meaning that the men of the tribe wore veils, presumably for protection in the harsh environment of the Sahara. These volunteers for holy war were steeped in the Malikite ideas taught by Ibn Yasin, which stressed strict adherence to the Quran and the example of the Prophet, and prohibited **Jews** and **Christians** from participating in government at the higher levels. The animosity towards the two older religions was for Europeans the outstanding characteristic of Murabit rule.

During the next three decades the Murabit united and consolidated their hold on Morocco, Ghana, and western Algeria. They were called in by the local Muslim rulers of Spain to fight against the Christian forces of the **Reconquista** in 1086. Alfonso VI of León had taken Toledo in 1085. The combined forces of Muslim Iberia and the Murabit, led by Yusuf ibn Tashufin, won a battle against Alfonso in October of 1086, but Toledo remained in Christian hands. Yusuf returned in 1089 and 1090 to attempt to oust the Christians, but the situation was complicated by the growing animosity between the Murabit and the Muslims of Spain. The Murabit turned on the Spanish Islamic kingdoms first, and used them as a base from which to inflict a number of defeats on the Christians. In 1093 Lisbon was lost, in 1097 Alfonso was again defeated at Consuegra, and in 1099-1102 Valencia was lost to the Murabit. By 1106 Yusuf was able to leave his son half of Spain, half of Algeria, and a united Morocco.

In about 1121 the Murabit, essentially members of the Sanhaja confederacy, were in their turn challenged by the Masmuda, one of the tribal confederacies that had traditionally rivaled them for power in the **Maghrib**. Resistance was centered in the central Moroccan part of the Atlas Mountains, and led by Muhammad ibn Tumart, who founded the **Muwahhid** (*Almohad*) dynasty. In 1147 their **jihad** against the Murabit had yielded them the capital, Marrakesh, and they moved on to replace their rivals in northern Africa and Spain.

MUSLIM. This word covers the multiple religious sects and sometimes political constructs dominated by followers of **Muhammad**. Only a very general overview can be given here, as a working guide to understanding basic political divisions.

It is important to see Muslim faith as responsive to Judaism, Christianity, and the culture of the ancient world. From the Muslim point of view, a belief in the Quran complements and completes the partial revelation of the divine order of each of these previous belief systems. Muslim believers were therefore free to investigate and use these earlier traditions, and where this freedom was embraced, it resulted in remarkable cultural and political advances. Christian Europe and **Byzantium** could offer neither the religious tolerance nor the scientific advancement that could be reached by Muslim society in the ninth through the 13th centuries. **Islam**, however, was no more a monolith than was **Christendom**, so there is considerable variation depending on which region is being studied. The early disagreements which created different sects and political structures focused on authority and leadership, as well as the degree of literalism with which the Quran was to be read. They were also very much influenced by regional differences among Muslim believers.

In general, the Arabic text of the Quran is regarded as the direct revelation of God to Muhammad, untranslatable and unique. This belief places fluency in Arabic in a privileged position in Muslim education and political life. The hadith are the actions and words of Muhammad, seen as a guide to right living, and evaluated both for moral consistency and the authority of the tradition by which individual stories are transmitted. The original Arab community of believers tended to form a ruling elite in conquered areas, and to be resented in consequence.

To simplify the ideological differences within Islam, the Shia looked for a legitimate replacement for Muhammad, a caliph related to the prophet who could combine the moral qualities of the religious leader with political oversight of the Muslim world. Sunnis saw the caliphate as a primarily political office, the role of which was protection for the community of believers, who were guided in religious matters by the religious scholars. In 632 A.D. the election of one of the prophet's companions to replace him displaced his cousin and son-in-law, Ali, who would have inherited the succession to the caliphate. There were regional factors as well as ideological ones: Iraq supported Ali against his opponents in Syria in the 650s. The Sunni believers, because they accepted the principles of election and majority consensus, were able to accept the line of Umayyad caliphs at **Damascus** (661-750) and **Abbasid** caliphs at **Baghdad** (750-1258).

The Shia rejected the election in favor of a hereditary succession, supporting Ali, which is the first division within Islam. The Shiites then divided among themselves over the question of the succession from Ali. The Twelvers, for instance, differed both from most Shiites and from the Ismailis over the succession from Ali. They believed that the twelfth in line from the true caliph had disappeared, and they waited for his return as Mahdi, who would bring justice to earth. The Ismailis believed in a succession that moved strictly from father to son, rather than being accessible to brothers in the same generation. For them, the legitimate line ran through the **Fatimid** dynasty of **Egypt**, which claimed its descent from the Prophet through his daughter Fatima. In 1021 a succession crisis in Egypt precipitated another split, between the Ismailis and the Druze; a slightly later split produced the Nizari (**Assassins**), and so on.

There were those who rejected the idea of the succession from either Muhammad's companions or from his family. The Kharijites (Khawarij), for instance, split from the Sunnis (657) in favor of a strict principle of election, based on both the spiritual and the political qualities of the potential leader and not limited to the original Arab community. For them, the other sectarian disputes still favored the family or tribe of the Prophet, and were exclusionary. Their egalitarian form of Islam was born in Khuzistan, between the Persian Gulf and the Caspian Sea, but became particularly powerful in northern Africa. Orthodox Muslims believed that the Quran could not be translated from the Arabic without grave insult to its meaning. This belief supported **Arab** supremacy in culture, education, and government. By contrast, until the 11th century, one of the Moroccan tribal confederacies claimed the validity of a Quran in the **Berber** language. The Berbers were also influenced, along with the rest of Islam, by the **Sufi** emphasis on purity and interior piety.

Within the orthodox or Sunni tradition and throughout Islam there is the practice of mysticism by the Sufis. The basis of mystical experience is a belief that it is possible to personally experience communion with God as a result of the Creator's immanence in the material as well as the spiritual world. The practice of or preparation for this experience is often one of a number of variations on practices of contemplative prayer and asceticism. Sufi belief, like other forms of mysticism, can be seen as a threat to both the establishment of orthodox doctrinal statements and/or a strict observance of **Islamic law**, in favor of the essentially nonrational and passive enjoyment of the vision of the deity.

One of the most influential Sufi writers was Abu Hamid al-Ghazali (d.1111). His autobiography, apologetics for the Sunni vs. Shia understanding of Islam, and response to the Muslim and Greek philosophers, established the primacy of revelation for the Muslim believer, with reason and experience playing a secondary role. Sufi belief is still part of the bedrock of Muslim culture, and was particularly prominent among the **Muwahhid** rulers of northern Africa and Spain.

MUWAHHID DYNASTY. This dynasty ruled the **Maghrib** from 1147-1269. In about 1121 **Murabit** dominance in northern Africa was challenged by the Harghi tribe of the central Moroccan part of the Atlas Mountains, who founded the Muwahhid dynasty.

Muhammad ibn Tumart (c.1080-c.1130) claimed to be the Mahdi, or divinely guided successor to **Muhammad**, and founded the Muwahhid ("the affirmers of God's unity," in Spanish *Almohad*) dynasty. The conquest of Tunisia, Morocco, and Algeria by his followers was well under way by 1147 and complete by 1160. Until 1230 their kingdom was the most powerful force in North African history since the Roman Empire.

Ibn Tumart was born in the Atlas Mountains but educated in **Baghdad**, where he came under the influence of the **Sufis**, **Muslim** mystics. He was a devotee of the ideas of Abu Hamid al-Ghazali (d.1111), "the most influential figure in medieval Islam after Muhammad" (Robinson, *Cambridge History of the Islamic World*, 217). Ibn Tumart was declared Mahdi by his tribe in 1128, when they went to war with the Murabit for control of northern Africa and Spain. They were able to unite all of northern Africa for the first time under a single **Berber** dynasty by 1160. They held off Norman **Sicily**'s attacks on the coast, and imposed a stricter version of **Islamic law** on Africa, by which even the People of the Book (**Jews** and **Christians**) were forcibly converted and women were secluded. Between 1163 and 1180 the Muwahhid empire was at peace and confident enough to enter into trade agreements with former enemies **Genoa** and **Pisa**. In 1195 they won a decisive battle against Christian Spain at Alarcos, but their real focus was a resistance to their rule based in the first instance in the Balearic Islands, but spreading to disperse their holdings in Tunisia, Morocco, and Algeria to local challengers.

The Muwahhid defeat by the forces of the **Reconquista** in 1212 at the battle of Las Navas de Tolosa is seen as a turning point in Spain. The real difficulty was internal to northern Africa, epitomized by six rival claimants to the throne between 1224 and 1236. By 1269 Muwahhid power was completely shattered, and northern Africa no longer had the cohesive force to serve as a base for a successful conquest of Iberia. The crusade of King **Louis IX of France** in Tunisia in 1270 makes little sense against this background, since by then the kingdom had excellent trade agreements with Christian Europe, and posed no immediate threat to it.

-N-

NAMUR. Count Henry the Blind (r.1136-96) ruled Luxembourg, Arlon, La Roche, and Durbuy along with Namur, and could raise an army of 250 knights. After his time the county was divided and was eventually taken over by the counts of **Flanders**.

NAVAL WARFARE. The crusades were as much about the importance of shipping and commerce in the Mediterranean as they were about religion. Increasing **Muslim** presence in shipping and trade was one of the factors that so alarmed the European powers about the spread of **Islam**. For instance, because of Muslim expansion into northern Africa and Spain, the Straits of Gibraltar were of strategic importance, along with islands that could be used as staging areas for invasion and supplies: the Balearic Islands, Corsica, Sardinia, **Sicily** for direct access to Europe, and **Cyprus** for the supply of crusades in the Holy Land. Ports such as **Barcelona** rose in the context of the struggle to control Mediterranean trade. The development of naval warfare is also one strand of the story of war and technology in this era. Beyond its obvious importance against enemy ports and in transport, naval expertise created a skilled labor force that could construct land **siege engines** as well as ships.

Navies in the modern sense of state-supported institutions training personnel and building ships for warfare did not exist in Europe before the 13th century. Boats were ordered for specific purposes, and typically owned by a group of merchants in "shares" or by a town commune or religious house. Medieval ships were constructed in small yards for local use, and hired or commandeered by states from merchant fleets. Ships could be built or ordered for particular expeditions as well, but time constraints were then added because of the lack of large, state-supported shipyards. Piracy was endemic to the Mediterranean, among and between **Christian** and Muslim powers. Crusade ideology was sometimes used to justify it.

For major and minor crusade expeditions, Western Europeans were supported during the crusade period by the Italian communes where the economy was based on commercial shipping, notably **Genoa**, **Pisa**, and **Venice**. On the Islamic side, **Alexandria** and Tunisia were particularly important ports, and shipbuilding technology was as advanced in the Muslim as in the Christian Mediterranean. By the late 11th century ships carrying 500 passengers and galleys powered by 140 oars could be built. Two-masted sailing ships in the following century ran about 200 tons, with some ports, such as Venice, able to field a battleship or floating "fortress" at 500 deadweight tons. Port towns in the **Levant** such as **Acre, Ascalon, Sidon, Tyre,** and **Tripoli** were hotly contested prizes. **Byzantine** power was concentrated in the land and sea walls of **Constantinople,** taken by Western Europeans with the help of the Venetians during the **Fourth Crusade.**

NAVAL WARFARE, FLEETS. In spite of the fact that from the **First Crusade,** European invaders were supplied by boat, and thereafter arrived by ship at the Christian-held ports in the Holy Land, local Islamic rulers were slow to build their own naval strength in response, preferring to concentrate on land forces to receive the intruders. Exceptions include the **Fatimid** dynasty of Egypt, whose fleet did offer some resistance to the First Crusade. There the evidence shows on paper at least an organized navy as an arm of the military, but there seem to have been endemic problems of supply and repair. By the 12th century that situation was only beginning to change. **Saladin**'s creation of an **Egyptian** fleet specifically for the Crusades in the 1170s is echoed by a similar effort by King **Richard I** of England during and after the **Third Crusade** in the 1190s. But Europeans themselves, dependent as they were on shipping for transport and supplies, were not well equipped for naval warfare at key moments in the 13th century such as the attack on Damietta by King **Louis IX** in 1248.

The difficulties in finding supplies and skilled labor are illustrated by the time lag between 1172, when Saladin decided to build a more effective Egyptian fleet, and the eventual results. To get access to necessary materials other than wood, he first had to make treaties with and buy supplies from his enemies, the communes of **Venice** and **Pisa.** Construction finally began in 1177. Two years later he had 60 galleys and 20 transports, 50 for defense of Egypt and 30 for attack on the 350 miles of coast held by the crusader states. Under the Fatimids, the supposed strength of the navy had been 70 galleys, but it is not clear that this was ever actually achieved. European numbers are equally difficult to come by. Estimates of European fleet size during the early crusades period average at about 50 ships. At Beirut in 1182 Saladin was met by 33 crusader galleys. The **Third Crusade** in 1191 is said to have brought 552 ships to the **siege of Acre.**

NAVAL WARFARE, PERSONNEL. The general medieval preference for battle on land added to the practical difficulties of creating a navy. One **Islamic** chronicler during the **Mamluk** period records that calling an **Egyptian** a sailor was an insult.

The men who rowed the galleys, for instance in the Italian city-communes, were not slaves. They were mercenaries, or citizens who owed military service, or in some situations, captives. Captives of Western European descent were normally sold for ransom or traded for political advantage rather than enslaved. Slavery resulted from war, and even then only **Muslims**, pagans, and heretics were enslaved. As enemies, they would not have been able to provide the mixed naval and fighting service expected of galley crews.

Using the galleys as a place of prison service was a 17th-century European practice rather than a medieval one. In the 13th century, most European galleys were powered by teams of two seated on a single bench, each wielding an oar. There was one deck, with very limited space below, and two triangular sails to take advantage of favorable winds. An armed galley carried about 140 oarsmen and 50 crew, all of whom would be expected to fight as well. A 500-ton ship used for cargo normally carried 100 men. "Armed," it carried several hundred.

In **Venice** before 1350 the 60 parishes that made up the city-commune selected crew by registering all men between the ages of 20 and 60 in groups of 12. The group of 12 drew lots to choose one to serve, and each paid him one lire a month to help meet his costs. He was responsible to provide his own weapons, but the government paid him another 5 lire a month. The **Doge**, or ruler of Venice, could close the port, or order all ships above a certain size to turn out for a military campaign. The ships would then sail in convoy under an admiral chosen by the Doge. But the discipline and decision making on board were relatively democratic, since all the crew were armed, and were normally citizens of the Republic. They had a right to load a certain amount of cargo without paying freight, and to bring their own supplies.

NAVAL WARFARE, WEAPONS. Very few detailed accounts of naval battles before the 13th century survive, so that while it is clear, for instance, that **horses** were transported on galleys designed with stern-quarter landing bridges, the details of their transport, and particularly the method of unloading them during a contested landing are largely unknown. One theory is that mounted **knights** were landed routinely in the 12th century, at least, and that fighting them head on was a losing proposition. Lashing galleys together to block a harbor or form a fighting platform is mentioned as having occurred, but would seem to offer insurmountable practical difficulties of maneuvering the ships against currents or attacks. The problems are not adequately addressed in the sources. The fatal flaw in using fire as a weapon is addressed: one should board a ship one has set on fire with great caution and with the wind. Otherwise there is a strong probability that the fire will spread to the attacker's ship as well.

The sea walls of **Constantinople** were gained by **Fourth Crusaders** crossing from the masts of assaulting ships by means of armored catwalks. **Weapons** suggested by later medieval manuals, but perhaps never used, include: burning tow soaked in oil, sulphur, or pitch; lime and dust to be thrown into the faces of the enemy; soft soap, launched in glass or ceramic containers so that it will break and make the enemy deck slippery; a battering ram with iron ends hung from the mast; holes bored into the hulls of enemy ships by divers; arrows and rigging hooks used so as to cut rigging and make holes in sails. The best position for attack was held to be trapping the enemy between your ship and the shore, or approaching him with your own ships in a half-moon shape, so that your flanks could surround him if he attacked your center.

European sailors used the crossbow, an improvement on the **Muslim** bow in this instance, while **Byzantines** and Muslims were more adept with Greek fire. Fighting ships, normally powered by oars in battle, could be fitted with **siege engines** such as the mangonel (a catapult) to throw Greek fire or stones. The use of these weapons on a galley led to very high casualties, and the reluctance of sailors on both sides to engage the enemy earns the disgust of the chroniclers pretty frequently.

Other popular methods of battle included using an old ship loaded with combustible material and set alight to destroy ships at anchorage. When the enemy was within range (200 or 300 hundred yards), longbows and various kinds of darts could be used. Once boarding occurred, personal weapons of the kind used on land came into play. The most effective weapons a medieval ship could carry were its personnel. An "armed" galley was first and foremost one that carried fighting men in addition to the oarsmen.

In the 15th century, cannon, whether mounted on ships or deployed against them from the shore, became the deciding factor in naval battles. The fall of Constantinople to the **Ottomans** in 1453, for instance, was the result of the use of shore batteries by the Turks against the **Venetian** war galleys. The victory spurred Ottoman interest in developing its naval power, and gave it the facilities at Constantinople to do so. By 1470 the approach of the Ottoman navy, at least according to a Venetian opponent, looked like a floating forest. There were reportedly over 300 ships. Technology (better artillery, better construction) and trained personnel became very much a concern according to the observers on both sides. For more on medieval naval powers, *see* **Genoa**; **Pisa**.

NAVARRE. Sancho III founded the medieval Spanish **Christian** states on his death in 1035 by leaving **Aragon** to Raimiro, his eldest son, and the kingdoms of Castile and **León** to a younger son, Fernando. In 1065 Fernando divided his estates among his sons, leaving Castile to Sancho and León to Alfonso. Sancho was assassinated in 1072, leaving Alfonso to reunite his father's conquests and use them as a base from which to take **Muslim** Toledo in 1085. *See* **Reconquista**.

NAZARETH. The crusader archbishopric was based at a shrine church, rebuilt over the fifth-century **Byzantine** structure by 1107. The city was important to **Christians** as the site of the early life of Christ. The church of the Annunciation contained shrines supposed to enclose the house in which Christ was brought up and the bed he used as a child. There was also the burial place of St. Joseph, the place where Mary sat to receive the angel, and the spot on which Gabriel stood to announce the birth of Christ and receive the submission of his mother. All of these supposed sites of biblical events were enclosed in a grotto on the north side of the church below the level of the nave, or main aisle of the church. A chapel in the church was supposed to be the birthplace of Mary. The tomb of the Virgin was restored by the crusaders before 1161 at the supposed site of Gethsemane.

Current attempts to reconstruct the iconography of the shrine stress the links between the Tomb of the Virgin, the Holy House, and the more important crusader shrine of the **Holy Sepulchre**. At Mount Tabor nearby a Benedictine abbey was founded on the site of the Transfiguration of Christ. Early in the history of the **Latin Kingdom of Jerusalem**, the abbot there held the office of archbishop.

A **Latin** bishop replaced the **Greek** Orthodox clergy at the shrine in 1109-10. Nazareth replaced Mount Tabor as the site of the archbishopric between 1125 and 1128. The church of the Annunciation was damaged by the earthquake of 1170 and was under construction to restore and enlarge it when the kingdom fell in 1187. Access to the shrine was regained by treaty during the **Sixth Crusade** (1229). The church was visited by King **Louis IX** of France in 1251 and destroyed by **Mamluk** Sultan **Baybars I** of **Egypt** in 1263. The set of sculptured capitals intended for the restored church has survived.

A 15th-century European legend successfully linked **pilgrimage** churches in Croatia and northern Italy to the shrine at Nazareth. According to this account, angels transported the house of the Virgin, which survived the Sultan Baybar's destruction of the church, to Croatia in 1291 and then to the town of Loreto in Italy in 1295. The 700th anniversary of the shrine of the Holy House at Loreto was celebrated in 1994. A similar story of the same era established the importance of the shrine to the Virgin at Walsingham, England.

The Franciscan Order built a new church over the crusader ruins in the 18th century. An archaeological dig in 1907-09 was supplemented by one in 1955-66 due to their decision to replace the church in the 20th century.

Archbishops of Nazareth and their reigning dates include: Bernard (bishop 1109-25); William I (1128-32); Robert I (1138-53); Lietard I (1154-8); Lietard II (1158-90).

NESTORIAN CHRISTIANS. The name derives from Nestorius, bishop of Constantinople (r.428-431). They are also called the "east Syrians" (or "Assyrians"), which refers not so much to Syria proper (*see* **Jacobite Christians**) as to **Anatolia** (Turkey), **Kurdistan**, upper Mesopotamia, and Persia (Iran). They spoke a dialect of Aramaic called Syriac, and resisted attempts to replace their liturgy with the **Greek** rites. In the early Middle Ages their missionary activity brought **Christianity** to Turkestan, India, and China. Traditions about the early history of this sect focus on **Edessa**, and the apocryphal *Acts of St. Thomas the Apostle* (*see* Atiya, under Byzantium in the bibliography).

Nestorius was excommunicated and deposed by the Council of Ephesus in 431, due to disagreements over the orthodox definition of the nature of Christ. He was exiled to Libya, where he wrote an apologetic, and died before the Council of Chalcedon in 451. Nestorianism was illegal in **Byzantium** by 553. The Nestorians fled to the Persian Empire as a result. By 652 **Islam** conquered Persia. The Nestorians, like the **Copts** and Jacobites, were protected by **Muslim** tolerance as long as they were willing to pay the tax on their religion. The **Mongols** also offered them tolerance after the initial massacres that accompanied conquest in the 1250s.

NICAEA. (Turkish: Iznik). An ancient city in northwest **Asia Minor** close to the Bosporus crossing the crusaders had to take from **Constantinople** on their way through to **Antioch**; Nicaea was the capital of the **Seljuk**

Turk kingdom of Rum (*see* **Anatolia**). The city existed from before Roman times, and its defenses have been attributed to the Emperor Justinian (r.527-65). It fell to the Turks in 1071 and changed hands twice in the 1080s. The inhabitants may still have been mostly **Christian** at the time of the crusades, with a Turkish garrison. An advance party of **First Crusaders**, often called the People's Crusade, led by **Peter the Hermit** was destroyed there by the Turks in 1096.

The city was built within a four-mile square of many-towered walls, each with a centered gate, so that from the middle of town one could look down the four main streets to the gates. The western wall was protected by Lake Ascanius, the others by a double ditch. The armies of the First Crusade besieged the city from 6 May until 19 June 1097, first blockading it and then vainly assailing the walls, which according to one account were defended by 240 towers. Their position was threatened by Kilij Arslan (r.1092-1107), Sultan of Rum, who brought an army against the attackers on 16 May. A pitched battle caused the Turkish army to retreat without aiding the city. The crusaders hurled the heads of captured Turks into the city in celebration of their victory.

The **Byzantine Empire** supported the crusaders by arranging for supplies (some of those who could not pay for them starved to death) and **naval** forces to stop the Nicaeans from receiving aid by way of the lake. Boats, some big enough to hold 50 or 100 men, were sent by the Byzantines and dragged seven miles overland by the crusaders in order to invest the lake. On at least four occasions during the **siege** attempts were made to undermine the walls or to take them by assault. The crusaders constructed and used portable armored shelters to conduct these attacks. The city surrendered upon the arrival of Byzantine troops, for reasons that are not clear from the sources. As a result, the European army was not permitted to sack Nicaea, and the emperor offered the crusaders a gift of money after the siege.

Nicaea remained a contested area between Byzantium and the Seljuks of Rum until **Mongol** conquest in 1308.

NORTHERN CRUSADES. *See* **Baltic Crusades; Swordbrethren; Teutonic Knights; Wends.**

NUR AL-DIN MAHMUD. Ruler of **Syria** from 1146-74, he succeeded his father **Zengi** as ruler of **Aleppo** in 1146. The fragmented political situation made it necessary for him to secure alliances with neighboring emirs and warlords, including his own brother at **Mosul** and **Turkmen**

tribes which had recently migrated to Syria. There was no unity among the **Muslim** forces as the **Second Crusade** approached.

Nur al-Din and his brother joined forces to advance on **Damascus**, but they had not reached the city when the crusaders abandoned the siege. Nur al-Din was able to ally with Mu'in al-Din Unur (d.1149), Turkish commander of Damascus, to defeat the army of Prince Raymond of **Antioch** in 1149. This victory and Raymond's death in battle increased Nur al-Din's prestige, so that he came to be looked upon as the champion of the faith. His career over the next 25 years laid the foundation for **Saladin**'s successful campaign against the crusader kingdom.

By 1154 he held all of Muslim Syria and the former **Latin** county of **Edessa**, earning recognition from the caliph in **Baghdad** as "the just king." Estimates of the strength of his army range from 10,000 to 15,000 horsemen in addition to infantry. In 1164 he was able to take crusader Banias (or Banyas), which controlled the main road from Damascus to Upper Galilee. He defeated a combined force of crusaders from Antioch and **Tripoli** while **Amalric I** was campaigning in Egypt. Nur al-Din's conquest of Mosul in 1170 increased his ability to threaten crusader Tripoli, where he continued his pressure on European defenses and resources.

His encouragement of Muslim unity under the banner of **jihad** extended to the patronage of schools and religious institutions; in 1169 he commissioned a pulpit destined for the mosque in Jerusalem, in anticipation of its reconquest. Saladin was able to install it in his honor. Nur al-Din died of an illness at Damascus on 15 May 1174, leaving a son too young to profit from his father's accomplishments.

-O-

ODO OF DEUIL. (d.1162). Historian of the **Second Crusade** who accompanied King **Louis VII** of France as chaplain on this expedition in 1147-49. Nothing is known of Odo's life beyond the fact that he was born in Deuil, in the valley of Montmorency, France, and that he was a monk at the Benedictine house of Saint-Denis.

THE OLD MAN OF THE MOUNTAIN. *See* **Assassins**.

OLIVER OF PADERBORN. Oliver was bishop of Paderborn 1224-25, and cardinal-bishop of Sabina 1225-27. He wrote a history of the **Fifth**

Crusade. He preached the expedition in Germany and accompanied it to **Egypt**. According to **Jacques de Vitry**, another crusade preacher, Oliver designed a much-celebrated **siege engine** used at Damietta in 1218.

ORDER OF ST. JOHN IN JERUSALEM. Also known as the Hospitallers, the order of St. John existed before the **First Crusade** to serve **pilgrims** and the sick. It became a **military order** along the pattern of the **Templars**, and like them adopted a rule and distinctive habit, in this case black robes with a white **cross** on the breast. From 1136 the order acquired **castles** on the borders of the crusader kingdoms, including the famous **Krac des Chevaliers** and in 1186 the fortress of Margat between Templar Tortosa and the port of Latakia. Both Margat and Krac survived **Saladin**'s assault on the kingdom in 1187. By the late 12th century a visitor put the number of Hospitaller knights at 400. After the fall of the crusader kingdom in 1291, the order moved to **Cyprus**. Between 1306 and 1310 the order conquered the island of Rhodes, which became their headquarters. In its turn Malta was the base and the Hospitallers became the Knights of Malta.

Histories of the order date its foundation to either 603, when it was reportedly a pilgrims' hospice, or c.1070, when a hospital was established by European merchants and run by the Benedictine monks of St. Mary Latin. The first master of the Hospital, Raymond of Le Puy (r.1120-60) compiled a rule for the order based on the rule attributed to St. Augustine and used by the canons of the **Holy Sepulchre**. In 1143 a newly established hospital to be staffed by Germans was placed under the order's control. The Hospitallers had a "quarter" of **Jerusalem**, actually within the Patriarch's Quarter, that included their own and neighboring institutions: a Benedictine convent named for St. Mary Magdalene, for instance, along with their conventual church of St. John the Baptist, and various other conventual buildings. Two other churches, Sts. Mary Minor (rebuilt in 1130) and Major (built by 1080) did not survive **Muslim** reconquest.

The hospital itself reportedly offered medical care to **Christians**, **Jews**, and Muslims. It could house 750-1,000 patients, double in an emergency. Salaried doctors, equipment such as beds and linen, and a diet geared to the sick were provided. Hospitals in medieval times also offered alms, meals, and sometimes housing to the poor and elderly. The Hospitallers fed 30 poor people daily. The administrative statutes were drawn up in 1182 under the Grand Master Roger des Moulins (r.1177-87).

Unlike the Templar order, which retired to France and was suppressed in 1312, the Hospitallers moved first to Cyprus and then to Rhodes. Their autonomous domain there is more reminiscent of the military orders founded during the **Baltic Crusades**, which became a force for colonial expansion. In 1374 the Hospitallers captured Smyrna on the coast of **Asia Minor**, the culmination of a series of raids carried out in alliance with Cyprus on the **Levantine** coast from **Syria** to **Egypt**. They were unable to take Greek territory and lost Smyrna to the **Ottoman Turks** in 1415 but took Halicarnassus instead. The Turks raided Rhodes in 1455 and 1480. The Ottomans were successful in driving the Hospitallers from Rhodes and therefore from the Aegean in 1522. The order was given property on Malta by the **Holy Roman Empire**.

ORDER OF ST. LAZARUS. Little information on this order survives. The first mention of a leper hospital outside the north wall of **Jerusalem** is in the third century. In the sixth century a **pilgrim** guidebook describes lepers washing in the Pool of Siloam. Under **Muslim** rule the leper hospital survived and was housed in St. Stephen's church. When the **First Crusade** arrived in 1099 "the Hospital" referred to three institutions under the same prior: St. Mary Latin, St. John the Almoner, and St. Lazarus. Sometime after 1120 St. Lazarus became a **military order**, under the Augustinian rule. They owned only two churches: the original one at Jerusalem and a hospital and chapel at Tiberias. Knights who contracted leprosy were by law entered into the community and fought as long as they were physically able. They wore a black and white robe with a green cross.

The first mention of knights fighting under the auspices of this order is not until 1244. They are reported to have accompanied **Saint Louis IX, King of France,** on his **Egyptian** crusade. Some stories have the master of the order assisting at the vain defense of **Acre** before its fall in 1291; others have it already based at Boigny in France by then. *See also* **Order of St. John.**

ORDER OF ST. THOMAS OF ACRE. This hospital in Acre was run by Augustinian canons and originally dedicated to care for the poor, **pilgrims**, and the sick. It was transformed into a military order in 1227 by the visiting bishop of Winchester, Peter of Roches. The bishop also contributed to the repair of the defenses of the cities of **Jaffa** and **Sidon**. Many of the recruits for this order came from England. After the fall of the crusader kingdom in 1291, the order moved to **Cyprus**. During the 14th century there was a schism between the order's members in Cyprus and in London, and by the end of the century the order had moved to England and abandoned its military character. *See* **Military Orders**; **Order of St. John in Jerusalem**; **Templars**.

OTTOMAN EMPIRE. The Ottoman Turks took **Constantinople** in 1453, **Egypt** in 1517, and effectively ruled most of southeastern Europe, western Asia, and northern Africa from the 16th century until World War I. The last expeditions that could reasonably be linked to crusading were aimed at stopping the Ottoman advance in **Asia Minor**. In 1395-96 the Ottomans demolished a crusading army recruited by the king of Hungary from the Western European countries at Nicopolis in Bulgaria. After the fall of Constantinople Pope Pius II again preached the crusade, but was ignored by the European monarchs and died as he set out in 1464.

-P-

PAPACY. The word *pope* came from the Greek word for bishops, and the popes were the bishops of Rome. *Papacy* denotes the system of government by which the pope is the head of the church. The Roman bishops claimed primacy over the other bishops of **Christendom** based on an interpretation of the New Testament that made St. Peter the head of the church, and a tradition that held that Peter had served as bishop of Rome and had been martyred there.

Between 955 and 1057 there were 25 popes. Thirteen were appointed by the local aristocracy in Rome. Twelve were appointed by the **Holy Roman Emperors**, who deposed five as well. The rhetoric that set the vicar of St. Peter above the judgment of any earthly power did not match the reality of papal elections. The church was also continually subject to simony, the purchase of church office by aristocratic families as career paths for second or third sons. The marriage of clergy complicated this pattern, as they in turn tried to provide careers in the church for their sons.

Between 1046 and 1057 the western emperor appointed a series of reform popes from among the German bishops. Pope Leo IX (r.1049-54), the bishop of Toul and the emperor's cousin, insisted that his imperial appointment be ratified by the clergy and people of Rome, according to canon (church) law. From this position of legitimacy, he launched a series of reform councils in Germany, France, and northern Italy, insisting on canonical election, punishment for simony, and clerical celibacy, all intended to safeguard the purity of the episcopate. At the Roman Curia (his court) he assembled scholars and reformers to replace the more usual household of Roman aristocrats. From this curia would emerge the most notable of the reform popes, **Gregory VII**.

In 1059 a council held at the Lateran palace established a new election procedure for the bishop of Rome. The cardinals, or senior clergy of Rome, were to be the electors, whose choice was to be acclaimed by the people and by the emperor. These cardinals were the 28 parish priests of the city of Rome, the seven holders of bishoprics around Rome, and the 19 deacons of the city.

At the same time papal policy replaced the emperors as the prime protectors of Rome's independence by allying with the Norman conquerors of **Sicily**. In return for papal legitimization of their conquests, the rulers of Apulia, Calabria (southern Italy), and Sicily agreed to hold their kingdoms as vassals of the pope. In 1061, when the Holy Roman Empire attempted to contest a papal election, Norman troops enforced it. In 1068 the king of **Aragon** made a similar arrangement. In both cases the extension of the vassal's domain was reconceived as part of a religious war against **Islam**, which allowed both Spanish and Sicilian warriors to call for help from Western Europe and to take advantage of crusade **indulgences** and status when those became available in the 12th century.

PELAGIUS. Pelagius was cardinal bishop of Albano, appointed by Pope **Innocent III** as papal legate in 1214. His original mission was to negotiate a peace between the **Latin Kingdom of Constantinople** and its **Greek** rival at **Nicaea**. One of his goals was to promote an effective union of the Greek Orthodox and Roman Christians, and as a step in that direction to encourage the Greeks to attend the Fourth Lateran Council in 1215. Pelagius would become the leader of the **Fifth Crusade**, which reached Syria in 1217.

PETER THE HERMIT. Peter preached and led the People's Crusade, which left in advance of **Godfrey of Bouillon**'s army in 1096, crossed into **Asia Minor**, and was defeated by the **Seljuk Turks** at **Nicaea** on 21 October 1096. Some of the survivors joined Godfrey's army to continue on the **First Crusade**. Peter traveled with **knights** led by Walter *de Pexeio*, or *Sine Habere/Senzavohir*, possibly from Boissy-Sans-Avoir in France, not far from Paris.

PETER OF VAUX-CERNAY. Historian of the **Albigensian Crusade**, Peter was an eyewitness who died in 1218/19. He was a Cistercian monk, nephew of Abbot Guy of Cîteaux. Guy was bishop of Carcassonne from 1212. Peter's account favors the established church and Simon of **Montfort** as a hero and saint. For the Cistercians, *see* **Bernard of Clairvaux**.

PILGRIMAGE. Pilgrimage in medieval Europe was a popular practice which generated **canon law**, literature, and art in support of and response to it. Journeys of varying lengths to sacred memorials could be undertaken for a number of reasons, from personal preference to imposed penance. Canon law regulated dress and behavior while on the journey, which ideally was a spiritual discipline undertaken in reverence and poverty. A passage from the New Testament, Hebrews 11:13, was one of the factors that led to medieval use of the idea of pilgrimage as an image of one's life on earth. The goal was the New **Jerusalem**, or Heaven.

The word used for crusaders in medieval chronicles is most often "pilgrim." Crusading has frequently been categorized as "armed pilgrimage." Both journeys begin with a vow. Both aim for a specific destination and often impose a time limit on departure, with penalties for delay. Both assume regulations (not always obeyed) on clothing and demeanor, and both aim for a hoped-for spiritual benefit. The goal of the pilgrimage was a spot where action of some pivotal kind had been taken, for instance the church of the **Holy Sepulchre**, the supposed site of Christ's resurrection, or where the **relic** of a saint was kept.

Most shrines had their own symbol or badge, and were constructed to allow for pilgrim traffic and special liturgies. Pilgrims brought income to the shrine and to the local economy, so that gifts, sales, and thefts of relics were important transactions. The creation of the shrine of **Sainte-Chapelle** in Paris by King **Louis IX** of France was impressive enough to warrant imitation by Henry III of England when he received the relic of the **Holy Blood** from the patriarch of **Jerusalem**. Throughout the crusade period, but particularly as the crusader kingdoms fell and access to Jerusalem became more difficult, there were increasing attempts to link pilgrimage sites in Western Europe to the lost relics and places of the Holy Land. *See also* **Nazareth**.

PISA, DESCRIPTION. Because of their geographical position and economies based on Mediterranean trade, both **Genoa** and Pisa suffered from **Muslim** attacks beginning in the 10th century. In 934/35 for instance, both cities were raided by the **Fatimids**, based at the time in northern Africa. Iberian Muslims captured Sardinia in 1015 and continued to plunder the cities and massacre or enslave their inhabitants. Genoa and Pisa united to take Sardinia in 1015-16 and by 1034 were carrying the fight to northern Africa. In the 1060s the Pisans offered naval assistance to the Normans in their conquest of Muslim **Sicily**. In 1087 a combined force of Genoese, Pisans, Romans, and Amalfitans, organized by Pope Victor III (r.1086-87), attacked the port city of Mahdia (in modern Tunisia). The papal legate, Bishop Benedict of Modena, led the expedition of 300 or more ships and 30,000 men. The prize was a large indemnity in gold, trading rights in Mahdia, and the promise of an end to North African attacks on Italian shipping.

Twelfth-century Pisa has been called "an episcopal republic." It was part of the marquisate of Tuscany. Customs of the association formed by the richest merchants of the city were confirmed by Pope **Gregory VII** in 1075 and **Holy Roman Emperor** Henry IV in 1081. Bishops Gerard (r.1080-85) and Daimbert (r.1089-1104) effectively ruled the city in consultation with an assembly of the chief citizens and a viscount with civil jurisdiction. In 1091 the city was raised to the status of an archbishopric with jurisdiction over Corsica. Daimbert, now an archbishop, attended the Council of Clermont in 1095 where Pope **Urban II** preached the **First Crusade**. The pope was normally closer than the emperor, and so more of a factor in Pisan politics. In the same way that rivalry between competing Muslim and **Christian** chiefs in the Iberian Peninsula came to be described by the rhetoric of the **Reconquista**, what might otherwise have been called simply piracy or territorial expansion in the Mediterranean borrowed the rhetoric of crusade and **jihad**.

PISA, IN THE CRUSADES. For the Italian cities the **First Crusade** was a natural progression from the success of the joint endeavor of 1087 (*see* **Pisa, description**). As with their other ventures, their involvement was based on a combination of motives including self-defense and a desire to expand their holdings and influence in the Mediterranean. Their first venture was similar to those of the other regional troops of the First

Crusade whose commanders chose to use them to carve out a lordship overseas.

A Pisan fleet of 120 ships arrived at the **siege** of Latakia (Laodicea, **Syria**) as the leaders of the crusade who chose to return home were traveling to **Constantinople** in the summer of 1099. The fleet was under the command of its archbishop, Daimbert, who had been effectively ruling the city/republic. The Pisans had wintered in Corfu and skirmished with the **Byzantine** navy out of the general ongoing rivalry between the **Greeks** and Italians for control of Mediterranean shipping. They joined **Bohemond of Taranto**, first crusader and de facto ruler of Byzantine **Antioch**, in his attack on the Greek port of Latakia.

When the other crusade leaders, **Raymond of Saint-Gilles, Robert of Normandy**, and Robert of **Flanders** arrived, they convinced Bohemond and Daimbert to give up the siege against **Christians**. Daimbert continued on to **Jerusalem** with Bohemond and **Baldwin of Boulogne**, ruler of **Edessa**, arriving at Christmas. **Godfrey of Bouillon**, who had assumed the title of Advocate of the **Holy Sepulchre**, was holding **Jerusalem**, the port of **Jaffa**, and little else, surrounded by hostile inhabitants and relying on the few hundred men who remained after the First Crusade army departed for home. He had failed to take either **Ascalon** or Arsuf, and desperately needed naval support to maintain his position.

Daimbert and the Pisan navy under his command helped Godfrey to fortify Jaffa and intimidate the **Muslim** rulers of Ascalon, **Acre**, and the **Transjordan**. The new ruler of Jerusalem was quick to make commercial treaties with these **Islamic** powers in his region. Godfrey then rewarded Daimbert by making him patriarch of Jerusalem (1099-1102) in place of the recently elected chaplain of Robert of Normandy. Bohemond and Godfrey became vassals of the new patriarch as a way of legitimizing their newly minted titles.

According to **William of Tyre**'s chronicle Daimbert demanded a fourth part of Jaffa and the city of Jerusalem. The agreement was made but then compromised by the death of Godfrey on 18 July 1100 and the departure of the Pisan fleet. When Godfrey died Daimbert was with **Tancred** of Tiberias at the siege of Haifa. The Pisans had been replaced by the **Venetians**. Without his Pisan navy, Daimbert's only hope of support against the new claimant to the throne, Baldwin of Boulogne, was his vassal the prince of Antioch. Bohemond was the captive of a **Danishmendid** chieftain at this juncture. When Daimbert crowned Baldwin I in **Bethlehem**, he still hoped to keep Jerusalem and part of Jaffa as his own domain. The new king of Jerusalem had other plans. Even after accepting help from the patriarch and a Pisan fleet in the siege of Caesarea in 1102, Baldwin was determined to escape Daimbert's demands. The Pisan patriarch was formally deposed by papal legate Robert of Paris at a church synod dominated by Baldwin's supporters on 8 October 1102.

The next major Pisan adventure was an attack on the Muslim Balearics. In 1113 Pope Paschal II authorized a crusade by the Pisans against the Muslims in the Mediterranean. Count Raymond Berenguer III (r.1097-1131) of **Barcelona** accepted leadership of this expedition in 1114, and went on to attack and briefly hold Majorca. Again, failure to consolidate and populate a territorial domain led to the loss of the islands to a Muslim force in 1119. Pisa did gain important trade agreements in Iberia in exchange for military assistance to its Christian rulers.

Losing those rights in the **Levant** prompted Pisan involvement in the **Third Crusade**, an attempt to repair the damage done by **Saladin**'s campaigns against the crusader kingdoms. In 1188 papal legate and Archbishop of Pisa Ubaldo commanded a fleet of 50 to 60 ships which reached **Tyre** in 1189. They joined the forces of the **Latin Kingdom of Jerusalem** under **Guy of Lusignan** at Acre during the summer of 1189. Determined to regain their commercial privileges, they attached themselves to King **Richard I** of England upon his arrival in 1191 as the best way to protect their interests in return for their assistance.

Their involvement in the crusades gave place to their war with the other Italian city-communes for dominance in Tuscany and in the Mediterranean. After their defeat at the hands of the Florentines in 1222 their focus turned to Italy.

PORTUGAL. Originally an administrative district of **León-Castile**, based on the town of Porto, in 1109 it passed to one of the daughters of Alfonso VI, Teresa, and her heirs. Between 1111 and 1117 Alfonso's heirs (Portugal, León, **Aragon**) fought for control of his holdings. Their rivals for Iberia were the **Murabit** from northern Africa, called in to assist the fragmented **Muslim** principalities, but by 1109 the major Muslim power in the peninsula.

Teresa (d.1130) was finally sent into exile after a war for control of her territory with her son, Alfonso Enríques (count 1112, d.1185). Alfonso won a major battle against Murabit forces at Ourique in southern Portugal in 1139. Up to this point he had stressed his descent from the dynasty of León-Castile. Beginning in 1140 he began to style himself "king" of Portugal. During the **Second Crusade** the assistance of the **Genoese** enabled the king of León to attack Almería, while a fleet composed of crusaders from Cologne, Flanders, Normandy, and England assisted the king of Portugal at the siege of Lisbon. Alfonso had positioned himself for such help by accepting his lands formally from the pope as a vassal in 1143. The crusade fleet which assembled at Dartmouth in May of 1147 was crucial to the conquest of Lisbon and therefore to the history of the territorial consolidation of Portugal. Alfonso's ability to call on them as crusaders assisted his successful attempt to recruit them as mercenaries.

The members of the crusade fleet had no allegiance to Alfonso and presumably little interest in his kingdom. The international assortment of crusaders began their expedition by forming a common association with judicial procedures and rules for sharing plunder. Their goal was **Jerusalem**, but when their 170 ships put in at Porto in June, the bishop there was able to convince them to earn their crusade **indulgence** in Portugal. Alfonso offered them the whole of the city's spoils, a remission of royal tolls, and rights of settlement. Even so, the crusaders demanded Portuguese hostages as guarantees of these arrangements. They would have far more at stake than the king at the **siege** of Lisbon. Alfonso brought only a small retinue, and the only other Portuguese troops were those of the bishop of Porto. The Germans and Flemish brought up ships with bridges to attack the walls that faced the Tagus estuary and a device that extracted foundation stones from the land walls. The Anglo-Normans built and manned a 95-foot siege tower. The expert who designed this and a second tower for them was a **Pisan** who died at the siege.

Portugal benefited in the same way from the **Third Crusade**. King Sancho I (r.1185-1211) was assisted at the siege of Silves in 1189 by a crusade fleet recruited from areas bordering the North Sea and the English Channel. Without the expertise and military/naval support of European crusaders, the ability of Portugal to advance its boundaries at the expense of Muslim Spain was doubtful at best. It is also clear, when the details of the arrangements between Portugal and its visitors are available, as they are for the siege of Lisbon, that religious motivation was not sufficient to bring that assistance to bear in Iberia.

-R-

RAMLA. Ramla was one of the most important secular lordships within the **Latin Kingdom of Jerusalem**; adjacent to Lydda, on the road from **Jaffa** to **Jerusalem**. The lords of Ramla had rights of court/jurisdiction and the minting of coins in return for military service to the kings of Jerusalem. The bishopric of Ramla/Lydda was established in 1099 by the crusading army, making the area an ecclesiastical lordship. Early in the kingdom's history the town of Jaffa was also fortified and given to Hugh II of Le Puiset, forming the basis for the secular lordship. The **Ibelin** family acquired the lordship by marriage after the death of Baldwin of Ramla, the son of one of the original crusaders, in 1138.

RAYMOND OF AGUILERS. Raymond was chaplain to Count **Raymond of Saint-Gilles**, one of the leaders of the **First Crusade**. The chronicle was written before 1105, and is particularly important for events during and after the **siege** of **Antioch** in 1098. There is an English translation by John H. Hill.

RAYMOND IV DE SAINT-GILLES. Raymond was the count of **Toulouse** (d. 1105) who founded a dynasty at **Tripoli** during the **First Crusade**. He may have been the first secular leader to take a **crusade vow**. A chronicle of the crusade was written by his chaplain, **Raymond of Aguilers**.

Raymond was related to the counts of **Barcelona** and was married to Elvira, the illegitimate daughter of King Alfonso VI of **León-Castile** (1030-1109). She accompanied him on the crusade. Alfonso had arranged his own and his children's marriages to support the **Reconquista** in Spain, a war which extended his domains considerably. His efforts were rewarded with the interest of warriors from southern France and the support of the **papacy**. When the **Murabit** dynasty retaliated against Alfonso in 1086 for his capture of Toledo, the king warned the French that without their help the **Muslims** would come through his domain and across the Pyrenees. Raymond was the first of the secular princes to respond to the call of Pope **Urban II** for the crusade in 1095.

Raymond was the most powerful lord in southern France, having inherited Rodez, Nîmes, Narbonne, Provence, and Toulouse. Urban selected **Adhémar**, bishop of Le Puy, as legate and leader of the First Crusade. The bishop led his own contingent of troops, but combined his forces with those of Raymond, who arguably led the largest of the regional armies that made up the expedition. At **Antioch** and **Jerusalem** Raymond's efforts to take secular leadership were foiled by **Bohemond of Taranto** and **Godfrey of Bouillon**. Both of them took territory that was claimed by Alexius **Comnenus**, ruler of **Byzantium**, to whose court Raymond returned after the crusade in 1100.

In 1101 Alexius put Raymond at the head of a large force of Europeans who had arrived in **Constantinople** on their way to the **Holy Sepulchre**. This army was wiped out by the Turkish sultans Kilij Arslan of **Iconium** and Malik-Ghazi ibn-**Danishmend** of Sebastia. Raymond was briefly held prisoner by **Tancred**, regent for Bohemond of Taranto, and made to swear that he would not try to establish a lordship to rival crusader Antioch.

Released, Raymond proceeded to do just that by taking Tortosa in 1102, building the **castle** of Mount Pilgrim as a base from which to take Tripoli in 1103. He died in February of 1105 without having taken the city. His troops remained at Mount Pilgrim until the arrival of Raymond's son Bertram in 1109. Bertram brought 4,000 men in **Genoese** ships, and like his father allied with the Byzantines against the crusader lords of Antioch.

Bertram's arrival precipitated a standoff outside Tripoli. Baldwin I of Jerusalem and **Baldwin Le Bourg** of **Edessa** backed Bertram against Tancred of Antioch. A compromise was reached that eventually gave Tancred Tortosa and Bertram Tripoli. When the city fell in July of 1109 Bertram held it as King Baldwin's vassal, and the Genoese received a third of the city in return for their assistance.

This victory founded the county of Tripoli but also led to the proclamation of a **jihad** against the crusaders by the **Seljuk Turk** sultan of Iraq. The commander who took up the fight in 1110 was Mawdud of **Mosul**.

RECONQUISTA. **Muslim** forces launched from northern Africa conquered Iberia in 711 A.D. During the 10th century, **Christian** kingdoms were founded in **Aragon, León**, and Castile. These kingdoms were made possible by the fact that by the 11th century Muslim Spain, or *al-Andalus*, was not a unified power itself, but rather a collection of principalities (or *taifas*) based at such centers as Córdoba, Seville, and Toledo. By 1250 most of Iberia was in Christian hands. Granada alone held out until 1492, when conquest of the last Muslim stronghold was combined with the expulsion of the **Jews** to create a united Christian Spain.

According to the traditional view of this contest, both societies were based on subsistence agriculture and the trade made possible by the rivers of the Iberian peninsula. By the 11th century, however, Muslim irrigation technology, based on the water- or animal-driven geared waterwheel, combined with the introduction of new crops from northern Africa to provide the base for a wealthier and more sophisticated society in the south than was possible in the emerging northern Christian domains.

Reliable numbers are always difficult to glean from medieval sources, but urban centers of over 50,000 were common in a Muslim Iberia of about 6,000,000, while the approximately 1,000,000 Christians of the peninsula could boast only small towns, based on an agricultural system that was not as well developed. Muslim trade took advantage not only of rivers and the old Roman roads, but also of the connection to northern Africa. Sunni was the dominant tradition, under the increasingly nominal auspices of the **Abbasid** caliphate in **Baghdad** (al-Andalus became an independent emirate in 756 and a caliphate in 929). One percent of the population of al-Andalus is estimated to have been Jewish, while the much-disputed Mozarabic and other Christian population numbers have been estimated at 30 percent. All of these groups were protected under **Islamic law** at the expense of a special tax.

Tensions between Muslim and Christian Spain were exacerbated when Alfonso VI of León-Castile conquered Toledo in 1085. Fragmented Muslim Iberia was unable to stop him, but was used to relying on northern African assistance. A number of **Berber** tribes coalesced in Morocco by 1056 under the **Murabit** dynasty, fought Alfonso in 1086, and emerged as an Iberian power by 1109. The Murabit were of the Malikite (after Malik ibn Anas, d.795) school of **Islam**, which disregarded the authority of the caliphs at Baghdad, and more importantly, of the Iberian Muslim powers, which they soon replaced. Until the death of the emir Ali ibn Yusuf (1106-43), the Murabit empire in northern Africa and Iberia was a serious threat to the tiny Christian principalities. From 1160 to 1230 the **Muwahhid** ("unitarian," in Spanish *Almohad*) dynasty, which replaced them, at various points controlled Morocco, Algeria, Tunisia, and al-Andalus. Toledo remained the focal point in the contest between Islamic and Christian Spain.

Pedro I, King of Aragon (r.1094-1104) responded to the dual threat of expanding León and the Murabit by renewing his homage to Pope **Urban II** in 1096 as a prelude to his attack on Muslim Huesca. By this allegiance Pedro gained European support for his expansion and discouraged any attack on him by Alfonso. He was able to take several other Muslim strongholds by 1100 with assistance from southern France. His brother and heir, Alfonso I (1104-34), followed up on his conquests, making possible the eventual union of the kingdom of Aragon and the county of **Barcelona**. In 1118-19 he was able to make considerable progress against the Murabit, taking both Córdoba and Tudela. Throughout this period, the contest for control of Iberia was as much a battle among rival Christian forces as with Islam.

The most famous among these various contenders for Spanish territory was Rodrigo Díaz de Vivar, given the titles the *Cid* (lord, or *campeador*, champion) by his victims. Without even as much of a territorial base as the counts of Barcelona, this redoubtable warrior began his career as a mercenary for the Muslim ruler of Saragossa (1081-87). Forced to work for himself after the Murabit incursion into the peninsula, Rodrigo managed to collect tribute from a number of Muslim towns, and finally to take Valencia in 1094. He held it until his death in 1099, when it was ruled by his wife Jimena Díaz until the Murabit took the city in 1102.

In spite of infighting among the tiny Christian principalities, the Murabit were in retreat by 1125-26, when Alfonso I of Aragon made a series of destructive raids on their empire in southern Spain. Over the course of the next 20 years Christian Spain made considerable advances, and in 1143 the powerful emir of the Murabit Empire died, leaving a fragmented Muslim state. In 1147 Pope Eugenius III (r.1145-53) offered the same crusading **indulgence** for three theaters of war: Iberia, the **Baltic** region, and the **Levant**. In 1148 the pope extended the indulgence to cover the campaign of the count of Barcelona against Tortosa. The assistance of the **Genoese** enabled the king of León to attack Almería, while a fleet composed of crusaders from Cologne, **Flanders**, and England assisted the king of **Portugal** at the **siege** of Lisbon. Other participants in the **Second Crusade** helped take Tortosa in 1148.

The "reconquest" stalled in the mid-12th century on both sides. The Christian rulers were primarily concerned to build their own power, as much by attacking each other as by attempting to interfere in the Muslim south. No Islamic ruler was able either to impose a unified regime on the Iberian states or escape the domination of northern Africa if their help was called in. The Berber tribes of the Murabit and then the Muwahhid who conducted the defense of Islam were both ferociously orthodox in the sense of being opposed to the brilliant culture of Muslim Spain, so that they sapped the military resources of the peninsula and its intellectual life. *See also* **Spanish Inquisition**.

RELIC. The transmission of relics by sale, theft, or gift is a characteristic of the medieval period in general, but also a notable by-product of the crusading movement. The stated goal of the crusader was often the **Holy Sepulchre**. The discovery of the **Holy Lance** at **Antioch** tipped the scales in morale at a crucial moment during the **First Crusade**. Gifts of the wood of the True **Cross** were particularly valued, and theft, as at the conquest of **Constantinople** during the **Fourth Crusade**, furnished many European houses with sacred objects (*see* **Holy Shroud**). Purchase of relics offered the benefits of verification of the pedigree of the artifacts. **Sainte-Chapelle**, in Paris, for instance, was built to contain the relics purchased by King **Louis IX**. King Henry III of England seems to have attempted to rival the king of France with a collection of relics at Westminster he acquired by gift or purchase, including the relic called the **Holy Blood**. When all else failed, relics could be acquired by miraculous translation, as was the case with the Holy House, transported by angels from **Nazareth** to Italy.

Relics are the physical remains of a holy person: clothing or any object used by the deceased, hair or bodily fluid (breast milk of the Virgin, blood of Christ, etc.), or bones. They were venerated by Christian believers as early as the second century A.D. By the 12th century bodies of saints were prepared for distribution by being eviscerated and boiled, so that the bones could be readied for distribution. Reliquaries, or containers for the bones, could take many forms (for instance jeweled caskets or churches), but again, by the 12th century often took the shape of the part of the body they contained. They could be decorated with scenes from the life of the saint represented. The belief in the impending physical resurrection of the body at the Last Judgment helped to endow the remains with tremendous power: the bones were, in popular belief, a conduit to the saint in heaven.

The iconography of the saint was also important. **Pilgrim** badges were decorated with symbols of the site or saint, and those who had been healed often had statuettes ("ex-votos") made of the body part that had been affected. By 1200 it had become fairly common to divide the bodies of clerics or ordinary people for burial at different sites, in order to benefit from the patronage of several saints. Medieval painting and sculpture sometimes celebrated the activities of the saints, and sometimes the translation of their relics, creating images that remain powerful, not only at the shrines and churches that have survived, but also as an aspect of European culture.

REYNALD OF CHÂTILLON. (d.1187). Reynald (or Reginald) has been seen as one of the key influences on the events which led to the fall of the crusader kingdoms in 1187 to **Saladin**. Born in c.1125 to the family of Donzy, he inherited the lordship of Châtillon-sur-Loire. Members of his family were nobles of Burgundy and counts of Chalon. Reynald came to the Latin East on the **Second Crusade**, and ruled **Antioch** 1153-61 as a result of his marriage to the heiress, Constance. He was captured by **Nur al-Din** in 1161 and held for 15 years at **Aleppo**. At Constance's death her principality passed to her son Bohemond III.

Reynald's actions as reported in **Ernoul**'s chronicle of the fall of the kingdom mark him as an impetuous, violent man. He was reported to have tortured the patriarch of Antioch and sacked the island of **Cyprus** during a dispute with the **Byzantine** emperor. King **Baldwin IV**, whose leprosy made a regency for the kingdom intermittently advisable, does not seem to have been troubled by these incidents, and **William of Tyre**'s recorded opinion of Reynald was that he was courageous and loyal to the king.

In spite of their previous enmity, Reynald negotiated an alliance between Manuel **Comnenus** and the **Latin Kingdom** in 1176. King Baldwin IV arranged his marriage to the heiress to the major fief of **Transjordan**, making Reynald the fourth most important lord in the kingdom. Upon the death of William of **Montferrat** in 1177, Reynald was made executive regent of the kingdom. He led the charge on Saladin's troops at the battle of Mont Gisard that year, in which the Europeans were successful against a much larger force.

In November of 1181, after heavy rains made the desert briefly accessible to **cavalry**, Reynald made a raid on Tarbuk in the Arabian Desert, 130 miles south of Eliat. A truce between Baldwin IV and Saladin was not due to expire until May of 1182. While in Tarbuk, which was on the **pilgrimag**e route from **Damascus** to Mecca, Reynald seized a caravan. He refused to release its members even after the king requested it.

In the winter of 1182-83 Reynald's five warships raided coastal areas on the Red Sea. His raids are known from Arabic sources rather than Christian chronicles. He seems to have had a force of 300 men, and to have created a threat to pilgrim traffic from **Egypt** to Mecca. No Christian naval force had been seen on the Red Sea for 500 years. **Al-Adil** countered this move with warships from **Alexandria** which he had carried overland from Cairo to the Red Sea.

Reynald did homage to **Guy of Lusignan** when he was crowned in 1186. Later that year, however, Reynald broke the kingdom's truce with Saladin by attacking a caravan, and defied Guy when the king attempted to insist on restitution.

Saladin followed through on his promise to behead Reynald personally when he was captured at **Hattin** in 1187.

RICHARD PLANTAGENET, Earl of Cornwall (r.1257-72). Richard was the son of King John of England (r.1199-1216), and the brother and heir of Henry III (r.1216-72). He left for the Holy Land in June of 1240, in spite of the resistance of the pope, who was at war with **Holy Roman Emperor** Frederick II. Frederick's treaty with **Egypt** during the **Sixth Crusade** had aroused controversy in Europe and in the **Levant**. The barons of the **Latin Kingdom of Jerusalem** had just assisted Count **Theobald of Champagne** in negotiating a similar truce with the **Ayyubid** sultan of **Egypt** for the return of a portion of the old crusader kingdom. The number of Europeans based at **Acre** was too small to hold the promised territory, especially given the ongoing war between the sultan of Egypt and the prince of **Damascus**.

Richard's expedition seemed particularly problematic to Pope Gregory IX (r.1227-41), because he feared the English army would pass through Italy. The Holy Roman Emperor and the pope were rivals for control of the peninsula, and Richard's sister was the empress, Isabel Plantagenet. Richard bypassed this situation and instead sailed from southern France, reaching Acre in October. Theobald of Champagne had just left with his troops, and the Levantine barons were caught between their shifting alliances with Damascus and Egypt. Richard took his army to **Jaffa**, where the sultan of Egypt renewed his promise to give the crusaders the territory surrounding **Jerusalem**, along with a string of fortresses that would assure their control of a corridor to the coast. This was a controversial offer for essentially the same reasons it had been problematic after the Sixth Crusade–both **Muslims** and **Christians** objected to an arrangement that had them sharing holy sites in the city. In addition, the land promised by the sultan could not be held in the face of a hostile Damascus.

Both sides prolonged negotiations until February 1241. Richard used the time to help in the refortification of **Ascalon**, a task begun by Theobald's forces. He rebuilt the city's defenses according to the plan that had been used there by King **Richard I** of England during the **Third Crusade**. He also buried those of Theobald's army whose corpses had been left on the field after the "battle" of Gaza in 1239, and arranged for the release of Christians who had been taken prisoner there. He then handed over Ascalon to the agent of Emperor Frederick II, regent for his son as king of Jerusalem, and left for home in 1241.

RICHARD I, LIONHEART. (1157-99), king of England (1189-99). Richard I was the patron of the **Lusignans** in the contest for control of the remains of the **Latin Kingdom** at **Acre** and **Cyprus**, and the leader of the more famous contingent of the **Third Crusade**. King Philip II Augustus (r.1180-1223) of France also brought troops, as did **Conrad**

of Montferrat, Henry of Champagne, and **Holy Roman Emperor Henry VI** (r.1190-97), who sent a force to Acre in 1197 led by Duke Henry of Brabant (r.1190-1235). *See* **Acre, siege of 1189**; **Ayyubid Dynasty**.

Richard was crowned at Westminster Abbey in 1189 and left on crusade with Philip Augustus in 1190, stopping in **Sicily** and Cyprus. On 12 May 1291 at Limassol on Cyprus Richard married Berengaria, the daughter of King Sancho VI of **Navarre**. Having conquered Cyprus in the course of his stay there, Richard spent 1191-92 recovering **Jaffa**, Acre, and **Ascalon** for the crusader kingdom. He won a notable victory over **Saladin**'s forces at Arsuf. Hearing of a plot against him by King Philip, who had gone home alone in 1191, Richard secured **Christian** access to **Jerusalem** for **pilgrimages** by means of a treaty with Saladin and departed for Europe. He was captured on his way home in 1192 in German territory and transferred to the care of Emperor Henry VI, who was paid by Philip to keep Richard imprisoned. In 1194 Richard secured his release with the payment of an enormous ransom.

Richard was mortally wounded by an arrow while he was planning the **siege** of a fortress at Chalus in Aquitaine in 1199. He was buried at the abbey of Fontevraud in Anjou (*see* **Robert of Arbrissel**).

ROBERT OF ARBRISSEL. (or Arbressec, c.1047-1116). Robert was born in Brittany in about 1047, and studied in Paris, possibly under Anselm of Laon. In 1089 he was archpriest at Rennes, where his zeal for **Gregorian** reform idealism led to his dismissal in 1093. He moved first to Angers and then to the forest of Craon to live with several companions as an ascetic. Among them were Bernard, the founder of Tiron, and Vitalis, the founder of Savigny, both monastic houses noted for the severity of their rule. Robert eventually founded a house of canons regular at La Roé in 1096. In the same year Pope **Urban II** commissioned him to preach the **First Crusade** in the Loire Valley.

By 1101 Robert had founded a second abbey at Fontevraud which accepted both men and women. The men practiced manual labor and asceticism, some of them seeking ordination, while the women devoted themselves to prayer and contemplation. Both groups lived in crude huts under the leadership of the first abbess, Petronilla, using a rule written by Robert. In 1116 when Robert died a church and leper hospital were under construction. The popularity of the Order of Fontevraud (*Fontevrault*) led to a rapid expansion and patronage by the nobility of Western Europe. By 1149 when Petronilla died Fontevraud had 88 affiliated houses in France, Spain, and England. Eleanor of Aquitaine (*see* **Second

Crusade) retired there, and both she and her son King **Richard I** of England were buried there.

See also **Bernard of Clairvaux**; **Gervase of Prémontré**; **Jacques de Vitry**.

ROBERT OF CLARI. (d.c.1216). Robert was a poor knight who went on the **Fourth Crusade** as a vassal of Peter of Amiens and wrote a chronicle of the expedition. Unlike Geoffrey of **Villehardouin**, who also chronicled this crusade, Robert returned to Europe rather than settling in the East.

ROBERT, DUKE OF NORMANDY. (r.1087-1106). Robert Curthose, one of the leaders of the **First Crusade**, was the eldest son of William the Conqueror (d.1187). He left France in the fall of 1096 with his cousin Robert II of **Flanders** and his brother-in-law, Stephen of Blois. In order to finance the voyage the duke mortgaged Normandy to his brother King William II for 10,000 marks of silver, raised by a tax on the clergy and people of England. He took as chaplain on expedition Arnulf of Chocques, who was to be the first patriarch of the **Latin Kingdom of Jerusalem**. His party traveled through Italy, stopping at Lucca to receive the blessing of Pope **Urban II**, and eventually sailing from Bari. They traveled through **Constantinople**, meeting the overland contingents under **Godfrey of Bouillon**, and assisting at the **sieges** of **Nicaea**, **Antioch**, and **Jerusalem**. Robert's party returned home after the battle of **Ascalon** of 1099. Robert's activities on crusade were chronicled by **Fulcher of Chartres**.

ROBERT (THE MONK) OF RHEIMS. Robert may have been present for Pope **Urban II's speech at Clermont** in 1095. His chronicle of the **First Crusade** was written in about 1107, and relies on the **Gesta Francorum** account. The *Historia Hierosolymitana/Jerusalem History* was translated by Carol Sweetenham.

RUM, SELJUK KINGDOM OF. *See* **Anatolia**.

-S-

ST. ANNE. The Benedictine church and convent of St. Anne were built before 1104, when King **Baldwin I** of **Jerusalem** placed his estranged wife there. The royal family continued to be patrons, which made this abbey one of the most important in the city. Tradition linked the site to the home of the Virgin's mother, Anne, and to a miracle by which Jesus healed a lame man. The crypt of the church was supposed to have been the birthplace of the Virgin. The conventual buildings were destroyed after 1187 but in 1192 **Saladin** converted the church into a college of **Islamic law**. In 1865 it was given to France for restoration by the **Ottoman Empire**.

ST. JOHN IN JERUSALEM. *See* **Order of St. John**.

ST. MARK'S CHURCH, VENICE. In the ninth century, two businessmen stole the remains of St. Mark the Evangelist from **Alexandria** and the great church in his honor was built in **Venice**. Each of the 60 Venetian parishes was centered on its church and patron saint. St. Mark provided a similar central identity for the city. The church buildings were expanded and renovated several times during the Middle Ages. The Campanile next to the church was lit by night as a beacon for ships. *See also* **Relic**.

SAINTE-CHAPELLE. This chapel was built in 1242-48 by Saint **Louis IX, King of France**, to house **relics** of the Crown of Thorns and True **Cross** purchased from one of the European emperors of the **Latin Kingdom of Constantinople**. Other relics of the passion such as the **Holy Lance** which pierced Christ's side and the sponge mentioned in the gospels, part of John the Baptist's skull, Moses' rod, etc., were collected and made the focus of an annual liturgy of healing on Good Friday. A procession was made through the streets of Paris by the king in March 1241, during which the Holy Cross was displayed.

The iconography of the chapel links the Capetian dynasty to the kings of the Old Testament by reference to Solomon's **temple**, Saul, and David. In 1249 King Louis unsuccessfully attacked **Egypt** as the key to **Muslim** dominance in the Middle East.

The King was canonized in 1299, and in 1306 his head was added to the relic collection in the church. Important foreign visitors were taken to the church and often given fragments of the relics it contained. Sainte-Chapelle is a good example of the tremendous influence of both the architecture and the iconography of the Holy Land in European church design and decoration during the crusading period.

For the rivalry between King Louis of France and King Henry III of England, *see* **Holy Blood**.

SALADIN. (r.1171-93). Saladin's victory against the **Latin Kingdom of Jerusalem** at the battle of **Hattin** in 1187 was a major step in effective **Islamic** response to the crusades, at least rivaling, if not surpassing, the victories of **Nur al-Din** at **Edessa** and the attacks of **Baybars I** on crusader strongholds from 1265 to 1271.

Ascalon, a city of strategic importance on the border of **Egypt**, fell to the crusaders in 1153. As a result, factions at the **Fatimid** court called on the **Muslim** Turkish ruler of **Syria** Nur al-Din for help. An army under the **Kurdish** general Shirkuh defended Egypt in 1168-69, after which his nephew, Salah al-Din Yusuf (Saladin), took Egypt for Nur al-Din (1171). The Syrian ruler intended to consolidate his holdings under the **Abbasid** caliphate, but died in 1174, leaving Saladin to create a coalition of Islamic forces under the banner of **jihad**. Not all of Syria rallied behind him. He was attacked twice (1174, 1176) by the **Assassins**, who managed to infiltrate the corps of **Mamluks** who belonged to his uncle Shirkuh. Saladin survived the second attempt only because he was wearing **armor** under his robes.

Sicily launched major offensives against Egypt at **Alexandria** in 1174-75. In 1176-77 Saladin feared a similar offensive by the **Byzantines**, who were as interested in blocking Sicilian expansion as they were in fighting Islam. He built an impressive citadel and defensive wall system at Cairo while undertaking the considerable task of building a **navy**. In 1177, his attack on **Jerusalem** was turned back at Mont Gisard by King **Baldwin IV**, whose reign is often seen as a turning point in the fortunes of the Latin Kingdom. In 1182-83, Saladin was campaigning in Syria while **Reynald of Châtillon** put a fleet of five warships on the Red Sea. They were the first **Christian** ships to be seen there in 500 years. **Al-Adil** countered the threat by sending warships overland from Cairo. Saladin ordered al-Adil's captives executed publicly at major **Ayyubid** cities. Two were killed at Mecca.

From 1174 until 1187 Saladin worked to establish himself as the successor to Nur al-Din in Egypt and Syria. His position was finally cemented by his success at the battle of **Hattin** against the crusader forces. He was able to take **Acre** and Jerusalem, decimating the Latin Kingdom, and to create a confederation of Islamic states under the leadership of his relatives.

In 1191 Saladin lost Acre to King **Richard I** of England during the **Third Crusade**, but was able to retain Jerusalem and prevent the reestablishment of the Latin Kingdom based in the Holy City. At his death in 1194 he had made his name as a warrior hero, and created the Ayyubid dynasty.

Biographies of leaders were rare in Islamic literature of this period, but two were written about Saladin by his advisors **Imad ad-Din al-Isfahani** (d.1201) and **Baha al-Din ibn Shaddad** (d.1234), making Saladin the best known of the jihad heroes. There are also extensive sections on his accomplishments in the general histories of Ibn al-Athir (d.1233) and Abu Shama (d.1258), and contemporary letters on his career were collected by another advisor, al-Qadi al-Fadil (*see* Gabrielli and Lyons in the Islam and Third Crusade sections of the bibliography).

SANTIAGO DE COMPOSTELA. The shrine church of Saint James at Compostela was a major **pilgrimage** site. The saint's **relics** were the only apostolic remains in Western Europe other than those of Sts. Peter and Paul in Rome. The relics were discovered late, not until the ninth century, which made the effort to authenticate them an ongoing concern of the bishops. Housing the relics involved allowing pilgrims access to them, which led to the construction of several churches in succession, including a major Romanesque cathedral planned from 1075. The shrine was the earliest focus for a Spanish **Christian** identity that promoted the ideal of the **Reconquista**.

The city of Compostela was in Galicia, an independent kingdom in northwest Spain that was taken by King Alfonso VI of **León** (1030-1109) in 1073 as part of a process of expansion that made him one of the heroes of the Reconquista. Compostela was the site of a fortress which commanded two Roman roads in the province of Asturia. According to tradition St. James had come to Iberia on a preaching mission before being martyred in **Jerusalem** in 44 A.D. His disciples had brought his remains to be buried in Spain, arriving at the port of Iria, the seat of the original Christian bishopric.

During the Roman persecutions of Christians the tomb at Iria was forgotten, but it was rediscovered by local people in about 813, when the first church was built at the site. Both Vikings and pilgrims were arriving by 844, when it was thought prudent to move the saint to a safer location inland at Compostela. Before 1103 the seat of the bishopric was transferred there as well.

In 899, when a second and larger church was consecrated to accommodate the growing number of visitors, Compostela became a focus of Christian devotion and a symbol of Spanish expansion at the expense of the **Muslims** of Iberia. When the enemy destroyed the church in 997 that devotion was intensified. Bishop Cresconio (c.1036-66) fortified the new church (consecrated in 1003) and held off Viking attack at the head of his own troops. Dalmatius (d. 1103), a monk from **Cluny**, was made bishop of Compostela in 1094, and accompanied Pope **Urban II** on the tour of Italy and France that culminated in the preaching of the **First Crusade** at Clermont in 1095. Because of the long-standing patronage of the kings of León, Cluny promoted the pilgrimage to Santiago in France, as well as helping to recruit warriors for the Reconquista.

The famous duly appeared on pilgrimage in the 12th century: a succession of legates, including Stephen, treasurer of Cluny in 1121, the daughter of the king of England in 1125, Duke William X of Aquitaine in 1127, the count of **Toulouse** in 1140, the bishops of Winchester and Cambrai in 1151 and 1153, and finally King **Louis VII** of France in 1154 after the **Second Crusade**.

Bishop Diego Gelmírez (c.1100-40) was invested by Alfonso VI with the barony of Compostela and used his troops to push back the Muslim advance in 1108 after the disastrous defeat of the king's forces at Uclés, where the heir to the throne of León was killed. He was rewarded with a grant to found the first seigniorial mint in the kingdom. Diego seems to have promoted the glory of his see by any means available, emphasizing the honor due to the apostolic relics. At some point in these early years Diego wrote to Archbishop Anselm of Canterbury (r.1093-1109), asking for English assistance in the Reconquista. There is some evidence that Diego sent money to aid the crusade in the Holy Land directly, and opened a correspondence with **Jerusalem patriarchs** Gormond and Stephen.

Bishop Diego was able to prevail upon Pope **Calixtus II** to raise his church to the status of an archbishopric in 1120 by insisting on the rights of an "apostolic" church. Diego, in his last year as papal legate, called a council at Compostela (January 1125) in which he preached the crusade in Spain. He issued a crusade **indulgence** for war in Iberia against the Muslims, and imposed the duty of preaching on the Spanish clergy. His biographer saw this appeal in the same light as the correspondence with Canterbury or Jerusalem: as a proclamation of Diego's status and the prestige of his church. The continued wars among the heirs of Alfonso VI of León prevented this appeal from accomplishing any immediate result. Combined with Diego's promulgation of the Peace and Truce of God the previous year, it shows an effort to use the crusade to divert the energies of the Spanish nobility towards the Muslims.

SARACEN. *See* **Arab**.

SAXO GRAMMATICUS. Very little is known about the author of the "History of the Danes," written between 1185 and 1215. He chronicled the Danish war against the pagan **Wends**, part of an effort to expand into the **Baltic** region between 1147 and 1505 that is known as the "Northern Crusades."

SECOND CRUSADE. Pope **Eugenius III** authorized this crusade in 1145; St. **Bernard of Clairvaux**, among others, preached it in 1146. The scope and preparations for this crusade were greater than any other, while the results in the **Levant** were negligible. Participants included King **Louis VII** of France and **Conrad III** of Germany (*see* **Holy Roman Empire**) who went to the **Latin Kingdom of Jerusalem**, while crusaders from England, France, Scandinavia, **Genoa**, and **Pisa** assisted in attacks on **Muslims** on the Iberian Peninsula and the **Wends** in the **Baltic** region.

This crusade is also famous for scandalous stories about the participation of Louis's queen, Eleanor of Aquitaine (d.1204), who reportedly recruited for the expedition in the costume of an Amazon. She rode with the army accompanied by ladies of her court. Their avowed purpose was to tend the wounded. Eleanor was the niece of Prince Raymond of **Antioch**. Rumor alleged that Eleanor and Raymond became lovers after her arrival in Antioch in 1148. Whatever the truth of the rumor, Louis moved on from Antioch and the possibility of military action there to a conference with other crusading bands and the king of Jerusalem at **Acre**. His marriage to Eleanor did not long survive their return to France (*see* **Robert of Arbrissel**).

During the summer of 1147 crusaders from England, Scotland, France, **Flanders**, and the Rhineland assisted King **Alfonso Enríques** of Portugal in capturing the Muslim port city of Lisbon. The **siege** took 17 weeks, after which many of the crusaders sailed on to the Levant. At the same time, crusaders from Genoa joined King Alfonso VII of **León-Castile** in the siege of Almeria. In 1148 another group led by Count Raymond Berenguer IV of Barcelona, regent of **Aragon**, attacked Tortosa. *See* **Caffaro**.

An extension of the crusade **indulgence** was granted to the Danes and the Saxons, who wanted to attack the Slavic Wends in the town of Dobin, north of the Elbe River, near the Baltic Sea. The Danes seem to have been involved in a long-term struggle to convert the pagan Wends by force. This particular attempt was not successful: the Wends converted in the face of the invading army in 1147 only to relapse upon its retreat. Attacks were also made on the settlement of Malchow and the **Christian** city of Stettin. The expedition established Denmark as a crusading state and led to further missions and expeditions near the Baltic. In 1169 King Valdemar invited the **Order of St. John** to Denmark, allotting it a tax of one penny per household for its work in the Holy Land.

The main crusade armies under Conrad and Louis proceeded in turn through Hungary and the **Byzantine Empire**. Louis was deflected from assisting Raymond of Antioch (see above). Conrad's troops were decimated by the Turks in **Asia Minor**. An assembly held in Acre in 1148 with King **Baldwin III** of Jerusalem identified **Damascus** as the proposed target. The siege failed, for reasons that are not clear due to the multiplicity of explanations in the sources. These range from the usual infighting among the military leaders to poor planning that led to a lack of water for the troops. King Louis's complaint that the Greeks had hampered his efforts may have been influenced by the enmity between his ally Roger of **Sicily** and the Byzantines. St. Bernard's explanation was that the combatants had not been pure of heart. For the perspective of local Islamic leaders *see also* **Nur al-Din**; **Zengi**.

SELJUK (SELCHUK/SELJUQ) TURKS. The Turks have a long history, but in the context of the crusades became known to the **Byzantines** as mercenary troops in the 11th century. They came from central Asia where they had contact with **Islam** through **Muslim** traders, and also served various Islamic rulers as mercenaries, especially in **Egypt** and Iran, from the ninth century.

To the sedentary population of the steppes "Turk" was a general term used to describe neighboring bands of pastoral nomads, rather than a geographic area or political organization. Seljuk is the name of a chief of the later 10th century who is the founder of the Selchükids or Seljuks, eventual conquerors of **Syria** and upper Mesopotamia (parts of modern Iran and Iraq) in the 1050s. Conquest of Iraq included the caliphate at **Baghdad**, traditional center of Islamic political power. The Turks did not replace the caliph, but controlled him as sultans, preferring to govern from military camps or alternative capitals such as Isfahan. Another branch of the Seljuks attacked Byzantine holdings in **Asia Minor** in the 11th century. Neither the **Abbasid** dynasty (the caliphs) nor the Seljuk sultans attached the same significance to the conquest of **Jerusalem** as did the Europeans or the local Muslim leaders. The **jihad** which eventually drove the crusaders out of Islamic territory was proclaimed by their neighbors: **Nur al-Din**, Turkish ruler of Syria, and **Saladin**, a **Kurd** who controlled Egypt.

On the eve of the **First Crusade**, the Turkish Sultanate of Iraq was the inheritance of the sons of Malik Shah (r.1072-92), Berkyaruk (Seljuk sultan 1094-1105), and Muhammad (Seljuk sultan 1105-18). Their preoccupation was the division of their legacy, which was not settled until 1104. The priorities of the Turkish commanders of **Levantine** communes were maintaining their practical independence from both Baghdad and Isfahan, and war with the Shia **Fatimid** dynasty of Egypt. The Turkish response to European invasion at **Antioch** in 1098, at **Edessa** in 1110, and in a proposed expedition of 1111-12 foundered due to a number of factors, including divisions among the various commanders. An army sent by the Turkish sultan in 1115 to oust the Europeans was met by a coalition of the Muslim cities of **Aleppo** and **Damascus**, which allied with the crusader principality of Antioch to defeat the sultan's army at the battle of Danith.

After this victory Muslim Aleppo took on its erstwhile allies at **Christian** Antioch, and defeated the crusader army in the battle of Balat (Field of Blood) in 1119. The histories of the four crusader principalities or counties (Antioch, Edessa, Jerusalem, **Tripoli**) imitate the Seljuk pattern, as the tiny European enclaves joined the mosaic of independent Turkish Levantine communes jockeying for preeminence through opportunistic battles and short-lived alliances. *See also* **Alp Arslan; Anatolia; Danishmends; Iconium.**

SEPULCHRE. *See* **Holy Sepulchre.**

SEVENTH CRUSADE. *See* **Louis IX**, king of France.

SHROUD. *See* **Holy Shroud.**

SICILY, DESCRIPTION. A Roman province from 241, the island was conquered for **Islam** by 965. Attempts by **Byzantium** to win it back began in 1038. Several members of the Hauteville family, named from their village in Normandy, were on **pilgrimage** to **Jerusalem** in the 1030s. On their way home they were hired as mercenaries by the Byzantine imperial forces in southern Italy. Along with some other renegades, they attacked their Greek masters and took the emperor's province of Apulia in 1041.

Another member of the Hauteville family, Robert (nicknamed Guiscard or "weasel" for his cunning), arrived in Apulia in 1046. When he died in 1085 Robert Guiscard controlled Apulia, Calabria, and Salerno, all in southern Italy. He had delegated the rule of Sicily to his youngest brother, Roger I (d.1101). Roger had begun his activities in the island by working with one of the **Muslim** warlords trying to establish preeminence there, and had employed Muslim troops. His cruelty and greed aroused such anger among the minority **Christian** population that they joined the Muslims to fight him in 1062. Roger responded by sending four camels loaded with plunder to Pope Alexander II (r.1061-73) in order to receive his blessing and a papal banner. The papal standard, or banner, recalls the one given to William Duke of Normandy for the conquest of England in 1066, a sign of St. Peter's protection. The chronicles of Roger's conquest of Sicily were not written until the 1090s, either during or after the **First Crusade**. One of the chroniclers added that the pope also granted the Normans in Sicily absolution for their sins (if they repented) in reward for their struggle against Islam. If this is true it constitutes an important precedent for the First Crusade.

SICILY, IN THE CRUSADES. Several members of the Hauteville family accompanied the **First Crusade**, including **Bohemond of Taranto**, son of Robert Guiscard. The family at this point was established as an enemy of the **Byzantines**. Robert had taken the port of Durazzo in 1081 and had been pushed back out of Macedonia by a combined imperial and **Venetian** force. Bohemond followed in his father's footsteps and managed during the crusade to create the principality of **Antioch** out of Byzantine lands. Meanwhile Roger I's son Roger II (r.1103-54), his grandson William I (r.1154-66), and his great-grandson William II (r.1166-89) held the kingdom of Sicily as vassals of the pope. As his vassals and heroes of the war against **Islam**, they also held the office of papal legate, giving them the freedom to appoint clergy to ecclesiastical offices and to handle all appeals from Sicilian church courts that would otherwise have been referred to Rome.

Count Roger I reportedly rejected Pope **Urban II**'s plea to join the First Crusade. Roger's widow, Adelaide, agreed to marry King **Baldwin I** of **Jerusalem** in 1113 on condition that her son Roger II inherit the kingdom. The marriage was barren, and annulled after three years, a humiliation to the Sicilians. By 1130 Roger II had attacked the Italian mainland and alienated the pope by interfering in a disputed papal election. The king of Jerusalem was alarmed by Roger's claim to the principality of Antioch on the death of Bohemond II in 1130. The prospect of his projected conquest of southern Italy made enemies not only of the Byzantines but of the Italian city-communes and the **Holy Roman Emperor**. In 1137 Emperor Lothair (r.1125-37) sent an army to southern Italy to settle complaints against Roger by the barons of Apulia, Venetian merchants whose trade he had intercepted in the Mediterranean, and the Byzantine emperor, who was enraged by Roger's invasion of Greece. By 1139 Roger II had not only deflected Lothair's troops, but also had beaten a papal army sent by Innocent II (r.1130-43) and recruited by St. **Bernard of Clairvaux**. General exasperation with Roger's pretensions cemented an alliance between the Byzantines and the emperors of the west.

In 1146 Byzantine Emperor Manuel **Comnenus** married the daughter of King **Conrad III** (r.1137-52) of Germany. Part of the agreement stipulated a joint expedition against Roger, the "invader of two empires," with the help of the Venetians. Fortunately for Roger, **Zengi** took **Edessa** in 1144, and the **Second Crusade** was being preached. King **Louis VII** of France secured an alliance with Sicily in 1146, accepting Roger's offer to join the expedition and provide supplies and transportation. But in 1147 Roger was temporarily outmaneuvered by Conrad III, who also joined the crusade. Louis VII was convinced to take the overland route through **Constantinople**, and Roger withdrew from the crusade rather than meet the Byzantines as allies. Instead he sent a fleet to take several Byzantine islands, including Corfu, and then sack wealthy Greek cities, including Athens, Thebes, and Corinth. Manuel sent a relief force and besieged Corfu, but in 1149 Roger's fleet sailed by them to raid the coast of Greece and Constantinople itself. The Sicilian fleet shot burning arrows into the imperial palace and raided the orchards. They also picked up King Louis VII and his queen Eleanor of Aquitaine, who were having their own difficulties with the Byzantines, and carried them to Italy. Roger met them on their way to Rome, and may have influenced Louis's presentation of the failure of the crusade as the fault of the Greeks.

One of the complaints against Roger was that he planned to take Africa. He sent regular raiding parties there and in 1146 he conquered Tripoli in northern Africa, following this with the conquest of Mahdia, Tunisia, in 1148. He used these two ports as a base from which to attack other cities along the North African coast. Roger's heir lost this African "colony" by 1160, but retained trading agreements with the North African Muslims. William II instead turned his attention to the Mediterranean, securing a 15-year truce with Germany (the Holy Roman Empire) in 1177. The king of Sicily sent men and money to support the **Latin**

Kingdom of Jerusalem, but his policy at home was one of tolerance for Islam, and he employed **Muslims** in his army and navy. In 1173 Shia nobles in **Egypt** sought an alliance with William against **Saladin**, who was replacing the **Fatimid** dynasty with a Sunni government. By the time William's navy, reportedly 200 galleys carrying 30,000 men, reached Alexandria in 1174, Saladin had heard of the plot and executed William's Egyptian allies. The inhabitants of the city delayed the Norman landing by sinking all the ships in the harbor, and after the **siege** had begun, managed to burn the **siege engines**. The Normans fled before Saladin himself could arrive.

In 1185 William attacked Greece by land and sea, hoping to take Constantinople itself. The main outcome of this war was a truce between the beleaguered Byzantine emperor and Saladin that helped the latter to take the crusader kingdom in 1187. In 1188 William sent help to **Conrad of Montferrat** at **Tyre**, and assisted the Europeans in holding Antioch and **Tripoli**.

SICILY, AND THE HOLY ROMAN EMPIRE. Upon William's death in 1189 there was a dispute over the Sicilian throne. **Holy Roman Emperor** Henry VI (r.1190-97) had been William's choice because of Henry's marriage to Roger II's daughter Constance. Some of William's nobles instead crowned Tancred of Lecce. William's widow, Joan, was the sister of King **Richard I** of England and opposed Tancred's election.

On his way to the **Third Crusade**, Richard stopped in Sicily to contest Tancred's coronation. By 1194 Tancred was dead and Henry VI had been crowned in his place. He could count on neither the inhabitants of Italy nor on the papacy for support in cementing his hold on his new kingdom. The popes could not afford to allow the Holy Roman Emperors to hold southern Italy in place of their Norman vassals. Henry launched his own crusade in 1195 partially to win over his opponents and establish his reputation as a papal ally. The army of German nobles that assembled for this crusade in southern Italy helped Henry to put down a rebellion there in 1197 before they left for **Acre**. Henry died in September, and civil war broke out in Germany, causing his crusaders to hurry home in 1198. *See* **Ayyubid Dynasty**.

Henry's heir, Frederick II, was crowned in Palermo in 1198, but was too young to rule. The Empire's holdings in Sicily and southern Italy effectively passed to the **papacy** as regents for the Germans. They were unable to maintain order there, and the south was turbulent during Frederick's regency, contested by various factions among the inhabitants, and threatened by **Muslim** or **Byzantine** invasion. By 1220 Frederick had assumed effective control but was distracted by his involvement in the long-standing German feud with the papacy and then was absent during the **Sixth Crusade**.

When Frederick died in 1250, in theory the Italian kingdoms passed to his son Conrad and then to his grandson, Conradin. However, in 1258 Frederick's natural son Manfred had himself crowned king of Palermo. The papacy did not support him, but instead eventually offered southern Italy to **Charles of Anjou** (1266), hoping to acquire a loyal vassal with the help of the Capetian monarchy.

Charles was less malleable than had been hoped, and the rebellion against French rule called the Sicilian Vespers, of 1282, was in some ways beneficial to the papacy. Pope Martin IV backed a French crusade in 1285 to retake the kingdom. The defeat of this expedition by King Peter III of **Aragon** (d.1285) led to a truce that divided the south, giving Sicily to the house of Aragon and Naples to Charles's heirs. Papal hopes to control the south and create a loyal ally there were dashed, but the threat to central Italy was much diminished by the division.

SIDON. An ancient Phoenician port, known from both Hebrew scripture and Greek poetry, Sidon was held by the **Fatimids** until the crusaders took it in 1110. **Saladin** reconquered it and leveled its defenses after 1187. It was taken by Europeans and **Muslim** powers in turn over the next hundred years, its defenses alternately rebuilt (1197, 1228, 1253) by crusaders and again leveled (1249, 1260). After the **Mongol** attack in 1260 the **Templars** made one more attempt to create a base there, but the last vestiges of the crusader kingdoms vanished in the **Levant** after the fall of **Acre** in 1291.

The city served as the base for a fief and fortress of the **Latin Kingdom of Jerusalem**, held by the descendants of Eustace Garnier (Grenier, *see* **Baldwin II**), to whom it was given in 1110. These include Gerard (d.1171) and his son Reynald Grenier. In 1169 Reynald married Agnes of Courtenay. *See* **Edessa** for the Courtenays and **Baldwin IV** for the succession crisis and Reynald of Sidon.

SIEGE. Pitched field battles were not as popular a medieval military strategy as were raids, ambushes, and sieges. Both **Muslim** and **Christian** armies favored the military barricade of a **castle** or town in order to starve out the garrison or inhabitants.

The 12th century saw a turning point in technology, when, in an ongoing attempt to create impregnable enclosures, stone replaced wood as the primary building material. Siege warfare was in response ingenious, flexible, adaptive to local conditions and supplies, and dependent as much on psychological factors as on more material weapons. When a surprise storming of a walled enclosure failed, complete isolation of the castle garrison or town inhabitants was desirable for success, with communication as well as access to water and food blocked, and morale attacked by various demonstrations (noisemaking or torture of hostages, for instance), bribery, and negotiations. Terms offered by the attacker and refused by the defenders could lead to a deliberately gruesome defeat, in which massacre and/or selective acts of terror were used to deter the next victim from resisting a siege.

Sieges often had to rely on both land and **naval** forces. The skilled labor necessary to build and equip ships easily translated into the construction of **siege engines** for use on land. The need for these combined skills made the involvement of Italian cities such as **Genoa**, **Pisa**, and **Venice** crucial to the crusade effort. Engineers who could claim expertise in designing siege weapons were increasingly valued.

SIEGE ENGINES. Clear medieval descriptions of the mechanisms of "siege engines," essentially rock throwers, apparently have not survived. There is considerable debate among historians about the meaning of and relationship between the Latin terms *mangonella*, *petraria*, *ballista*, *catapulta*, and *tormentum* as used by medieval writers who may not have been experts on either Latin or **weapons**. There is also a considerable literature on weapons by modern amateurs and experts who have built replicas. There is not much agreement on details, and there are various estimates of the range and force of such weapons.

The mangonel was a large swing beam rock thrower used against fortifications, and needing either a lever mechanism or considerable manpower. The ballista was a smaller version, more suitable to throwing bolts or arrows against people. It worked by torsion. The word ballista can also refer to a wheeled or stationary crossbow which required several men for its operation. Steel-tipped darts shot from a replica torsion device have been thrown with force over 800 yards, inflicting damage on one or more combatants depending on the size of the projectiles, distances, and the strength of the armor worn by those hit. The intended effect was certainly to punch through metal and/or leather gear. A handheld crossbow, slower to use than a **Muslim** bow but more accurate and powerful, could punch through armor at 60 yards (the English longbow, famous for penetrating armor, was not used until the 14th century). Any kind of catapult could be used to throw bottles or clay jars filled with "Greek fire," a naphtha-based compound supposedly of Byzantine origin, instead of rock. Damaged structures might be pulled down by infantry using poles, hooks, or other tools.

Roman and Chinese sources give more detail on exactly how torsion and lever devices worked than do medieval European or Middle Eastern ones. Torsion rock throwers with either one or two arms were used as early as the Roman period. They worked by means of springs made of twisted rope or animal sinew and tendons. They were difficult to construct and heavy (about two tons) to move. Lever artillery, using a counterweight, is thought to have been used by Europeans starting in the 12th century because it was lighter and easier to build. Lever artillery originated in China before the seventh century and was in use by **Byzantium** and **Islam** when the **First Crusade** arrived in the East.

It is difficult to be sure from chronicle accounts what the size of the projectile and range of an individual counterweight machine was. Modern replicas have been built to test this, producing machines which can throw an object weighing about 160 pounds to about 200 yards. Obviously the size of the machine is decisive. Fedden and Thomson, in their work on *Crusader Castles*, noted 600-pound stones they thought were used as projectiles in the ruins of the castle of Saone, captured by **Saladin** in 1188 (p. 81).

Machines of this kind were tricky to use, requiring a knowledgeable crew as well as a competent designer. Projectiles are described as falling out of the device onto those manning it, or sometimes being accidentally projected back onto the besieging army. Wheels needed to be attached to the machines to move them. Some experts feel the wheels would have had to have been removed for stability during use. Others argue that without the wheels, the force needed in operation would have damaged the device. Accuracy in hitting a target was low.

Wheeled towers, covered in hides doused in vinegar to deter fire, were used to bring archers, sappers, and ramming equipment close to the walls of the fortification. Four-storied towers of wood, using lead, iron, copper, or just earth and animal skins for protective cover could be used to bring the attackers to a place where they could leap the distance between the tower and the walls, allowing the siege army to enter the city. Bridges to assist them in this process were improvised out of a number of materials. During the siege of Crema in 1160, **Holy Roman Emperor** Frederick Barbarossa used a bridge specially constructed to put a large number of invaders on the walls. It was reportedly 60 feet long, with an armored roof. Sappers protected by siege towers or by portable armored roofs could use tunnels to undermine and collapse sections of fortification walls. In 1154-55 the count of **Barcelona** used a floating siege tower large enough to hold 200 men at Arles. It was pulled along the Rhone River from the banks and guided by small boats.

Towers could also be built aboard ships to bring attackers close to sea walls. Simpler strategies included filling in moats, ramming the gate with a tall tree held by many attackers, and using ladders and ropes to scale the walls. Defenders showered the attackers with arrows, stones, or debris, dug countertunnels, deflected the ram with grappling hooks, or used Greek fire in their turn. Counterforts, constructed by a besieging army against towers or to encircle a city or other large defensive system, were a standard method of assault.

At sieges involving a harbor or lake it was possible to tie a number of boats together to create a blockade. At the siege of Bari, for instance (1068-71), Robert Guiscard chained boats together and then improvised wooden bridges between them and the land to create a defensible sea wall. The conquest of southern Italy in the 12th century is a good example of medieval strategy. R. Rogers, in *Latin Siege Warfare*, analyzed the career of Roger II, ruler of **Sicily** (1103-54), finding that more than 80 sieges are reported by the sources, 50 of which were successful (p. 119). *See* **castles** for building techniques designed to deter sieges.

SIXTH CRUSADE. Emperor Frederick II (r.1215-50) took the **cross** at his coronation in Aachen in 1215. Embroiled in a struggle for power with the **papacy**, the Emperor formally promised in 1225, under pain of excommunication, to go on crusade by August 1227. He became seriously ill in September of that year, having missed the deadline, but more importantly, angered Pope Gregory IX (r.1227-41) so that Gregory was deaf to his attempts at reconciliation. The immediate cause of their dispute was the succession of the kingdom of **Sicily**. In June of 1228 Frederick decided to depart for the Holy Land without papal absolution, as a public declaration of his willingness to be reconciled and the pope's intransigence. Meanwhile the pope ignored Frederick's status as a crusader by invading imperial lands in Italy.

Beyond the polemic with Gregory IX, Frederick's preparation for the crusade included his marriage in 1225 to Isabel, daughter of **John of Brienne** (d.1237) and heiress to the **Latin Kingdom of Jerusalem**. In spite of a previous agreement with John, who had expected to hold the regency of the kingdom for his daughter until his own death, Frederick immediately claimed the title and effective control of the kingdom, which had been based at **Acre** since the loss of the kingdom in 1187.

He had ordered a fleet to be constructed for the expedition as early as 1224, which included 50 large galleys and 100 smaller ones designed to allow mounted **knights** to be landed directly on shore. He planned to use the fleet to transport 1,000 knights, and to maintain them for two years at his own expense. Beyond that, the agreement of 1225 between Frederick and the papacy stipulated that he also pay the transport costs of an additional 2,000 knights with their entourages and 6,000 **horses**. The additional agreement means that Frederick's own army of 1,000 must also have been planned to include at least three horses each. It is not known how many of these projected forces actually arrived at Acre in 1228, but even a portion of them would have effectively threatened Damietta and Cairo, in contrast to the smaller navies brought unsuccessfully by both the **Fifth Crusade** and King **Louis IX** of France in 1248.

Frederick's campaign was technically successful, in that he regained access to **Bethlehem**, **Nazareth**, and **Jerusalem** by means of a treaty with **al-Kamil**, sultan of **Egypt** in 1229. Both rulers earned the criticism of their own followers for making the agreement. Frederick entered Jerusalem in defiance of the **patriarch** of the city, who had placed it under interdict to prevent the excommunicated Frederick's coronation as ruler of the Latin Kingdom. The Emperor's army completed their **pilgrimage** on March 18 by visiting the **Holy Sepulchre**, where Frederick crowned himself.

Frederick fought the troops of the patriarch of Jerusalem in Acre, while John of Brienne, backed by the pope, raised an army against the Emperor in Italy. Leaving a garrison to protect his interests in Acre, Frederick, pelted with garbage by the inhabitants, left for Italy in order to take up arms against the pope.

SPANISH INQUISITION. The **Inquisition** as a legal process originated under papal supervision in southern France after the **Albigensian Crusade**. It was a method of questioning suspects and assembling proofs in order to identify **Christian** heretics. The Spanish Inquisition, founded by papal bull on 1 November 1478, arose in the context of the **Reconquista**, the crusade against the **Muslims** of Iberia, but was aimed in the first instance at **Jews** who had converted to Christianity. From 1232 clerics had been commissioned to inquire into the **Cathar** heresy in Spain, as they had been in southern France. The papal bull of 1478 was not acted on until 1480, but it commissioned inquisitors to look into Christian heresy promulgated by converted Jews, and it put appointment of the inquisitors in the hands of the Spanish monarchy. On 27 September 1480 the **Dominicans** Juan de San Martín, Miguel de Morillo, and Juan Ruiz de Medina were appointed by Ferdinand II king of Castile (r.1474-1504 as Ferdinand V), **Aragon** (r.1479-1504) and then Spain (r.1504-16) to identify and eliminate the threat from "judaizers."

From the decisive battle of Las Navas de Tolosa against the **Muwahhid** dynasty in 1212, Spain's offensive against Muslim powers in the peninsula was essentially a consolidation of victory. By 1391, a year of considerable economic hardship, the Muslim population of Iberia was politically defeated but much larger than that of the Jewish minority. Christians rioted, aiming violence at two minorities blamed in a confused way for economic difficulties: aristocrats and Jews.

Before the **First Crusade**, the crusaders led by **Emicho of Flonheim** in 1096 had paused in Germany to murder Jews, theorizing that the enemies of Christ could be found at home before they were eliminated in **Jerusalem**. The slaughter of Jews in that case preceded the massacre of the Muslim inhabitants of the Holy City in 1099. In Iberia, a similar logic applied, in the sense that crusading increased hostility against Jews as well as against the Muslim enemy. Judaism was to be outlawed in 1492, and Islam in 1502, after a century of outright war against the last Muslim stronghold at Granada and a concurrent series of legal moves to isolate and expel the Jewish population. The reason given in official documents for laws aimed against Islam and Judaism was the danger these alternative religions offered to the salvation of Christian believers.

The riots of 1391 were aimed at the aristocracy and at the Jews, who in general constituted an educated middle class of artisans, traders, physicians, and translators. Reliable population numbers are not available for medieval Spain. Some estimates of the loss of life due to the riots of 1391 put the number massacred to one-fourth of the population in some areas. Jewish residence was concentrated in the cities, and in some cases the governors and other officials vainly attempted to protect them. In some cities so many people were massacred that the Jewish quarter ceased to exist after the riots. Some were able to save themselves by accepting baptism.

Forced conversions were not sanctioned by either ecclesiastical or secular law, but many who had survived the riots of 1391 by accepting forced baptism kept their status as converts. Technically, the status of Christian entitled them to previously forbidden authority in government and the military. Some scions of converted families eventually entered the church, even becoming bishops. At the same time, the "Old Christians" continued to recognize the converts as Jews. There is evidence that the *conversos* responded by taking pride in their mixed identity of Jewish descent and Christian belief. From 1255 political anxiety arising out of the mixed races and religions of the Iberian Peninsula had created laws forbidding Christians to convert to Islam or Judaism. Anxiety over the influence of the Jews and *conversos* in particular led to the establishment of regional or local laws attempting to restrict Jewish residences and professions. In 1467 and 1473 there were riots against *conversos* in Toledo and Segovia. Numbers are unknown, but by 1480 when the crowns of Aragon and Castile were united in the persons of Ferdinand and Isabella there were considerable minority populations of converted Jews and Muslims. The problem of the position of these converts within the realm appeared to contemporaries to be acute. Jewish *conversos* were accused of a range of harmful activities, from practicing Judaism in private to the ritual murder of Christian infants. The process of the Inquisition was put into practice in 1480 essentially to identify Jews and Muslims among those who had converted, and to neutralize the perceived threat they offered to Spanish society.

Those who had never converted were by law exempt from the *inquisition*, a formal process used in ecclesiastical courts to identify Christian heretics. The Muslim majority waited its turn in the early 16th century. The Inquisitors began by putting pressure on the Jewish community to assist in denouncing the *conversos*. This led to denunciations by both Christians and Jews against a mixed group of converted Christians: those Jews whose families had been baptized 90 years earlier and may really have assimilated, along with those who had accepted conversion as a path to improved legal status or better economic opportunity. Accusations of "judaizing" ranged from not working on Saturday to not knowing the creed. Practices which were common among Christians were taken as proofs of heresy against those who were identified as *conversos*. By 1492 commissions of inquiry had multiplied, and tribunals continued to be established in major population centers. In Castile, for instance, these included Ávila, Córdoba, Jaén, Medina del Campo, Segovia, and Sigüenza, Toledo, and Valladolid. In addition, a council which had been set up to oversee all the regional courts in 1488 led to the creation of the office of "Inquisitor General."

As "heretics" were identified, laws were passed in various dioceses expelling all Jews, including those who had helped the Inquisition, from those regions. Some towns forced Jews out without the benefit of law. During the decade of these piecemeal expulsions, the 1480s, the resources of the state were dedicated to a final victory over the Muslims of Iberia in their last stronghold, Granada. In January of 1492 Granada fell, partially as a result of negotiations which assured Muslim believers of toleration in the now politically Christian peninsula. In March, on the advice of the Dominican Inquisitor General Tomás de Torquemada (d.1498), the Jews were formally expelled from Spain. The decree outlawed Judaism and (ironically) offered Jews baptism as the only alternative to expulsion. Otherwise they were to depart the realm by the end of July.

There was an expectation that Jews would choose conversion over expulsion, and many high-ranking or "court" Jews did so. A recent estimate puts the total Jewish population of Spain at 80,000 people. Export of gold and silver was forbidden, making it difficult for those who chose exile to finance their departure even if they had something to sell. Perhaps as many as half converted. Thousands emigrated to Italy, southern France, and northern Africa. The question of emigration numbers is clouded by the fact that many were forced to return, due to similar persecution in their chosen refuges.

The economic cost of Ferdinand's policy and the role of the papacy in promoting the Inquisition have been much debated. On 18 April 1482, for instance, Pope Sixtus IV (r.1471-84) who had issued the decree founding the Inquisition issued another decree allowing appeals to Rome. The reason given was the disgust Christians felt at the injustice many of the accused had suffered. Future popes would make similar objections, but the crown, once in control of the Inquisition, refused to relinquish it. The pope's protest led only to the promotion of Torquemada to oversight of all the regional inquiries, establishing him in a position to advise the crown on the expulsions of 1492.

Ferdinand presumably saw this quarrel as a test of his authority. A similar incident occurred in 1484 when the city magistrates in Teruel refused entrance to the inquisitors and were deprived by excommunication of their offices. Ferdinand enforced obedience to the inquisitors with troops. In 1484 Ferdinand responded to protests from the regional authorities in Barcelona that "no cause or interest, however great, will make us suspend the Inquisition" (see Kamen, p. 52, under Reconquista in the bibliography).

The process worked as follows: an initial period of grace was given in each area, during which *conversos* could confess voluntarily and pay a fine. Normally those who did so were immune from further prosecution, but there were cases when people were denounced after their original penance. Accusations of those who did not come forward voluntarily were investigated with torture. Those who did not flee were eventually burnt at the stake. Again, estimates of the numbers of persons involved vary widely. The final death toll for the period 1481-1530 may have been 2,000. Only a minority failed to take the options of voluntary confession or flight. Typical auto-da-fé executions saw only a few burnt but dozens condemned in absentia. The inquisitors took the large number of voluntary confessions as proof that heresy existed. The public display of these tactics drove some *conversos* back to Judaism.

Reliable numbers of Muslims and Jews in the total population of Spain are not known. Although it is known that the Inquisition targeted moral issues, Protestantism, and witchcraft as well as heresy, an analysis of the gender, ethnic background, and social status of the accused and the convicted overall is also not available.

STEPHEN OF BLOIS. One of the leaders of the **First Crusade**, Stephen deserted at the **siege** of **Antioch** and returned in 1101 to the Holy Land with a group led by William, earl of Poitou. Stephen was killed at **Ramla** in 1101, leaving his wife Adela, fourth daughter of William the Conqueror, as regent of Blois and Chartres. Adela (c.1062-1137) hosted the marriage of **Bohemond,** Prince of Antioch, to Constance, daughter of King Philip I of France in 1108. Stephen's story is told in the chronicle of **Fulcher of Chartres.**

SUFISM. **Islamic** mysticism, usually compatible with Sunni **Muslim** orthodoxy, had a great popular appeal even where it was viewed with suspicion by the educated. The search for individual experience of the divine led to a profusion of masters, each with a different discipline, and eventually to institutionalized orders, or organizations, with rules and levels of asceticism. Some branches of Sufism offer ecstatic practices such as eating glass, walking on fire, or piercing the body with skewers. Others incorporate local "saints" or rituals. The Yezidi order, for instance, influential among **Kurds**, was founded in the 12th century and posits a group of seven Holy Beings to whom the Creator assigned the running of the world. There was a shrine, supposedly the burial place of the founder of the sect, at Lalish, Iraq, which attracted the condemnation of orthodox Muslims. Other orders contradict Muslim practices, allowing, for instance, the eating of pork.

SWORDBRETHREN. The Swordbrethren were also known as the Militia of Christ of Livonia. They were a **military order** founded by Bishop **Albert** of Livonia at Riga in 1202 to protect **Christian** settlements and enforce conversion on the local inhabitants. The order of **Dobrin** in Prussia was established at about the same time and for the same reasons. The Swordbrethren wore white mantles with their symbol on their left shoulders: a red sword and the **cross**. Both orders were absorbed into the **Teutonic Knights** in the 1230s. *See also* **Templars**.

SYRIA. Syria was not a territorial state in the Middle Ages. The area was conquered between 1071 and 1079 by the **Seljuk Turks** and divided into principalities with shifting boundaries, nominally subject to the **Ayyubid** and then to the **Mamluk** dynasties and in theory loyal to the caliph in **Baghdad**. **Mongol** incursion after 1250 further complicated the political organization of Syria. Its history is written from the perspective of the various contenders for regional power operating from the larger cities. The "Jazira" refers to a territory between the Tigris and Euphrates Rivers. *See also* **Aleppo**; **Damascus**.

-T-

TANCRED. He was the nephew of **Bohemond of Taranto**, a **First Crusader**, who played a notable role in the foundation of the **Latin Kingdom of Jerusalem**. He left for the crusade of 1096 at the age of 20 in the company of his uncle, who became prince of **Antioch**. Tancred carved out a lordship for himself with 80 of his **knights** after the **siege of Jerusalem** in 1099, taking Nablus, Tiberias, Baisan (or Bethsan), and Haifa. This territory put him on the frontier between the new crusader state and **Muslim Damascus** in southern Syria, and made him one of the tenants-in-chief of the kingdom.

Tancred gave up this lordship in 1101 to become regent of Antioch. The garrison there had sent urgently for him to take over the defense of the city when his uncle was captured by the **Danishmends**. Tiberias became one of the major fiefs of the Latin Kingdom and was given to Hugh of Falkenberg.

As regent Tancred took the **Cilician** cities of Mamistra, Adana, and Tarsus, as well as the **Byzantine** port of Latakia. Bohemond was released and resumed power in 1103. He and Tancred went to the assistance of **Baldwin of Le Bourg** and Joscelin, his chief vassal, in 1104 at Harran, 23 miles south of Baldwin's city of **Edessa**. The emirs of Mardin and **Mosul** had combined forces and were able to decimate the crusader troops, capturing Baldwin and Joscelin. Tancred escaped with difficulty to briefly become regent of Edessa. However, Bohemond left for Italy, and Tancred was once again installed as regent of Antioch. He made Edessa a dependent fief under the rule of Richard of the Principate of Salerno (1104-08).

Baldwin of Le Bourg was released in 1108 and went to war with Tancred for the restoration of his county. Edessa was returned to him in September, but an angry Tancred allied with the Muslim lord of **Aleppo**, Ridwan, against Baldwin in the fall, defeating the lord of Edessa at a battle near the fortress of Tell Bashir. Both crusaders returned to their fiefs after this falling out.

Tancred died in December of 1112. Roger of Salerno succeeded him as regent of Antioch.

TEMPLARS, MILITARY ORDER OF THE. Hugh of Payns (d.1136) and nine companions consecrated themselves to the protection of **pilgrims**, creating the first **military order** of monks in 1119-20. Their original vow was directed to the authority of the patriarch of **Jerusalem**, and they took the Augustinian rule of communal poverty in imitation of the canons of the **Holy Sepulchre**. Their first name was the Poor **Knights** of Christ. They were housed on the **Temple** Mount, in what was at the time a royal palace. Eventually there was a complex of buildings on the Temple Mount close to the city walls for their use, with a gate they controlled to exit or enter the city. A 13th-century observer testified that they continued to observe "poverty, chastity, and obedience," the keynotes of the monastic life. At the Council of Troyes, in January 1128, their rule was elaborated with the help of **Bernard of Clairvaux**, whose tract, *In Praise of the New Knighthood*, laid the theoretical groundwork for the military orders.

The 11th century in Europe saw the establishment of secular confraternities, organized to protect ecclesiastical institutions and pilgrims from local threats. In the same era, there are reports of monks in Spain fighting **Muslims**. The key differences between these organizations and the military orders are, first, that unlike members of a secular confraternity, laymen in the military orders took vows to lead a religious life according to a rule. Then, unlike monks who may have been moved to fight in exceptional circumstances, the Templar rule established fighting rather than prayer as the primary duty of the order. Like other religious orders, they adopted distinctive dress as a symbol of their identity, in this case white cloaks marked with red **crosses**. Only the chaplains of the order were ordained; the knights were laymen living according to a rule.

The Templars were widely influential, prompting the transformation of charitable institutions like the **Order of St. John** into military orders. The pattern was imitated in Iberia as well, with the foundation of orders such as Santiago and Mountjoy.

In the **Levant**, the order was given two marches to defend: the Amanus frontier northwest of **Antioch** and the plain between **Tripoli** and the Orontes River. The Templars bought the fortress of Beaufort in 1260, but it was lost in 1268. After 1187 the order built Chastel Pèlerin on a peninsula near Mount Carmel as a defensive retreat. It was never taken by **siege**. The knights abandoned it after Acre fell in 1291. They continued to hold Ruad, a fortified but waterless island two miles off the coast of Tortosa until 1303.

Grand Masters with the dates during which they held office include Robert of Craon, 1136-48; Everard of Barres, 1148-49; Bernard of Tremelay, 1151-53; Bertrand of Blancfort, 1154-65; Philip of Milly, 1165-70; Odo of St. Amand, 1171-79; Arnold of Toroge, 1180-84; Gerard of Ridefort, 1185-89.

TEMPLARS, TRIAL AND SUPPRESSION. In 1291, when the crusader kingdom fell, the headquarters of the **Orders** of the **Templars, St. John,** and **St. Thomas** moved to **Cyprus**. On 13 October 1307 Templars who were in France were arrested and charged with heresy, idolatry, and immorality, including the encouragement of homosexual acts. It is not clear where the initiative for prosecution originated, but the pope ordered further arrests in all of Europe by 22 November. There was some resistance, especially in Spain, and some brothers fled, but a large number were in custody by 1308 in June, when 72 of them were brought before Pope Clement V at Poitiers, and almost all confessed. Proceedings were to be brought against others by local authorities, acting in concert with **inquisitors**. By March of 1310 numerous trials had taken place in Italy, **Cyprus**, **Aragon**, Majorca, Castile, **Portugal**, and England, and 600 brothers assembled in Paris to defend the order. Many confessed and were punished, including 54 condemned by the archbishop of Sens and burnt on 12 May. Under considerable pressure from King Philip IV, Clement V suppressed the order at the Council of Vienne in 1312, and transferred its property to the **Hospitallers**.

Scholars continue to debate the causes of the prosecution and the meaning of the confessions, which were obtained using torture. The king of France profited by holding the property of the order during the trials and being compensated for relinquishing it to the court after 1312. Philip supported giving their holdings to the Hospitallers. Templar houses in France were small and staffed by sergeants rather than **knights**, so that they did not threaten royal jurisdiction. What is known is that there was considerable criticism of all of the **military orders**, especially in the 14th century, due to the loss of the **Levant** and the slow progress against the **Muslims** in Spain. Medieval critics focused on possible mismanagement of funds and poor morale as well as on the sins listed in the indictment as explanations for failure to defeat an enemy which would continue to threaten Europe's dominance in the Mediterranean until the end of the 17th century.

TEMPLE. Medieval people associated the Temple of Solomon with two buildings which were part of the temple complex in **Jerusalem**: the Dome of the Rock and the al-Aqsa mosque. The original Temple of Solomon was supposed by both **Muslims** and **Jews** to have been built on the site where Abraham prepared to sacrifice his son Isaac (medieval **Christians** located this event on Golgotha). The first Temple was destroyed when the Ark of the Covenant was lost, in 587 B.C., and the second was destroyed in 70 A.D. by the Romans. The ground supposed to have been covered by these early temple complexes is a discrete area within the city of Jerusalem, called "the Noble Sanctuary" by Muslims, on which a number of buildings and monuments stand.

Muslim conquest of Jerusalem in 638 led to the building of the Dome of the Rock as a shrine to commemorate Abraham's obedience and also both Enoch and **Muhammad**'s ascent into heaven, supposedly from the same spot. The crusaders referred to this building as "the Temple of the Lord." The al-Aqsa mosque, a complement to the shrine enclosing the rock, was built close by in 709, also to commemorate Muhammad's ascent at the end of his "Night Journey," and enlarged by the Crusaders as "the Temple of Solomon" after 1099. The **Templars** were housed in this mosque early in their history.

Crusader conquest led to the use of these two buildings for a church and a palace, respectively. An additional building was constructed to house the Augustinian canons who served the church in the Dome of the Rock. This building was destroyed in 1187.

Although the crusaders certainly were concerned to identify and refurbish **pilgrimage** sites, it was the allegorical or spiritual meaning of the sites that was important. Medieval Europeans writing about the Temple in some ways rejected the material remains in favor of the prophetic meaning of historical events, in order to show a clearer contrast between Christianity and Judaism. The "Temple" was a key term in Christian exegesis, which could mean the spiritual purification of the soul, or Christ himself, or the Church as a whole, or the role of the Temple in pre-Christian Judaism. In St. **Bernard of Clairvaux**'s writing on the new order of the Templars, for instance, whatever interest the buildings of the Temple complex may have had to pilgrims or historians is completely eclipsed by an idea with a long history in Christian exegesis about the role of the church in the world.

In the same way, the Dome of the Rock had a number of spiritual meanings for Muslims and Jews that devalued the material. As the place of ascent to heaven, or the spot where the Holy of Holies stood in the original Temple, or even the gate to the Garden of Eden, it is the center of the world, or a place of connection between earth and heaven. Muhammad's night journey, during which the angel Gabriel carried him from Mecca to the Temple Mount so that he could ascend to heaven, can be understood as a physical or as a spiritual event. Below the rock is a cave in which, according to tradition, Abraham, David, Solomon, and Elijah prayed. *See also* **Holy Sepulchre**; **Relic**.

TEUTONIC KNIGHTS. Like the **Orders of St. John** and **St. Lazarus**, this order grew out of a hospital, in this case established by "Germans" in **Acre** before the **Third Crusade** (1190). In 1193 Count **Henry of Champagne** assigned the order the defense of part of the wall that protected Acre. In 1198 German crusaders arranged for the house to have a two-part rule: the rule of the Hospitallers for the hospital and care of **pilgrims**; and the rule of the **Templars** for its military activities. Through the 13th century the order had considerable possessions in the **Levant** and in Spain. Eventually, its focus on the Northern or **Baltic Crusades** would be more important to its history.

In 1211 King Andrew II of Hungary gave the order frontier territory to the north of the Transylvanian Alps. Members of the order came to the district of Burzenland by 1212 and successfully defended it from the Cumans, thus extending their own holdings and benefiting the Hungarians by protecting their borders. Disputes with the king over property rights led to his expulsion of them in 1225.

Conrad of Masovia in Poland offered the order the district of Culmerland, and the **Holy Roman Emperor** Frederick II encouraged their expansion by confirming the grant and offering them whatever they could conquer in Prussia. Both the **Swordbrethren** and the order of **Dobrin** were absorbed into the Teutonic Knights in the 1230s, which extended the Knights' activities into Livonia and **Estonia**.

In spite of revolts in 1242 and 1260, the Knights were in **Lithuania** by the 14th century. From 1280 one of their characteristic square castles, Marienburg, was the seat of the order in West Prussia. In 1291, when the crusader kingdom in the Levant fell to the Muslims, the order moved its headquarters to **Venice**, equidistant from the frontiers on the Mediterranean and the Baltic. The Battle of Tannenberg in 1410 when an army of Poles and Lithuanians decimated the main army of the order was the beginning of its decline. *See* **Military Orders**.

THEOBALD IV. Theobald was count of Champagne (1201-53), and king of **Navarre** (1234-53). The truce arranged by **Holy Roman Emperor** Frederick II to end the **Sixth Crusade** was to expire in 1239. Anticipating this, Pope Gregory IX (r.1227-41) called for a new crusade starting in 1234, realizing the importance of raising funds for a plan which called for maintaining troops in the Holy Land for 10 years after the projected arrival date (1239-49).

Theobald took the **cross**, intending to go to **Acre**, but was asked by the pope to instead assist **John of Brienne**, once titular king of Jerusalem but now hard-pressed ruler of the **Latin Empire of Constantinople**. The crusade to Acre was to leave in August 1239, to be led by Frederick II, while the one to Constantinople was to depart in 1238. In the event, John's son and heir requested money rather than troops. Then, Frederick II, at odds with the **papacy** again over imperial rights in Italy (*see* **Sicily**; **Charles of Anjou**), was excommunicated in March of 1239. Frederick was guardian and regent for his son, the heir to Jerusalem, and had offered both support and leadership for the crusade.

In August, urged by the pope, the crusade left without the emperor. The army was essentially French, and led by Theobald and another peer of the realm, the duke of Burgundy. Champagne was a crusading family (*see* **Henry II of Champagne**), and Theobald, like many a crusader before him, left home at a moment when he was in serious trouble. He had rebelled against King **Louis IX of France** in 1226 and his legal status as a **pilgrim** protected him from the reprisals that had not yet caught up with him.

The barons of the Holy Land advised the army to stop at **Cyprus** in order to take council with them about the military situation of the **Ayyubid** dynasty, which controlled **Egypt**, the lands of the old **Latin Kingdom of Jerusalem**, and **Damascus** (southern **Syria**). Delayed by a storm in the Mediterranean, Theobald landed instead at Acre in September. He was met by the barons and the leaders of the **military orders**: the **Hospitallers**, the **Templars**, and the **Teutonic Knights**. Also on hand was Walter of Brienne, Theobald's vassal (and the nephew of John of Brienne), to whom Emperor Frederick II had given the county of **Jaffa**.

The crusader council decided to take **Ascalon**. This city, originally part of the Latin Kingdom, had been taken by **Saladin** in 1187 and then returned, its fortifications razed, to the Europeans as part of the treaty between **al-Kamil** and Frederick II after the Sixth Crusade. Its refortification would have extended and protected the county of Jaffa.

On 2 November 1239, the army, reportedly composed of 4,000 **knights**, half local and half from France, left for the south. At Jaffa Theobald lost control of the army, and a raiding party of 400 to 600 knights raced ahead to scout for the rumored approach of the sultan's forces, in order to make a name for themselves. Among them was Walter of Brienne, but he and about half the raiding party fled when the raiders were ambushed by the sultan's army near Gaza. Part of the group was slaughtered, while about 80 knights were captured. An attempt at rescue failed when the sultan's army retreated rather than meet the main crusade army head on. Instead of either pursuing the **Muslims** or fortifying Ascalon, the crusaders retreated in their turn to Acre. Meanwhile the local Muslim commander offered the tiny garrison in Jerusalem their lives in return for handing over the city at the end of the truce period. The garrison was offered no assistance by Theobald, so they also left for Acre, and Jerusalem reverted peacefully to Muslim control.

Instead, Theobald allied with the Muslim prince of Damascus against the sultan of Egypt, and marched south again to Jaffa. Both the count's supporters and the army of Damascus were against the alliance, and when the allies met the sultan's forces near Jaffa, general confusion ensued. Many of the Damascenes went over to the sultan's side, while the **Christians** fled to Ascalon. The sultan of Egypt in his turn offered an alliance to Theobald, who accepted.

This truce, which confirmed and extended the one negotiated during the Sixth Crusade, was unpopular with everyone but Theobald, who visited the Holy City and then left for home in September of 1240. It gave the local European barons Jerusalem and a wide corridor of access to it, as well as Ascalon and other important fortresses. The question was whether they would be able to keep these places, given the small number of Europeans to hold the territory and their role in the war between Egypt and Damascus. The only immediate hope lay in the expected arrival of **Richard of Cornwall** and a party of troops from England. The barons returned to Acre, leaving a small garrison to begin the reconstruction of the fortifications at Ascalon.

THIRD CRUSADE. An international venture, led by the kings of France and England, the crusade took **Acre** and Arsuf, establishing the second **Latin Kingdom** in the **Levant**. **Frederick Barbarossa** and the German army took the land route, but disbanded after the emperor's death in **Cilicia** in 1190. King Philip II Augustus of France (r.1180-1223) arrived at Acre in 1191 and left at the end of the campaign season, while King **Richard I** of England (r.1189-99) stayed for a year in the Frankish East. The crusade was a response to the fall of the Latin Kingdom of **Jerusalem** at **Hattin** in 1187. It accomplished little in terms of reconquering territory beyond establishing **Guy of Lusignan** on the throne of **Cyprus** and **Henry of Champagne** as king of the crusader territory in the Levant by virtue of his marriage to **Amalric I**'s daughter Isabel (d.1205).

The crusade ended in a truce between Richard and **Saladin** which gave the Europeans a strip of territory from **Jaffa** to **Tyre**, with parts of the crusader county of **Tripoli** and principality of **Antioch**.

TOULOUSE, COUNTS. *See* **Albigensian Crusade**; **First Crusade**; **Tripoli**.

TRANSJORDAN. This lordship of the **Latin Kingdom of Jerusalem** controlled the land route from Cairo to **Damascus** with a string of **castles** from the Dead Sea to the Gulf of Aqaba. King **Baldwin I** of Jerusalem built Montreal, two forts at Petra, and Aila on the Gulf of Aqaba. Kerak, the greatest of these castles near the Dead Sea, was built in 1142.

The lordship became even more important when **Saladin** established the **Ayyubid** dynasty's rule over **Egypt** and **Syria**. The crusader lords of the region extended their jurisdiction into the southern Sinai Desert, including by 1169 the monastery of St. Catherine at Mount Sinai. Saladin was encroaching on the outskirts of Transjordan by 1170 to ensure the safety of the **pilgrimage** route to Mecca.

TRIPOLI. This was in the first instance a port city on the coast of what is now Lebanon, used to supply **Damascus**. At the time of the **First Crusade** it was held by the **Fatimids** of **Egypt**. It became one of four principalities or counties which made up the crusader kingdoms: Jerusalem, **Antioch**, and **Edessa** were the other three. At the peak of crusader power in the **Levant**, the early 12th century, the fief of Tripoli could field 300 **knights**, and unlike Antioch, which was autonomous, owed knight service to the **Latin Kingdom of Jerusalem** of 100 men.

Tripoli was held by the family of the counts of Toulouse between 1109 and 1187. Count **Raymond of Saint-Gilles**, one of the leaders of the First Crusade, died besieging Tripoli in 1105. The **castle** of Mount Pilgrim was built by Raymond in 1103 just outside the walls as a base from which to attack the city. When the city fell in 1109, Raymond's son Bertram (r.1109-12) claimed the lordship. *See* **Nur al-Din**.

Raymond III of Tripoli (r.1152-87) played a key role in the fall of the Latin Kingdom. He was regent during the minority of **Baldwin IV**, but then was replaced by **Reynald of Châtillon**. His claim to the Latin Kingdom of Jerusalem was equivalent to that of the princes of Antioch, so that their rivalry prevented either family from making an effective bid for power during the illness of the young king. Raymond married the heiress to Galilee, making him the greatest landholder in the kingdom.

In 1180 Raymond entered the kingdom with troops, presumably to take over during the succession crisis of that year, when the king's sister and heir, Sybil (d.1190), was widowed and seeking a suitable husband. Sybil was married to **Guy of Lusignan**, much to the disgust of Raymond and the **Ibelins**. In 1181 Guy began to be associated with Sybil and the king in royal acts, and in 1182 Raymond again appeared at the border of the kingdom with troops. He was denied access to the king, but the High Court advised a reconciliation, given the imminent danger posed by **Saladin**. The truce between Baldwin IV and Saladin expired in May 1182.

In 1183 Guy was given command of a large force to meet Saladin's invasion but the engagement was inconclusive, due either to his inexperience or to the unwillingness of the barons of the kingdom to accept his leadership, or both. Baldwin IV had Sybil's son crowned as **Baldwin V** and attempted to have her marriage to Guy annulled. Guy's defiance of calls to court allowed the king to begin the process of depriving him of his fiefs. Raymond had again been made regent in 1185 when Baldwin IV died. He refused to do homage when Guy of Lusignan was crowned in 1186 after the death of Baldwin V. Guy attempted to disseize him. Raymond responded by allying himself with Saladin, and allowing **Muslim** troops into Tiberias.

He was reconciled with Guy when Saladin attacked the kingdom in 1187, and fought with the king at **Hattin**. Escaping the battle, he returned to Tripoli, where he fell ill and died in September. His death ended his dynasty. The county passed to the control of the princes of Antioch.

Bohemond VII, count of Tripoli (r.1275-87), was the last of the crusader lords of this county. In the spring of 1285 the **Mamluk** sultan of Egypt took the **Hospitaller** fortress of Margat, among other strongholds in the region, isolating Tripoli by removing possible allies. In 1287 Bartholomew Embriaco took over the government of the city in concert with a Genoese merchant, Benito Zaccaria. Egypt suspected **Genoa** of trying to found a commercial empire in the Levant, and mobilized in 1289. They took the city, and encouraged by their success, prepared to take **Acre** as well. Benito Zaccaria retaliated by attacking **Alexandrian** shipping. The sultan made a treaty with Genoa in 1290, resolving these differences, but died the same year without completing his preparations against Acre.

The Latin bishops of Tripoli and their office dates include: Albert of St. Erard, fl.1104-10; Gerard, c.1137-45; William, fl.1149-52; John, 1183-84; Aimery, 1186-90; Peter of Angoulême, c.1191-96; Geoffrey, fl.1217; Gregory of Montelongo, bishop-elect 1249-51; Opizo, c.1252-59; Paul, 1261-85; Cinthius de Pinea, bishop-elect 1285-86; Bernard of Montmajour, 1286-91. Bernard, the last bishop, was in Rome when Tripoli was sacked in 1289, and sailed to Acre at the head of a papal fleet of galleys in 1290 in a vain attempt to prevent its fall in 1291. Bernard was a Benedictine monk who after the fall of the Latin Kingdom moved first to Cyprus, then to England, and died at Monte Cassino (Italy) in 1296.

TUDEBOD(E), PETER. A priest and crusader from Poitou, France, Peter wrote a chronicle of the **First Crusade**, the *Historia de Hierosolymitano Itinere*, in about 1110, apparently using the anonymous **Gesta** account.

TURKMEN. (Turcoman, Turkoman). In readings about the crusades, this word usually refers to bands or tribes of nomadic Turks from central Asia not identified with any particular political organization. Turkoman is now the official language of Turkmenistan. *See* **Seljuk Turks.**

TYRE. This Mediterranean port, the capital of ancient Phoenicia, was conquered by **Islam** in the seventh century. The first rulers of the **Latin Kingdom of Jerusalem** made the conquest of the seaports a priority, battling Egypt for **Ascalon**, **Jaffa**, and Tyre in the early 12th century. Tyre was captured by a joint effort of the **Venetian** navy and the forces of the Latin Kingdom in 1124. After **Saladin**'s victory over the armies of the Latin Kingdom in 1187, Tyre remained as the only coastal city south of Tripoli that did not fall immediately into **Muslim** hands. By September of 1187 the Crusader army had lost Beirut, Jaffa, Ascalon, and **Sidon**, and had assembled in Tyre to wait for reinforcements. Refugees from inland cities and fortresses joined them, and reinforcements arrived in the person of **Conrad of Montferrat**, who resisted Saladin's offer to release Conrad's father, William, in return for the surrender of the town. Tyre fell in the weeks following the **Egyptian** conquest of **Acre**, which had been garrisoned with the full resources of the crusader kingdom for the siege of 1291. The population in the mid-12th century is estimated at 30,000.

Tyre's importance was due to its location and defenses. It was a place of refuge for the Muslim inhabitants of the Mediterranean littoral in the 1120s as it was for the Europeans after Saladin's victory of 1187. In 1124, when the crusaders finally captured it, it was supported by troops from **Damascus** and a **Fatimid** navy. It was defended by water and a double sea wall on three sides, with a triple, many-towered wall to the east, the only feasible location for approach. The European army held off the land forces to the east, but it was the Venetian blockade, maintained for five-and-a-half months, that induced the garrison to surrender.

The **castles** of Toron, built by Hugh of St. Omer in the Galilean hills in 1103, followed by Scandelion in 1116, were built to act as bases from which to attack Tyre. The citadel of the city was built in 1210 to improve its defenses.

-U-

URBAN II, POPE. (c.1035-99). Odo/Eudes prior of **Cluny** c.1070, was made cardinal-bishop of Ostia by Pope **Gregory VII**. He was acting as the pope's legate in Germany when Gregory died in 1085. For the first few years of Urban's pontificate, which began in 1088, his election was disputed and it was not safe for him to live in Rome. He followed the pattern set by the **papacy** in 1059, of relying on the Norman conquerors of southern Italy and **Sicily** for protection from the **Holy Roman Empire** and the citizens of Rome.

Urban moved to Rome and secured his election by 1094. He held a council at Piacenza to consolidate his position in March 1095, where he received an appeal from the **Byzantine** emperor for warriors to assist in fighting the **Seljuk Turks**. That summer the pope visited Cluny, where he dedicated the main altar of the abbey church and confirmed a number of gifts made to it and its daughter houses. His speech at Clermont in November echoes the reform idealism of his monastic background and of his predecessor, Gregory. He spoke of a church "chaste from all contagion of evil, and free from secular power" (Duffy, *Saints*, 99).

URBAN II, SPEECH AT CLERMONT. There are four accounts of what Pope **Urban II** said at the council of Clermont in 1095 to launch the **First Crusade.** (*See* **Historians.**)

Adhémar of Monteil, bishop of Le Puy, came forward to vow that he would go to **Jerusalem**, and was named leader of the expedition by the pope. Urban directed the clergy at the council to preach the crusade and ordered that all who took the vow to go should sew cloth **crosses** on the shoulders of their garments as a sign of their intention. He seems to have asked for warriors to go to the relief of the eastern church, emphasizing the potential role of "the **Franks**" as a people chosen by God. He also chastised the warriors of Europe for fighting at home, and urged them to seek plunder in the **Levant** instead. Urban promised the crusaders "a new way of salvation" as **knights**, without having to give up their secular profession. More immediately, he promised them an **indulgence**, or the remission of all other penalty imposed for their confessed sins, as the reward for their **pilgrimage** to Jerusalem. Clergy were not to go without permission from their superiors, and other noncombatants were not to go at all.

The pattern that Urban seems to have envisioned was that potential warriors would take a **crusade vow**, witnessed by their local clergy, who would guarantee, under threat of excommunication, the safety of their family and possessions while they were gone. Those signed with the cross were also threatened with anathema if they turned back before reaching the **Holy Sepulchre**. On the other hand, if they died from any cause while on the journey, they died as **martyrs**, due to their vow.

Urban directed all the clergy who attended the council to preach the crusade, and sent a number of letters to regional leaders. During the summer of 1096, he commissioned **Robert of Arbrissel** and Gerento, abbot of St. Bénigne of Dijon, to preach the crusade in the Loire Valley, Normandy, and England. He commissioned other preachers in various regions as well, such as the two bishops he sent to **Genoa**, and whose efforts led to the creation of a fleet of 13 ships which set out in July of 1097. **Peter the Hermit** preached so successfully that he was able to lead an advance guard of "the poor" to **Nicaea**, where most were massacred. Another group, roused in advance of the main armies in 1096, participated in the massacres of **Jews** in the Rhineland led by **Emicho of**

Leiningen. Urban died before learning of the success of the **siege of Jerusalem**.

For other crusade procurators, *see* **Gervase of Prémontré**; **Jacques de Vitry**.

USAMA IBN MUNQIDH. (1095-1188). The chronicler was an Arab patrician of northern **Syria**, whose autobiographical *Book of Learning* contains stories of contacts with crusaders. Usama lived at the court of the **Fatimids** as well as in Syria. Frequently translated by European scholars, the stories from his autobiography are essentially morality tales, intended to amuse and instruct rather than to provide a chronological record of events.

-V-

VALDESIUS. *See* **Waldensians**.

VENICE. For Venice the crusades were part of a process of expansion that started in the 10th century, when the city began to rise to prominence in Mediterranean in addition to river commerce. A population estimated at 80,000 in 1200 made Venice one of the three or four largest cities in Europe. The nobility numbered about 1,200 men from 150 families in 1300. The city was physically about 60 island parishes with local customs, grandees, and businesses, tied together by the leadership of the wealthier merchants and the **Doge**, or ruler.

Like its rivals **Genoa** and **Pisa**, Venice was a republic based on sea trade and plunder rather than acquisition of territory. The roots of the rivalry went back to the early crusade period. The Italian cities routinely traded naval support in war for commercial privileges. In 1082 Venice traded privileged trade status in **Constantinople** for alliance with the **Byzantine Empire** against the Guiscards of **Sicily**. During the **First Crusade**, in 1096-99, Genoa's assistance earned it a trade agreement with the **Latin Kingdom of Jerusalem**, finalized in 1104. Venice was delayed by a tussle with Pisa over trade with "Romania" (Greece) as both fleets met at Rhodes in 1099 on their way to the crusade. The Pisans were defeated and sailed on to land their archbishop and ruler, Daimbert, at **Jaffa** and to assist **Godfrey of Bouillon** in building the defenses at the only port the crusaders held at the time. When the Pisan navy left in July of 1100, the Venetians took their turn at trading commercial agreements with the new Latin Kingdom of Jerusalem for their help in taking Haifa.

The **Levant** was not the primary focus of Italian attention. The Venetians were equally concerned with Norman expansion in the Mediterranean and the threatened independence of the Adriatic coastal region of Dalmatia (parts of Bosnia, Serbia, Albania). The latter was in a position to threaten Venice's preeminence, and was protected by the **Christian** kings of Hungary (*see* **Zara**). These concerns kept Venice out of the Levant after the First Crusade until 1123, when their fleet came to the rescue of Jaffa, under attack by the **Fatimids** of **Egypt**. The Venetians lured the Fatimid fleet out of **Ascalon** with an advance guard that looked like a trading vessel carrying **pilgrims**, a tempting target for **Muslim** attack. The Venetian victory allowed them to cruise down the coast collecting plunder from Egyptian ships, and then return to assist in the successful crusader **siege** of **Tyre** in 1124. They were able to negotiate favorable trade agreements with the crusaders as a result, and eventually their own quarter at the port of **Acre**. On their way home they raided Romania and several Greek islands to revenge themselves on the Byzantines, who had failed to renew commercial treaties with them in 1118.

Tension mounted in the following decade as the Byzantines alternated between allying with Venice and trying to play it off against its rivals. In 1171, for instance, the arrest of all Venetians in imperial territory and confiscation of their goods was revenged by raids on Greek cities. In 1182 there was a massacre of all Western Europeans in Constantinople by the inhabitants of the city. Competition in the Ionian and Aegean Seas among the Italian cities, the Muslims, the Byzantines, and the Normans of Sicily led to further raids and the enslavement of Greek women and children. It also seems to have prevented extensive Venetian involvement in the **Third Crusade**, in spite of the fact that the city held considerable territory in the Latin Kingdom in 1187, including a quarter in Tyre. Venice did send a fleet to assist in the blockade of Acre in 1189, but took no role in the struggle for the throne between **Guy of Lusignan** and **Conrad of Montferrat**. In contrast, Genoa and Pisa went to war over the issue in February 1192, each trying to protect their interests in the crusader kingdom. Instead, Venice seems to have been concentrating on its other interests, and especially in negotiating a resumption of Byzantine trade between 1187 and 1192.

During the **Fourth Crusade** Venice took three-eighths of the city of Constantinople, establishing a colony of thousands in the Latin Empire there. The Western European emperor who would rule the city was to be elected by a panel of six Venetians and six of the crusading barons. The Venetians voted in a block for Baldwin IX (r.1194/95-1205), count of **Flanders**, rather than for Boniface of **Montferrat**, who was an ally of the Genoese. Even more significantly, they were able to prohibit any state at war with them from being received in imperial territory. They then used the situation to establish bases at Crete and Negroponte, in the Aegean. In the Adriatic they established a base at Ragusa, and in the Ionian Sea, at Modon and Coron. This "colonial empire" allowed them to dominate the eastern Mediterranean.

Genoa retaliated by supporting the deposed Greek emperors in 1260, and was rewarded with its own colony when Venice and the crusader kingdom were defeated in 1261. Open war broke out between Genoa and Venice four times between 1253 and 1381. The first quarrel originated in Acre when a Venetian murdered a Genoese, and the Genoese pillaged the Venetian quarter of the city in retaliation.

The rivalry was based on a desire to control the lucrative trade with the Levant, Greece, and the Black Sea. Venice profited first from **Mongol** protection of the trade routes to Asia after the 1250s and then from resisting **Ottoman** expansion into Byzantine territory in the 14th century. Their focus remained commercial success, and especially rivalry with Genoa. The Venetian Republic acted as a buffer between inhabitants and the Turks in the absence of Greek control of Durazzo, Scutari, Lepanto, Patras, Argos, Nauplia, and Athens. The Italian cities were able to continue to attack each other in the early 15th century because the Ottomans were distracted by Tamerlane's approach through Central Asia. *See also* **Arsenal**; **Naval Warfare**; **St. Mark's Church**.

VILLEHARDOUIN. (Geoffrey of). Marshal of Champagne and then of Romania (Greece), negotiator and chronicler of the **Fourth Crusade**, Geoffrey founded the principality of Achaea (or Achaia) in the **Latin Kingdom of Constantinople** (d.1213).

Geoffrey was one of a committee of 24, half **Venetians** and half **Franks**, who drew up a pact in 1204 assessing the territory of Byzantium and distributing it to the Fourth Crusaders who had decided to stay in the east. The committee used the tax registers from 1203 and the arrangements of the pact made by the crusaders in preparation for the **siege** of **Constantinople** as guides. The tax registers contained references to land not actually held by the emperor in 1203, and the arrangements depended on the ability of the crusaders to take and subdue territory after the division.

In 1205 the rapid conquests of the first year were threatened by the Vlacho-Bulgars, who had been contained in the Balkans by the **Byzantines**. Their leader in 1204 was Kalojan, known to the crusaders as Johanitsa (d.1207). His offer of alliance was repulsed by the Western Europeans, and he became a formidable enemy. The conquests of central Greece made under the leadership of Boniface of **Montferrat** proved more sustainable than those in the region of the imperial city. Geoffrey's nephew, Geoffrey I of Villehardouin, arrived in Greece in 1205 and joined Boniface's army, eventually inheriting his uncle's conquests as prince of Achaea (1209-29). Achaea was the northern portion of the Peloponnesian Peninsula, which was called the Morea by the Latins. Geoffrey was one of those who had abandoned the Fourth Crusade to go to **Syria**, but returned to fight for the chance to establish a lordship in Greece.

Geoffrey II, son of Geoffrey I, was prince of Achaea in his turn (r.1229-46). The family allied itself to the ruling dynasty in Constantinople. Geoffrey II married Agnes de Courtenay in 1217, the daughter of the newly crowned Latin emperor Peter. Peter's brother Robert (1221-28) inherited the throne of Constantinople. Geoffrey II's brother, William II, succeeded him (1246-78), but at this point the Villehardouin luck ran out. The Greek resistance to French rule became powerful enough after the campaigns of 1263-64 that in 1267 William surrendered his fief to **Charles of Anjou**, accepting Charles as his overlord. Charles was the brother of King **Louis IX** of France. He was invested by the **papacy** with the Kingdom of Naples and **Sicily** in 1265. He called on his new vassal in 1268 to send troops to Sicily.

William and 400 knights from the Morea went to Charles's aid in the battle of Tagliacozzo on 23 August. In return, Charles sent troops to Greece in 1271 under his marshal in Sicily, Dreux de Beaumont. Isabel, William's daughter and heir (d.c.1311) was the last of the Villehardouin dynasty in Achaea. Strategically, the fief became part of the holdings of the Kingdom of Naples and Sicily in the Mediterranean, rather than a crusader outpost.

-W-

WALDENSIANS (THE POOR OF LYON). Waldensian believers were identified by the Roman Catholic church hierarchy as heretics. A crusade was launched against them in 1487 in three principalities in the southwestern Alps: Dauphiné, Savoy, and Piedmont. According to the most reliable sources for this crusade, about 160 Waldensians were killed.

References to Waldensians can be found in Western Europe from the 12th to the 16th century, when some became Calvinists. Their original resistance to Catholicism stemmed from their application, denied by the church, to preach. Episcopal license based on adequate training was necessary for either the *monito*, moral exhortation that could be practiced by members of religious orders, or in some cases, laypersons, or *praedicato*, dogmatic teaching reserved for ordained clergy.

In spite of a tradition that traces Waldensianism back to the early church, the movement seems to have started with a wealthy merchant in Lyon, Valdesius, in 1173. He heard a street preacher, who urged the value of voluntary poverty as a means of salvation, and after confirming the message with local clergy, he gave away his goods. His self-imposed mission was public: he gave away money on the street and talked to passersby about why he had done so. As a result, by 1177 he had founded a community of like-minded followers. They had portions of scripture translated from Latin into the vernacular, and began to recite verses publicly.

The merchant and his community attended the Third Lateran Council in 1179, where their lay "order" was approved, but they were instructed not to preach unless asked to do so by local clergy. They were again warned not to preach at the Council of Lyon in 1180-81 by the archbishop and the cardinal legate. The Waldensians refused to obey the hierarchy, instead claiming a higher duty imposed by God. As a result they were excommunicated and expelled from Lyon sometime between 1182 and 1184. At the Council of Verona in 1184 they were listed among heretics such as the **Cathars**. The canon condemning them specifically excommunicated all who preached publicly or privately without permission from the clergy.

The Waldensians were forced to emigrate, and became concentrated in Provence (southern France) and Lombardy (northern Italy), where they preached against the Cathars. In spite of Rome's concern with the rise of Catharism in these regions, the Waldensian preaching of Catholic doctrine continued to be anathematized as disobedience, and disobedience as heresy. Some Waldensians did preach the Donatist heresy that the sinfulness of the priest disqualified him for office, but even here, the issue was one of authority rather than of theology.

Valdesius died in c.1205. Some of his followers were apparently converted back to orthodoxy by Bishop Diego of Osma, who had brought St. **Dominic** to southern France. He debated with the new sect in 1207 at Pamiers. Like the Cathars, the Waldensians became a focus for the **Inquisition**, which replaced the **Albigensian Crusade** as the papal response to heresy. In 1487-88 the inquisitorial process was followed by a crusade **indulgence** granted to those who hunted down Waldensian believers in the duchy of Savoy and the principalities of Piedmont and Dauphiné. A disputed number of heretics were killed, others were captured and fined. Those who agreed to abjure their faith were readmitted to the orthodox church at a ceremony held before the cathedral at Embrun on 27 April 1488.

Penances of various kinds were imposed as a condition of absolution, including the wearing of a yellow **cross** sewn into the clothes. Some heretics were allowed to buy back confiscated land or pay to have the penance revoked. Money was also collected from Catholic individuals and communes which had sheltered the Waldensians. In 1507 the conduct of this crusade and the penalties imposed on the heretics came under review, first by a papal commission, and then by an ecclesiastical court at Paris. The Waldensian Alpine communities were represented by lawyers who were able to obtain a judgment in their favor in 1509.

Waldensians who fled the diocese of Embrun for southern Italy were persecuted by the Inquisition in 1560 as a result of having called in Protestant ministers. Soldiers were called in to arrest and execute Waldensians, about 84 of whom had their throats slit. Other marginally heretical groups who did not become targets of full-scale crusades include the Humiliati, Publicani, and Patarenes.

WEAPONS. Standard weapons for both **Muslim** and **Christian** included bow and arrow, crossbow, sword, dagger, lance, and mace (metal head either smooth or spiked with a long handle). The war **horse** itself was both an offensive weapon during the charge and defensive in retreat, and could be armed by European warriors with plate **armor** and even an iron helmet. As with armor, weapons very much reflected what the wearer could afford or could pick up on the battlefield.

Common problems for the European warrior were the weight of armor developed for combat in a cooler climate, and difficulties with terrain in the East. Shipping horses from Europe by land or sea was a problem, as was using European fighting techniques in the sand dunes or in the dust of a recently plowed field in a dry climate. In general the Muslim **knight** used a lighter horse and strategic planning to encircle and harass an enemy, shooting arrows from horseback and retreating in response to a charge. In general, Europeans relied on armor to deflect Muslim arrows and lances, and used heavier horses during the battle to charge at the defenders. The ax, either handheld or thrown, was an ancient European weapon, but obviously widely available to both groups.

Convention has Muslims fighting with curved scimitars, but in fact straight swords were the common weapon for all warriors before the 14th century. Sword and lance sizes varied considerably, as did types of bows. Warriors also carried short lances or javelins for throwing, as well as knives and shields.

Western European horsemen in general did not use the bow, leaving that weapon to the infantry. Wooden bows were common in Europe and known in the **Levant**, but Muslim armies favored the composite bow, in use in ancient **Egypt** and Iran. There was a core of wood, reinforced on the outside by horn and sinew. The materials, craftsmanship, and curve of the weapon could make it more powerful than the European version. Arrows were made of reeds or wood, with flights made from birds of prey. The Muslim archer drew with his thumb, while the European used his fingers. The crossbow was used by infantry in the Levant in the 12th century, because of its greater accuracy, its power even against armored enemies, and the relatively little training needed to use it. Pedestal crossbows that shot multiple arrows were used by both European and Muslim warriors during **siege** warfare.

Fire was used in various situations by both sides, but Muslim armies apparently had more sophisticated incendiary missiles than Europeans. The **Byzantine** "Greek fire" so composed that it was difficult to put out, was much admired. Many combinations of liquid petroleum or pitch, as well as resin, sulphur, quicklime, saltpeter (potassium nitrate), and bitumen were used to create missiles or spray burning liquid. Clay or glass containers of various sizes could be affixed to arrows or shot from slingshots, or mangonels (trebuchets–both words refer to throwing machines of various sizes and constructions). In 1291 the use of exploding devices thrown by **siege weapons** was crucial to the fall of crusader **Acre**. Cannon were used by Islamic and European armies as early as the middle of the 13th century. Smaller models, including early handguns, were used to make noise and against personnel; larger ones were an improvement on lever or pivot siege engines, allowing stones of 800 pounds to be projected.

These sophisticated weapons did not replace the ingenious use of whatever was at hand: rocks, boiling wax or water (or any other liquid), dung or even body parts from fallen combatants. Fire wheels were invented independently at sieges from the Baltics to Malta, consisting of hoops treated with, in one case, brandy, oil, and gunpowder, and in another, caulking and pitch. Wells were poisoned, booby traps of various kinds were devised, hostages were torn limb from limb or hanged as their compatriots watched. In one case **Holy Roman Emperor Frederick Barbarossa** reportedly tied hostages to his **siege engines**, which did not keep the besieged from trying to destroy his weapons.

See also **Castles**; **Cavalry**; **Naval Warfare**.

WENDS. The crusade against the Slavic Wends in 1147 was the first of the "Northern Crusades" in the **Baltic** region, an effort of conquest and colonization that was accompanied by papal **indulgences** from 1147 to 1505. In the case of the Wends, there were no indulgences granted after 1147. After the initial battle, technically part of the **Second Crusade**, the advance against the Slavs was waged piecemeal by local leaders such as King Valdemar I of Denmark (r.1157-82), and **Henry XII, the Lion**, duke of Saxony.

On 13 April 1147 Pope **Eugenius III** issued the Bull *Divina dispensationse*, which offered the crusade indulgence to those who would offer baptism or death to the heathen Wends. The expedition was to be led by the Premonstratensian bishop of Havelberg, Anselm, who was to accept no truce or tribute. Anselm was joined by the archbishop of Bremen, a force of Danes, and a contingent of Saxons under Duke Henry XII. The archbishop and the Saxons forced the garrison at Dobin to accept baptism and retreated without plundering the countryside. Anselm marched to Demmin with the bishops of Brandenburg, Halberstadt, Mainz, Merseburg, Münster, and Olmutz. They burnt a temple with pagan idols at Malchow.

As with the expedition to **Jerusalem** in 1099, there was an association by the preachers of this expedition with the battle between good and evil believed to be the prelude to the Last Judgment. Like the concurrent attack on **Damascus**, this crusade was a failure. Those who had been forcibly converted abandoned their new faith as soon as the crusade left their area. Although other leaders received crusade indulgences for expeditions in other Baltic areas, after 1147 the territorial war of the Saxons and Danes against the Wends was neither authorized nor directed by the **papacy**.

See also chroniclers **Helmhold**; **Saxo Grammaticus**. Eric Christiansen's *The Northern Crusades* (2nd ed., London: Penguin, 1997) contains maps and descriptions of the Baltic region giving more detail on regional nomenclature for tribes and peoples.

WILLIAM, ARCHBISHOP OF TYRE. (c.1130-c.1185). William was born in the **Latin Kingdom,** probably in **Jerusalem,** and was fluent in French, Arabic, Greek, and Latin, with some knowledge of Hebrew and Persian. He was commissioned by **Amalric I** to write a history of the Latin Kingdom after the king's **Egyptian** campaign of 1167. William had studied in France and Lombardy before 1165, and became **Baldwin IV**'s tutor in 1170, when the heir to the throne was nine. He was made archbishop of **Tyre** and chancellor of the Latin Kingdom of Jerusalem in 1175. The latter office gave him control over the royal archives.

The archbishop made two voyages to Rome, including one in 1178-79 to attend the Lateran Council, and twice stayed at the court of **Constantinople** for extended periods. His history covers the crusader kingdoms from 1099 until 1184 in 23 books, the last of which is unfinished. Continuations usually referred to as **Eracles** and **Ernoul,** were compiled by unknown authors and are important sources for events through the **Fifth Crusade.**

-X, Y, Z-

ZARA. The **Fourth Crusade** was diverted to the **siege** of this city on the coast of Dalmatia. Unable to pay the previously agreed passage money, the French and German contingents consented to the **Venetian** insistence that the army earn an extension on payment of the debt for their passage by assisting in an attack on Zara. The Venetians justified the siege on the grounds that the inhabitants were guilty of piracy, which contemporary chroniclers interpreted as simple economic rivalry between the two cities for trade in the Adriatic.

Envoys from the city came to camp to request peace in the wake of a letter received from Pope **Innocent III** which threatened the army with excommunication if they attacked. The city belonged to the king of Hungary, who had himself taken **crusade vows,** which put his domains under papal protection. In spite of these excellent reasons for desisting, only the Cisterican abbots of Vaux-de-Cernay, Pairis, and Cercanceaux, along with Simon of **Montfort** refused to join the assault (the abbot of Perseigne had already traveled on to the **Levant**). They took their forces instead to Barletta, and embarked for the Holy Land. Simon fought overseas for a year, and returned to become the hero of the **Albigensian Crusade.**

Zara was razed by the crusade army, and they were therefore excommunicated. The crusade army asked for and quickly received pardon, but was again diverted to **Constantinople** in order to place the future Alexius IV on the throne and receive his much-needed assistance for their expedition to the Holy Land. The Venetians refused to seek papal approval and carried out the siege of Constantinople under the ban of excommunication.

IMAD AL-DIN ZENGI. (d.1146). Zengi was the ruler of **Syria** whose capture of **Edessa** in 1144 sparked the **Second Crusade**. From 1108 Zengi served in the armies of powerful Turkish commanders, following in the footsteps of his father, Aq Sunqur, governor of **Aleppo** from 1087/88-1094. In 1122-23 the **Seljuk** sultan appointed Zengi military governor of Basra and Wasit in southern Iraq. In 1127 he became governor of **Mosul** in northern Iraq. In 1128 he conquered Aleppo. In 1135 citizens of **Damascus**, tired of a weak government which had attracted the attention of the crusader kingdom, invited Zengi to take over the defense of the city. In the event, a local military commander was able to move into Damascus more quickly, and Zengi withdrew. His interest in Syria continued, moving him to attack the city of Homs in 1137.

European and **Byzantine** forces were unable to stop his expansion into Syria. In 1140 the crusader kingdom formed an alliance with Damascus against Zengi, whose ultimate goal according to the Damascenes was **Jerusalem**. Zengi laid **siege** to Edessa in 1144, taking the city after 28 days. He then set about consolidating **Christian** territory nearby, defeating an army assembled by the local Europeans in 1145. He died the following year. The same Islamic chroniclers who relished tales of his legendary cruelty lauded him as a **martyr** in the **jihad**. The fall of Edessa can be seen as the first of the great Muslim victories which culminated in the battle of **Hattin** in 1187. Zengi's possessions were divided between his sons Saif al-Din Ghazi in Mosul and **Nur al-Din** in Aleppo.

Bibliography

This bibliography offers a starting point for the history of the crusades to the English-speaking reader. The works listed cover not just the expeditions, but also an introduction to the great range of topics and regions covered by the movement. In each section there are three types of entries: general histories accessible to a wide audience; scholarly works which offer further bibliography; and individual works which offer a starting place for further information on culture, including art, dress, food, and religious practice. For those who seek recent academic scholarship on the crusades, the international Society for the Study of the Crusades and the Latin East has over 450 members and publishes its own *Bulletin*, which lists recent publications. In addition, officers of the Society have joined with Ashgate Press, Aldershot, United Kingdom, and Burlington, Vermont, to publish a journal called *Crusades*.

Since the crusades originated in Europe, the list begins with European history and technology. Sections on Byzantine, Islamic, and Jewish history offer other perspectives on crusading. Some primary sources are included, especially where translations into English are available. They are listed at the beginning of each section, followed by atlases and dictionaries, and then by secondary sources. Sections offering suggestions for further reading on individual countries follow the general histories of Europe and of Islam. The major European categories are: general history, the organized church and popular religious practice, architectural history (since medieval buildings were important pieces of a military system), and warfare.

Sections on Byzantium, Islam, Jerusalem, and Judaism are followed by the general "Crusades" section, and then by major expeditions in roughly chronological order (see the chronology for more information). Information on the crusader kingdoms in the Levant is listed under the First Crusade, on Cyprus under the Third Crusade, and in Byzantine territory under the Fourth Crusade. Publication dates separated by commas usually indicate paperback editions following a year or two after the original. Dates separated by semicolons indicate when the most recent reprint and then the original edition were published. Revised editions are noted.

Comprehensive overviews of Islam have proliferated since the attack on the World Trade Center, and they can represent mutually exclusive views of Muslim civilization. Listing them all is not possible. Instead, a few selections with further bibliography are listed. To get a sense of the opposing points of view, students might start with the pair of articles by

Bernard Lewis and Edward W. Said, listed in the "Islam" section, below. See John Tolan for a recent overview of the debate, listed in the same section.

Bibliography Contents

General: Europe in the Middle Ages 233
    France 234
    Germany 235
    Great Britain 235
    Hungary 236
    Italy...236
    The Low Countries 237
    Spain 237
The Church and Religious Practice in Western Europe..............................237
Architecture and Design: General and Military..240
Warfare: Military Technology, Orders, and History...................................242
Byzantium..246
Islam 247
    Africa 251
    Anatolia...251
    Armenia 251
    Egypt...251
    Iran..252
    Iraq..252
    Kurds 252
    Mongols..252
    Palestine..252
    Syria..252
    Turkey...253
Jerusalem 253
Jewish History and the Crusades 254
Crusades 256
    Reconquista...259
    The First Crusade and the Latin Kingdom of Jerusalem.......................261
    The Second Crusade 265
    The Third Crusade and the Kingdom of Cyprus 267
    The Fourth Crusade and the Latin Kingdom at Constantinople............268
    The Albigensian Crusade..269
    The Fifth Crusade 270
    The Northern Crusades 270

General: Europe in the Middle Ages

These sources offer an overview of the geography and history of Western Europe during the Middle Ages, chosen either for coverage and bibliography or for their relevance to the crusade movement. Atlases are followed by a bibliography, and then by Strayer's dictionary. Other useful reference works include the *Catholic Encyclopedia*, in three editions. Students will also find bibliography in Tierney's clear, chronological, and thorough overview of the period. More recent overviews like that of Backman contextualize Western Europe as part of a Mediterranean civilization group, along with Byzantium and Islam, and are particularly interesting to students of the crusades. Works on technology provide a background for those seeking information on weapons and warfare, which form their own subcategory after the section on the church. Following the general works, which can be only a selection of the many books available on medieval Europe, there are regional studies that offer information on the crusades.

McEvedy, Colin. *The New Penguin Atlas of Medieval History*. London: Penguin, 1992

Pounds, Norman J.G. *An Historical Geography of Europe, 450 BC–AD 1330*. Cambridge: Cambridge University Press, 1973.

International Medieval Bibliography. Edited by Robert S. Hoyt, et al. Leeds: Leeds University Press, semiannual, 1967-.

Backman, Clifford R. *The Worlds of Medieval Europe*. Oxford: Oxford University Press, 2003.

Strayer, Joseph R., ed. *The Dictionary of the Middle Ages*. New York: Charles Scribner's Sons, 1982.

Tierney, Brian. *Western Europe in the Middle Ages: 300-1475*. 6th edition. Boston: McGraw-Hill, 1999.

Abulafia, David. *The Western Mediterranean Kingdoms 1200-1500: The Struggle for Dominion*. Harlow, United Kingdom: Longman, 1997.

Blanks, David R., and Michael Frassetto, eds. *Western Views of Islam in Medieval and Early Modern Europe: Perception of the Other*. New York: St. Martin's, 1999.

Burns, J.H., ed. *The Cambridge History of Medieval Political Thought, c. 350-c.1450*. Cambridge: Cambridge University Press, 1988.

Colish, Marcia L. *Medieval Foundations of the Western Intellectual Tradition*. New Haven, Conn.: Yale University Press, 1997.

Gies, Frances, and Joseph Gies. *Cathedral, Forge, and Waterwheel: Technology and Invention in the Middle Ages*. New York: Harper, 1994.

Gillingham, John. *The Angevin Empire*. 2nd ed. Oxford: Oxford University Press, 2001.

Kelly, H.A. *Inquisitions and Other Trial Procedures in the Medieval West*. Aldershot, United Kingdom: Variorum, 2001.

Marshall, Anne. *Medieval Wall Painting in the English Parish Church*. http://www.paintedchurch.org/index.htm, 2002 [accessed 9 January 2003].

Murphy, T.P., ed. *The Holy War [Papers]*. Columbus: Ohio State University Press, 1976.

Murray, Peter, and Linda Lefevre. *The Oxford Companion to Christian Art and Architecture*. Oxford: Labyrinth Books, 1996.

Phillips, J.R.S. *The Medieval Expansion of Europe*. 2nd ed. Oxford: Oxford University Press, 1998.

Piponnier, Françoise, and Perrine Mane. *Dress in the Middle Ages*. New Haven, Conn.: Yale University Press, 1997.

Reese, Lyn. "Eleanor of Aquitaine." *Women in World History Curriculum 2001*. http://www.womeninworldhistory.com/heroine2.html [accessed 9 January 2003].

Rupert, Alen, and Anna Marie Dahlquist. *Royal Families of Medieval Scandanavia, Flanders, and Kiev*. Kingsburg, Calif.: Kings River Publications, 1997.

Schiller, Gertrud. *Iconography of Christian Art*. 2 vols. Translated by Janet Seligman. Greenwich, Conn.: New York Graphic Society, 1971.

Schmitt, Jean-Claude. *Ghosts in the Middle Ages: The Living and the Dead in Medieval Society*. Chicago: University of Chicago Press, 1998.

Scully, Terence. *The Art of Cookery in the Middle Ages*. Woodbridge, United Kingdom: Boydell and Brewer, 1995.

Southern, Richard. *The Making of the Middle Ages*. New Haven, Conn.: Yale University Press, 1953.

———. *Western Views of Islam in the Middle Ages*. Rev. ed. Cambridge, Mass.: Harvard University Press, 1992.

Tolan, John V. *Saracens: Islam in the Medieval European Imagination*. New York: Columbia University Press, 2002.

France. See also the Albigensian Crusade, below.

Bouchard, Constance Brittain. *"Those of My Blood": Constructing Noble Families in Medieval Francia*. Philadelphia: University of Pennsylvania Press, 2001.

Dunbabin, Jean. *France in the Making, 834-1180.* Oxford: Oxford University Press, 1985.
Gillingham, John. *The Angevin Empire.* 2nd ed. Oxford: Oxford University Press, 2001.
Hallam, E.M. *Capetian France, 987-1328.* Harlow, United Kingdom: Longman, 2001.
Jordan, William Chester. *Ideology and Royal Power in Medieval France. Kinship, Crusades, and the Jews.* Aldershot, United Kingdom: Ashgate, 2001.
———. *Louis IX and the Challenge of the Crusade. A Study in Rulership.* Princeton, N.J.: Princeton University Press, 1979.

Germany

Abulafia, David. *Frederick II: A Medieval Emperor.* Oxford: Oxford University Press, 1992.
Arnold, Benjamin. *Princes and Territories in Medieval Germany.* Cambridge: Cambridge University Press, 2002.
Barraclough, G. *Medieval Germany, 911-1250.* 2 vols. Oxford: B. Blackwell, 1938.
Fuhrmann, Horst. *Germany in the High Middle Ages, c. 1050-1200.* Trans. Timothy Reuter. Cambridge: Cambridge University Press, 1986.
Haverkamp, Alfred. *Medieval Germany, 1056-1273.* Oxford: Oxford University Press, 1988.
Hiestand, Rudolf. "Kingship and Crusade in Twelfth-Century Germany." In *England and Germany in the High Middle Ages,* ed. Alfred Haverkamp and Hanna Vollrath. Oxford: Oxford University Press, 1996.
Leyser, Karl. *Medieval Germany and Its Neighbors, 900-1250.* London: Hambledon, 1982.
Robinson, Ian S. *Henry IV of Germany.* Cambridge: Cambridge University Press, 2000.
Wilson, Peter H. *The Holy Roman Empire, 1495-1806.* New York: St. Martin's, 1999.

Great Britain

Foster, R.F., ed. *The Oxford History of Ireland.* Oxford: Oxford University Press, 1992.
Hollister, C. Warren. *The Making of England: To 1399.* 8th ed. Boston: Houghton Mifflin, 2001.
Keen, M.H. *England in the Later Middle Ages. A Political History.* London: Methuen, 1973.

Macquarrie, Alan. *Scotland and the Crusades, 1095-1560.* Edinburgh: J. Donald, 1997.
Mayer, H.E. "Henry II of England and the Holy Land." *English Historical Review* 97 (1982): 721-39.
Thomas, Hugh M. *Vassals, Heiresses, Crusaders, and Thugs. The Gentry of Angevin Yorkshire, 1154-1216.* Philadelphia: University of Pennsylvania Press, 1993 [and see John Gillingham, under France, above].
Tyerman, Christopher. *England and the Crusades, 1095-1588.* Chicago: University of Chicago Press, 1988.
Vaughan, Richard. *The Chronicles of Matthew Paris.* Gloucester, United Kingdom: A. Sutton, 1984.
Vincent, Nicholas. *King Henry III and the Westminster Blood Relic.* Cambridge: Cambridge University Press, 2002.

Hungary
Berend, Nora. *At the Gate of Christendom: Jews, Muslims, and "Pagans" in Medieval Hungary, c.1000-c.1300.* Cambridge: Cambridge University Press, 2001.
Engel, Pál. *The Realm of St. Stephen: A History of Medieval Hungary, 895-1526.* Trans. Tamás Pálosfalvi. London: I.B. Tauris, 2001.

Italy
Abulafia, David. *Commerce and Conquest in the Mediterranean, 1100-1500.* Aldershot, United Kingdom: Ashgate, 1993.
———. *Italy, Sicily, and the Mediterranean, 100-1400.* Aldershot, United Kingdom: Ashgate, 1987.
Day, Gerald W. *Genoa's Response to Byzantium, 1155-1204: Commercial Expansion and Factionalism in a Medieval City.* Urbana: University of Illinois Press, 1988.
Epstein, Steven A. *Genoa and the Genoese, 958-1528.* Chapel Hill: University of North Carolina Press, 1996.
Heywood, William. *A History of Pisa, Eleventh and Twelfth Centuries.* Cambridge: Cambridge University Press, 1921.
Holmes, George, ed. *The Oxford Illustrated History of Italy.* Oxford: Oxford University Press, 1997.
Houben, Hubert. *Roger II of Sicily.* Cambridge: Cambridge University Press, 2002.
Lane, F.C. *Venice: A Maritime Republic.* Baltimore, Md.: Johns Hopkins University Press, 1973.

Loud, G.A. *The Age of Robert Guiscard. Southern Italy and the Norman Conquest.* Harlow, United Kingdom: Longman, 2000.

Matthew, Donald. *The Norman Kingdom of Sicily.* Cambridge: Cambridge University Press, 1992.

The Low Countries: Flanders, Hainaut, Namur, etc.

Dept, Gaston G. "Les Influences anglaise et française dans le comté de Flandre au début du XIIIme siècle." *Recueil de Travaux publiés par la Faculté de philosophie et lettres* 59 (1928): 9-227.

Nicholas, David. *Medieval Flanders.* Harlow, United Kingdom: Longman, 1992.

Nicholas, Karen S. "The Role of Feudal Relationships in the Consolidation of Power in the Principalities of the Low Countries, 1000-1300." In *Law, Custom, and Social Fabric in Medieval Europe: Essays in Honor of Bruce Lyon.* Ed. Bernard S. Bachrach and David Nicholas. Kalamazoo, Mich.: Western Michigan University Press, 1990.

Spain and the Spanish Inquisition. See the Reconquista, in the Crusades section, below.

The Church and Religious Practice in Western Europe

For Eastern Christianity, see **Byzantium**, below, and especially Atiya, for the Copts, Nestorians, etc. Again, these works are a selection from what is available on medieval Western European religious beliefs and practice. The Cistercian reform was so closely connected with the crusades in ideology, recruitment (*see* St. **Bernard of Clairvaux**), and, in the **Baltic Crusades**, settlement, that one example of primary source texts on the movement is given below. For medieval topics the earlier editions of the *Catholic Encyclopedia* are often useful as a place to start, but the information should be checked against recent works on specialized topics. All of these works offer further bibliography. For an example of a relic with a pedigree which dates to the crusades and is still extant, see the website (as of December 2002) for the Shroud of Turin: http://sindone.torino.chiesacattolica.it/en/museo.htm.

Emerton, Ephraim, ed. *The Correspondence of Pope Gregory VII: Selected Letters from Registrum.* New York: Octagon Books, 1966; 1932.

Matarasso, Pauline, ed. *The Cistercian World. Monastic Writings of the Twelfth Century.* London: Penguin, 1993.

The Catholic Encyclopedia. 15 vols. New York: Robert Appleton, 1907-12.

The New Catholic Encyclopedia. 18 vols. New York: McGraw-Hill, 1967-88; 2nd ed. in 14 vols., Detroit: Thomson/Gale, 2003.

Duffy, Eamon. *Saints and Sinners. A History of the Medieval Popes*. New Haven, Conn.: Yale University Press, 1997.

Baschet, Jérôme. "Medieval Abraham: Between Fleshly Patriarch and Divine Father." *Modern Language Notes* 108 (1993): 738-58.

Berman, Constance Hoffman. *The Cistercian Evolution. The Invention of a Religious Order in Twelfth-Century Europe*. Philadelphia: University of Pennsylvania Press, 2000.

Bolton, Brenda. *Adrian IV, The English Pope, 1154-1159: Studies and Texts*. Aldershot, United Kingdom: Variorum, 2002.

Brett, Edward Tracy. *Humbert of Romans: His Life and Views of Thirteenth-Century Society*. Toronto: Pontifical Institute of Medieval Studies, 1984.

Brown, Peter. *The Rise of Western Christendom. Triumph and Diversity, AD 200-1000*. Cambridge, Mass.: Blackwell, 1996.

Brox, Norbert. *A Concise History of the Early Church*. Trans. John Bowden. New York: Continuum, 1995.

Bynum, Caroline Walker. *The Resurrection of the Body in Western Christianity, 200-1336*. New York: Columbia University Press, 1995.

Constable, Giles. *Cluny from the Tenth to the Twelfth Centuries. Further Studies*. Aldershot, United Kingdom: Ashgate, 2000.

Cowdrey, H.E.J. *The Cluniacs and the Gregorian Reform*. Oxford: Clarendon, 1970.

———. *The Crusades and Latin Monasticism, 11th-12th Centuries*. Aldershot, United Kingdom: Ashgate, 1999.

———. *Pope Gregory VII, 1073-1085*. Oxford: Clarendon Press, 1998.

Drodge, Arthur J., and James D. Tabor. *A Noble Death. Suicide and Martyrdom among Christians and Jews in Antiquity*. San Francisco: Harper, 1992.

Dunn, Marilyn. *The Emergence of Monasticism: From the Desert Fathers to the Early Middle Ages*. Oxford: Blackwell, 2000.

Dvornik, Frances. *The Ecumenical Councils*. New York: Hawthorn Books, 1961.

Geary, Patrick J. *Living with the Dead in the Middle Ages*. Ithaca, N.Y.: Cornell University Press, 1994.

Golding, Brian. *Gilbert of Sempringham and the Gilbertine Order, c. 1130-c. 1300*. Oxford: Clarendon, 1995.

Hamilton, Bernard. "Ideals of Holiness: Crusades, Contemplatives, and Mendicants." *International History Review* 17 (1995): 693-712.
———. *The Medieval Inquisition*. New York: Holmes and Meier, 1981.
Harper, John. *The Forms and Orders of Western Liturgy from the Tenth to the Eighteenth Century*. Oxford: Oxford University Press, 1991.
Head, Thomas, and Richard Landes, eds. *The Peace of God. Social Violence and Religious Response in France around the Year 1000*. Ithaca, N.Y.: Cornell University Press, 1992.
Keck, David. *Angels and Angelology in the Middle Ages*. Oxford: Oxford University Press, 1998.
Lambert, Michael. *Medieval Heresy: Popular Movements from the Gregorian Reform to the Reformation*. 3rd ed. Oxford: Blackwell, 2002.
McGinn, Bernard. *Visions of the End. Apocalyptic Traditions in the Middle Ages*. New York: Columbia University Press, 1998.
Moore, John, ed. *Pope Innocent III and His World*. Aldershot, United Kingdom: Variorum, 1999.
Morris, Colin, and Peter Roberts, eds. *Pilgrimage, The English Experience from Becket to Bunyan*. Cambridge: University Press, 2002.
Muldoon, James. *Canon Law, the Expansion of Europe, and World Order*. Aldershot, United Kingdom: Ashgate, 1998.
Ousterhout, Robert. *The Blessings of Pilgrimage*. Urbana: University of Illinois Press, 1990.
Peters, Edward. *Inquisition*. New York: Free Press, 1988.
Raitt, Jill, ed. *Christian Spirituality: High Middle Ages and Reformation*. New York: Crossroad, 1987.
Sandoval, Annette. *The Dictionary of Saints. A Concise Guide to Patron Saints*. New York: Penguin, 1995.
Sayers, Jane. *Innocent III, Leader of Europe, 1198-1218*. Harlow, United Kingdom: Longman, 1994.
Schiller, Gertrud. *Iconography of Christian Art*. 2 vols. Trans. Janet Seligman. Greenwich, Conn.: New York Graphic Society, 1971-72.
Snoek, G.J.C. *Medieval Piety from Relics to the Eucharist: A Process of Mutual Interaction*. Leiden: Brill, 1995.
Somerville, Robert. *Papacy, Councils, and Canon Law in the Eleventh and Twelfth Centuries*. Aldershot, United Kingdom: Variorum, 1990.
Southern, Richard. *Western Society and the Church in the Middle Ages*. New Haven, Conn.: Yale University Press, 1961.
Sumption, Jonathan. *Pilgrimage: An Image of Medieval Religion*. New York: Faber and Faber, 1975.

240 • Bibliography

Tellenbach, Gerd. *The Church in Western Europe from the Tenth to the Early Twelfth Century*. Trans. by Timothy Reuter. New York: Columbia University Press, 1993.
Tongeren, Louis van. *Exaltation of the Cross: Toward the Origins of the Feast of the Cross in Early Medieval Liturgy*. Leuven, Belgium: Peeters, 2000.
Vauchez, André. *The Laity in the Middle Ages. Religious Beliefs and Devotional Practices*. Ed. Daniel E. Bornstein, trans. Margery J. Schneider. Notre Dame, Ind.: University of Notre Dame Press, 1993.
Ward, Benedicta. *Miracles and the Medieval Mind. Theory, Record, and Event, 1000-1215*. 2nd edition. Aldershot, United Kingdom: Variorum, 1987.
Webb, Diana. *Pilgrims and Pilgrimage in the Medieval West*. New York: St. Martin's, 2001.

Architecture and Design, General and Military
The reader will find more on weapons and ships in the following section on warfare. For information on the history of technology, see the general history section on Europe, above.

Fortress: The Castles and Fortifications Quarterly. Liphook, United Kingdom, 1989-.

Boas, Adrian J. *Crusader Archaeology. The Material Culture of the Latin East*. London: Routledge, 1999.
Boase, T.S.R. *Castles and Churches of the Crusading Kingdom*. London: Oxford University Press, 1967.
Edwards, Robert W. *The Fortifications of Armenian Cilicia*. Washington, D.C.: Dumbarton Oaks Research Library and Collection, 1987.
Elgood, Robert, ed. *Islamic Arms and Armour*. London: Scolar, 1979.
Fahmy, Aly Mohamed. *Muslim Sea-Power in the Eastern Mediterranean from the Seventh to the Tenth Century AD*. Cairo: National Publication and Print House, 1966.
Fedden, Robin, and John Thomson. *Crusader Castles*. London: J. Murray, 1957.
Folda, Jaroslav. *The Art of the Crusaders in the Holy Land, 1098-1187*. Cambridge: Cambridge University Press, 1995.
———. *Crusader Manuscript Illumination at Saint Jean d'Acre, 1275-1291*. Princeton, N.J.: Princeton University Press, 1976.

———. *The Nazareth Capitals and the Crusader Shrine of the Annunciation.* University Park: Pennsylvania State University Press, 1986.
Gardiner, Robert. "Crusader Turkey: the Fortifications of Edessa." *Fortress* 2 (1989): 23-35.
Hill, Donald Routledge. *Islamic Science and Engineering.* Edinburgh: Edinburgh University Press, 1993.
Hillenbrand, Carole. "Armies, Arms, Armour and Fortifications," in her *The Crusades. Islamic Perspectives* (New York: Routledge, 2000), 431-510.
Hillenbrand, Robert. *Islamic Architecture. Form, Function, and Meaning.* New York: Columbia University Press, 1999.
Hourani, George Fadlo, and John Carswell. *Arab Seafaring in the Indian Ocean in Ancient and Early Medieval Times.* Expanded editon. Princeton, N.J.: Princeton University Press, 1995.
Johns, C.N. *Pilgrims' Castle ('Atlit), David's Tower (Jerusalem), and Qual'at ar-Rabad ('Ajlun). Three Middle Eastern Castles from the Time of the Crusades.* Ed. Denys Pringle. Aldershot, United Kingdom: Ashgate, 2000.
Keegan, John D.P. *A History of Warfare.* New York: Alfred A. Knopf, 1993.
Kennedy, Hugh. *Crusader Castles.* Cambridge: Cambridge University Press, 1994.
Kinder, Terryl N. *Cistercian Europe. Architecture of Contemplation.* Grand Rapids, Mich.: Wm. B. Eerdmans, 2002.
Müller-Wiener, Wolfgang. *Castles of the Crusaders.* New York: McGraw-Hill, 1966.
Pringle, Denys. *Fortification and Settlement in Crusader Palestine.* Aldershot, United Kingdom: Ashgate, 2000.
———. *Secular Buildings in the Crusader Kingdom of Jerusalem. An Archaeological Gazetteer.* Cambridge: Cambridge University Press, 1997.
Von Simson, Otto. *The Gothic Cathedral. Origins of Gothic Architecture and the Medieval Concept of Order.* 3rd edition. Princeton, N.J.: Princeton University Press, 1988.
Warner, Philip. *The Medieval Castle. Life in a Fortress in Peace and War.* New York: Taplinger, 1971.
Weiss, Daniel. *Art and the Crusade in the Age of Saint Louis.* Cambridge: Cambridge University Press, 1998.

———. "Biblical History and Medieval Historiography: Rationalizing Strategies in Crusader Art." *Modern Language Notes* 108 (1993): 710-37.

Warfare: Military Technology, Orders, and History
For the Assassins, see also authors Bartlett, *Assassins*, and Daftary, *Ismailis*, under **Islam**; and Mirza, under Islamic regions, Syria. This section begins with a bibliographical guide, a journal that publishes articles on naval warfare, and an illustrated atlas. The works on various aspects of medieval warfare which follow also offer bibliography. For histories of medieval technology see the general history of Europe section, above.

Crosby, Everett U. *Medieval Warfare. A Bibliographical Guide.* New York: Garland, 2000.

The Mariner's Mirror. London: Society for Nautical Research, 1-, 1911-.

Hooper, Nicholas, and Matthew Bennett. *The Cambridge Illustrated Atlas of Warfare: The Middle Ages, 768-1487.* New York: Cambridge University Press, 1996.

Anderson, R.C. *Oared Fighting Ships: From Classical Times to the Coming of Steam.* London: Percival Marshall, 1962.
Arnold, Benjamin. *German Knighthood 1050-1300.* Oxford: Clarendon, 1985.
Ayalon, David. *Gunpowder and Firearms in the Mamluk Kingdom: A Challenge to Medieval Society.* 2nd ed. London: F. Cass, 1978.
Barber, Malcolm, and Helen Nicholson, eds. *The Military Orders.* 2 vols. Aldershot, United Kingdom: Variorum, 1994.
———. *The New Knighthood. A History of the Order of the Temple.* Cambridge: Cambridge University Press, 1996.
———. *The Trial of the Templars.* Cambridge: Cambridge University Press, 1993.
Bradbury, Jim. *The Medieval Siege.* Woodbridge, Suffolk, United Kingdom: Boydell, 1992.
Burns, Robert I. "Piracy as an Islamic-Christian Interface in the Thirteenth Century." *Viator* 11 (1980): 165-78.
Byrne, E.H. *Genoese Shipping in the Twelfth and Thirteenth Centuries.* Cambridge, Mass.: Harvard University Press, 1930; repr. 1970.

Davis, R.C. *Shipbuilders of the Venetian Arsenal.* Baltimore, Md.: Johns Hopkins University Press, 1991.

DeVries, Kelly. *Guns and Men in Medieval Europe, 1200-1500. Studies in Military History and Technology.* Aldershot, United Kingdom: Ashgate, 2002.

———. *Medieval Military Technology.* Peterborough, Ontario: Broadview, 1992.

Ehrenkreutz, A.S. "The Place of Saladin in the Naval History of the Mediterranean Sea." *Journal of the American Oriental Society* 75 (1955): 100-16.

Elgood, Robert. *Islamic Arms and Armour.* London: Scolar, 1979.

Elm, Kaspar. *Umbilicus mundi: Beiträge zur Geschichte Jerusalems, der Kreuzzüge, des Kapitels vom Hlg. Grab in Jerusalem und der Ritterorden.* Brugge: Sint-Trudo-Abij, 1998.

Elm, Kaspar, and Cosimo Damiano Fonseca, eds. *Militia Sancti Sepulcri, idea e istituzioni: atti del colloquio internazionale tenuto presso la Pontificia univerisità del Laterano, 10-12 aprile 1996.* Città del Vaticano: n.p., 1998.

Elton, Hugh. *Warfare in Roman Europe, A.D. 350-425.* Oxford: Oxford University Press, 1998.

Forey, Alan. *The Fall of the Templars in the Crown of Aragon.* Aldershot, United Kingdom: Ashgate, 2001.

———. *Military Orders and Crusades.* Aldershot, United Kingdom: Ashgate, 1994.

———. *The Military Orders from the Twelfth to the Early Fourteenth Centuries.* Toronto: University of Toronto Press, 1992.

Fowler, Kenneth. *Medieval Mercenaries.* Volume 1, *The Great Companies.* Malden, Mass.: Blackwell, 2001.

Friel, I. *The Good Ship: Ships, Shipbuilding, and Technology in England, 1200-1250.* London: British Museum Press, 1995.

Gardner, Charles W. "Weaponry." *Military History* 6 (1989): 16, 70-74.

Graff, David A. *Medieval Chinese Warfare, 300-900.* London: Routledge, 2001; 2002.

Haidu, Peter. *The Subject of Violence: The Song of Roland and the Birth of the State.* Bloomington: Indiana University Press, 1993.

Hamblin, W. "The Fatimid Navy during the Early Crusades 1099-1124." *American Neptune* 46 (1986): 77-83.

Hassan, Ahmed Yusuf, and Donald Routledge Hill. *Islamic Technology: An Illustrated History.* Cambridge: Cambridge University Press, 1986.

Hillenbrand, Carole, on Muslim warriors and weapons. See *Islamic Perspectives*, under Islam, below.
Housley, Norman. *Crusading and Warfare in Medieval and Renaissance Europe*. Aldershot, United Kingdom: Ashgate, 2001.
Hutchinson, G. *Medieval Ships and Shipping*. London: Leicester University Press, 1994.
Johnson, James Turner, and John Kelsay, eds. *Cross, Crescent, and Sword. The Justification and Limitation of War in Western and Islamic Tradition*. New York: Greenwood, 1990.
―――. *The Holy War Idea in Western and Islamic Traditions*. University Park: Pennsylvania State Press, 1997.
Kaeuper, Richard W. *Chivalry and Violence in Medieval Europe*. Oxford: Oxford University Press, 1999; 2000.
Keen, Maurice. *Medieval Warfare*. Oxford: Oxford University Press, 1999.
―――. *Nobles, Knights, and Men-at-Arms in the Middle Ages*. London: Hambledon, 1996.
―――. *The Outlaws of Medieval Legend*. London: Routledge, 2000.
Kennedy, Hugh. *The Armies of the Caliphs. Military and Society in the Early Islamic State*. London: Routledge, 2001.
Lewis, A.R., and T.J. Runyan. *European Naval and Maritime History, 300-1500*. Bloomington: Indiana University Press, 1985.
Luttrell, Anthony. *The Hospitallers of Rhodes and Their Mediterranean World*. Aldershot, United Kingdom: Ashgate, 1992.
―――. *The Hospitaller State on Rhodes and Its Western Provinces, 1306-1462*. Aldershot, United Kingdom: Ashgate, 1999.
―――. *The Making of Christian Malta from the Early Middle Ages to 1350*. Aldershot, United Kingdom: Ashgate, 2002.
Marshall, Christopher. *Warfare in the Latin East, 1192-1291*. Cambridge: Cambridge University Press, 1996; 1992.
Menache, Sophia. "The Templar Order: A Failed Ideal?" *Catholic Historical Review* 79 (1993): 1-21.
Mollat du Jourdan, Michel. *Europe and the Sea*. Oxford: Blackwell, 1993.
Nicholson, Helen. *The Knights Hospitaller*. Woodbridge, United Kingdom: Boydell and Brewer, 2002.
Nicolle, David C. *Arms and Armour of the Crusading Era*. Revised and updated ed. London: Greenhill, 1999.
―――. *Warriors and Their Weapons around the Time of the Crusades. Relationships between Byzantium, the West, and the Islamic World*. Aldershot, United Kingdom: Ashgate, 2003 (forthcoming at this writing).

Parry, Vernon J., and M.E. Yapp, eds. *War, Technology, and Society in the Middle East.* London: Oxford University Press, 1975.

Prestwich, Michael. *Armies and Warfare in the Middle Ages. The English Experience.* New Haven, Conn.: Yale University Press, 1996.

Pryor, J.H. "The Crusade of Emperor Frederick 1220-9: the Implications of the Maritime Evidence." *American Neptune* 52 (1992): 113-32.

———. *Geography, Technology and War: Studies in the Maritime History of the Mediterranean 649-1571.* Cambridge: Cambridge University Press, 1988.

———. "The Transportation of Horses by Sea during the Era of the Crusades: Eighth Century to 1285 A.D." *The Mariner's Mirror* 68 (1982): 9-27, 103-25.

Renna, Thomas. "Early Cistercian Attitudes toward War in Historical Perspective." *Cîteaux* 31 (1980): 119-29.

Riley-Smith, Jonathan. *The Knights of St. John in Jerusalem and Cyprus, c. 1050-1310.* London: Macmillan, 1967.

Rodger, N.A.M. *The Safeguard of the Sea: A Naval History of Great Britain, Volume I, 660-1649.* London: Harper-Collins, 1997.

Rodgers, W.L. *Naval Warfare under Oars, Fourth to Sixteenth Centuries.* Annapolis, Md.: Naval Institute Press, 1967.

Rogers, R. *Latin Siege Warfare in the Twelfth Century.* Oxford: Oxford University Press, 1997; 1993.

Rose, Susan. *Medieval Naval Warfare, 1000-1500.* London: Routledge, 2002.

Selwood, Dominic. *Knights of the Cloister: Templars and Hospitallers in Central-Southern Occitania, c.1100-c.1300.* Woodbridge, United Kingdom: Boydell and Brewer, 1999.

Seward, Desmond. *The Monks of War. The Military Religious Orders.* New York: Penguin, 1995; 1972.

Sire, H.J.A. *The Knights of Malta.* New Haven, Conn.: Yale University Press, 1994; 1996.

Smail, R.C. *Crusading Warfare 1097-1193.* 2nd ed. Cambridge: Cambridge University Press, 1995.

Upton-Ward, J.M. *The Rule of the Templars. The French Text of the Rule of the Order of the Knights Templar.* Woodbridge, United Kingdom: Boydell and Brewer, 1997; 1992.

Woodcock, Thomas, and John Martin Robinson. *The Oxford Guide to Heraldry.* Oxford: Oxford University Press, 1988.

Byzantium. For a survey of Christian groups, see Atiya.
Eastern Christianity is normally treated as a separate phenomenon due to the split between Constantinople and Rome on issues of primacy and practice in 1054. The Byzantine Empire, based at Constantinople, was at various times an ally and an enemy of Western Europe during the crusades. Histories of Christian Armenia are listed in regional studies under Islam, below. Anna Comnena's chronicle is the most important Byzantine source on the First Crusade available in an English translation. John Cinnamus (c.1144-c.1203) was secretary to Emperor Manuel I Comnenus, and wrote his history in the early 1180s about events in Byzantium from 1118 to 1176. Nicetas Choniates (c.1140-1213) wrote an account of the fall of the city of Constantinople to the Fourth Crusaders. Eustathius (d.1194/95) wrote an account of events in his city after 1180. See also the Western European sources under the Fourth Crusade, below.

Anna Comnena. *The Alexiad of Anna Comnena.* Trans. E.R. Sewter. New York: Penguin Putnam, 1979.

Brand, Charles M., ed./trans. *Deeds of John and Manuel Comnenus, by Joannes Cinnamus.* New York: Columbia University Press, 1995; 1976.

Dawes, Elizabeth A. *The Alexiad of Princess Anna Comnena.* New York: AMS Press, 2002.

Eustathius of Thessalonika. *The Capture of Thessaloniki.* Ed./trans. John R. Melville Jones. Canberra: Australian Association for Byzantine Studies, 1987; 1988.

Magoulias, Harry J. *O City of Byzantium: Annals of Niketas Choniates.* Detroit, Mich.: Wayne State University Press, 1984.

Rosser, John H. *Historical Dictionary of Byzantium.* Lanham, Md.: Scarecrow Press, 2001.

Angold, Michael. *The Byzantine Empire, 1025-1204. A Political History.* 2nd ed. Harlow, United Kingdom: Addison Wesley, 1997.

———. *The Byzantine Government in Exile: Government and Society under the Laskarids of Nicaea, 1204-1261.* Oxford: Oxford University Press, 1975.

———. *Church and Society in Byzantium under the Comneni, 1081-1261.* Cambridge: Cambridge University Press, 1995.

Atiya, Aziz Suryal. *History of Eastern Christianity.* Notre Dame, Ind.: University of Notre Dame Press, 1968.

Gouma-Peterson, Thalia. *Anna Komnene and Her Times*. New York: Garland, 2000.
Jenkins, Romilly. *Byzantium: The Imperial Centuries, A.D. 610-1071*. Toronto: University of Toronto Press, 1987.
Jotischky, A. "Manuel Comnenus and the Reunion of the Churches: The Evidence of the Conciliar Mosaics in the Church of the Nativity in Bethlehem." *Levant* 26 (1994): 207-23.
Laiou, Angeliki E., and Roy Parviz Mottahedeh, eds. *The Crusades from the Perspective of Byzantium and the Muslim World*. Washington, D.C.: Dumbarton Oaks Publishing Service, 2001.
Lilie, Ralph-Johannes. *Byzantium and the Crusader States, 1096-1204*. Trans. J.C. Morris and Jean E. Ridings. Oxford: Oxford University Press, 1993.
Magdalino, Paul. *The Empire of Manuel I Komnenos, 1142-1180*. Cambridge: Cambridge University Press, 1993.
Mango, Cyril, ed. *The Art of the Byzantine Empire, 312-1453*. Toronto: University of Toronto Press, 1986.
Matthew, Gervase. *Byzantine Aesthetics*. New York: Viking Press, 1971.
Meyendorff, John. *Byzantine Theology*. Fordham, N.Y.: Labyrinth, 1979.
Morris, Rosemary. *Monks and Laymen in Byzantium, 843-1118*. Cambridge: Cambridge University Press, 1995.
Obolensky, Dimitre. *The Byzantine Commonwealth: Eastern Europe, 500-1453*. London: Sphere, 1974.
Pelikan, Jaroslav. *The Spirit of Eastern Christendom (600-1700)*. Chicago: University of Chicago Press, 1977; 1974.
Raevskaia-Kh'iuz, Ol'ga, and Boris Gasparov, eds. *Christianity and the Eastern Slavs*. Berkeley: University of California Press, 1993.
Regan, Geoffrey. *First Crusader: Byzantium's Holy Wars*. New York: Palgrave Macmillan, 2003; 2001.
Vasiliev, A.A. *History of the Byzantine Empire, 324-1453*. 2nd English ed. Madison: University of Wisconsin Press, 1973.
Ware, Timothy. *The Orthodox Church*. Harmondsworth, United Kingdom: Penguin, 1964.

Islam

There is a tremendous volume of material available on Islam. Students should be aware that there are serious disagreements among scholars on how to present and interpret the history of Islamic states. This select bibliography focuses on the crusades and shows some of the range of opinion. Several sources in translation begin the list, followed by an atlas and two overall histories. Ibn Jubayr (1145-1217), whose *Travels* heads the list, was secretary to the Muslim governor of Granada, made the pilgrimage to Mecca in 1183/85 and returned through the Latin Kingdom of Jerusalem just before its fall to Saladin in 1187. Gabrielli's edition of Arabic sources gives further information on Muslim authors. The *History of the Patriarchs* offers the perspective of the Copts under Muslim rule.

Histories of the medieval Islamic empires based at Damascus and Baghdad follow, showing a range of opinion from that of Bernard Lewis, who has been criticized for taking a view that values the civilization of Western Europe over other world systems, to the ideas of Edward Said, who has responded with a critique of what he sees as colonial scholarship. More recent works, such as Molly Greene's history of both cultures as a product of the Mediterranean region, and Carole Hillenbrand's analysis of the Islamic world during the crusades are recommended as balanced introductions for senior students, along with Tarif Khalidi's overview of Muslim civilization. The Esposito and Robinson overviews are good places to start for those with little background in history. Regional studies follow the general section on Islam.

Broadhurst, R.J.C., trans. *The Travels of Ibn Jubayr*. New Delhi: Goodwood, 2001; 1952.

Gabrielli, Francesco, ed./trans. *Arab Historians of the Crusades*. Translated from the Italian by E.J. Costello. Berkeley: University of California Press, 1984; 1969.

Gibb, H.A.R. *The Damascus Chronicle of the Crusades*. Mineola, N.Y.: Dover: 2003; 1932.

Hitti, Philip K. *An Arab-Syrian Gentleman and Warrior in the Period of the Crusades: Memoires of Usamah ibn-Munqidh*. New York: Columbia University Press, 2000; 1929.

Khs-Burmester, O.H.E., and Yassa 'Abd al-Masih, ed./trans. *History of the Patriarchs of the Egyptian Church*. 4 vols. Cairo: Publications de la Société de l'archéologie Copte, 1943-74.

Maqrizi, Ahmad ibn 'Ali. *A History of the Ayyubid Sultans of Egypt*. Ed./trans. Ronald J.C. Broadhurst. Boston: Twayne Publishers, 1980.

Atlas of the Arab World and the Middle East. Introduction by C.F. Beckingham, created by Djambatan Publishers and Cartographers. London: Macmillan, 1960.

Esposito, John L. *The Oxford History of Islam*. Oxford: Oxford University Press, 2000.

Robinson, Francis. *The Cambridge Illustrated History of the Islamic World*. Cambridge: Cambridge University Press, 1998; 1996.

Somel, Selcuk Aksin. *Historical Dictionary of the Ottoman Empire*. Lanham, Md.: Scarecrow Press, 2003.

Abu-Izzeddin, Nejla M. *The Druzes: A New Study of Their History, Faith, and Society*. Leiden: Brill, 1984; 1993 repr. with corrections.

Amitai-Preiss, Reuven. *Mongols and Mamluks: The Mamluk-Ilkanid War, 1260-1281*. Cambridge: Cambridge University Press, 1995.

Bartlett, W.B. *The Assassins: The Story of Islam's Medieval Secret Sect*. Harlow, United Kingdom: Longman, 2001. See also: Mirza, under Syria, below.

Berkey, Jonathan P. *The Formation of Islam: Religion and Society in the Near East, 600-1800*. Cambridge: Cambridge University Press, 2002.

Blair, Sheila S., and Jonathan M. Bloom. *The Art and Architecture of Islam, 1250-1800*. New Haven, Conn.: Yale University Press, 1994.

Bloom, Jonathan, and Sheila Blair. *Islam: A Thousand Years of Faith and Power*. New Haven, Conn.: Yale University Press, 2002.

Daftary, Farhad, ed. *Medieval Ismaili History and Thought*. Cambridge: Cambridge University Press, 2001.

Ettinghausen, Richard, et al. *The Art and Architecture of Islam, 650-1250*. 2nd ed. New Haven, Conn.: Yale University Press, 2001.

Gibb, H.A.R. *The Arab Conquests in Central Asia*. London: University Press, 1923; repr. New York: AMS Press, 1970; 1923.

Greene, Molly. *A Shared World: Christians and Muslims in the Early Modern Mediterranean*. Princeton, N.J.: Princeton University Press, 2000.

Hillenbrand, Carole. *The Crusades: Islamic Perspectives*. New York: Routledge, 2000.

Holt, P.M. *The Age of the Crusades. The Near East from the Eleventh Century to 1517*. Harlow, United Kingdom: Longman, 1986.

Humphreys, Steven R. *Islamic History. A Framework for Inquiry*. 2nd ed. Princeton, N.J.: Princeton University Press, 1991.

Kennedy, Hugh. *The Prophet and the Age of the Caliphates: The Islamic Near East from the Sixth to the Eleventh Century*. Harlow, United Kingdom: Longman, 1986.

Khalidi, Tarif. *Classical Arab Islam: The Culture and Heritage of the Golden Age*. Princeton, N.J.: Darwin Press, 1985.

Kreyenbrock, Philip, and Christine Allison, eds. *Kurdish Culture and Identity*. London: Zed Books, 1996.
Laiou and Mottahedeh, on the Crusades from Islamic perspective. See above, under Byzantium.
Lewis, Bernard. *The Arabs in History*. 6th ed. Oxford: Oxford University Press, 1993.
———. *The Assassins*. New York: Basic Books, 1968.
———. *Islam and the West*. Oxford: Oxford University Press, 1993.
———. *What Went Wrong? Western Impact and Middle Eastern Response*. New York: Oxford University Press, 2002.
———. "The Revolt of Islam." *The New Yorker* (19 November 2001): 50-63.
———, ed. *Islam and the Arab World: Faith, People, Culture*. New York: Knopf, 1976.
———, with Peter M. Holt, eds. *Historians of the Middle East*. London: Oxford University Press, 1962.
Lippman, Thomas W. *Understanding Islam. An Introduction to the Muslim World*. 2nd rev. ed. New York: Penguin, 1995.
Maalouf, Amin. *The Crusades through Arab Eyes*. Trans. Jon Rothschild. New York: Schocken Books, 1989; 1985.
Nagel, Tilman. *The History of Islamic Theology from Muhammad to the Present*. Princeton, N.J.: Markus Wiener, 2000.
Peters, Rudolf F. *The Jihad in Classical and Modern Islam*. Princeton, N.J.: Markus Wiener, 1996.
Sachedina, Abdulaziz A. "The Development of *Jihad* in Islamic Revelation and History." In *Cross, Crescent, and Sword. The Justification and Limitation of War in Western and Islamic Tradition*, ed. James Turner Johnson and John Kelsey. New York: Greenwood, 1990.
Said, Edward W. *Covering Islam*. New York: Pantheon, 1981.
———. "Impossible Histories. Why the Many Islams Cannot Be Simplified." *Harper's Magazine* (July 2002): 69-74.
———. *Orientalism*. Harmondsworth, United Kingdom: Penguin, 1995; 1978.
Spuler, Bertold. *The Age of the Caliphs: A History of the Muslim World*. Princeton, N.J.: Markus Wiener, 1999.
———. *The Mongol Period: A History of the Muslim World*. Princeton, N.J.: Markus Wiener, 1996; 1994.
Tolan, John Victor. *Saracens: Islam in the Medieval European Imagination*. New York: Columbia University Press, 2002.

Watt, W.M. *The Influence of Islam on Medieval Europe*. Edinburgh: Edinburgh University Press, 1972.

Wheatcroft, Andrew. *The Ottomans*. London: Penguin, 1993.

Africa (the Maghrib). See also Egypt.

Oliver, Roland A., and Anthony Atmore. *The African Middle Ages, 1400-1800*. Cambridge: Cambridge University Press, 1981.

Powers, David S. *Law, Society, and Culture in the Maghrib, 1300-1500*. Cambridge: Cambridge University Press, 2002.

Shillington, Kevin. *The History of Africa*. Rev. ed. New York: St. Martin's Press, 1995.

Anatolia (Turkey)

Cahen, C. *Pre-Ottoman Turkey. A General Survey of the Material and Spiritual Culture and History c. 1071-1330*. New York: Taplinger, 1968.

Kuloglu, Abdullah. "The Anatolian Seljuk State (1077-1308)." *Revue internationale d'histoire militaire* 46 (1980): 15-30.

Armenia. There is a French translation of a chronicle written by Smbat the Constable (1208-76), brother of King Hethum I of Cilicia, which covers the years 1159-1272.

Dédéyan, Gérard, ed./trans. *La Chronique attribuée au Connétable Smbat*. Paris: P. Geuthner, 1980.

Boase, T.S.R. *The Cilician Kingdom of Armenia*. Edinburgh: Scottish Academic Press, 1978.

Hamilton, Bernard. "The Armenian Church and the Papacy at the Time of the Crusades." *Eastern Churches Review* 10 (1978): 61-87.

Hovannisian, Richard G. *The Armenian People from Ancient to Modern Times*. 2 vols. New York: St. Martin's Press, 1997.

Egypt. See also the primary sources listed at the beginning of this section.

Adams, William Yewdale. *Nubia: Corridor to Africa*. Princeton, N.J.: Princeton University Press, 1977.

Ayalon, David. *Gunpowder and Firearms in the Mamluk Kingdom: A Challenge to a Mediaeval Society*. 2nd ed. London: F. Cass, 1978.

Irwin, Robert. *The Middle East in the Middle Ages: The Early Mamluk Sultanate 1250-1382*. Carbondale: Southern Illinois University Press, 1986.

Khuwaytir, A.A. *Baibars the First: His Endeavors and Achievements*. London: Green Mountain, 1978.

Lev, Yaacov. *State and Society in Fatimid Egypt*. Leiden: Brill, 1991.

Meinardus, Otto Friedrich August. *Atlas of Christian Sites in Egypt*. Cairo: Société d'Archéologie Copte, 1962.

Petry, Carl F., and Martin W. Daly. *The Cambridge History of Egypt*. 2 vols. Cambridge: Cambridge University Press, 1999.

Thorau, P. *The Lion of Egypt: Sultan Baybars I and the Near East in the Thirteenth Century*. Harlow, United Kingdom: Longman, 1995.

Iran

Boyle, J.A. *The Saljuq and Mongol Periods*. Vol. 7 of *The Cambridge History of Iran*, ed. W.B. Fisher. Cambridge: Cambridge University Press, 1968-91.

Mackey, Sandra. *The Iranians: Persia, Islam, and the Soul of a Nation*. London: Dutton, 1996.

Morgan, David. *Medieval Persia, 1040-1797*. Harlow, United Kingdom: Longman, 1988.

Iraq

Fink, H.S. "Mawdud of Mosul, Precursor of Saladin." *Muslim World* 43 (1953): 18-27.

Roux, Georges. *Ancient Iraq*. 3rd ed. New York: Penguin, 1992.

Kurds. See Kreyenbrock, under Islam, above.

Mongols. See Spuler, and Amitai-Preiss, under Islam, above.

Palestine

Gil, Moshe. *A History of Palestine, 634-1099*. Cambridge: Cambridge University Press, 1992.

Syria. There is a French translation of the chronicle of Michael the Syrian, Jacobite patriarch of Antioch (1126-99) by Chabot. The chronicle of Bar Hebraeus (1226-86) on world history covers events in Syria from the Jacobite Christian perspective.

Chabot, Jean, ed./trans. *Chronicle*. 4 vols. Paris: Ernest Leroux, 1899-1924.

Wallis-Budge, Ernest, ed./trans. *The Chronography* [Bar Hebraeus]. 2 vols. Oxford: Oxford University Press, 1932.

Downey, Glanville. *A History of Antioch in Syria: From Seleucus to the Arab Conquest.* Princeton, N.J.: Princeton University Press, 1961; 1966.

Fink, H.S. "The Role of Damascus in the History of the Crusades." *Muslim World* 40 (1950): 41-53.

Hitti, Philip K. *Syria, a Short History; Being a Condensation of the Author's History of Syria, Including Lebanon and Palestine.* New York: Collier, 1961; 1959.

Humphreys, Stephen R. *From Saladin to the Mongols: The Ayyubids of Damascus, 1193-1260.* Albany: State University of New York Press, 1977.

Mirza, Nasser Ahmad. *Syrian Ismai'ilism: The Ever-Living Line of the Imamate, A.D. 1100-1260.* Richmond, United Kingdom: Curzon, 1997.

Shatzmiller, Maya, ed. *Crusaders and Muslims in Twelfth-Century Syria.* Leiden: Brill, 1993.

Turkey (*see* Anatolia)

Jerusalem

In this section are works emphasizing the importance of the city for three major religions, and giving information on pilgrimage patterns, practices, and facilities in the Middle Ages. John Wilkinson translated the pilgrim account of John Phocas, a Greek Orthodox visitor to Jerusalem in 1185. Leontios (c.1110-85) was Greek patriarch of Jerusalem until 1185. His disciple Theodosius Goudeles wrote the *Life* in about 1203.

Tsounkarakes, Dimitris, ed./trans. *The Life of Leontios, Patriarch of Jerusalem.* Leiden: Brill, 1993.

Wilkinson, John, et al., eds. *Jerusalem Pilgrimage, 1099-1185.* London: Hakluyt Society, 1988.

Armstrong, Karen. *Jerusalem: One City, Three Faiths.* New York: Alfred A. Knopf, 1996.

Auxientios, Bishop. *The Paschal Fire in Jerusalem: A Study of the Rite of the Holy Fire in the Church of the Holy Sepulchre.* 3rd ed. Berkeley, Calif.: St. John Chrysostom Press, 1999.

Boas, Adrian. *Jerusalem in the Time of the Crusades: Society, Landscape, and Art in the Holy City under Frankish Rule.* London: Routledge, 2001.
Cole, Penny J. "Christians, Muslims, and the 'Liberation' of the Holy Land." *The Catholic Historical Review* 84 (1998): 1-10.
Coüasnon, Charles. *The Church of the Holy Sepulchre in Jerusalem.* Trans. J.P.B. Ross and Claude Ross. London: Oxford University Press, 1974.
Cousins, Ewert. "The Humanity and the Passion of Christ." In *Christian Spirituality: High Middle Ages and Reformation,* ed. Jill Raitt. New York: Crossroad Press, 1987.
Elad, Amikam. *Medieval Jerusalem and Islamic Worship: Holy Places, Ceremonies, Pilgrimage.* 2nd ed. Leiden: Brill, 1999.
Gibson, Shimon, and Joan E. Taylor. *Beneath the Church of the Holy Sepulchre, Jerusalem: The Archaeology and Early History of Traditional Golgotha.* London: Palestine Exploration Fund, 1994.
Hamilton, Bernard. "The Impact of Crusader Jerusalem on Western Christendom." *The Catholic Historical Review* 80 (1994): 695-713.
Levine, Lee I., ed. *Jerusalem: Its Sanctity and Centrality to Judaism, Christianity, and Islam.* New York: Continuum, 1999.
Linder, Amnon. "The Liturgy of the Liberation of Jerusalem." *Mediaeval Studies* 52 (1990): 110-31.
Pringle, Denys. *The Churches of the Crusader Kingdom of Jerusalem. A Corpus.* 2 vols. Cambridge: Cambridge University Press, 1993-98.
Renna, Thomas. *Jerusalem in Medieval Thought, 400-1300.* Lewiston, N.Y.: E. Mellon, 2002.
Schein, Sylvia. "Between Mount Moriah and the Holy Sepulchre: The Changing Traditions of the Temple Mount in the Central Middle Ages." *Traditio* 40 (1984): 175-95. [For the Temple as an idea rather than as a building, *see* Thomas Renna, under the Second Crusade, below.]
——. *Gateway to the Heavenly City. Crusader Jerusalem and the Catholic West (1099-1187).* Aldershot, United Kingdom: Ashgate, 2003 (forthcoming at this writing).
Wharton, A.J. "The Baptistery of the Holy Sepulchre in Jerusalem and the Politics of Sacred Landscape." *Dumbarton Oaks Papers* 46 (1992): 313-26.

Jewish History and the Crusades

The emphasis here is on the massacres perpetrated by the People's Crusade in the Rhineland in 1096 rather than on a comprehensive history of the Jews during the period of the crusades. The first two works offer Jewish sources in translation for the massacres. Rabbi Benjamin of Tudela's *Itinerary* is an important 12th-century source on the Holy Land. Judah ha-Levi (c.1075-1141) wrote a Jewish apologetic with some comments on contemporary crusading. There are then three works which indicate to beginning students how broad the spectrum is of available scholarship: a dictionary, a work on the history of Jewish law and practice, and Niditch's introduction to Judaism in history. There is then a selection of works on Western Europe and the Jews during the crusades. For more on the Jews in Spain, see the Reconquista section, below, and in particular works on the Spanish Inquisition.

Chazan, Robert. *European Jewry and the First Crusade.* Berkeley: University of California Press, 1987.
———. "The First Crusade as Reflected in the Earliest Hebrew Narrative." *Viator* 29 (1998): 25-38.
Eidelberg, Shlomo, ed./trans. *The Jews and the Crusaders: The Hebrew Chronicles of the First and Second Crusades.* Madison: University of Wisconsin Press, 1977.
Judah ha-Levi. *The Kuzari. Kitab al Khazari: An Argument for the Faith of Israel.* Trans. Hartwig Hirschfeld. New York: Schocken Books, 1964.
Signer, M.A., ed./trans. *The Itinerary of Benjamin of Tudela: Travels in the Middle Ages.* Malibu, Calif.: J. Simon, 1987.

The Oxford Dictionary of the Jewish Religion. R.J. Zwi Werblowsky and Geoffrey Wigoder, eds. in chief. New York: Oxford University Press, 1997.
Cohen, Abraham. *Everyman's Talmud.* New York: Schocken Books, 1995.
Niditch, Susan. *Ancient Israelite Religion in Historical Perspective.* Oxford: Oxford University Press, 1998.

Berger, David. "The Attitude of St. Bernard of Clairvaux toward the Jews." *Proceedings of the American Academy of Jewish Research* 40 (1972): 89-108.
Biale, David, ed. *Cultures of the Jews. A New History.* New York: Schocken Books, 2002.
Chazan, Robert. *God, Humanity, and History: The Hebrew First Crusade Narratives.* Berkeley: University of California Press, 2000.
———. *In the Year 1096: The First Crusade and the Jews.* Philadelphia: Jewish Publication Society, 1996.

Nirenberg, David. "Conversion, Sex, and Segregation: Jews and Christians in Medieval Spain." *American Historical Review* 107 (2002): 1065-93.

Prawer, Joshua. *The History of the Jews in the Latin Kingdom of Jerusalem.* Oxford: Clarendon Press, 1988.

Shepkaru, Shmuel. "To Die for God: Martyrs' Heaven in Hebrew and Latin Crusade Narratives." *Speculum* 77, no. 2 (April 2002): 311-41.

Stow, Kenneth R. *Alienated Minority: The Jews of Medieval Latin Europe.* Cambridge, Mass.: Harvard University Press, 1992; 1994.

Crusades

The most famous and widely read history of the crusades is by Steven Runciman, in three volumes. The Setton history, in six volumes, is a comprehensive overview with maps, timelines, and bibliography. In some cases it is outdated and should be replaced by recent monographs. A 2002 collection of essays on key aspects of crusading, edited by Thomas Madden, offers students an accessible one-volume introduction to the best of new scholarship.

Examples of different kinds of primary sources available in English translation begin this list, followed by an atlas and the Oxford one-volume histories, which are particularly accessible to students. There are not always narratives of individual crusades available, a situation which makes the general histories of the movement as a whole important secondary sources. Again, only a selection of what is available can be given here, and all of the works listed offer further bibliography. The Cistercian and Cluniac orders are covered in the bibliography on the Western European Church, while the medieval military orders are covered under Warfare. A work on the Premonstratensian Order, which became involved in recruitment, is listed below. Works on the history of the crusader kingdoms are listed under the First Crusade. See also sections on particular expeditions.

Hallam, Elizabeth, ed. *Chronicles of the Crusades: Nine Crusades and Two Hundred Years of Bitter Conflict for the Holy Land Brought to Life in the Words of Those Who Were Actually There.* New York: Weidenfeld and Nicolson, 1989.

Noffke, Suzanne. *The Letters of Catherine of Siena.* 2 vols. Tempe, Ariz.: Arizona Center for Medieval and Renaissance Texts and Studies, 2000, 2001.

Peters, Edward, ed. *Christian Society and the Crusades, 1198-1229. Sources in Translation, Including the Capture of Damietta by Oliver of Paderborn.* Philadelphia: University of Pennsylvania Press, 1971.

Shirley, Janet, ed./trans. *Crusader Syria in the Thirteenth Century: The Rothelin Continuation of the History of William of Tyre with Part of the Eracles or Acre Text*. Aldershot, United Kingdom: Ashgate, 1999.

Slack, Corliss K. *Crusade Charters, 1138-1270*. Tempe, Ariz.: Arizona Center for Medieval and Renaissance Texts and Studies, 2001.

William, Archbishop of Tyre. *A History of Deeds Done beyond the Sea*. 2 vols. Ed./trans. A.C. Krey and E.A. Babcock. New York: Columbia University Press, 1943.

Kontam, Angus. *Historical Atlas of the Crusades*. New York: Facts on File, 2002.

Madden, Thomas, F., ed. *The Crusades: The Essential Readings*. Oxford: Blackwell, 2002.

Setton, Kenneth Meyer, gen. ed. *A History of the Crusades*. 2nd ed. 6 vols. Madison: University of Wisconsin Press, 1969-89. Volume 6 includes a general bibliography.

Smith, Jonathan Riley, ed. *The Oxford History of the Crusades*. 2nd ed. Oxford: Oxford University Press, 2002.

―――, ed. *The Oxford Illustrated History of the Crusades*. Oxford: Oxford University Press, 1995.

Abulafia, David. *Frederick II*. Oxford: Oxford University Press, 1992.

Ashtor, E. *Levant Trade in the Later Middle Ages*. Princeton, N.J.: Princeton University Press, 1983.

Asiedu, F.B.A. "Anselm, the Ethics of Solidarity, and the Ideology of Crusade." *American Benedictine Review* 53 (March 2002): 42-59.

Brundage, James A. "*Cruce Signari:* The Rite for Taking the Cross in England." *Traditio* 22 (1966): 289-310.

―――. *The Crusades, Holy War, and Canon Law*. Aldershot, United Kingdom: Ashgate, 1991.

―――. *Medieval Canon Law*. Harlow, United Kingdom: Longman, 1996.

―――. *Medieval Canon Law and the Crusader*. Madison: University of Wisconsin Press, 1969.

―――. "A Note on the Attestation of Crusaders' Vows." *Catholic Historical Review* 52 (1966): 234-39.

Burns, Robert I., S.J. *Diplomatarium of the Crusader Kingdom of Valencia*. 3 vols.; vol. 1 is in English with an introduction and bibliography. Princeton, N.J.: Princeton University Press, 2001.

Cheney, C.R. "Gervase, Abbot of Prémontré: A Medieval Letter-Writer." In Cheney, *Medieval Texts and Studies*, pp. 242-76. Oxford: Clarendon Press, 1973.
Christianson, Karen. "Reconstructing the Growth of an Order: Fontevraud and the Charter Evidence." Paper delivered at the 117th Annual Meeting of the American Historical Association, Chicago, January 2-5, 2003.
Cole, Penny J. *The Preaching of the Crusades to the Holy Land, 1095-1270.* Cambridge, Mass.: Medieval Academy of America, 1991.
Edbury, Peter W., and John Gordon Rowe. *William of Tyre: Historian of the Latin East.* Cambridge: Cambridge University Press, 1988.
Edgington, Susan B., and Sarah Lambert, eds. *Gendering the Crusades.* New York: Columbia University Press, 2002.
Flori, Jean. *Guerre sainte, jihad, croisade: Violence et religion dans le christianism et l'islam.* Paris: Éditions du Seuil, 2002.
Jacoby, David. *Studies on the Crusader States and on Venetian Expansion.* Aldershot, United Kingdom: Ashgate, 1999.
Jordan, William Chester. *Louis IX and the Challenge of the Crusade: A Study in Rulership.* Princeton, N.J.: Princeton University Press, 1979.
Jotischiky, A. *The Perfection of Solitude: Hermits and Monks in the Crusader States.* University Park: Pennsylvania State University Press, 1995.
Kedar, Benjamin Z., et al., eds. *Crusades.* Aldershot, United Kingdom: Ashgate, 2002.
Kienzle, Beverly Mayne. *Cistercians, Heresy and Crusade in Occitania, 1145-1229: Preaching in the Lord's Vineyard.* York, United Kingdom: York Medieval Press, 2001.
Leopold, Antony. *How to Recover the Holy Land: The Crusade Proposals of the Late Thirteenth and Early Fourteenth Centuries.* Aldershot, United Kingdom: Ashgate, 2000.
Lewis, Archibald Ross. *Nomads and Crusaders, A.D. 1000-1368.* Bloomington: Indiana University Press, 1991; 1988.
Maier, Christoph T. "Crisis, Liturgy, and the Crusade in the Twelfth and Thirteenth Centuries." *Journal of Ecclesiastical History* 48 (1997): 628-57.
———. *Crusade Propaganda and Ideology: Model Sermons for the Preaching of the Cross.* Cambridge: Cambridge University Press, 2000.
Mayer, Hans Eberhard. *The Crusades.* Trans. John Gillingham. Oxford: Oxford University Press, 1981.

Pennington, Kenneth. "The Rite for Taking the Cross in the Twelfth Century." *Traditio* 30 (1974): 429-35.
Phillips, Jonathan. "Hugh de Payne and the 1129 Damascus Crusade." In *The Military Orders: Fighting for the Faith and Caring for the Sick*. Proceedings of the International Conference on the Military Orders, London, 3-6 September 1992. Ed. Malcolm Barber. Aldershot, United Kingdom: Variorum, 1994.
Powell, James M., ed. *Innocent III. Vicar of Christ or Lord of the World?* Washington, D.C.: Catholic University of America Press, 1994.
Prawer, Joshua. *The Latin Kingdom of Jerusalem: European Colonialism in the Middle Ages*. London: Weidenfeld & Nicolson, 1973.
Premonstratensian Order. *The Day of Pentecost: Constitutions of the Order of Canons Regular of Prémontré, with Appendices*. 3rd English edition. De Pere, Wis.: St. Norbert Abbey, 1998.
Richard, Jean. *The Crusades, c.1071-1291*. Trans. Jean Birrell. New York: Cambridge University Press, 1999.
———. *Francs et Orientaux dans le monde des croisades*. Aldershot, United Kingdom: Ashgate, 2003 (forthcoming at this writing).
Runciman, Stephen. *A History of the Crusades*. 3 vols. Cambridge: Cambridge University Press, 1951-55.
Siberry, Elizabeth. *Criticism of Crusading, 1095-1274*. Oxford: Clarendon, 1985.
———. *The New Crusaders. Images of the Crusades in the Nineteenth and Early Twentieth Centuries*. Aldershot, United Kingdom: Ashgate, 2000.
Strickland, Debra Higgs. *Saracens, Demons, and Jews. Making Monsters in Medieval Art*. Princeton, N.J.: Princeton University Press, 2003.
Tyerman, Christopher. *The Invention of the Crusades*. Houndmills, Basingstoke, United Kingdom: Macmillan, 1998.
Undset, Sigrid. *Catherine of Siena, 1347-1380*. Trans. Kate Austin-Lund. New York: Sheed & Ward, 1954.
Vicaire, M.H. "Humbert de Romans." *Dictionnaire de Théologie Catholique*, vol. 7, pp. 1108-1116. Paris: Beauchesne, 1969.

Major Expeditions/Crusades, in chronological order (also see the Crusades and Islam sections above):

Reconquista. See also the Second Crusade, below.
The war against Islam in Spain predated the First Crusade and lasted far beyond the fall of Acre in 1291. A selection of works on the Spanish king-

doms, the Islamic African kingdoms, pilgrimage to Compostela, and the conflict in general are offered below.

Gerli, Michael, ed. *Medieval Iberia. An Encyclopedia*. London: Routledge, 2002.

Biggs, Anselm Gordon. *Diego Gelmirez, First Archbishop of Compostela*. Washington, D.C.: Catholic University of America Press, 1949.

Bishko, Charles Julian. *Studies in Medieval Spanish Frontier History*. London: Variorum, 1980.

Bisson, Thomas N. *The Medieval Crown of Aragon. A Short History*. Oxford: Oxford University Press, 1991; 1986.

Bulliet, Richard W. *Conversion to Islam in the Medieval Period: An Essay in Quantitative History*. Cambridge, Mass.: Harvard University Press, 1979.

Davidson, Linda Kay, and Maryjane Dunn, eds. *The Pilgrimage to Compostela in the Middle Ages*. New York: Garland, 1996; 2000.

De Oliveira Marques, A.H. *History of Portugal*. 2 vols. New York: Columbia University Press, 1972.

Fletcher, Richard. *The Quest for El Cid*. Oxford: Oxford University Press, 1991.

Hunt, Jocelyn. *Spain, 1474-1598*. London: Routledge, 2000; 2001.

Kamen, Henry. *The Spanish Inquisition. A Historical Revision*. New Haven, Conn.: Yale University Press, 1998.

Kennedy, Hugh. *Muslim Spain and Portugal. A Political History of al-Andalus*. Harlow, United Kingdom: Longman, 1996.

Linehan, Peter. *The Spanish Church and the Papacy in the Thirteenth Century*. Cambridge: Cambridge University Press, 1971.

Livermore, H.V. *A New History of Portugal*. 2nd ed. Cambridge: Cambridge University Press, 1976.

Mackay, John. *The Other Spanish Christ*. Eugene, Oreg.: Wipf & Stock, 2001; 1933.

O'Callaghan, Joseph F. *Reconquest and Crusade in Medieval Spain*. Philadelphia: University of Pennsylvania Press, 2002.

Reilly, Bernard F. *The Contest of Christian and Muslim Spain (1031-1157)*. Cambridge, Mass.: Blackwell, 1992; 1995.

———. *The Kingdom of León-Castilla under King Alfonso VI, 1065-1109*. Princeton, N.J.: Princeton University Press, 1988.

———. *The Medieval Spains*. Cambridge: Cambridge University Press, 1993.

———. *Santiago, St.-Denis, and Saint Peter: The Reception of the Roman Liturgy in León-Castile in 1080*. New York: Fordham University Press, 1985.

Smith, Damian. *Innocent III and the Realms of Aragon and Catalonia: The Limits of Papal Authority*. Aldershot, United Kingdom: Ashgate, 2004 (forthcoming).

UNESCO. *General History of Africa*. Vol. 3 (of 8). London: Heinemann Educational Books, 1981-1993.

First Crusade and the Latin Kingdom of Jerusalem, 1096-1187

This section includes works on the organization of the crusader kingdom, along with some information on the families of crusade leaders and nonmilitary religious orders founded by Europeans in the Holy Land. A number of the sources available in translation are listed first, followed by secondary sources. The *Livre au roi* is an account of the laws of the Latin Kingdom before 1187, but was not compiled until c.1205 for the king of Cyprus. John of Ibelin/Jaffa wrote a treatise on the laws of the Latin Kingdom and practices of the High Court before he died in 1266. For information on the crusader kingdom in Cyprus and on the family of Montferrat see the Third Crusade section, below. For the massacres of Jews in the Rhineland that preceded the First Crusade, see "Jews" above, in this bibliography.

Archambault, Paul J., ed./trans. *A Monk's Confession: The Memoirs of Guibert of Nogent*. University Park: Pennsylvania State University Press, 1996.

Bachrach, Bernard S., and David S. Bachrach, ed./trans. *The Gesta Tancredi of Raoul Caen: A History of the Normans on the First Crusade*. Aldershot, United Kingdom: Ashgate, 2004 (forthcoming).

Belgrano, Luigi T., ed. *Annali genovesi de Caffaro e de'suoi continuatiori, dal MXCIX al MCCXCII*. 2nd ed., 5 vols. Genoa: Tipografia del Senato Istituto sordo-muti, 1929.

Bernard of Clairvaux. "In Praise of the New Knighthood." Trans. Conrad Greenia, in *The Works of Bernard of Clairvaux*, vol. 7. Kalamazoo, Mich.: Cistercian Publications, 1977.

Edwards, Bede, ed./trans. *The Rule of Saint Albert*. Aylesford, United Kingdom: Carmelite Priory Press, 1973.

Fulcher of Chartres, ed./trans. Harold S. Fink and Frances Rita Ryan, S.S.J. *A History of the Expedition to Jerusalem, 1095-1127*. New York: Norton, 1973; 1969.

262 • Bibliography

Guibert of Nogent, ed./trans. Robert Levine. *The Deeds of God through the Franks/Gesta Dei per Francos*. Woodbridge, United Kingdom: Boydell, 1997.

Hill, Rosalind T., ed./trans. *Gesta Francorum et aliorum Hierosolymitanorum/The Deeds of the Franks and Other Pilgrims to Jerusalem*. Oxford: Clarendon Press, 1962; 1972.

Krey, A.C. *The First Crusade: The Accounts of Eye-Witnesses and Participants*. Princeton, N.J.: Princeton University Press, 1921.

Le Livre au roi. Edited by Myriam Greilsammer. Paris: Académie des Inscriptions et Belles-Lettres, 1995.

"Livre de Jean d'Ibelin." Edited in *Recueil des historiens des croisades, Lois*, I, pp. 1-432. Paris: Imprimerie royale, 1841-43 [See Edbury, *John of Ibelin*, and *Recueil*, below].

Munro, Dana Carleton. *Urban and the Crusaders*. 3rd ed. New York: AMS Press, 1971; 1897.

Peters, Edward, ed./trans. *The First Crusade*. 2nd ed. Philadelphia: University of Pennsylvania Press, 1998.

Raymond of Aguilers, ed. John Hugh Hill and Laura Lyttleton Hill. *Raimundus d'Aguilers. Historia Francorum qui ceperunt Iherusalem*. Philadelphia: American Philosophical Society, 1968.

Recueil des historiens des croisades. 16 vols. in 5 series: *Historiens occidentaux, Historiens grecs, Historiens orientaux, Lois. Assises de Jérusalem, Documents arméniens*. Corporate author: Académie des Inscriptions et Belles-Lettres. Paris: Imprimerie Royale, 1841-1906.

Robert (the Monk) of Rheims, ed./trans. Carol Sweetenham. *History of the First Crusade. The Historia Iherosolimitana*. Aldershot, United Kingdom: Ashgate, 2003 (forthcoming at this writing).

Shirley, Janet. *Crusader Syria in the Thirteenth Century. The Rothelin Continuation of the History of William of Tyre with Part of the Eracles or Acre Text*. Aldershot, United Kingdom: Ashgate, 1999.

Tudebod(e), Peter, ed./trans. John Hugh Hill and Laurita Lyttleton Hill. *Petrus Tudebodus. Historia de Hierosolymitano itinere*. Philadelphia: American Philosophical Society, 1974.

William, Archbishop of Tyre. *A History of Deeds Done beyond the Sea*. 2 vols. Ed./annotated Emily Atwater Babcock; ed. A.C. Krey. New York: Octagon, 1976; 1943.

Asbridge, Thomas S. *The Creation of the Principality of Antioch, 1098-1130*. Rochester, N.Y.: Boydell and Brewer, 2000.

Bachrach, Bernard S. *Fulk Nerra, the Neo-Roman Consul (987-1040)*. Berkeley: University of California Press, 1993.

———. *State-Building in Medieval France. Studies in Early Angevin History*. Aldershot, United Kingdom: Ashgate, 1995.

Baldwin, M.W. *Raymond III of Tripolis and the Fall of Jerusalem (1140-1187)*. New York: AMS Press, 1978; 1936.

Barber, Malcolm. "The Order of Saint Lazarus and the Crusades." *The Catholic Historical Review* 80 (1994): 439-56.

Brundage, J.A. "Adhémar of Puy, the Bishop and His Critics." *Speculum* 34 (1959): 201-12.

Buchthal, Hugo. *Miniature Painting in the Latin Kingdom of Jerusalem*. London: Pindar, 1984; 1957.

Chazan, Robert. "The First Crusade as Reflected in the Earliest Hebrew Narrative." *Viator* 29 (1998): 25-38.

Cowdrey, H.E.J. "The Genesis of the Crusades: The Springs of the Holy War." In *Popes, Monks, and Crusaders*. London: Hambledon, 1984. Previously published in *The Holy War*, ed. Thomas Patrick Murphy. Columbus: Ohio State University Press, 1976.

———. *Pope Gregory VII, 1073-1085*. Oxford: Clarendon Press, 1998.

Edbury, Peter W., ed. *Crusade and Settlement: Papers Read at the First Conference of the Society for the Study of the Crusades and the Latin East. Presented to R.C. Smail*. Cardiff, United Kingdom: University College of Cardiff Press, 1985.

———. *John of Ibelin and the Kingdom of Jerusalem*. Woodbridge, United Kingdom: Boydell Press, 1997.

———. *Kingdoms of the Crusaders. From Jerusalem to Cyprus*. Aldershot, United Kingdom: Ashgate, 1999.

Elm, Kaspar. *Quellen zur Geschichte des Ordens vom Hlg. Grab in Nordwesteuropa aus deutschen und niederländischen Archiven (1191-1603)*. Brussels: Académie Royale de Belgique, 1976.

———. *Umbilicus mundi: Beiträge zur Geschichte Jerusalems, der Kreuzzüge, des Kapitels vom Hlg. Grab in Jerusalem und der Ritterorden*. Brugge: Sint-Trudo-Abij, 1998.

Evergates, Theodore. *Feudal Society in the Bailliage of Troyes, under the Counts of Cbampagne, 1152-1284*. Baltimore, Md.: Johns Hopkins University Press, 1990; 1975.

———. "Louis VII and the Counts of Champagne." In *The Second Crusade and the Cistercians*, ed. Michael Gervers. New York: St. Martin's, 1992.

Flori, Jean. *Pierre l'Ermite et la Première Croisade*. Paris: Fayard, 1999.

France, John. "The Destruction of Jerusalem and the First Crusade." *Journal of Ecclesiastical History* 47 (1996): 1-17.

———. *Victory in the East: A Military History of the First Crusade.* Cambridge: Cambridge University Press, 1994.

Hamilton, Bernard. *The Latin Church in the Crusader States: The Secular Church.* London: Variorum Publications Ltd., 1980.

———. *The Leper King and His Heirs: Baldwin IV and the Crusader Kingdom of Jerusalem.* Cambridge: Cambridge University Press, 2000.

Hill, John Hugh, and Laurita Lyttleton Hill. *Raymond IV, Count of Toulouse.* Westport, Conn.: Greenwood Press, 1980; 1962.

Hintlian, Kevork. *History of the Armenians in the Holy Land.* Jerusalem: Armenian Patriarchate, 1989; 1976.

Jessee, W. Scott. *Robert the Burgundian and the Counts of Anjou, ca. 1025-1098.* Washington, D.C.: Catholic University of America Press, 2000.

Kedar, B.Z., et al., eds. *Outremer: Studies in the History of the Crusading Kingdom of Jerusalem Presented to Joshua Prawer.* Jerusalem: Yad Izhak Ben-Zvi Institute, 1982.

———. *The Horns of Hattin: Proceedings of the Second Conference of the Society for the Study of the Crusades and the Latin East, Jerusalem and Haifa, 2-6 July 1987.* Jerusalem: Israel Exploration Society, 1992.

Lamonte, J.L. "The Houses of Lusignan and Châtellerault, 1150-1250." *Speculum* 30 (1955): 374-84.

Mayer, Hans Eberhard. "The Origins of the Lordships of Ramla and Lydda in the Latin Kingdom of Jerusalem." *Speculum* 60 (1985): 535-52.

Morgan, M.R. *The Chronicle of Ernoul and the Continuations of William of Tyre.* Oxford: Oxford University Press, 1973.

Morris, Colin. "The Aims and Spirituality of the First Crusade as Seen through the Eyes of Albert of Aachen." In *Saints and Saints' Lives: Essays in Honour of D.H. Farmer.* Ed. Anne E. Curry. Reading, United Kingdom: University of Reading Press, 1990.

Murray, Alexander. "Baldwin II and His Nobles: Baronial Factionalism and Dissent in the Kingdom of Jerusalem, 1118-1134." *Nottingham Medieval Studies* 38 (1994): 60-84.

———. "The Army of Godfrey of Bouillon: Structure and Dynamics of a Contingent on the First Crusade." *Revue Belge de philologie et d'histoire* 70 (1992): 301-29.

Painter, Sidney. "The Lords of Lusignan in the Eleventh and Twelfth Centuries." *Speculum* 32 (1957): 27-47.

Pryor, J.H. "The Crusade of Emperor Frederick II, 1220-9: The Implications of the Maritime Evidence." *American Neptune* 52 (1992): 113-32.

Riley-Smith, Jonathan. *The Feudal Nobility and the Kingdom of Jerusalem, 1174-1277*. London: Macmillan, 1973.
———. *The First Crusaders, 1095-1131*. Cambridge: Cambridge University Press, 1997.
Runciman, Steven. *The Families of Outremer: The Feudal Nobility of the Crusader Kingdom of Jerusalem, 1099-1291*. London: University of London Press, 1960.
———. "The Holy Lance Found at Antioch." *Analecta Bollandiana* 68 (1950): 197-209.
Smet, Joachim. *The Carmelites. A History of the Brothers of Our Lady of Mount Carmel ca. 1200 AD until the Council of Trent*. Darien, Ill.: Camelite Spirituality Center, 1988; 1975.
———, and Kaspar Elm. *Pre-Tridentine Reform in the Carmelite Order*. Berlin: Duncker & Humblot, 1989.
Stow, Kenneth. "Conversion, Apostasy, and Apprehensiveness: Emicho of Flonheim and the Fear of Jews in the Twelfth Century." *Speculum* 76 (2001): 911-33.
Webster, Jill R. *Carmel in Medieval Catalonia*. Leiden: Brill, 1999.

Second Crusade, 1148

David, Charles W., ed./trans. *The Conquest of Lisbon*. New York: Columbia University Press, 2000; 1936.
Edgington, Susan, trans. The text of the *Lisbon Letter* is translated into English in the appendix of her essay "Albert of Aachen, St. Bernard, and the Second Crusade." In *The Second Crusade. Scope and Consequences*. Ed. Jonathan Phillips. Manchester, United Kingdom: Manchester University Press, 2001.
Gibb, H.A.R. *The Damascus Chronicle of the Crusades*. Mineola, N.Y.: Dover, 2003; 1932.
James, B.S., ed./trans. *The Letters of St. Bernard of Clairvaux*. New York: AMS Press, 1988; 1953.
Odo of Deuil. *De profectione Ludovici VII in Orientem/The Journey of Louis VII to the East*. Ed./trans. by Virginia Gingerick Berry. New York: Norton, 1948.

Barton, Simon F. "A Forgotten Crusade: Alfonso VII of León-Castile and the Campaign for Jaén (1148)." *Historical Research* 73 (2000): 312-20.
Edgington, Susan. "The Lisbon Letter of the Second Crusade." *Historical Research* 69 (1996): 328-39 [Latin text with discussion of the content].

Evans, G.R. *St. Bernard of Clairvaux*. Oxford: Oxford University Press, 2000.
Gervers, Michael, ed. *The Second Crusade and the Cistercians*. New York: St. Martin's, 1992.
Hillenbrand, Carole. "'Abominable Acts': The Career of Zengi." In *The Second Crusade: Scope and Consequences*. Ed. Jonathan Phillips. Manchester, United Kingdom: University of Manchester Press, 2001.

———. "A Neglected Episode of the Reconquista: A Christian Success in the Second Crusade." *Revue des études islamiques* 54 (1988): 163-70.
Jorden, Karl. *Henry the Lion*. Trans. P.S. Falla. Oxford: Oxford University Press, 1986.
Mayr-Harting, H. "Odo of Deuil, the Second Crusade, and the Monastery of St. Denis." In *The Culture of Christendom: Essays in Medieval History in Commemoration of Denis L.T. Bethell*. Ed. Marc C. Mayer. London: Hambledon, 1993.
Phillips, Jonathan. "The Murder of Charles the Good and the Second Crusade: Household, Nobility, and the Traditions of Crusading in Medieval Flanders." *Medieval Prosopography* 19 (1998): 55-75.

———. "Saint Bernard of Clairvaux, the Low Countries, and the Lisbon Letter of the Second Crusade." *Journal of Ecclesiastical History* 48 (1997): 485-97.

———, and Martin Hoch, eds. *The Second Crusade: Scope and Consequences*. Manchester, United Kingdom: Manchester University Press, 2001.
Renna, Thomas. "Bernard of Clairvaux and the Temple of Solomon." In *Law, Custom, and Social Fabric in Medieval Europe: Essays in Honor of Bruce Lyon*. Ed. Bernard S. Bachrach and David Nicholas. Kalamazoo, Mich.: Western Michigan University Press, 1990.
Segal, Judah Benzion. *Edessa, the Blessed City*. Oxford: Clarendon Press, 1970.
Taylor, Pegatha. "Moral Agency in Crusade and Colonization: Anselm of Havelberg and the Wendish Crusade of 1147." *International History Review* 22 (2000): 754-84.
Walker, Curtis H. "Eleanor of Aquitaine and the Disaster at Cadmos Mountain on the Second Crusade." *American Historical Review* 55 (1949-50): 857-61.
Wheeler, Bonnie, and John C. Parsons, eds. *Eleanor of Aquitaine: Lord and Lady*. New York: Palgrave Macmillan, 2002.

Williams, John Bryan. "The Making of a Crusade: The Genoese Anti-Muslim Attacks on Spain, 1146-8." *Journal of Medieval History* 23 (1997): 29-53.

Third Crusade, 1189-91, and the Kingdom of Cyprus

Baha-ed-Din. *The Life of Saladin, or What Befel Sultan Yusuf.* Ed./trans. C.W. Wilson and C.R. Conder. London: Palestine Exploration Fund, 1897.
Crawford, Paul, ed./trans. *The Templar of Tyre. The Deeds of the Cypriots.* Aldershot, United Kingdom: Ashgate, 2002.
Delaborde, H.F., ed./trans. *Oeuvres de Rigord et Guillaume le Breton, historiens de Philippe Auguste.* 2 vols. Paris: Librairie Renouard, 1882-85.
Edbury, Peter W., ed./trans. *The Conquest of Jerusalem and the Third Crusade. Sources in Translation.* Aldershot, United Kingdom: Ashgate, 1996; 1998.
La Monte, John, and M. Hubert, trans. *Philip de Novare:The Wars of Frederick II vs. the Ibelins in Syria and Cyprus.* New York: Columbia University Press, 1979; 1936.
Massé, Henri. *La conquête de la Syrie et de la Palestine par Saladin.* Paris: Librairie orientaliste Paul Geuthner, 1972.
Mierow, Charles Christopher, and Richard Emery. *The Deeds of Frederick Barbarossa/Otto of Freising and His Continuator, Rhahewin.* Toronto: University of Toronto Press, 1994; 1953.
Nicholson, Helen J., ed./trans. *The Chronicle of the Third Crusade. A Translation of the Itinerarium Peregrinorum et Gesta Regis Ricardi.* Aldershot, United Kingdom: Ashgate, 1997.
Richards, D.S., ed./trans. *The Rare and Excellent History of Saladin, by Baha'al Din Ibn Shaddad (1144-1234).* Aldershot, United Kingdom: Ashgate, 2001.

Coureas, Nicholas. *The Latin Church in Cyprus.* Aldershot, United Kingdom: Ashgate, 1997.
Edbury, Peter W., and Janet Shirley. *Guillaume de Machaut. The Capture of Alexandria.* Aldershot, United Kingdom: Ashgate, 2001.
———. *The Kingdom of Cyprus and the Crusades, 1191-1374.* Cambridge: Cambridge University Press, 1991, 1994.
Ehrenkreutz, Andrew S. *Saladin.* Albany: State University of New York Press, 1972.
Gibb, H.A.R. *The Life of Saladin from the Works of Imad ad-Din and Baha'ad-Din.* Oxford: Clarendon Press, 1973.

268 • Bibliography

Gillingham, John. *Richard I*. New Haven, Conn.: Yale University Press, 1999.

———. "Richard I, Galley Warfare and Portsmouth: The Beginnings of a Royal Navy." In *Thirteenth Century England*, vol. 6, ed. M. Prestwich, R.H. Britnell, and R. Frame. Woodbridge, United Kingdom: Boydell Press, 1997.

Jacoby, David. "Conrad Marquis of Montferrat and the Kingdom of Jerusalem (1187-1192)." In *Dai Feudi Monferrini E dal Piemonte Ai Nuovi Mondi Oltre Gli Oceani*, ed. L. Balletto. Alessandria: Società Di Storia Arte E Archeologia, 1993.

Lyons, Malcolm C., and David E.P. Jackson. *Saladin: The Politics of the Holy War*. Cambridge: Cambridge University Press, 1997; 1982.

Munz, Peter. *Frederick Barbarossa: A Study in Medieval Politics*. Ithaca, N.Y.: Cornell University Press, 1969.

Turner, Ralph V., and Richard R. Heiser. *The Reign of Richard the Lionheart: Ruler of the Angevin Empire, 1189-1199*. Boston: Addison-Wesley, 2000.

Fourth Crusade, 1204, and the Latin Kingdom at Constantinople (1204-61)
Listed below are the Western European accounts of the expedition. For the Byzantine perspective, see above, under Byzantium in the bibliography.

Andrea, A.J., ed./trans. *The Capture of Constantinople: The "Hystoria Constantinopolitana" of Gunther of Paris*. Philadelphia: University of Pennsylvania Press, 1997.

———. "Holy War, Holy Relics, Holy Theft: The Anonymous of Soissons' *De Terra Iherosolimitana*: An Analysis, Edition, and Translation." *Historical Reflections* 18 (1992): 147-75.

McNeal, Edgar Holmes, ed./trans. *The Conquest of Constantinople, by Robert of Clari*. Toronto: University of Toronto Press, 1996.

Shaw, M.R.B., ed./trans. *Joinville and Villehardouin: Chronicles of the Crusades*. London: Penguin, 1963.

Secondary Sources:

Andrea, A.J. "Cistercian Accounts of the Fourth Crusade: Were They Anti-Venetian?" *Analecta Cisterciensia* 41 (1985): 3-41.

Lock, Peter W. *The Franks in the Aegean 1204-1500*. Harlow, United Kingdom: Longman, 1995.

Madden, Thomas F. *Enrico Dandalo and the Rise of Venice*. Baltimore, Md.: Johns Hopkins University Press, 2003.

Queller, Donald E., and Thomas F. Madden. *The Fourth Crusade: The Conquest of Constantinople, 1201-1204*. 2nd ed. Philadelphia: University of Pennsylvania Press, 1997.

Wolff, R.L. "Baldwin of Flanders and Hainaut, 1172-1205." *Speculum* 27 (1952): 281-322.

Albigensian Crusade, 1204-29

Shirley, Janet, ed./trans. *The Song of the Cathar Wars: A History of the Albigensian Crusade by William of Tudela and an Anonymous Successor*. Aldershot, United Kingdom: Ashgate, 1996.

Tugwell, Simon, ed./trans. *Jordan of Saxony: On the Beginnings of the Order of Preachers*. Chicago: Parable, 1982.

Auth, Charles R., et al. *A Dominican Bibliography and Book of Reference, 1216-1992: A List of Works in English by and about Members of the Order of the Friar Preachers, Founded by St. Dominic de Guzman (c.1171-1221) and Confirmed by Pope Honorius III, Dec. 22, 1216*. New York: P. Lang, 2000.

Andrews, Frances. *The Early Humiliati*. New York: Cambridge University Press, 1999.

Arnold, John H. *Inquisition and Power. Catharism and the Confessing Spirit in Medieval Languedoc*. Philadelphia: University of Pennsylvania Press, 2001.

Barber, Malcolm. *The Cathars: Dualist Heretics in Languedoc in the High Middle Ages*. Harlow, United Kingdom: Longman, 2000.

Biller, Peter. *The Waldenses, 1170-1530. Between a Religious Order and a Church*. Aldershot, United Kingdom: Ashgate, 2001.

Cameron, Euan. *Waldenses: Rejections of Holy Church in Medieval Europe*. Oxford: Blackwell, 2000.

Hamilton, Bernard. *Crusaders, Cathars, and the Holy Places*. Aldershot, United Kingdom: Ashgate, 1999.

Kay, Richard. *The Council of Bourges, 1225. A Documentary History*. Aldershot, United Kingdom: Ashgate, 2002.

Lambert, Malcolm. *The Cathars*. Oxford: Blackwell, 1998.

Mundy, John Hine. *Men and Women at Toulouse in the Age of the Cathars*. Toronto: Pontifical Institute of Medieval Studies, 1990.

270 • Bibliography

———. *Society and Government at Toulouse in the Age of the Cathars*. Toronto: University of Toronto Press, 1997.
Pegg, Mark Gregory. *The Corruption of Angels: The Great Inquisition of 1245-1246*. Princeton, N.J.: Princeton University Press, 2001.
Strayer, Joseph. *The Albigensian Crusades*. 2nd ed. Ann Arbor: University of Michigan Press, 1992.
Sumption, Jonathan. *The Albigensian Crusade*. London: Faber, 1999; 1978.
Vicaire, M.-H. *St. Dominic and His Times*. Trans. K. Pond. New York: McGraw-Hill, 1964.
Wakefield, Walter L. *Heresy, Crusade, and Inquisition in Southern France, 1100-1250*. London: G. Allen & Unwin, 1974.
Weis, René. *The Yellow Cross: The Story of the Last Cathars' Rebellion against the Inquisition, 1290-1329*. New York: Knopf, 2001.

Fifth Crusade, 1213-21

Armstrong, Regis J., and Ignatius C. Brad, ed./trans. *Francis and Clare: The Complete Works*. New York: Paulist Press, 1982.
Huygens, R.B.C., ed. *Lettres de Jacques de Vitry*. Leiden: Brill, 1960.
Jacques de Vitry/Jacobus, de Vitriaco Cardinal. *A History of Jerusalem: A.D. 1180* [sic]. Ed./trans. Aubrey Stewart. New York: AMS Press, 1971; 1896.
Oliver of Paderborn. *The Capture of Damietta*. Ed./trans. Father John J. Gavigan. New York: AMS Press, 1976; 1946.

Donovan, Joseph P. *Pelagius and the Fifth Crusade*. Oxford: Oxford University Press, 1950.
Powell, James M. *Anatomy of a Crusade, 1213-1221*. Philadelphia: University of Pennsylvania Press, 1986.
Richard, Jean. *Saint Louis, Crusader King of France*. Trans. Jean Birrell; ed. Simon D. Lloyd. Cambridge: Cambridge University Press, 1992.

The Northern or Baltic Crusades

Brundage, James A. *The Chronicle of Henry of Livonia*. Madison: University of Wisconsin Press, 1990; 1961.
Fudge, Thomas A. *The Crusades against Heretics in Bohemia, 1418-1437. Sources and Documents for the Hussite Crusades*. Aldershot, United Kingdom: Ashgate, 2002.
Helmhold. *The Chronicle of the Slavs*. Ed./trans. Francis Joseph Tschan. New York: Octagon Books, 1966; 1935.

Saxo Grammaticus. *History of the Danes.* Ed./trans. Peter Fisher and Hilda Davidson. 2 vols. Cambridge: D.S. Brewer, 1979-80.

Christiansen, Eric. *The Northern Crusades.* 2nd ed. London: Penguin, 1997.

Jordan, Karl. *Henry the Lion: A Biography.* Trans. P.S. Falla. Oxford: Clarendon Press, 1986.

Murray, Alexander, ed. *Crusade and Conversion on the Baltic Frontier 1150-1500.* Aldershot, United Kingdom: Ashgate, 2001.

Tschan, Francis J. "Helmhold: Chronicler of the North Saxon Missions." *Catholic Historical Review* 16 (1931): 379-412.

About the Author

Corliss K. Slack received a D.Phil. from Balliol College, Oxford, in 1988. She teaches European history and the crusades at Whitworth College in Spokane, Washington. Her first book was a collection of charters left by crusaders departing from northern Europe between 1138 and 1275. She has also published articles on the reform of the secular church in the century between 1050 and 1150, and on the activities of the Premonstratensian Order in crusade preaching and procuration.

```
D 155  .S53 2003
Slack, Corliss Konwiser,
 1955-
Historical dictionary of th
 crusades
```